ART OF SADHANA

a guide to daily devotion

ART OF SADHANA

a guide to daily devotion

Swami B.P. Puri Maharaja

A Bhakti Siddhanta Vani Publication

MANDALA
publishing group

ISBN:
Cloth: 1-886069-02-6
Paper: 1-886069-03-4

Published for
Bhakti Siddhanta Vani

by the

Mandala Publishing Group

1585-A Folsom Street
San Francisco, CA 94103
phone: 415 621 2336 fax: 415 626 1510
mandala@mandala.org www.mandala.org

Readers interested in the subject matter may also contact:

Gopinath Gaudiya Maths in India

Ishodyan, Mayapur
District Nadia, West Bengal
Phone: 91-347-245-307

Chakratirtha Road
Jaganath Puri, Orissa
Phone: 91-6752-25690

Old Dauji Mandhir
Gopeswara Road
Vrindavana, U.P. 281121
Phone: 91-565-444-185

Printed in China through Palace Press International

Contents

Introduction

guru vaiṣṇava bhagavān tinera smaraṇa
tinera smaraṇe haya vighna-vināśana
anāyāse haya nija vāñchita pūraṇa

"I meditate on the guru, the Vaishnavas, and the Lord. By remembering them, all obstacles are destroyed and one quickly attains the fulfillment of all desires."
(*Chaitanya Charitāmṛta* 1.1.20-21)

With these words, Krishnadāsa Kavirāja Gosvāmī begins his *Chaitanya Charitāmṛta.* This prayer is his *maṅgalācaraṇa,* or auspicious invocation. Following in Krishnadāsa's footsteps we invoke the mercy of gurudeva. By remembering Krishna, "the abode of all good fortune," in accordance with the directions of His devotees, it is possible to quickly attain the Lord's mercy.

yasya prasādād bhagavat-prasādo
yasyāprasādān na gatiḥ kuto'pi

"The guru is the best of Krishna's devotees and non-different from His beloved Rādhārāṇī. Therefore when guru is pleased, Krishna is also pleased."

The conclusion of the *mahājanas* is that there is no way of gaining the Lord's pleasure other than through the guru. Thus, we pray that our beloved gurudeva be pleased with us and that the devotees of Krishna, all of whom, as His expansions, are non-different from Him, will also look upon us with pleasure. We pray that their combined mercy will result in our obtaining the great fortune of Krishna's satisfaction. May Śrī Guru, Gaurāṅga, Gāndharvikā, and Giridhārī be ever glorious, and may they bestow all auspiciousness upon us.

In the *Mahābhārata*, King Yudhiṣṭhira and the other Pāṇḍavas were challenged to answer questions by Yamarāja, who had disguised himself as a heron. Of the five brothers, only Yudhiṣṭhira was able to answer all the questions, thus passing Yamarāja's test. In answer to the question about the genuine spiritual path, the eldest Pāṇḍava stated that only the path followed by the *mahājanas* was free of all obstacles, and that everyone should therefore cast aside all intellectual criticism and simply follow that path. Anyone who disregards the path of the *mahājana's* for another will soon find that they are no longer headed toward the divine abode, Goloka, but rather in the completely opposite direction—toward a hellish existence. It is therefore necessary for us to ascertain who the *mahājanas* are, find the path they have left for us, and learn how we should follow it. This path is the "art of sādhanā"—the means to achieving the supreme goal of spiritual life.

While recounting the story of Ajāmila in the *Śrīmad Bhāgavatam's* sixth canto, Śukadeva names twelve *mahājanas*, all of whom are said to know the inner secrets of the path to God. These *mahājanas* are Svāyambhū, Nārada, Śambhu, the four Kumāras, Kapila, Manu, Prahlāda, Janaka, Bhīṣma, Bali, Vaiyāsaki and Yamarāja. The Kapila spoken of here is the son of Kardama and Devahūtī and not the atheistic author of Sāṅkhya philosophy. All of these great personalities were followers of the path of devotion and all of them demonstrated, each in his own way, the excellence of this path.

bhagavān brahma kārtsnyena
trir anvīkṣya manīṣayā
tad adhyavasyat kūṭastho
ratir ātman yato bhavet

> "Lord Brahmā, for instance, carefully studied the Vedic literature three times and came to the conclusion that attachment to the Supreme Self is the Vedic literature's ultimate goal." (*Śrīmad Bhāgavatam* 2.2.34)

Just as munis read a scripture two or three times over in order to understand it properly, so Brahmā also decided to play the part of a seeker, even though he is all-knowing. He thus took on the character of a muni—just as it is said in the *Śrutis*, *sa munir bhūtvā samacintayat*, "He became a muni and started to think carefully." Brahmā carefully studied the Vedas three times in their entirety just to show how difficult it is to extract the essence of the scriptures and find their ultimate meaning. When Brahmā completed his study he came to the conclusion that attachment to the Supreme Lord Hari, or *bhakti-yoga*, is the genuine fruit of such scholarly research.

"It is necessary for us to ascertain who the mahajanas are, find the path they have left for us, and learn how we should follow it"

na hy ato 'nyaḥ śivaḥ panthā
viśataḥ saṁsmṛtāv iha
vāsudeve bhagavati
bhakti-yogo yato bhavet

> "There is no more auspicious a path for the souls who have entered the world of repeated birth and death than the path which leads to Lord Vāsudeva's devotional service." (*Śrīmad Bhāgavatam* 2.2.33)

Although there are many paths to liberation, none is more reasonable, easily performed or safer than the process by which one pleases the Supreme Lord and, as a result, attains devotion or love for His lotus feet. There is no doubt that direct devotional service is superior to other processes such as *karma-yoga*, by which one offers the results of one's activities to the Lord.

The superiority of devotional service over other paths of spiritual life is clearly stated in the concluding verses of the *Bhagavad-gītā*'s sixth chapter: *tapasvibhyo'dhiko yogī* (6.46) and *yoginām api sarveṣām* (6.47). Furthermore, the most confidential instructions of the Lord, at the end of the *Gītā*'s eighteenth chapter (*man-manā bhava* and *sarva-dharmān parityājya)*, also indicate clearly that the ultimate goal of the Vedic literature is Bhakti yoga.

"When Brahma had completed his study, he came to the conclusion that attachment to the Supreme Lord Hari, or bhakti-yoga, is the genuine fruit of such scholarly research"

Many conflicting ideas about religion have developed throughout history. According to the authority of the *Śrīmad Bhāgavatam* (1.2.6), however, the ultimate religious activity for all human beings is devotion to the Supreme Lord, Śrī Krishna, who lies beyond empirical validation. At its apex, such devotion (characterized by activities such as hearing and chanting about Krishna) must be causeless; that is, the performer should be free from any selfish motive. Devotion must also be uninhibited; nothing must be allowed to interfere with its performance, and it must be independent and spontaneous.

In the sixth canto of the *Śrīmad Bhāgavatam*, it is said that bhakti, devotional service, is primarily executed in the form of *saṅkīrtana*:

etāvān eva loke 'smin
puṁsāṁ dharmaḥ paraḥ smṛtaḥ
bhakti-yogo bhagavati
tan-nāma-grahaṇādibhiḥ

"Therefore, the supreme religious activity for people in this world is devotional service to the Lord, performed by such acts as repeating His divine names."
(*Śrīmad Bhāgavatam* 6.3.22)

Lord Brahma, the creator.

Śrī Chaitanya Mahāprabhu also confirmed this statement from the *Bhāgavatam* in His own words:

bhajanera madhye śreṣṭha nava-vidhā bhakti
kṛṣṇa-prema, kṛṣṇa dite dhare mahā-śakti
tāra madhye sarva-śreṣṭha nāma-saṅkīrtana
niraparādhe laile nāma pāya prema-dhana

"Of the many ways of executing devotional service, there are nine varieties which are considered to be the best, for they possess a great capacity to deliver love for Krishna and thus Krishna Himself. Of these nine processes of devotional service, the most important is the chanting of the Lord's Holy Name, for if one chants without committing offenses, the treasure of love for the Lord will be obtained."
(*Chaitanya Charitāmṛta* 3.4.70-71)

In the twelfth chapter of the *Bhagavad-gītā*, it is said that remembering, contemplating and meditating on the Lord depends on inner purification; thus, these activities are not easily perfected by ordinary people. On the other hand, since *saṅkīrtana* is an activity executed by the external senses, it is within the grasp of anyone, even the disturbed human beings of this Age of Kali. The most merciful Śrī Chaitanya Mahāprabhu, who appeared in this age to give the great gift of love of God in the mood of Krishna's associates in Vraja, testified to this end when He emotionally embraced His most confidential associates,

Svarūpa Dāmodara and Rāmānanda Rāya, and said:

harṣe prabhu kahena śuna svarūpa rāma-rāya
nāma-saṅkīrtana kalau parama upāya

"Chanting the Holy Names is the supreme means of salvation in this age of Kali."
(*Chaitanya Charitāmṛta* 3.20.8)

From this statement we can easily understand that the Lord invested some special powers in the chanting of His Holy Names in this particularly fortunate age of Kali. This special power is its capacity to awaken affectionate attachment or *rāga* for the Lord. This is thus the best process by which one can develop *rāga-bhakti*, or devotional service in spontaneous affection.

"Such greed, which mirrors the eternal attachment that the residents of Vraja have for their Lord, is the price that one has to pay to purchase a consciousness imbued with devotional sentiment"

Even though Chaitanya Mahāprabhu has stated that through devotional service based on rules and regulations one cannot attain the type of love of God that is found in Vraja, (*vidhi-bhaktye vraja-bhāva pāite nāhi śakti—Chaitanya Charitāmṛta* 1.3.15), if one takes up *harināma-saṅkīrtana* on the *vidhi-bhakti* platform according to the directions given by Chaitanya Mahāprabhu, then one will quickly attain the qualifications necessary for the inner awakening of such a spontaneous service attitude. Mahāprabhu told Svarūpa Dāmodara and Rāmānanda Rāya how one should chant the Holy Name in order to awaken his dormant love for Krishna:

tṛṇād api sunīcena
taror iva sahiṣṇunā
amāninā mānadena
kīrtanīyaḥ sadā hariḥ

"One should chant the Holy Name of the Lord while thinking oneself to be lower than the grass. He should be more tolerant than the tree, take no respect for oneself and give all respect to others." (*Chaitanya Charitāmṛta* 3.20.21)

Thus, if anyone follows Mahāprabhu's direction and chants the Holy Name in the manner described in this verse, he or she will quickly develop transcendental greed or intense hankering. Such greed, which mirrors the eternal attachment that the residents of Vraja have for their Lord, is the price that one must pay to purchase a consciousness imbued with devotional sentiment. This is called *rāgānugā bhakti*, and it is the merciful manifestation of Krishna's pleasure potency, *hlādinī-śakti*.

Expertise in devotional service is measured by the extent to which one is able to satisfy the senses of the Lord. An advanced devotee who has this expertise is one who has taken exclusive shelter of Krishna. He is free from any tendency to criticize others, and seeks only to be absorbed in the pastimes of the Divine Couple of Vraja. Such a devotee is very dear to Krishna and is certainly rare in this world. To see such a devotee, to associate with him, or to serve him are manifestations of good fortune on a level seldom experienced. Only if Krishna bestows His mercy on someone can he experience the blessing of such association. To inform everyone of this important aspect of spiritual life, *mahājanas* such as Bhaktivinoda Ṭhākura have prayed for the contact of a person who is expert in devotional service:

kabe śrī caitanya more karibena dayā
kabe āmi pāiba vaiṣṇava-pada-chāyā

"When will Śrī Chaitanya Mahāprabhu be merciful unto me? When will I find shelter in the shade of a Vaishnava's lotus feet?"
(*Kalyāṇa-kalpataru, Dainyamayī prārthanā*, 1)

This kind of consciousness, imbued with a taste for devotion to Krishna, is obtained by the grace of a great soul who has traveled the *rāgānugā bhakti* path. Millions and millions of births filled with pious acts will not bring about the same result.

After taking shelter of a spiritual master, one should engage with absolute dedication in the worship of the Holy Name, in the association of devotees and in the deepest solitude. Through this worship, the devotee's understanding of the object of worship (*upāsya*), the worshiper (*upāsaka*) and the process of worship (*upāsanā*) will be clarified. This advancement in spiritual life will awaken an intense desire or spiritual greed to attain the mood of Krishna's associates in Vraja. Even so, everyone should remember the warning of the *Kaṭha Upanishad*:

kṣurasya dhārā niśitā duratyayā
durgaṁ pathas tat kavayo vadanti

"The path of spiritual realization is very difficult; it is sharp like a razor's edge. That is the opinion of learned transcendentalists." (*Kaṭha Upanishad* 1.3.14)

If one swerves even slightly from the path laid out by the spiritual master, he will fall down. If one gives any consideration to desires for profit, adoration or prestige, or if one allows himself to succumb to political intrigues, the growth of his devotional creeper will be stunted. In this matter, the devotee who is dear to Krishna is the only one who can save us. The scriptures say that the type of perfection one attains depends on the thoughts one has while engaged in spiritual practice (*yādṛśī bhāvanā yasya siddhir bhavati tādṛśī*). If we concentrate with transcendental greed on obtaining the association of a devotee who is expert in the science of serving the Lord, then Krishna will surely appear Himself in the form of such an advanced soul.

On the other hand, if we have some other objective in mind, we may encounter many people who merely present themselves as religious leaders or as saintly persons but who have no substance. We may be confused by their powers or popularity and lose our bearings, wandering ever further from the genuine goal of pure devotion. Far from achieving love for Krishna in Vrindavan, we will become totally confused and thus inevitably lose our soul on the path to oblivion.

It has been said that the path of religion is established by God Himself—*dharmaṁ tu sākṣād bhagavat-praṇītam*. If one has no understanding of this basic principle of spiritual life, no matter how intellectually gifted he may be, his grasp of the truth will be skewed and he will become indifferent to the true, eternal, spiritual religion of the soul. Such persons promote the idea of a secular state where everyone is indifferent to the practice of religion. One should never, however, be indifferent to the true, eternal, spiritual religion. The secularist is wrong when he thinks that one who adheres to the supreme truth of spiritual life is affected by a sectarian or ungenerous spirit.

"After taking shelter of a spiritual master, one should engage with absolute dedication in the worship of the Holy Name in the association of devotees and in the deepest solitude"

"If one swerves even slightly from the path laid out by the spiritual master, he will fall down. If one gives any consideration to desires for profit, adoration or prestige, or if one allows himself to succumb to political intrigues, the growth of his devotional creeper will be stunted"

"We may encounter many people who merely present themselves as religious leaders or as saintly persons but who have no substance. We may be confused by their powers or popularity, wandering ever further from the genuine goal of pure devotion"

The Supreme Lord is eternal, true, permanent and everlasting; the living being also has these same qualities. The relationship between them is thus eternal and indissoluble. The Supreme Lord is infinite consciousness. By His omnipotent desire, the atomic conscious particle (the individual living being) is brought into being. Despite this difference—the Lord being infinite and the living being atomic—the aspect of consciousness and spirituality is common to both. Thus the relation of the individual to the Supreme Lord is described as being one of simultaneous oneness and difference. Since it is impossible for one to understand how two things can be simultaneously one and distinct, the Gauḍīya *mahājanas* have added the adjective *acintya* or "inconceivable" to this definition, calling their doctrine, *acintya-bhedābheda*. The implication is that one can only know this relationship through revealed scripture and accept it on faith.

In this world, people have presented many doctrines about spiritual life and religion without an understanding of this basic relation between the individual soul and God. As it is said in the *Bhāgavatam*: "Thus, due to their different natures, human beings have a variety of different understandings" (*evaṁ prakṛti-vaicitryād bhidyante matayo nṝṇām*). Since people are under the influence of the qualities of material nature, namely goodness, passion and ignorance, they differ in their perceptions of reality and thus conflicts inevitably arise between them. Since Mahāprabhu's religion of love is universal, the secular state should promote it, for under its influence alone can all quarrels and conflicts be eliminated. Mahāprabhu's religion of love is the unique route to lasting world peace.

"If one has no understanding of this basic principle of spiritual life, no matter how intellectually gifted he may be, his grasp of the truth will be skewed"

Only a true saint, fixed in the eternal religion of devotion to the one supreme truth, can harmonize all conflicting points of view and produce lasting peace. Krishna is the source of all incarnations, the complete whole and is all-pervading. All apparent contradictions are resolved in Him. Similarly, the devotee who is exclusively devoted to the Lord is capable of harmonizing all different philosophical positions from his transcendental vantage point. Therefore, when one shows preference to such a devotee, one is in fact following a policy of non-preferential treatment towards any religious denomination.

In the second of the *Śrīmad Bhāgavatam's* invocatory verses, the non-envious saint has been described as a person who is uniquely qualified to engage in the true, eternal religion from which all cheating tendencies have been discarded. The word *mātsarya* (envy) indicates the inability to tolerate another's good fortune or happiness. Enviousness within individuals does not allow proper distinction between the inner self and the material self. Such envy creates philosophical ideas based on distinctions between that which one possesses and that which belongs to others. Such envy is the source of war and other disruptions. Of course, varieties exist in the divine dimension, but the lack of unity arising from such varieties does not result in any real conflict because each individual is firmly fixed in the non-dual supreme truth, the source of spiritual harmony.

On the other hand, it is impossible to harmonize the materialistic propensity with the spiritual. The futile efforts to legislate harmony between these mutually opposing realities merely contribute to further unrest and disharmony. The sun, which allows us to see, cannot compromise with the darkness that obstructs vision. Similarly, the non-envious nature cannot accommodate the envious nature of the mundane; rather, it drives it away and proclaims its conquest, just as the rising sun dispels darkness and brings auspiciousness to the world. In this way, supreme peace comes to reign in the world.

At first, the *Bhāgavata* appears to condemn spiritual practices such as work in the spirit of renunciation or the cultivation of knowledge. It does accept, however, the necessity for work performed for the satisfaction of the Supreme Lord and the cultivation of knowledge in the categories of *sambandha, abhidheya,* and *prayojana* in relation to Krishna. When placed in the context of devotion to Krishna, these contradictory visions of spiritual practice are thus harmonized. To Mahāprabhu, the *Śrīmad Bhāgavatam* is the only authoritative scripture; thus, it sets the standard for Vaishnava behavior and doctrine. True peace in the world can only be achieved on the basis of the pure philosophical conclusions established by the *Bhāgavatam*. In this publication, *The Art of Sādhanā*, various aspects of the Vaishnava scriptures—the *Śrīmad Bhāgavatam*, *Hari-bhakti-vilāsa* and *Chaitanya Charitāmṛta*—are cited to highlight different aspects of the path of devotion.

Chaitanya Mahaprabhu

Every single living being is in essence a part of the single non-dual Supreme Truth. As one takes shelter of this Supreme Truth and deepens his knowledge of that eternal relationship (*sambandha*), his understanding of the process (*abhidheya*) by which to reach the ultimate perfection of life (*prayojana*) becomes clear. As this development takes place, true vision of equality and friendship between living beings becomes a reality.

When we speak of the *Bhāgavata*, we mean two different things. The first is the scripture, *Śrīmad Bhāgavatam*. The second is the *Bhāgavata* devotee who has established a relation with *Bhagavān,* the Supreme Lord. Svarūpa Dāmodara instructed the brahmin from East Bengal to go and study the *Bhāgavatam* from a Vaishnava.

jāha bhāgavata paṛa vaiṣṇavera sthāne
ekānta āśraya kara caitanya-caraṇe
caitanya bhakta-gaṇera nitya kara saṅga
tabe ta jānibe siddhānta-samudra-taraṅga

> "Go and study the *Bhāgavatam* from a Vaishnava. Take exclusive shelter of Chaitanya Mahāprabhu's lotus feet. Always associate with Chaitanya Mahāprabhu's devotees. If you do all this, you will be able to plunge into the ocean of His divine teachings." (*Chaitanya Charitāmṛta* 3.5.131-132)

"Mahaprabhu's religion of love is the unique route to world peace"

siddhānta baliye citte nā kara alasa
ihā haite kṛṣṇa lāge sudṛḍha mānasa

> "Do not, out of laziness, neglect to meditate on the conclusions of the scriptures. From knowledge of the *siddhānta*, the mind will become fixed on Krishna." (*Chaitanya Charitāmṛta* 1.2.117)

A saintly person who is free from envy and who has studied the art of *sādhanā* as taught by Śrī Chaitanya has entered into the Lord's most confidential teachings. By hearing the *Bhāgavata* from such a person, it is possible to learn its true meaning and gain the ultimate auspiciousness. By the grace of Śrī Chaitanya's art of *sādhanā*, it becomes possible to understand the transcendental nature of Krishna Chaitanya Mahāprabhu's body. From that knowledge, one can come to understand that the jewel in the center of the nine islands of Nabadwip, the divine garden of Īśodyāna[1], is similarly transcendental, as is the whole of Mahāprabhu's abode.

"As one starts to experience the divine joy of the eternal realm, one will be able to have direct perception of Sri Chaitanya Mahaprabhu's transcendental form, which will then appear like the rising full moon"

The Lord says, "Both the divine sound and the divine form are My eternal bodies" (*śabda-brahma paraṁ brahma mamobhe śāśvatī tanū*). The sound vibration which designates the Supreme Lord is known as the divine sound or *śabda brahma.* Chaitanya Mahāprabhu's gospel is just such a divine sound. By careful attention to it anyone can achieve an understanding of the form of the Param Brahman, or divinity in its highest, personal aspect. This leads to relishing His ever-fresh and delightful name, form, attributes, and pastimes—a fortune that puts to rest any residual attraction that one may have for material sense pleasures. As one starts to experience the joy of the eternal realm, one will be able to have direct perception of Śrī Chaitanya Mahāprabhu's transcendental form, which will then appear like the rising full moon. May this book, *The Art of Sādhanā*, based on the teachings of the Lord and the great devotees, be ever victorious.

RADHA AND KRISHNA, THE DIVINE COUPLE

CHAPTER I

PERFECTION IN WORSHIP

The word *vedānta* means "the end result of knowledge." It is a reference to the *Upanishads,* the final books of the Vedic revelation or *Śruti*. These books contain the mystic insights of the rishis and are considered to be the basis for all spiritual knowledge in India. The Lord's incarnation, Vedavyāsa, the compiler of the Vedic literature, also composed the *Vedanta sutras,* or *Brahma sutras,* in order to summarize the teachings of the *Upanishads.* The word sutra means "aphorism," or "code," a short, enigmatic statement meant to remind one of an entire aspect of the Upanishadic teaching.

Thus, the *Vedanta Sutras* are the texts which stand as the basis of all religious philosophy in India. Indeed, the founders of every school of Indian philosophy (Śaṅkara, Rāmānuja, Vallabha, Vishnusvāmī, Mādhva and Nimbārka) have all written commentaries or *bhāṣyas* on the sutras in order to explain their understanding of the supreme truth. The Gauḍīya Vaishnava school founded by Chaitanya Mahāprabhu also has an authoritative commentary on this important scripture, the *Govinda-bhāṣya* of Baladeva Vidyābhūṣaṇa. For the Gauḍīyas, however, the unblemished commentary on the *Vedanta Sutra* is the *Śrīmad Bhāgavatam*, also composed by Vyāsadeva, where the three aspects of spiritual knowledge, *sambandha, abhidheya* and *prayojana,* are clearly enunciated.

The *Vedanta Sutra* is divided into four chapters or *adhyāyas*, and each is further subdivided into four *pādas*. The first and second chapters deal with *sambandha-tattva*, the third with *abhidheya-tattva,* and the fourth with *prayojana*.

The first chapter of the *Vedanta Sutra* is called *samanvaya,* or "synthesis," for it organizes all the ideas of the Vedas and the *Upanishads* into an orderly whole centered around the concept of Brahman, the Supreme Truth. The second chapter is called *avirodha*, which means "consistency" or "harmony." According to Baladeva Vidyābhūṣaṇa, in this chapter all apparently inconsistent scriptural statements are shown to point harmoniously to the one Brahman, or Supreme Lord[1] (*tad evam aviruddhānāṁ śrutīnāṁ samanvayaḥ sarveśvare siddhaḥ*). The third chapter is named *sādhana*, or "the means." It discusses devotion, which is the only means for attaining Brahman. The fourth chapter is known as *phala*, or "the result." The term *prayojana*, or "ultimate purpose," is also used to indicate the attainment of Brahman.

Śrī Chaitanya Mahāprabhu made the teachings of the Vedanta more explicit to His disciples and His explanations were mercifully recorded by Krishnadāsa Kavirāja Gosvāmī in the *Chaitanya Charitāmṛta*:

> *veda-śāstra kahe sambandha abhidheya prayojana*
> *kṛṣṇa prāpya sambandha bhakti prāptyera sādhana*
> *abhidheya-nāma bhakti prema prayojana*
> *puruṣārtha-śiromaṇi prema mahā-dhana*

> "The Vedic knowledge is subdivided into three parts known as *sambandha* ("relations"), *abhidheya* ("procedure") and *prayojana* ("the aim or end"). The knowledge of Krishna as the goal of spiritual life is called *sambandha*. The knowledge that devotion is the means of attaining Him and acting accordingly is called *abhidheya*. The ultimate goal of life, or *prayojana*, is love of Krishna or *prema*. This *prema* is the greatest treasure of spiritual life and is foremost amongst all the objectives of human life."
> (*Chaitanya Charitāmṛta* 2.20.124-125)

Elsewhere, Krishnadāsa repeats the same thing even more succinctly:

> *veda-śāstre kahe sambandha abhidheya prayojana*
> *kṛṣṇa kṛṣṇa-bhakti prema tina mahā-dhana*

> "The Vedic knowledge is subdivided into three parts known as *sambandha* ("relations"), *abhidheya* ("procedure") and *prayojana* ("the aim or end"). These three great treasures are Krishna, devotion to Krishna, and love for Krishna."

In the *Bhakti-rasāmṛta-sindhu*(1.1.1) Krishna is stated to be the *akhila-rasāmṛta-mūrti* or personification of all twelve aesthetic and relational experiences known as *rasa*. According to *sambandha* knowledge, Krishna is the Supreme Truth. The only means to attain Him is bhakti or devotion, and love for Him is the ultimate objective of spiritual practices.

SAMBANDHA

In the *Bhagavad-gītā*, Lord Krishna says,

> *vedaiś ca sarvair aham eva vedyo*
> *vedānta-kṛd veda-vid eva cāham*

> "I am the object to be known by all the Vedic literatures. I am the composer of the *Upanishads* or Vedanta and the knower of the true meaning of the Veda."
> (*Gītā* 15.15)

In the *Śvetāśvatara Upanishad* the Supreme is described as the attributeless Brahman:

eko devaḥ sarva-bhūteṣu gūḍhaḥ
sarva-vyāpī sarva-bhūtāntarātmā
karmādhyakṣaḥ sarva-bhūtādhivāsaḥ
sākṣī cetāḥ kevalo nirguṇaś ca

"There is but one Divine Entity, who is hidden within all beings. All-pervading, He is the dwells within every created thing; He is the overseer of all activities, the refuge of all creatures, the witness, the consciousness, the one existing thing. He has no attributes." (*Śvetāśvatara Upanishad* 6.11)

The *Śrīmad Bhāgavatam*, however, shows that there is an aspect of the divine beyond even this Brahman. It is *parātpara*, or "beyond that which lies beyond":

vadanti tat tattva-vidas
tattvaṁ yaj jñānam advayam
brahmeti paramātmeti
bhagavān iti śabdyate

"Knowers of the truth have ascertained that the supreme non-dual substance is named in three ways: as Brahman, as Paramātman, and as Bhagavān."
(*Śrīmad Bhāgavatam* 1.2.11)

The Bhagavān, or personal aspect of the Supreme, is known as Krishna—*kṛṣṇas tu bhagavān svayam* (*Śrīmad Bhāgavatam* 1.3.28).

harir hi nirguṇaḥ sākṣāt
puruṣaḥ prakṛteḥ paraḥ

"The Supreme Lord Hari is untouched by the material qualities. He is the supreme person, beyond the material nature." (*Śrīmad Bhāgavatam* 10.88.5)

ABHIDHEYA

Hari or Krishna is the *pratyag-ātmā*, the innermost soul of every individual, and is only understandable through bhakti, or devotion.

"Hari or Krishna is
the pratyag-atma,
the innermost soul
of every individual, and
is only understandable
through bhakti,
or devotion"

tvaṁ pratyag-ātmani tadā bhagavaty ananta
ānanda-mātra upapanna-samasta-śaktau
bhaktiṁ vidhāya paramāṁ śanakair avidyā-
granthiṁ vibhetsyasi mamāham iti prarūḍham

"By engaging in intense devotion to the Supersoul, the Supreme Lord who is infinite, defined by joy alone, and in whom all potencies are present, you will slowly cut the tight knots of ignorance based in the concepts of 'I' and 'mine.'"
(*Śrīmad Bhāgavatam* 4.11.30)

Brahman is said to be unknowable, ineffable, unmanifest and imperceptible by the material senses. Even so, it must not be said that He is completely unattainable. If we think that He can never be attained, then we will lose hope, and that is a serious impediment to ever taking up devotional service. For this reason, Baladeva quotes a line from the *Kaivalya Upanishad*: *śraddhā-bhakti-dhyāna-yogād avaiti*—"One can have direct knowledge of Him through the discipline of faith, devotion, and meditation."

Baladeva further explains, "Faith is firm belief; devotion is a reference to the numerous devotional practices beginning with hearing; and meditation means thinking of Brahman uninterruptedly—one's thought being like a stream of oil. The word 'yoga' in the text means that the discipline combines all three of these practices. The word *avaiti*, 'he knows,' means to have *sākṣātkāra*—direct perception or experience of Brahman." (*Govínda-bhāṣya*)

"If one engages properly in the course of devotional practices, then the Lord becomes accessible even to our senses"

In the *Bhagavad-gītā*, Krishna says that He can only be known by devotion (*bhaktyā mām abhijānāti*). He confirms the same to Uddhava in the *Bhāgavatam: bhaktyāham ekayā grāhyaḥ* (11.14.21). The *Māṭhara-śruti* further glorifies bhakti:

bhaktir evainaṁ nayati
bhaktir evainaṁ darśayati
bhakti-vaśaḥ puruṣaḥ
bhaktir eva bhūyasī

"Devotion attracts Him, devotion reveals Him; the Lord is influenced by devotion. Nothing is more powerful than bhakti."

All these texts confirm that although the Lord is inconceivable and unmanifest, devotion has the power to reveal His form.

A well-known aphorism from the *Vedanta Sutras* (3.2.24)—*api saṁrādhane pratyakṣānumānābhyām*—also broaches the same subject. The sutra arises in the context of the possible objection that the Supersoul or the Param Brahman cannot be perceived by sight and the other senses. The first word of the aphorism, *api*, specifically condemns the idea. If one is properly engaged in devotional practices (*saṁrādhane*), the Lord becomes accessible even to our senses. This is confirmed by the *Śruti* (*pratyakṣa*) and the *Śmṛti* (*anumāna*).[1]

In the *Govinda-bhāṣya* commentary to this sutra, Baladeva quotes two verses from the *Śruti* and two from the *Bhagavad-gītā* (*Smṛti*) to support the idea that certain devotees fixed in knowledge do indeed see the Lord:

parāñci khāni vyatṛṇat svayambhūs
tasmāt parāṅ paśyati nāntarātman
kaścid dhīraḥ pratyag-ātmānam aikṣad
āvṛtta-cakṣur amṛtatvam icchan

"The Self-born Creator pierced holes facing outward (making eyes in the body); therefore men look outward and do not see the soul within. Desiring immortality, some wise men turn their eyes inward and see the atman, who dwells within."
(*Kaṭha Upanishad* 2.1.1)

na cakṣuṣā gṛhyate nāpi vācā
nānyair devais tapasā karmaṇā vā
jñāna-prasādena viśuddha-sattvas
tatas tu taṁ paśyati niṣkalaṁ dhyāyamānaḥ

"Though He cannot be seen by the eyes, described by words, revealed by the gods, or understood through austerities or rituals, one whose very being has been purified by [scriptural] knowledge can see Him in His entirety by meditation."
(*Muṇḍaka Upanishad* 3.1.8)

In the *Bhagavad-gītā* also, Krishna further confirms the possibility of a direct vision of the Lord:

nāhaṁ vedair na tapasā
na dānena na cejyayā
śakya evaṁ-vidho draṣṭuṁ
dṛṣṭavān asi māṁ yathā

bhaktyā tv ananyayā śakya
aham evaṁ-vidho 'rjuna
jñātuṁ draṣṭuṁ ca tattvena
praveṣṭuṁ ca parantapa

"I cannot be seen in the same way that you have seen Me simply through a study of the Veda, nor through serious penances, charity, or worship. O Arjuna, it is only through undivided devotional service that I can be known in this way, that I can be seen, and indeed, entered into." (*Gītā* 11.53-54)

A gopi serves the Lord

The phrase "in the same way" (*evaṁ-vidho*) in these verses refers to Krishna's human form. Baladeva concludes: "Therefore, by the perfect performance of devotional service (*samyag-bhaktyā*) the Lord can indeed be perceived. At this time, the eyes and the other senses are saturated with devotion and this gives them the ability to know him."[2]

Once a person (the "wise individual" or *dhīra* in the *Kaṭha Upanishad* verse quoted above) stops seeking the satisfaction of his own senses, he attains love of Krishna, in which he seeks only the pleasure of Krishna's senses. In the context of Baladeva's comments on the *Vedanta Sutra*, such a person obtains divine sight when his eyes are smeared with the unguent of love. This gives him the qualification to behold Śyāmasundara's divine form of unparalleled beauty.

The Different Forms of Yoga

In some places, the scriptures glorify ritual activity or disinterested works as being the best means for spiritual accomplishment, or *abhidheya*; in others, they glorify knowledge. These are also known as yogas, or spiritual disciplines. Yoga also means "uniting with the supreme." The abovementioned yogas are thus known as *karma-yoga* and *jñāna-yoga*. It is a fact however, that the topmost process for achieving spiritual perfection is devotion, or Bhakti yoga. Bhakti is completely independent of any other kind of process, whereas *karma*, *jñāna* and *yoga* all rely on bhakti to give their full rewards. This is stated in the *Chaitanya Charitāmṛta* (2.22.17):

kṛṣṇa-bhakti haya abhidheya pradhāna
bhakti-mukha-nirīkṣaka karma-yoga-jñāna

> "The primary rewards of *karma*, *jñāna*, and mystic yoga, namely sense enjoyment, liberation and mystic powers, are all considered by the devotees to be most insignificant. These processes have no independent power to bestow rewards on the practitioner. Even liberation itself stands with hands folded, waiting for the opportunity to serve bhakti. The other goals of life—religiosity, wealth, and sense enjoyments—are even more dependent on bhakti and stand quietly waiting for her glance of mercy."

Although the entire *Bhagavad-gītā* deals with the subject of yoga, the sixth chapter in particular discusses the meditational form of yogic discipline (the eightfold yogic system) that is usually equated with the term yoga. At the end of that chapter, two verses clearly state that of all the yogas, Bhakti yoga, or the discipline of devotion, is the best.[3]

In his explanation of these verses, our predecessor *ācārya* Bhaktivinoda Ṭhākura has explained the meaning of the term yoga and discussed the differences between the different types of yogic practice: "A fruitive worker (*sakāma-karmī*) cannot be called a yogi, for this term is only applicable to the disinterested worker, the philosopher, the follower of the eightfold mystic path, and the practitioner of devotional service. The word yoga itself refers to the gradual path of spiritual development. Any person who takes to yoga is on the road to a direct experience of the Supreme Spirit.

"The yoga of desireless action is the first step along this path, and when knowledge and renunciation are added to such action, the aspirant advances to the stage of *jñāna-yoga*. When direct meditation on the Supreme Lord is added to the other qualities, then one advances to the stage of practicing the eightfold yogic system, or *aṣṭāṅga yoga*. The fourth and highest stage is when the feeling of love for the Supreme Person is added to these disciplines.

"Any person who takes to yoga is on the road to a direct experience of the Supreme Spirit"

"The seeker of the ultimate good will veritably engage in the spiritual discipline of yoga. As one takes to the practices of each successive stage of development, a necessity to develop strong determination and faith in its practices will ensue. However, as he advances, he will ultimately have to discard his strict adherence to the detailed practices of that particular stage. If one remains attached to one or the other of these stages without going on further, he is identified with the partial yogic practice to which he has been limited. As a result, some persons are known as *karma-yogis*, some are *jñāna-yogis*, while others are *aṣṭāṅga-yogis* or *bhakti-yogis*.

"Krishna says, 'Therefore, O Arjuna, anyone who makes it his exclusive goal to engage in devotion to Me alone is superior to the three other kinds of yogi. You should therefore become a yogi, that is, a *bhakti-yogi*. Through the yoga of desireless action one advances in knowledge; through the yoga of knowledge, one advances to the yoga of meditation on the Supreme Lord and from there, one finally progresses to the yoga of devotion, characterized by love for the Supreme Person.' "

In his commentary to these verses, Viśvanātha Cakravartī writes: *karmī jñānī ca yogī mataḥ/ aṣṭāṅga-yogī yogitaraḥ/ śravaṇa-kīrtanādi-bhaktimāṁs tu yogitama ity arthaḥ:* "The *karmī* and *jñānī* are considered yogis. The *aṣṭāṅga-yogi*, the follower of the eightfold yoga system of Patañjali, is considered to be a greater spiritualist than the aforementioned two. But the best of all yogis is one who practices devotional acts like hearing and chanting."

Thus a devotee takes no interest in other practices of yoga, which are partial. The devotee considers them not only incomplete, but even defective because of the presence of ego desire implicit in their practice. The Lord made the following statement to Uddhava:

Sri Radha, the Queen of Vrindavana

tasmād mad-bhakti-yuktasya
yogino vai mad-ātmanaḥ
na jñānaṁ na ca vairāgyaṁ
prāyaḥ śreyo bhaved iha

yat karmabhir yat tapasā
jñāna-vairāgyataś ca yat
yogena dāna-dharmeṇa
śreyobhir itarair api

sarvaṁ mad-bhakti-yogena
mad-bhakto labhate'ñjasā
svargāpavarge mad-dhāma
kathaṁcid yadi vāñchati

na kiṁcid sādhavo dhīrā
bhaktā hy ekāntino mama
vāñchanty api mayā dattaṁ
kaivalyam apunarbhavam

> "For the devoted yogi who has surrendered his thoughts to Me, neither knowledge nor renunciation are considered to be the sources of true good in this world. All the results obtained through ritual practices, penance, philosophy, renunciation, yogic discipline, charity or performance of prescribed duties, are easily obtained by My devotees through the practice of devotional service to Me. My saintly, patient and single-minded devotees desire nothing of all this; nevertheless, I still bestow all these rewards on them, even including liberation and freedom from rebirth." (*Śrīmad Bhāgavatam* 11.20.31-34)

Therefore, other than devotional service, mystical practices are like the teats on the neck of a goat—they serve no worthwhile function. For this reason, an intelligent person gives up the useless tendency to seek out sense enjoyment and liberation and cultivates pure devotion through the practice of Bhakti yoga.

The Perfect Process of Worship

The word *saṁrādhanā* found in the *Vedanta Sutra* aphorism quoted earlier is also significant. It comes from the verb root *rādh*, which means "to worship." The prefix *sam* means "complete or perfect." Also derived from the same root is the name of Krishna's internal potency, Śrī Radha. Rādhārāṇī is the perfect worshiper of Krishna, as indicated by the *Bhāgavatam* verse spoken by the *gopīs* in the description of the *rāsa-līlā:*

anayārādhito nūnaṁ
bhagavān harir īśvaraḥ
yan no vihāya govindaḥ
prīto yām anayad rahaḥ

"Radharani is the perfect worshiper of Krishna"

"Truly the Supreme Lord, the supreme controller, has been perfectly worshiped by Her (Radha). It is for this reason that Govinda was so pleased with Her that He took Her to a secluded spot, leaving all of us behind."
(*Śrīmad Bhāgavatam* 10.30.28)

Chaitanya Mahāprabhu's teachings can be summarized as follows:

ārādhyo bhagavān vrajeśa-tanayas tad-dhāma vṛndāvanam
ramyā kācid upāsana vraja-vadhū-vargeṇā va kalpitā
śrīmad-bhāgavataṁ pramāṇam amalaṁ premān pumartho mahān
śrī-caitanya-mahāprabhor matam idaṁ tatrādaraḥ naḥ paraḥ

"The object of worship (*ārādhya*) is the Lord in His form as the son of the King of Vraja. His abode is Vrindavan and the cowherd girls who live there with Him, chief amongst whom is Rādhikā, are His perfect worshipers, or *sāṁrādhikās*. The most enchanting method of worshiping the Supreme Lord is that devised by these *gopīs*. The most authoritative source of divine revelation is the *Śrīmad Bhāgavatam*. Love for Krishna or *prema* is the fifth and ultimate goal of human life. These are the basic principles of Śrī Chaitanya Mahāprabhu's belief and we thus consider this doctrine to be supreme."

The conclusion is that worshiping Krishna by following Śrīmatī Rādhārāṇī is the spiritual process justifiably named *saṁrādhanā*, "the most perfect process of worship." Any activity of worship in which the element of *prema* is absent will not result in a direct vision of the Supreme Person.

The following couplets are found in the *Chaitanya Charitāmṛta*:

jñāna-karma-yoga-dharme nahe kṛṣṇa vaśa
kṛṣṇa-vaśa-hetu eka prema-bhakti-rasa

"The most enchanting method of worshiping the Supreme Lord is that devised by these gopis"

"By following the paths of speculative philosophical knowledge, fruitive activity or mystic yoga to control the senses, one cannot win Krishna over. The only way of winning His love is through the taste of devotion in ecstatic love."
(*Chaitanya Charitāmṛta* 1.17.75)

aiche śāstra kahe karma jñāna yoga tyaji
bhaktye kṛṣṇa vaśa haya bhaktye tāṅre bhaji

"Such scriptures say that one should give up fruitive activity, speculative knowledge and the mystic yoga system. By devotion, Krishna is won over. Therefore, I worship him with devotion." (*Chaitanya Charitāmṛta* 2.20.136)

Without pure devotion, the awakening of ecstatic love is an impossibility. Pure devotion or *uttamā bhakti* as described by Rūpa Gosvāmī is the culture of Krishna consciousness characterized by the absence of desire for anything but Krishna. Rūpa Gosvāmī further notes that such culture must not be enfeebled by the admixture of practices appropriate to the paths of philosophical speculation and fruitive action. After repeating this same description in the *Chaitanya Charitāmṛta*, Krishnadāsa Kavirāja goes on to say:

ei śuddha-bhakti ihā haite premā haya
pañcarātre bhāgavate ei lakṣaṇa kaya

"This is the definition of pure devotional service from which ecstatic love is developed. The characteristics of such love are described in literatures like the *Bhāgavata* and *Pañcarātra*."[4] (*Chaitanya Charitāmṛta* 2.19.169)

The *Pañcarātra* specifically defines devotional service as the engagement of the senses in the service of the Proprietor of the Senses. It adds that this service is to be free from any contamination by identity with the body and unblemished through being exclusively fixed on the Lord (*Bhakti-rasāmṛta-sindhu* 1.1.12; *Chaitanya Charitāmṛta* 2.19.170):

sarvopādhi-vinirmuktaṁ
tat-paratvena nirmalam
hṛṣīkeṇa hṛṣīkeśa-
sevanaṁ bhaktir ucyate

"Without pure devotion, the awakening of ecstatic love is an impossibility"

And in the *Bhāgavatam*, the following extended description of pure bhakti is given by Kapiladeva to his mother Devahūti:

mad-guṇa-śruti-mātreṇa
mayi sarva-guhāśaye
mano-gatir avicchinnā
yathā gaṅgāmbhaso 'mbudhau

lakṣaṇaṁ bhakti-yogasya
nirguṇasya hy udāhṛtam
ahaituky avyavahitā
yā bhaktiḥ puruṣottame

"The primary sign that pure union in devotion, free from any material quality, has appeared in someone's heart comes when, upon hearing about My qualities, that person's thoughts are drawn immediately and irresistably towards Me, the indweller of every being, in the same way that the waters of the Ganges flow toward the sea. Like the flow of the Ganges, such devotion to the Supreme Person is unmotivated and unimpeded." (*Śrīmad Bhāgavatam* 3.29.10-11)

sālokya-sārṣṭi-sāmīpya-
sārūpyaikatvam apy uta
dīyamānaṁ na gṛhṇanti
vinā mat-sevanaṁ janāḥ

sa eva bhakti-yogākhya
ātyantika udāhṛtaḥ

yenātivrajya tri-guṇaṁ
mad-bhāvāyopapadyate

> "Unless he is assured of having service to the Lord, a pure devotee does not accept any kind of liberation, whether it be residence on the same planet, equal opulences to the Lord, proximity to Him, having the same form as the Lord, or monistic union—even though they may be offered to the devotee by the Lord.
> "Thus I have described the superlative stage of that which is known as Bhakti yoga. By mastering this discipline, one can overcome the three qualities of material nature and attain true feeling (*bhāva*) for Me." (*Bhāgavatam* 3.29.12-13)

The above quotations show that the *Bhāgavata* and the *Pāñcarātrika* schools of thought ultimately reach the same conclusion.

Anyone who engages in the practice of devotional service is gradually freed of the bad habits (*anarthas*) that hold him back from making spiritual progress. As the *anarthas* recede, he becomes firmly fixed in his devotional practices and this firmness allows him to execute his practices with purity and deep attachment. The devotee then goes on developing a real taste (*ruci*) which, when strengthened, develops into the divine emotion and preliminary ecstasies of the *bhāva* stage. From there it is not long before he attains the stage of ecstatic love known as *prema*. A devotee's progress does not stop at this stage of perfection, however. There are numerous stages which develop within ecstatic love, namely *sneha, māna, praṇaya, rāga, anurāga, bhāva,* and *mahābhāva.*

Prayojana

The fourth chapter of the *Vedanta Sutra* is called "the results." The first section or *adhikaraṇa* of this chapter is called *āvṛtty-adhikaraṇa*, or "repetition." The sutra after which this section is named is *āvṛttir asakṛd upadeśāt*: "One must engage in the repeated practice of hearing and chanting, or the uninterrupted meditation on the Supreme, for this instruction has been given again and again." (*Vedanta Sutra* 4.1.1)

Baladeva Vidyābhūsaṇa understands this instruction to be contained in the words repeated nine times to Śvetaketu in the *Chāndogya Upanishad*: *sa ya eṣo'ṇimaitad-ātmyam idaṁ sarvaṁ tat satyaṁ sa ātmā tat tvam asi śvetaketo*: "That which is the smallest of the small is that of which all that exists is made, O Śvetaketu. It is the truth and it is the Self. You are that, O Śvetaketu." The Self here means the Supreme Brahman. The words *tat tvam asi* can also be understood as "you are His."

Thus it is quite logical that the emphasis on sound is found again at the end of the *Vedanta Sutra* in its final aphorism: *anāvṛttiḥ śabdād anāvṛttiḥ śabdāt*—"Revelation tells us that we never come back. Revelation tells us that we never come back." (*Vedanta Sutra* 4.4.22)

The purport is that when one knows the Lord's true identity, one attains His abode of Goloka by the influence of His devotional service. Once he is so liberated, he never again returns to this world of repeated birth and death. The proof of this is found in "sound," or revelation (*śabda*).

The relevant passages Baladeva cites from the revealed scriptures are:

etena pratipadyamānā imaṁ mānavam āvartaṁ nāvartante

"Those who have taken shelter of Brahman and are thus liberated never return to this mortal world of repeated birth and death."

sa khalv evaṁ vartayan yāvad āyuṣaṁ brahma-lokam abhisampadyate
na ca punar āvartate na ca punar āvartate

"The liberated person remains as such throughout his life and then after death goes to the Brahmaloka, whence he never returns, whence he never returns."
(*Chāndogya Upanishad* 8.15.1)

Krishna confirms this statement in the *Gītā* with two important verses:

mām upetya punar janma
duḥkhālayam aśāśvatam
nāpnuvanti mahātmānaḥ
saṁsiddhiṁ paramāṁ gatāḥ

ābrahma-bhuvanāl lokāḥ
punar āvartino 'rjuna
mām upetya tu kaunteya
punar janma na vidyate

"The great devotees who attain the status of participating in My divine pastimes, once having reached Me, never again accept a transitory birth, which is the dwelling house of agony. O Arjuna, from the planet of Lord Brahmā downwards, the residents of all planets are naturally subjected to repeated birth and death. But, upon reaching Me, O Kaunteya, there is no rebirth." (*Gītā* 8.15-16)

Lord Vishnu

The repetition of the phrase *anāvṛttiḥ śabdāt* is an indication that the *Vedanta Sutra* ends with these words.[5]

Of course, for the devotees, *prema*, which is bhakti in its purest form, is its own reward. Devotees are therefore ready to take birth in any lowly species as long as they can be assured of some service to the Lord, which is the highest good as far as they are concerned. This attitude is exemplified by Lord Brahmā in his prayers to Gopāla Krishna:

tad astu me nātha sa bhūri-bhāgo
bhave'tra vānyatra tu vā tiraścām
yenāham eko'pi bhavaj-janānāṁ
bhūtvā niṣeve tava pāda-pallavam

"O my lord, allow me to have that great good fortune, either in this life or in another, even if it be in the body of a lowly creature, whereby I can live amongst your intimate devotees and serve Your lotus feet."
(*Śrīmad Bhāgavatam* 10.14.30)

Śrīla Bhaktivinoda Ṭhākura repeats the same sentiment in one of the songs in his *Gītāvalī*:

janmāobi moe icchā jadi tora
bhakta-gṛhe jani janma ha-u mora
kīṭa janma hau jathā tuwā dāsa
bahirmukha brahmā nāhi āśa

"O Lord, if it is your wish that I should take birth again, grant me birth in the house of a devotee. I will even gladly become a worm or an insect as long as I can be Your servant, but I have no interest in becoming a Brahmā who has no interest in Your service." (*Śaraṇāgati* 11)

"A devotee is therefore ready to take birth in any lowly species as long as he can be assured of some service to the Lord, which is the highest good as far as he is concerned"

What is Sādhanā Bhakti?

In this way, bhakti is both the *abhidheya* and the *prayojana*, both the means to perfection and perfection itself. It is said there are three levels of bhakti: devotion in practice (*sādhanā-bhakti*), devotion on the level of ecstasy (*bhāva-bhakti*), and devotion on the level of pure love (*prema-bhakti*). *Bhāva-bhakti* is attained when the devotional service in practice has become mature and when intensified it becomes *prema-bhakti.*

Devotional service in practice is defined by Rūpa Gosvāmī in the *Bhakti-rasāmṛta-sindhu* as follows:

kṛti-sādhyā bhavet sādhya-
bhāvā sā sādhanābhidhā
nitya-siddhasya bhāvasya
prākaṭyaṁ hṛdi sādhyatā

"That devotion which is executed by the senses and which aims at the attainment of *bhāva* is called *sādhanā-bhakti.* The *bhāva* which it seeks is eternally perfect and simply becomes manifest in the heart of the practitioner." (*Bhakti-rasāmṛta-sindhu* 1.2.2)

Here, Rūpa Gosvāmī warns against a misunderstanding of the term *sādhanā.* Through the execution of the regulative principles of devotion one does not create or produce *bhāva-bhakti,* or devotional feeling. Devotional feeling or *bhāva* is a manifestation of Krishna's internal potency and thus eternally perfect or *nitya-siddha.* Devotion is the eternal natural mood of the living being, and through the practice of devotional service, it is revealed in the heart of the devotee. This is how one should understand the object of the practice. Krishnadāsa Kavirāja Gosvāmī explains this verse as follows:

śravaṇādi-kriyā tāra svarūpa-lakṣaṇa
taṭastha-lakṣaṇe upajāya prema-dhana
nitya-siddha kṛṣṇa-prema sādhya kabhu naya
śravaṇādi-śuddha-citte karaye udaya

"The activities of hearing, chanting, remembering and so forth make up the essential characteristic (*svarūpa-lakṣaṇa*) of devotional service. Its marginal characteristic (*taṭastha-lakṣaṇa*) is that it awakens pure love for Krishna. It is never possible to create pure love for Krishna; rather, it appears in the heart which has been purified by devotional practices like hearing and chanting." (*Chaitanya Charitāmṛta* 2.22.103-4)

In his *Amṛta-pravāha-bhāṣya*, Bhaktivinoda Ṭhākura elaborates on these verses as follows: "The essential characteristic of devotional service consists of activities like hearing and chanting about Krishna with the appropriate attitude. This characteristic results in the treasure of *prema* manifesting when the practitioner gives up all other desires and cuts off all relation to fruitive activities and the search for liberation. Love for Krishna is *nitya-siddha* (eternally self-manifest). It cannot be attained by any means other than pure devotional service. It wells up in the mind which has been purified by the process of devotional service in practice. Therefore, activities such as pure chanting and hearing are the essential elements of devotional service in practice."

Vaidhī Bhakti

Devotional service in practice is of two types: *vaidhī bhakti* ("devotion based on regulative principles") and *rāgānugā bhakti* ("devotion which follows in the wake of spontaneous love"). These have also been explained in the *Chaitanya Charitāmṛta*:

rāga-hīna jana bhaje śāstrera ājñāya
vaidhī bhakti bali tāre sarva-śāstre gāya

> "One who has no spontaneous attachment for the Lord worships Him because it is ordained in the scriptures. All scriptures call such devotional service *vaidhī bhakti*." (*Chaitanya Charitāmṛta* 2.22.106)

The word *rāga* means a natural desire for the Supreme Soul, a natural attachment or affection. If such a natural affection has not arisen in one's heart, but he has developed faith in the scriptural injunctions after hearing from the saintly persons, he may perform devotional service beginning with accepting a guru. Such devotional service is called *vaidhī bhakti*. There are sixty-four different activities and prohibitions which make up this type of regulated devotion. The three main regulations are taking shelter of a spiritual master, being initiated by him and serving him. Among the other sixty-one activities, five are considered to be the most important: associating with devotees, singing the Holy Names, hearing the *Bhāgavatam*, residing in Mathurā (i.e., the holy *dhāma*), and worshiping the deity with faith. Only a small amount of effort in these activities will result in the practitioner developing love for Krishna. The great authorities or *mahājanas* say that whether you practice only one of these five activities or all of them, unless you practice with constancy or *niṣṭhâ*, you will not be washed by the waves of *prema*. *Niṣṭhā* has been defined by Jīva Gosvāmī as *avikṣepeṇa sātatyam*, or steadfastness without distraction. The idea is that one should be fixed in a particular practice with unshakable faith.

"Devotional feeling or bhava is a manifestation of Krishna's internal potency"

eka aṅga sādhe keha sādhe bahu aṅga
niṣṭhā haile upajaya premera taraṅga

> "Whether a person executes only one or many of the processes of devotional service, the waves of love of Godhead will arise if he or she practices with fixed determination or *niṣṭhā*." (*Chaitanya Charitāmṛta* 2.22.130)

Elsewhere, Mahāprabhu says that the nine types of devotion named by Prahlāda are the best amongst the sixty-four devotional practices. Of these nine, the first three (hearing, chanting and remembering) are considered superior. Of these three, *kīrtana* is the best.

Kīrtana itself is subdivided into several categories: glorification of Krishna's names, His form, His attributes and His activities. Of these, pride of place is given to the chanting of His names. Anyone who takes up the chanting of the Holy Names with constancy is sure to obtain the mercy of the Name and he will quickly relish the taste of love of God.

"The three main regulations are taking shelter of a spiritual master, being initiated by him and serving him"

RĀGĀNUGĀ BHAKTI

The great authorities or *mahājanas* say that the practice of devotion purely on the strength of the scriptural injunctions leads to the Lord's majestic feature in the abode of Vaikuṇṭha, not to that aspect of the Lord which resides in Vraja. To attain Vraja, one must take up the practice of *rāgānugā bhakti*. This is stated in the *Chaitanya Charitāmṛta* (1.3.15):

sakala jagate more kare vidhi-bhakti
vidhi-bhaktye vraja-bhāva pāite nāhi śakti

"Everyone throughout the world worships Me according to scriptural injunctions; but by this process of *vaidhī bhakti* one cannot attain the loving moods of Vraja."

The preceding verses certainly tell us that only worship on the *rāga* path can result in obtaining the service of Krishna in Vraja. However, what we must try to understand here is the following: if one thinks on that basis that the various regulative principles of the *vidhi-mārga* can be dispensed with before acquiring a readiness for the manifestation of *rāgānugā bhakti*, such a person will become a religious hypocrite, a pretender and a *prākṛta-sahajiyā*. For this reason, Bhaktivinoda Ṭhākura has written in his song *Kṛṣṇa-nāma dhare kata bal?*:

vidhi-mārga-rata jane svādhīnatā ratna dāne
rāga-mārge karān praveśa
rāga-vaśavartī haiyā pārakīya bhāvāśraye
labhe jīva kṛṣṇa-premāveśa

"To the person fixed in the regulative principles, the Holy Name gives the jewel of independence, placing him on the path of spontaneous devotion. That person, overcome by spontaneous attachment to the Lord, takes shelter of the *parakīyā* mood and goes on to become absorbed in love for Krishna."

"To attain Vraja, one must take up the practice of raganuga bhakti"

One who aims for the ultimate goal of pure love for Krishna should start by taking shelter of a spiritual master according to the scriptural injunctions and following the *vidhi-mārga* by continuously chanting the Holy Names of the Lord. He will thus very quickly obtain the qualifications necessary for the manifestation of spontaneous affection. As the undesirable elements of one's character (*anarthas*) are destroyed, spontaneous affection automatically awakens. On the other hand, if one does not rid himself of these undesirable elements, the discussion of subjects for which he is not qualified will in all likelihood have disastrous consequences.

It is premature to think that as soon as one has taken shelter of his spiritual master he has the right to relish books like the *Bhāgavata's Rāsa-pañcādhyāya*, *Gopīgītā*, *Uddhava-saṁvāda*, or *Govinda-līlāmṛta* and *Kṛṣṇa-bhāvanāmṛta*, the songs of Caṇḍīdāsa and Vidyâpati, *Jagannātha-vallabha-nāṭaka*, *Kṛṣṇa-karṇāmṛta*, *Gītā-govinda*, and other books of this type. The inevitable consequence of such precocious entry into the subjects of Krishna's conjugal pastimes is that one falls into illicit sexual activity.

Faith is the Seed of the Devotional Creeper

Faith is the seed of the devotional creeper. The seed of the creeper of *vaidhī bhakti* is faith in the regulative principles given in the scripture; the seed of the creeper of *rāgānugā bhakti* is faith based on intense desire for the spontaneous love of the residents of Vraja. One who has faith is eligible for the practice of devotion (*śraddhāvān jana haya bhakti-adhikārī—Chaitanya Charitāmṛta* 2.22.64). If one does not have this faith based in intense desire (*lobha-mūlā śraddhā*), then various pitfalls are inevitable in the practice of *rāgānugā bhakti*. On the other hand, if he has acquired such faith, he will be able to constantly listen to the nectarean pastimes of Vrajendranandana, such as the *rāsa-līlā*, and the supreme devotion which arises of such attachment will cleanse his heart of the disease of material desire. With the dissolution of mundane desire, an intense urge arises to serve the senses of Madana-mohana, the transcendental Cupid who enchants the mundane Cupid with His beauty. It is only at this point in one's spiritual development that one will be able to properly engage in the practices of *rāgānugā bhakti* such as hearing, chanting and meditating on the *aṣṭa-kālīya līlās*. As long as material desires are present in the heart, it is very possible that a concerted effort to enter into erotic subject matter such as those described in Jayadeva's *Gītā-govinda* will have inauspicious results.

A Gopi fans the Lord with a camara.

One must thus be careful to follow the direction of the guru closely; there are many dangers in trying to follow the *vraja-bhāva* on one's own. One should follow the process as given by a bonafide guru, carefully engaging in the devotional activities as prescribed by him. As the disciple does so, he will gradually clear his heart of all unwanted elements and then with good fortune, progress through the stages described by Rūpa Gosvāmī—*niṣṭhā, ruci, āsakti,* then *bhāva* and *prema.* One should pay careful attention not to fall into the dangerous trap of thinking himself to be an advanced devotee. Since Mahāprabhu has assured us that *nāma-bhajana* is the best of all devotional practices and the source of all perfection, we should lay to rest any doubts that *nāma-bhajana* is inappropriate for any stage of devotional life, whether one is a beginner, a practitioner or a perfected soul.[6]

"The seed of the creeper
of raganuga bhakti
is faith based
in the intense desire
for the spontaneous love
of the residents of Vraja"

sadā nāma laibe yathā-lābhete santoṣa
ei ta ācāra kare bhakti-dharma-poṣa

> "One should always chant the Holy Name and be satisfied with whatever comes to him as his lot. Such behavior is propitious for the development of devotion."
> (*Chaitanya Charitāmṛta* 1.17.30)

Since chanting the Holy Name is the only practice, and since the Holy Name alone is the only object of practice, one should endeavor with great determination to take shelter of the Holy Name in all times and circumstances. If we are able to do this, the Holy Name will bestow His mercy on us and destroy all the *anarthas* in our hearts and cause all auspiciousness to manifest there. When a purified feeling of love for Krishna's name arises, then the same kind of purified love for the Named also arises. At this point the purified feelings of *rāga* become possible.

īṣat vikaśi punaḥ dekhāya nija-rūpa-guṇa
citta hari laya kṛṣṇa pāśa
pūrṇa vikaśita hañā vraje more jāya lañā
dekhāya nija svarūpa vilāsa

"When the Name is even slightly revealed, it shows me my own spiritual form and characteristics. It steals my mind and takes it to Krishna's side. When the Name is fully revealed, it takes me directly to Vraja, where it shows me my personal role in the eternal pastimes." (*Śaraṇāgati*)

"When a purified feeling of love for Krishna's name arises, then the same kind of purified love for the Name also arises"

The conclusion, then, is that the worship of the Holy Name is the best means of developing one's devotional attitude and is thus the means through which one's Vraja mood is revealed. To take up the chanting of the Holy Name is thus to embark on the way to the perfection of worship.

Chapter II

The Purifying Power of Service

In the *Bhagavad-gītā*, the Lord states,

daivī hy eṣā guṇamayī
mama māyā duratyayā
mām eva ye prapadyante
māyām etāṁ taranti te

"The external energy consisting of the three qualities is divinely empowered and thus impossible to overcome. Whoever surrenders to Me, however, can cross over this maya." (*Bhagavad-Gītā* 7.14)

Viśvanātha Cakravartī notes that this verse prompts the question, "In view of the great benefits which come from surrendering to the Lord, why then aren't there more intelligent people who do so?" The succinct answer given by Viśvanātha is that those people may think themselves to be intelligent, but in fact they are not. The truly intelligent, the truly learned, will indeed surrender to the Lord. Those who lack such piety go on to be *kupaṇḍitas* rather than *supaṇḍitas*—people whose learning has been used for personal gain and self-aggrandizement rather than for the satisfaction of the Lord. To clarify this, Krishna goes on to say:

na māṁ duṣkṛtino mūḍhāḥ
prapadyante narādhamāḥ
māyayāpahṛta-jñānā
āsuraṁ bhāvam āśritāḥ

"The wicked do not surrender to Me. They are foolish and the lowest of mankind; their intelligence has been robbed of them by illusion and they have taken refuge in a demoniac mentality." (*Gītā* 7.15)

Śrīla Viśvanātha Cakravartī Ṭhākura comments on this verse that there are four kinds of wicked people (*duṣkṛtin*) who do not surrender to the Lord: (1) the foolish (*mūḍhāḥ*), (2) the lowest of humankind (*narādhamāḥ*), (3) those whose knowledge has been robbed by illusion (*māyayāpahṛta-jñānāḥ*) and (4) those who are of a demonic mentality (*āsuraṁ bhāvam āśritāḥ*). He goes on to analyze the characteristics of each of these types:

(1) The foolish. *Eke mūḍhāḥ paśu-tulyāḥ karmiṇaḥ*. These are the fruitive workers who are on a par with the animals. They have no regard for the eternal delights of Krishna conscious philosophy but seek rather the fleeting pleasures of sense gratification in this world and later in heaven.

(2) The lowest of humankind (*narādhamāḥ*). These people have accepted the principles of devotion for a short time at some point in their lives and thus can be considered to have achieved the status of human beings. However, before achieving the goal of devotional practice they give it up, thinking it not worth the effort. Such a voluntary rejection of bhakti is the symptom of their being the lowest of humankind.

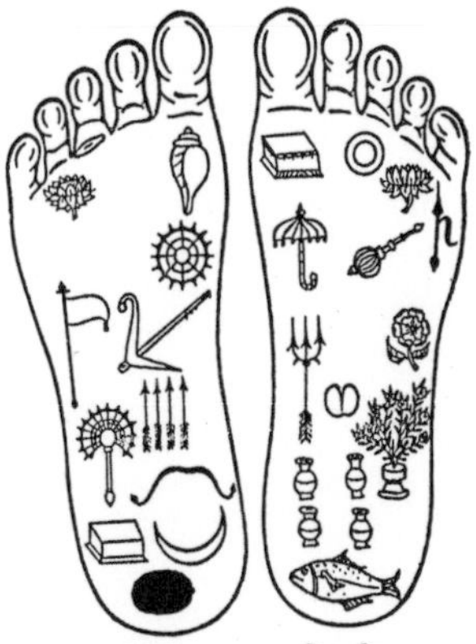

শ্রীশ্রীনিত্যানন্দপ্রভুর শ্রীচরণচিহ্ন

Nityananda's lotus feet

(3) The next class are those who, despite having studied and even taught the scriptures, have lost their powers of discrimination due to the influence of the Lord's external energy. These people think that the divine form of Nārāyaṇa in Vaikuṇṭha alone is worthy of our eternal praise and devotion, but they take Rāma and Krishna not to be similarly worthy, thinking them to be ordinary human beings. It is for such persons that the Lord spoke the verse, *avajānanti māṁ mūḍhāḥ mānuṣīṁ tanum āśritam* (9.11): "Fools have no respect for Me when I take a human form." Though these people may give the appearance of being surrendered devotees, this is not the case.

(4) The demons are those who have become the enemies of the Lord. They are like Jarāsandha who saw the form of the Lord but shot arrows at it. Such persons argue falsely that because Krishna's form can be seen, it is therefore the same as other forms visible in the material world. They project this belief even onto Nārāyaṇa in Vaikuṇṭha and try to cut up His body of eternity, consciousness and bliss. As a result, they never surrender to Him.

THOSE WHO COME TO DEVOTIONAL SERVICE

In the *Gītā*'s next verse, Lord Krishna goes on to describe four sorts of people who do surrender to Him:

catur-vidhā bhajante māṁ
janāḥ sukṛtino' rjuna
ārto jijñāsur arthārthī
jñānī ca bharatarṣabha

"Four kinds of pious persons worship Me, O Arjuna. These are the afflicted, those who seek wisdom, those who seek gain, and the wise." (*Gītā* 7.16)

The afflicted (*ārta*) are those suffering from disease or some other hardship who seek freedom from these sufferings. The one who seeks wisdom (*jijñāsu*) may be either someone looking for knowledge of the self, or a student with interests in some other field of learning like grammar. Those seeking gain (*arthārthī*) wish to enjoy sense objects like land, beautiful women and money. The wise (*jñānī*) are those who are internally purified and renounced. Viśvanātha states that the pious (*sukṛtiṇaḥ*) are those who are religiously engaged in following the prescribed duties of the *varṇāśrama-dharma.*

The first three of these pious types are householders who still have mundane desires whereas the last is a desireless renunciate, a sannyasi. All four, however, are performers of mixed devotion: the first three engage in devotion mixed with karma (*karma-miśrā bhakti*), while the last engages in devotion mixed with knowledge (*jñāna-miśrā bhakti*), or the *yoga-miśrā bhakti* which is described in the *Gītā*'s eighth chapter (see also 8.12). When devotion is not mixed with any of these other elements, it is called *kevalā,* or exclusive devotion; this is known as pure bhakti and is described in a number of verses in the *Gītā*:

> "Those who seek gain (artharthi) wish to enjoy sense objects like land, beautiful women and money. The wise (jnani) are internally purified and renounced"

mayy āsakta-manāḥ pārtha
yogaṁ yuñjan mad-āśrayaḥ
asaṁśayaṁ samagraṁ māṁ
yathā jñāsyasi tac chṛṇu

"Now hear, O son of Pṛthā, how by engaging in yoga while taking shelter of Me and with your mind attached to Me, you can know Me fully, free from doubt." (*Gītā* 7.1)

ananya-cetāḥ satataṁ
yo māṁ smarati nityaśaḥ
tasyāhaṁ sulabhaḥ pārtha
nitya-yuktasya yoginaḥ

"For the yogi who is always disciplined and unceasingly remembers Me without deviation, I am easy to obtain, O son of Pṛthā." (*Gītā* 8.14)

mahātmānas tu māṁ pārtha
daivīṁ prakṛtim āśritāḥ
bhajanty ananya-manaso
jñātvā bhūtādim avyayam

satataṁ kīrtayanto māṁ
yatantaś ca dṛḍha-vratāḥ
namasyantaś ca māṁ bhaktyā
nitya-yuktā upāsate

"O son of Pṛthā, the great souls who take shelter of the divine nature worship Me with undivided attention because they know My unlimited opulences. They are constantly chanting My glories, endeavoring fully while keeping firm in their vows, bowing down to Me with devotion and worshiping Me, permanently united with Me." (*Gītā* 9.13-14)

ananyāś cintayanto māṁ
ye janāḥ paryupāsate
teṣāṁ nityābhiyuktānāṁ
yoga-kṣemaṁ vahāmy aham

"I personally assume responsibility for protecting and acquiring all the necessities of life for My fully dependent devotees who are always absorbed in thought of Me alone and who worship Me exclusively in all respects." (*Gītā* 9.22)

In His very last instruction in the *Bhagavad-gītā* (*sarva-dharmān parityājya mām ekaṁ śaraṇaṁ vraja*), Lord Krishna states that one should abandon all duties previously prescribed in the Vedic scriptures, including the *varṇāśrama-dharma*, or other regulations governing the bodily activities or thought. Further, one should concentrate on the most confidential teaching of the scripture—the personal nature of the Supreme Lord—and surrender exclusively to Him. Thus the kind of piety (*sukṛti*) needed to attain this pure or exclusive devotion is that which is directed to worshiping the Supreme Lord (*bhakty-unmukhī*).

THE TRANSITION FROM IMPIETY TO SURRENDER

Śrīla Saccidānanda Bhaktivinoda Ṭhākura gives an expanded discussion of these verses in his translation of the *Bhagavad-gītā*, explaining how one goes from reluctance to engaging in the Lord's service to enthusiasm. He paraphrases the *Bhagavad-gītā* verses as follows: "The Lord says, 'It is almost impossible for those who are impious to engage in My devotional service because they are not on the path of progressive development. Even so, there are occasionally some unregulated or impious individuals who are exceptions to this rule and take suddenly to the path of devotion.

"It is almost impossible for those who are impious to engage in My devotional service because they are not on the path of progressive development"

"Among the pious who follow a regulated lifestyle, there are four types who engage in My service. Anyone who seeks the fulfilment of material desires suffers when his or her hopes are frustrated. In the midst of such suffering, such people remember Me. I call these people *ārta*, 'the distressed.' Impious people who do not follow a regulated lifestyle, however, never think of Me even when distressed.

"The previously mentioned foolish persons (*mūḍhas*), the godless empiricists and logicians, come around to remembering Me when they begin to feel a need for the concept of a supreme being in their researches. These are the *jijñāsus*.

"Those whom I have described as 'the lowest of mankind' (*narādhama*) accept the principle of deity as a necessity for ethics, but not that ethics are founded in the principle of the deity. When these people become dissatisfied with their inadequate concept of God and realize that the deity stands above ethics, they become devotees on the path of *vaidhī bhakti*, seeking some return for their devotional practice as *arthārthīs*.

"Those whom I have called *māyayāpahṛta-jñānāḥ* worship Shiva or Brahmā but do not have accurate knowledge of *sambandha*—they do not recognize that the Supreme Lord eternally possesses potencies, that the *jīva* is an eternally individual spark of consciousness, and that the *jīva*'s relation to the unconscious material energy is temporary. Most of all they don't recognize that their relationship of service to the Supreme Lord is their eternal constitutional position. As a result, even though they study the Vedanta and other philosophical works, their knowledge is covered. When a *jīva* whose intelligence has been stolen by the illusory energy recognizes that the Brahman and Paramātman conceptions of the Supreme Truth are incomplete and takes shelter of the personal conception of the deity, Bhagavān, the Lord Himself removes the covering over his intelligence. The *jīva* then recognizes that he is the eternal servant of the Lord and takes up the sixfold path of surrender (*prapatti*).[1]

Sri Krishna embraces His devotee upon returning home to the spiritual world.

"Thus, when the distressed person's covering of desire is removed, when the seeker of knowledge (*jijñāsu*) gives up the covering which restricts him to ethically-based knowledge, the seeker of profit (*arthārthī*) gives up the trivial desire for sensual happiness in the hereafter, and the philosophers (*jñānī*) give up their attachment to merging into the impersonal aspect of the truth and their belief that the personal aspect is a temporary manifestation, then these four kinds of persons can also become eligible for devotional service. As long as these impurities remain, they will at best engage in mixed devotional service. Only when the impurities are removed can someone engage in *kevalā, akiñcanā,* or *uttamā bhakti*."

The word used by Bhaktivinoda Ṭhākura for impurity is *kaṣāya*. All impurities have at their base the desire for the satisfaction of one's own senses. When the distressed, the curious, the materially motivated and the learned give up their sensually based desires and begin thinking of how they can please the Lord, their devotion becomes free of impurities—this is pure devotional service.

The Lord Holds the Pure Devotee Most Dear

Lord Krishna continues His discussion in the *Gītā*'s seventh chapter by specifying that, of the four types of people who take up devotional service, the *jñānī* is supreme:

teṣāṁ jñānī nitya-yukta
eka-bhaktir viśiṣyate
priyo hi jñānino 'tyartham
ahaṁ sa ca mama priyaḥ

> "Of these four types of worshipers, the philosopher situated in knowledge of Me who is permanently engaged in single-minded devotion stands out. I, in My form as Śyāmasundara, am most dear to such a philosopher and he is most dear to Me." (*Gītā* 7.17)

udārāḥ sarva evaite
jñānī tv ātmaiva me matam
āsthitaḥ sa hi yuktātmā
mām evānuttamāṁ gatim

> "All these devotees are undoubtedly magnanimous souls, but the philosopher is My very soul. Being ever in union with Me, he is convinced that I am the unexcelled goal of life." (*Gītā* 7.18)

We cannot say that the Lord has no affection whatsoever for the distressed person, the seeker of wealth and the curious person who have taken up His devotional service. The Lord is like a desire tree and to some extent He awards all of His worshipers the objects of their desires. And of course, these devotees gladly accept them. The truly knowledgeable philosopher, however, does not ask anything of the Lord, whether it be life in heaven or salvation from all material involvement. This is why he is so dear to the Lord. He has realized that more than the formless aspect of Brahman, the Lord's form as the beautiful blackish boy is the unexcelled goal of life. The Lord holds this desireless philosopher to be so dear that He considers him to be equal to Himself.

"The Lord considers the exclusive, pure devotee to be even dearer than Himself"

The Lord considers the exclusive, pure devotee to be even dearer than Himself. He therefore says to Uddhava:

na tathā me priyatama
ātma-yonir na śaṅkaraḥ
na ca saṅkarṣaṇo na śrīr
naivātmā ca yathā bhavān

"No one is as dear to Me as you, O Uddhava, not My son Brahmā, not Shiva who was born out of My very body, not My brother Saṅkarṣaṇa, not Lakṣmī, My consort who dwells on My chest, not even My own body."
(*Śrīmad Bhāgavatam* 11.14.15)

Elsewhere in the *Bhāgavatam*, the Lord says,

nāham ātmānam āśāse
mad-bhaktaiḥ sādhubhir vinā
śriyaṁ cātyantikīṁ brahman
yeṣāṁ gatir ahaṁ parā

"O brahmin, I have no desire to enjoy My transcendental bliss and My supreme opulences without the saintly devotees for whom I am the only goal in life."
(*Śrīmad Bhāgavatam* 9.4.64)

The Association of Devotees is the Purifying Force

In Śrīla Viśvanātha Cakravartī's opinion, the three types of devotees—the *ārta, jijñāsu* and *arthārthī*—all have desires, whereas the *jñānī* is desireless. Krishnadāsa Kavirāja Gosvāmī, however, differs somewhat. He writes that the *ārta* and *arthārthī* have material desires, while the *jijñāsu* and *jñānī* are desirous of attaining liberation. If they develop the kind of piety which leads to devotion (*bhakty-unmukhī sukṛti*), then they can give up their desires and begin worshiping the Lord.

ārta arthārthī dui sakāma-bhitare gaṇi
jijñāsu jñānī dui mokṣa-kāma māni
ei cāri sukṛti haya mahā-bhāgyavān
tat-tat-kāmādi chāḍi haya śuddha-bhaktimān

"I consider the distressed person and the seeker of wealth to be materialistic devotees, while I take the curious person and the philosopher to be desirous of liberation. All four of these types of pious individuals are to be considered greatly fortunate for they gradually give up the desires which rule them and become pure devotees." (*Chaitanya Charitāmṛta* 2.24.95-96)

SELF-DECEPTION AND CHEATING—THE DESIRES FOR BHUKTI AND MUKTI

The spotless authority for spiritual knowledge is the *Śrīmad Bhāgavatam*. Its purpose is to describe a religious system that is free from all self-deception. This is stated in the introductory verses of the *Bhāgavatam*: *dharmaḥ projjhita-kaitavo 'tra paramo nirmatsarāṇāṁ satāṁ* (*Śrīmad Bhāgavatam* 1.1.2). Although all the four objects of human life are considered to be *kaitava*, or self-deception arising out of ignorance, the desire for liberation is the deepest darkness of all because it can completely eradicate any gains one makes on the path of devotion.

Śrīdhara Svāmī, named by Vaishnavas as the prime preserver of devotion for his commentary on the *Śrīmad Bhāgavatam*, explains the words *projjhita-kaitava* in the following way: "The prefix *pra* indicates that the desire for liberation is completely rejected." (*pra-śabdena mokṣābhisandhir api nirasta iti—Chaitanya Charitāmṛta* 1.1.93)

On this basis, the purity of devotion is measured by the extent to which it is free of desire for sense gratification and liberation, or the four goals of life—religiosity, material achievements, sense enjoyment and salvation. Elsewhere Krishnadāsa Kavirāja Gosvāmī speaks of all auspicious or inauspicious actions (*śubhāśubha-karma*) as being the darkness of ignorance which interferes with the attainment of bhakti (*Chaitanya Charitāmṛta* 1.1.94). Thus the words of this introductory *Bhāgavata* verse lead one to the definition of pure devotion given by Rūpa Gosvāmī—that it is free from any other desire (*anyābhilāṣitā-śūnyam*) other than for the pleasure of the Lord.

"The causeless mercy of Gaura-Nitai results in the destruction of this ignorant self-deception and permits the knowledge of pure devotion to rise like the sun in the darkness"

The causeless mercy of Gaura-Nitāi results in the destruction of this ignorant self-deception and permits the knowledge of pure devotion to rise like the sun in the darkness.

Rūpa Gosvāmī also compares the desires for sense gratification and liberation to a witch:

bhukti-mukti-spṛhā yāvat
piśācī hṛdi vartate
tāvad bhakti-sukhāmbodheḥ
katham abhyudayo bhavet

"How is it possible for the ocean of devotional happiness to appear in the heart as long as the witches of desire for sense enjoyment and liberation remain present there?" (*Bhakti-rasāmṛta-sindhu* 1.2.22, *Chaitanya Charitāmṛta* 2.19.176)

But just as such desires interfere with the development of pure devotion, devotional service is the only means by which they can be destroyed. The basis of all sinful desire is ignorance or the rejection of Krishna. The seed of all sin, i.e., the tendency to sin, is present in this ignorance. From there sinful activity is inevitable. The word *kleśa* is used to refer to ignorance, sin and the seed of sin (*kleśas tu pāpaṁ tad-bījam avidyā ceti te tridhā*). Only the process of devotional service consisting of hearing and chanting as given by the spiritual master can destroy these *kleśas.*

> *kleśaghnī śubhadā mokṣa-*
> *laghutā-kṛt sudurlabhā*
> *sāndrānanda-viśeṣātmā*
> *śrī-kṛṣṇākarṣiṇī ca sā*

"The basis of all sinful desire is ignorance or rejection of Krishna"

"The six characteristics of bhakti are (1) it destroys all *kleśas*, (2) it bestows all auspiciousness, (3) it renders liberation insignificant, (4) it is very rare, (5) it contains at its core an especially intense blissfulness, (6) it is capable of attracting Krishna." (*Bhakti-rasāmṛta-sindhu* 1.1.18)

DEVOTIONAL SERVICE PURIFIES DESIRES

The king of elephants, Gajendra, who gave up all hope of saving his life and simply prayed for the Lord's mercy in his affliction, is considered to be an example of someone who came to devotion out of his distress (*ārta*). Śaunaka and the rishis are taken as the example of those who gave up an ordinary desire for knowledge to become devotees (*jijñāsu*). At a certain point Dhruva Mahārāja realized that his desire for becoming a great king was a waste of time and that the real value (*artha*) in life is the *paramārtha* of spiritual life. He then became a devotee. And finally, the four Kumāras, Śukadeva, and the Nava Yogīndra all gave up following the philosophical path to seek exclusive devotion to the Lord. In each of these cases the piety leading to devotion (*bhakty-unmukhī sukṛti*) brought them this good fortune.

Bad association has the effect of gradually awakening desires for liberation, sense gratification, or mystic powers in a person. The association of devotees, however, has the opposite effect. Through their company, the individual develops spiritual intelligence and faith in pure devotional service. As a result, one realizes the insignificance of liberation, sense gratification and mystic power and takes up the practice of Bhakti yoga with great intensity.

"In all circumstances of life, regardless of motivation, the only duty of every living being is to engage in pure and causeless devotional service"

This was stated by Śukadeva when he said that in all circumstances of life, regardless of motivation, the only duty of every living being is to engage in pure and causeless devotional service:

> *akāmaḥ sarva-kāmo vā*
> *mokṣa-kāma udāra-dhīḥ*
> *tīvreṇa bhakti-yogena*
> *yajeta puruṣaṁ param*

"The person of expansive intelligence should worship the Supreme Person by the process of intense Bhakti yoga, whether he is a pure devotee without any personal desire, or someone filled with all kinds of desires, or one who seeks liberation." (*Śrīmad Bhāgavatam* 2.3.10)

In his discussion of this verse, Krishnadāsa Kavirāja Gosvāmī analyses the word *udāra-dhīḥ* ("of expansive intelligence") as follows:

buddhimān-arthe yadi vicāra-jña haya
nija-kāma lāgiha tabe kṛṣṇere bhajaya
bhakti binu kona sādhana dite nāre phala
saba phala deya bhakti svatantra prabala
ajā-gala-stana-nyāya anya sādhana
ataeva hari bhaje buddhimān jana
udāra mahatī jāṅra sarvottamā buddhi
nānā kāme bhaje tabu pāya bhakti-siddhi
bhakti-prabhāva sei kāma chāṛāñā
kṛṣṇa-pade bhakti karāya guṇe ākarṣiyā

"The meaning of the word 'intelligent' is to have good judgment. It is a sign of good judgment to engage in devotional service, even if one has desires for sense gratification or liberation. This is because no other process can yield its promised results unless supplemented by bhakti. Bhakti, however, is so strong and independent that it can give all results on its own. These other practices are unable to yield their results. Knowing this, an intelligent person worships Krishna exclusively. One who has this kind of broad, deep and superior intelligence serves the Lord even if he has some motive, with the result that he eventually attains the perfection of devotion. The power of devotion is such that it makes one give up all material desires and, by attracting one to the transcendental qualities of the Lord, bestows devotion at Krishna's feet."
(*Chaitanya Charitāmṛta* 2.24.91-95)

"Bad association has the effect of gradually awakening desires for liberation, sense gratification, or mystic powers"

Viśvanātha Cakravartī interprets the word *tīvreṇa* ("intensely") as meaning the devotee should engage in transcendental loving service without any mixture of *karma* or *jñāna* practices. (See also the commentary on *Śrīmad Bhāgavatam* 5.19.26.)

The power of even basic devotional acts is such that one can be liberated by them.

kṛṣṇa tomāra haṅa jadi bale eka-bāra
māyā-bandha haite kṛṣṇa tāre kare pāra

"If someone says just once, 'Krishna, I am Yours,' then Krishna delivers him from bondage in the illusory energy." (*Chaitanya Charitāmṛta* 2.22.33)

Lord Rāmacandra Himself made this assurance when telling Sugrīva about His meeting with Vibhīṣaṇa:

sakṛd eva prapanno yas
tavāsmīti ca yācate
abhayaṁ sarvadā tasmai
dadāmy etad vrataṁ mama

"It is My promise that if someone truly surrenders to Me and says just once, 'I am Yours,' asking for freedom from fear, then I grant him fearlessness for all eternity."

Bhakti transforms the devotee, even if the motivation of one's service is based on other kinds of desires, as the external acts of devotion attract Krishna's mercy. The Lord is so merciful that He quickly cleanses the heart of such a worshiper, ridding it of the desires for sense gratification and liberation. He even goes so far as to give him love of God, even if this was not the original object of his performance of devotional practice. Śrīla Krishnadāsa Kavirāja Gosvāmī has also written:

bhukti-mukti-siddhi-kāmī subuddhi jadi haya
gāḍha-bhakti-yoge tabe kṛṣṇere bhajaya
anya-kāmī jadi kare kṛṣṇera bhajana
nā māgiteha kṛṣṇa tāre dena sva-caraṇa
kṛṣṇa kahe āmā bhaje māge viṣaya-sukha
amṛta chāṛi viṣa māge ei baṛa mūrkha
āmi vijña ei mūrkhe viṣaya kene diba
sva-caraṇāmṛta diyā viṣaya bhulāiba
kāma lāgi kṛṣṇe bhaje pāya kṛṣṇa-rase
kāma chāṛi dāsa haite haya abhilāṣe

"Due to bad association, the living entity desires material happiness, liberation (merging into the impersonal aspect of the Lord), or engages in mystic yoga for material power. If such a person actually becomes intelligent, he takes to Krishna consciousness by engaging himself in intense devotional service to Lord Śrī Krishna. If someone engages in devotional service while harboring selfish desires, the Lord still gives him shelter at His lotus feet, even though He was not asked for it. The Lord says to Himself, 'This foolish person is worshiping Me and at the same time is looking for material sense gratification. He is discarding divine nectar in order to drink poison. I am wise enough to not give the poison of sense gratification to this fool. Instead, I will give him the ambrosia of My lotus feet and make him forget such inferior sensual pleasures.' Those who worship Krishna with some other objective still get a taste of the joys of devotional service. They thus give up their desires and begin to crave only to become His servant." (*Chaitanya Charitāmṛta* 2.22.37-41)

"The power of devotion is such that it makes one give up all material desires and, by attracting one to the transcendental qualities of the Lord, bestows devotion at Krishna's feet"

The above series of verses from the *Chaitanya Charitāmṛta* have been commented on by Śrīla Bhaktivinoda Ṭhākura in his *Amṛta-pravāha-bhāṣya* as follows: "As a result of bad character and bad association, a living entity develops desires for sense enjoyment, liberation, or mystic powers. If by some chance one comes into contact with pure devotees it is still possible to develop the clear intelligence to abandon all desire for such things. Those who desire sensual pleasures, salvation or mystic prowess are bereft of any desire for pure devotion. Nevertheless, if out of some good fortune they come to engage in the practices of pure devotion, then Krishna is so merciful to them that He will bestow *prema* upon them, even if that was not their objective.

"Krishna says to Himself, 'This person was seeking something else but still has engaged in My service; however a lower nature continues to infect his heart. He has given up the nectarean cup of *prema* and wants to drink from a poison chalice, which demonstrates how foolish he is. This inability to pray for the nectar of immortality is a sign of ignorance. Even so, I am both wise and experienced; I know what is needed for the perfection of life, so I will give him a taste of the nectar of My lotus feet. This ecstasy causes one to forget forever the bitter taste of material pleasures.'"

The demigods thus sing the following verse in the *Bhāgavatam* about the nature of the Lord's mercy:

satyaṁ diśaty arthitam arthito nṛṇāṁ
naivārthado yat punar arthitā yataḥ
svayaṁ vidhatte bhajatām anicchatām
icchā-pidhānaṁ nija-pāda-pallavam

Lord Vishnu lies in the Causual Ocean

"It is true that Lord Krishna fulfills one's desire whenever someone petitions Him to do so. However, He does not award anything which, once having been received, will be asked for again and again. Even if these worshipers show no desire for His lotus feet, the Lord personally bestows this benediction on them whereby they forget all their transitory material desires." (*Śrīmad Bhāgavatam* 5.19.27)

kāma lāgi kṛṣṇe bhaje pāya kṛṣṇa-rase
kāma chāḍi dāsa haite haya abhilāṣe

"Someone who engages in Lord Krishna's devotional service out of egotistical motivation instead acquires a taste to serve Krishna. As a result one gives up his material desires and longs to become the Lord's eternal servant."
(*Chaitanya Charitāmṛta* 2.22.51)

According to Bhaktivinoda Ṭhākura, "If someone has the good fortune to come into the association of the devotees and take up devotional service to Krishna as a means to achieving some selfish mundane purpose, these objectives are soon revealed to be of little value as a result of the higher taste obtained from bhakti. Krishna worship is so pure and holy a thing that anyone who comes into contact with it soon rejects their other desires and seeks to become a servant of the Lord." (*Amṛta-pravāha-bhāṣya*)

"Someone who engages in Lord Krishna's devotional service out of egotistical motivation instead acquires a taste to serve Krishna. As a result one gives up their material desires and longs to become the Lord's eternal servant"

This power of bhakti to make one forget material desires was demonstrated by the great child devotee Dhruva who refused the boon which the Supreme Lord offered him saying:

sthānābhilāṣī tapasi sthito'haṁ
tvāṁ prāptavān deva-munīndra-guhyam
kācaṁ vicinvann api divya-ratnaṁ
svāmin kṛtārtho smi varaṁ na yāce

"O my Lord, I took up the practice of penance and austerities out of a wish to become a great ruler. Now that I have attained You, who remain hidden to even great demigods, saintly persons and kings, I feel like someone who had been searching for fragments of glass but has found instead a most valuable jewel. I am now so fulfilled that there is no benediction left for me to ask of You."
(*Hari-bhakti-sudhodaya,* 7.28; quoted at *Chaitanya Charitāmṛta* 2.22.42 and 2.24.219)

Prabhupāda Bhaktisiddhānta Sarasvatī Ṭhākura comments in *Anubhāṣya*, "The association of pure devotees, Krishna's mercy and devotion to Krishna share this common characteristic: they rid one of all taste for associating with non-devotees, or for any good fortune arising from the illusory energy, as well as any tendency to take up the paths of *karma, jñāna* and *yoga.*" (*Chaitanya Charitāmṛta* 2.24.104)

The Transformation of the Desires for Knowledge and Liberation

Śrīla Viśvanātha Cakravartī Ṭhākura writes in his commentary on *Śrīmad Bhāgavatam* 1.1.4 that the seers led by Śaunaka were originally contaminated by attachment to works based in desire (*sakāma-karma*). As a result of hearing the Puranic literature from Romaharṣaṇa and reflecting on its contents, they came to the stage of desiring knowledge (*jijñāsu*). Later, as a result of the association of the saintly Ugraśravā, they came to aspire for the taste of devotion. The idea that they were originally engaged in fruitive activity is evidenced by their words to Sūta Gosvāmī:

karmaṇy asminn anāśvāse
dhūma-dhūmrātmanāṁ bhavān
āpāyayati govinda-
pāda-padmāsavaṁ madhu

> "We were engaged in the performance of this sacrifice, the fruits of which are uncertain due to the many imperfections in the ritual, until our bodies were blackened by smoke. But you came and revived us by giving the honey nectar from Govinda's lotus feet to drink." (*Śrīmad Bhāgavatam* 1.18.12)

After they entered the devotional path, the curiosity of the sages became a less dominant motivation and their sacrificial performance was carried out for the purpose of going to the abode of Hari, Vaikuṇṭha.

The speaker of the *Bhāgavatam*, Śukadeva Gosvāmī, also told Mahārāja Parīkṣit that he had been firmly fixed in oneness with the undifferentiated Brahman when the nectar of Krishna *kathā* attracted his mind.

pariniṣṭhito 'pi nairguṇya
uttama-śloka-līlayā
gṛhīta-cetā rājarṣe
ākhyānaṁ yad adhītavān

> "O saintly King, even though I was certainly situated in perfect transcendence, my mind was forcibly attracted by the delineation of the pastimes of the Lord, who is described by enlightened verses. And so I took up its study." (*Śrīmad Bhāgavatam* 2.1.9)

Elsewhere, the same was stated by Sūta Gosvāmī:

harer guṇākṣipta-matir
bhagavān bādarāyaṇiḥ
adhyagān mahad ākhyānaṁ
nityaṁ viṣṇu-jana-priyaḥ

"The greatly powerful Śukadeva Gosvāmī, son of Vyāsadeva, was overcome with attraction to the qualities of Hari. He thus underwent the study of this great narration of the *Śrīmad Bhāgavatam* and became eternally dear to the devotees of Vishnu." (*Śrīmad Bhāgavatam* 1.7.11)

The following account is found in the *Brahma-vaivarta Purana*. While his son Śukadeva was absorbed in *samādhi* in the midst of the jungle, Vyāsadeva found a way to make him hear some verses he had written glorifying the Lord. These verses were so powerful that Śukadeva's *samādhi* was disrupted when he heard them. Their sweetness so attracted Śuka that he began to regret the time he had lost in his Brahman meditation and showed his displeasure by saying '*dhik*.' Being omniscient, he knew that the verses were from the *Bhāgavatam* and that their author was his own father. As a result, he immediately went to Vyāsa and asked to be instructed in the *Bhāgavatam*. In this way, the goddess of devotion conquered the father and son, both of whom had direct experience of Brahman, and thus brought the entire universe under her control.

The four Kumāras were sages who after having direct realization of Brahman became attracted to devotional service.

tasyāravinda-nayanasya padāravinda-
kiñjalka-miśra-tulasī-makaranda-vāyuḥ
antar-gataḥ sva-vivareṇa cakāra teṣāṁ
saṅkṣobham akṣara-juṣām api citta-tanvoḥ

"When the breeze carrying the aroma of *tulasī* leaves from the toes of the lotus feet of the lotus-eyed Lord entered the nostrils of those sages, their bodies and minds were disturbed, even though they were fixed in consciousness of the imperishable Brahman." (*Śrīmad Bhāgavatam* 3.15.43)

The nine great yogis, the Nava Yogīndras, were also knowers of Brahman who were attracted by Lord Krishna's qualities and then took up His devotional service. The scriptural evidence is found in the *Bhakti-rasāmṛta-sindhu*:

akleśāṁ kamala-bhuvaḥ praviśya goṣṭhīṁ
kurvantaḥ śruti-śirasāṁ śrutiṁ śrutajñāḥ
uttuṅgaṁ yadu-pura-saṅgamāya raṅgaṁ
yogīndrāḥ pulaka-bhṛto navāpy avāpuḥ

"Though those nine great masters of yoga were already free from distress and conversant in Vedic knowledge, they came to Lord Brahmā's assembly and heard the *Gopāla-tāpanī Upanishad*, the topmost portion of the Veda. When they thus learned about the supremacy of Krishna, they were covered with ecstatic symptoms and developed a great enthusiasm for visiting Lord Krishna's city of Dvārakā." (*Bhakti-rasāmṛta-sindhu* 3.1.20, *Chaitanya Charitāmṛta* 2.22.140)

Krishnadāsa Kavirāja Gosvāmī summarizes the above descriptions of these Brahma *jñānīs* who were later attracted by devotion to Krishna as such:

janma haite śuka-sanakādi brahma-maya
kṛṣṇa-guṇākṛṣṭa hañā kṛṣṇere bhajaya
sanakādyera kṛṣṇa-kṛpāya saurabhe hare mana
guṇākṛṣṭa hañā kare nirmala bhajana
vyāsa-kṛpāya śukadevera līlādi-smaraṇa
kṛṣṇa-guṇākṛṣṭa hañā karena bhajana
nava-yogīśvara janma haite sādhaka jñānī
vidhi-śiva-nārada-mukhe kṛṣṇa-guṇa śuni

"Although Śukadeva Gosvāmī and the four Kumāras were always absorbed in the thought of impersonal Brahman and thus considered Brahmavādīs, they were nonetheless attracted by the transcendental pastimes and qualities of Krishna and started to worship Him. By Krishna's mercy, the minds of the four Kumāras were attracted by His aroma. Attracted by His qualities, they took up His pure devotional service. By Vyāsa's mercy, Śukadeva started to remember Lord Krishna's pastimes. Thus attracted by Krishna's transcendental qualities, he also became a devotee and engaged in His service. The nine great mystics were practitioners on the path of knowledge from their very births. However, they were transformed by hearing Lord Krishna's qualities from Lord Brahmā, Lord Shiva, and the great sage Nārada." (*Chaitanya Charitāmṛta* 2.24.115-118)

bhaktira svabhāva brahma haite kare ākarṣaṇa
divya deha diyā karāya kṛṣṇera bhajana
bhakta-deha pāile haya guṇera smaraṇa
guṇākṛṣṭa hañā kare nirmala bhajana

"The nature of devotion is such that it attracts the mind away from the joys of Brahman realization. It gives the devotee a transcendental body so he can engage in Lord Krishna's service. Once he has such a body, the devotee meditates on Krishna's transcendental qualities. After being attracted to these qualities, he engages in pure devotional service."

(*Chaitanya Charitāmṛta* 2.24.110-111)

All these examples of liberated souls being attracted by the qualities of the Lord give weight to the claim of Sūta Gosvāmī, who told the sages at Naimiṣāraṇya:

ātmārāmāś ca munayo
nirgranthā apy urukrame
kurvanty ahaitukīṁ bhaktim
ittham-bhūta-guṇo hariḥ

"Though freed from all material ties, all the different types of *ātmārāmas* who take pleasure in the self engage in causeless devotional service unto the Lord of glorious feats. Truly, the Lord possesses transcendental qualities and therefore can attract everyone, including liberated souls." (*Śrīmad Bhāgavatam* 1.7.11)

Even Śaṅkarācārya writes in his commentary on the *Nṛsiṁha-tāpanī Upanishad* that liberated souls willingly take a body so that they can worship the Lord (*muktā api līlayā vigrahaṁ kṛtvā bhagavantaṁ bhajante*). This characteristic of devotional service is called *mokṣa-laghutā-kṛt*, meaning that it diminishes the attraction of liberation.

Devotion Must Ultimately Be Exclusive

In view of the preceding discussion, the conclusion is clear:

ata eva māyā-moha chāṛi buddhimān
nitya-tattva kṛṣṇa-bhakti karena sandhāna

"Therefore an intelligent person gives up his enchantment with this illusory material world and searches out the eternal truth of devotion to Krishna."

The power of devotion to destroy desire is applicable to any of the five principal devotional activities.

sat-saṅga kṛṣṇa-sevā bhāgavata nāma
vraje vāsa ei pañca sādhana pradhāna
ei-pañca-madhye eka svalpa yadi haya
subuddhi janera haya kṛṣṇa-premodaya
udāra mahatī jāṅra sarvottamā buddhi
nānā kāme bhaje tabu pāya bhakti-siddhi
bhakti-prabhāva sei kāma chāṛāñā
kṛṣṇa-pade bhakti karāya guṇe ākarṣiyā

The sages at Naimisaranya.

"The five most powerful aspects of devotional service are association with devotees, serving Lord Krishna's deity form, hearing the *Śrīmad Bhāgavatam*, chanting the Holy Names, and residing in Vraja *dhāma*. If intelligent persons come into even minimal contact with any one of these five types of devotional practice, their dormant love for Krishna is awakened. Those who have this kind of broad, deep, and superior intelligence serve the Lord even if they have some motive, with the result that they eventually attain the perfection of devotion. The power of devotion is such that it makes one give up all material desires and bestows devotion to Krishna's feet by attracting one to the transcendental qualities of the Lord."

(*Chaitanya Charitāmṛta* 2.24.187-188, 190,192)

Śrīla Krishnadāsa Kavirāja Gosvāmī also named these five principle devotional activities in the twenty-second chapter of the *Chaitanya Charitāmṛta's Madhya-līlā*. But there he mentions that without determined and faithful adherence to these practices, one cannot expect the fruit of love of Godhead to manifest. Here also, the symptoms of superior intelligence are given: "Having given up both gross and subtle sense gratification, one who dedicates oneself to the satisfaction of Krishna's senses is truly intelligent." True love for Krishna has absolutely no element of self-directed sensual desire. If one has come to this understanding, then such a person deserves the title *udāra-dhī*, as mentioned in the *Bhāgavatam* verse quoted above (*Śrīmad Bhāgavatam* 2.3.10): "Whether persons desire everything or nothing, or they desire to merge into the existence of the Lord, such individuals are intelligent only if they worship Lord Krishna, the Supreme Personality of

Godhead, by intensely rendering transcendental loving service."

Without this kind of perspicacity, one will confuse pure devotion with other kinds of devotion that are mixed or dominated by philosophical speculation or other purposes. One will take such kinds of ignorance as wisdom, sectarianism as liberality, and will ultimately be misled. In the material world, people think that any single spiritual path is just as good as another—*jata mata tata patha*. In fact, there is only one way to reach the abode of Krishna, Goloka Vrindavan. That path is the discipline of Bhakti yoga. This is made clear both in the *Bhagavad-gītā* and the *Srīmad Bhāgavatam*.

"True love for Krishna has absolutely no element of self-directed sensual desire"

This kind of exclusiveness is also described in the glorification of the *Bhagavad-gītā*, *Gītā-māhātmya*:

ekaṁ śāstraṁ devakī-putra-gītam
eko devo devakī-putra eva
eko mantras tasya nāmāni yāni
karmāpy ekaṁ tasya devasya sevā

> "There is only one scripture—that which was sung by the Son of Devakī.
> There is only God—He who is known as the Son of Devakī.
> There is only one hymn to be sung—the names of the Son of Devakī.
> There is only one duty—the service of this one supreme God."

The next chapter explores how one attains the great fortune of coming to devotional service and the manner in which it is cultivated.

CHAPTER III

THE BEGINNINGS OF SERVICE

It is said that only after wandering for many lifetimes throughout the fourteen worlds[1] does a fortunate living soul meet the Vaishnava guru through the mercy of Krishna. Through the guru, one gets the seed of the devotional creeper.

bhramite bhramite jadi sādhu-vaidya pāya
tāṅra upadeśa-mantre piśācī palāya
kṛṣṇa-bhakti pāya tabe kṛṣṇa nikaṭe jāya...
tāte kṛṣṇa bhaje kare gurura sevana
māyā-jāla chuṭe pāya tabe kṛṣṇera caraṇa

"After wandering through the universe in this bewildered condition, if the *jīva* can somehow find a saintly person to act as an exorcist, then through such a person's instructions, which act as a powerful spell, the witch of Maya's mastery is overcome and she is forced to run for her life. The fortunate individual then finds pure devotion to Krishna and a place by His side. There, he worships Krishna while continuing to serve the guru's lotus feet. As a result he is freed from the illusory entanglements of material life and attains Krishna's lotus feet." (*Chaitanya Charitāmṛta* 2.22.14-15, 25)

kona bhāgye kāro saṁsāra kṣayonmukha haya
sādhu-saṅge tabe kṛṣṇe rati upajaya

"When by some good fortune, it is time for one's material entanglement to come to an end, then an attraction to Krishna develops within them in the association of devotees." (*Chaitanya Charitāmṛta* 2.22.45)

King Mucukunda stated this idea in the prayers he spoke to Lord Krishna after being delivered by Him:

bhavāpavargo bhramato yadā bhavej
janasya tarhy acyuta sat-samāgamaḥ
sat-saṅgamo yarhi tadaiva sad-gatau
parāvareśe tvayi jāyate ratiḥ

Without the association of devotees, no one can take up the practice of devotional service.

"O infallible Lord! When the time has come for those wandering throughout the universes to be finished with their material existence, they come into contact with devotees. Only as a result of such association with devotees can one develop an attraction for You, the destination of the saintly, the Lord of the universe."
(*Śrīmad Bhāgavatam* 10.51.53)

Without the association of devotees, no one can take up the practice of devotional service. Without such practice, no one can be rid of sinful tendencies with the result that no one can reach the goal of love for Krishna. However, no one gets the association of devotees without first having the kind of piety that leads to devotional service (*bhakty-unmukhī sukṛti*). Therefore, Krishnadāsa Kavirāja Gosvāmī says:

kṛṣṇa jadi kṛpā kare kona bhāgyavāne
guru-antaryāmi-rūpe śikhāya āpane
sādhu-saṅge kṛṣṇa-bhaktye śraddhā jadi haya
bhakti-phala prema haya saṁsāra jāya kṣaya
mahat-kṛpā vinā kona karme bhakti naya
kṛṣṇa-bhakti dūre rahu saṁsāra nahe kṣaya

Deities of Chaitanya Mahaprabhu and Nityananda Prabhu

"When Krishna decides to be kind to some fortunate soul, He then personally directs that person from within as the Supersoul and from without as the spiritual master. If one's faith in devotional service to Krishna is awakened through the association of devotees, then one develops dormant love for Krishna by which material, conditional existence comes to an end. Unless one is favored by a great devotee, no activity can be considered to take on the characteristics of devotional service. One cannot even be relieved from the bondage of material existence, what to speak of attaining Krishna bhakti."
(*Chaitanya Charitāmṛta* 2.22.47,49,51)

The Piety Which Leads to Devotion

In the texts quoted above, the word "fortune" is a reference to the kind of previous pious activity that ultimately leads to bhakti. This kind of predisposition to spiritual life causes the awakening of a desire for association with people advanced in spiritual matters. Through this kind of association, a taste for devotional service is developed.

bhaktis tu bhagavad-bhakta-
saṅgena parijāyate
sat-saṅgaḥ prāpyate pumbhiḥ
sukṛtaiḥ pūrva-sañcitaiḥ

> "Devotion is born out of the association with devotees of the Lord. Contact with such saintly persons is given to those who have accumulated pious merit in previous lifetimes." (*Bṛhan-nāradīya Purana, Hari-bhakti-vilāsa* 10.279)

Śrīla Bhaktivinoda Ṭhākura explains this development in his *Amṛta-pravāha-bhāṣya* (2.22.45): "The devotional scriptures call the results of one's past piety 'good fortune.' Past piety is of three types depending on whether it leads to devotion, sense gratification or to liberation. All acts in this world that give rise to pure devotion are called *bhakty-unmukhī sukṛti,* while those that lead to sense gratification bring *bhogonmukhī sukṛti* and those which lead to liberation give *mokṣonmukhī sukṛti*. The pious activities that awaken the *jīva*'s constitutional activity of devotional service to the Lord bring entanglement in material nature to an end."

The pious activities that awaken the jiva's constitutional activity of devotional service to the Lord bring entanglement in material nature to an end.

The conclusion is that the association of devotees comes about as a result of pious activities connected to devotional service, or *bhakty-unmukhī sukṛti*. This type of piety originates in accidental service to Vishnu or the Vaishnavas. One need not have spent a great amount of time in the company of devotees. A *lava* is equal to 4/45ths of a second, the time that it takes to blink. It is said that even as little as a *lava*'s time of association with advanced devotees will result in the attainment of all perfections. This is the extent of the transcendental potency of such association:

sādhu saṅga sādhu saṅga sarva śāstra kaya
lava-mātra sādhu saṅge sarva siddhi haya

> "All the scriptures again and again glorify the association of devotees. Just a moment's association with devotees results in all perfection." (*Chaitanya Charitāmṛta* 2.22.54)

tulayāma lavenāpi
na svargaṁ nāpunar-bhavam
bhagavat-saṅgi-saṅgasya
martyānāṁ kim utāśiṣaḥ

> "We cannot compare heaven or liberation to even the briefest moment of association with the companions of the Lord. If this is so, then how can the miserable benedictions of the worldly be considered their equal?" (*Śrīmad Bhāgavatam* 1.18.13, *Chaitanya Charitāmṛta* 2.22.55)

Sri Krishna

FAITH

The piety that comes from contact with a saintly person results in a growing detachment from this world with its fleeting pleasures and frustrations. This in turn leads to a desire to associate with people who are cultivating the eternal truth. Upon hearing the Krishna conscious discourses from the lips of a saintly person, the fortunate soul develops faith, or the certain belief that by engaging in devotion to Krishna, all his other obligations will be fulfilled.

When one hears the explanation of the *Bhagavad-gītā* from a devotee, he learns that although Krishna at first seems to give value to various spiritual paths, such as Vedic sacrifice, *karma-yoga,* and *jñāna-yoga,* in the final analysis, these paths are relegated to a secondary status and Bhakti yoga is given precedence. Krishna's final order prescribes devotional service as the topmost process of spiritual realization. The general rule is given that where there are conflicting instructions, the last instruction should be given precedence—*pūrva-parayor para-vidhir balavān.* Thus *Gītā* verses such as *man-manā bhava mad-bhakto mad-yājī māṁ namaskuru* and *sarva-dharmān parityājya mām ekaṁ śaraṇaṁ vraja* are to be taken as Krishna's final word. The living being who has faith in this final instruction will become a devotee, renounce all other activities, and engage in Krishna bhajana.

The word sraddha refers to a firm and confident belief that by engaging in devotion to Krishna alone, all other duties will be fulfilled.

In an important verse in the *Bhāgavatam,* Lord Kapiladeva instructs his mother Devahūtī about the development of faith beginning with the association of devotees and the hearing of Krishna conscious topics from them. Such faith implies the taking up of disciplined devotional activity. Once one begins such practice, one's inner life develops through *rati* or *bhāva,* the stage of devotional feeling, and from there to devotion in its pure state, *prema.*

satāṁ prasaṅgān mama vīrya-saṁvido
bhavanti hṛt-karṇa-rasāyanāḥ kathāḥ
taj-joṣaṇād āśv apavarga-vartmani
śraddhā ratir bhaktir anukramiṣyati

Chaitanya Mahaprabhu's shoes and water pot

"My heroic pastimes are very pleasing to the ear and satisfying to the heart when heard in the association of pure devotees. As a result of joyfully relishing these pastimes in such association, one quickly advances on the path of liberation, passing through the stages of faith (*śraddhā*), the revelation of one's divine relationship with Krishna (*rati*), and true love for Him (*bhakti*)."

(*Śrīmad Bhāgavatam* 3.25.25)

Krishnadāsa Kavirāja Gosvāmī has defined faith (*śraddhā*) in the following way:

śraddhā-śabde kahe viśvāsa sudṛḍha niścaya
kṛṣṇa-bhakti kaile sarva-karma kṛta haya

"The word *śraddhā* refers to a firm and confident belief that by engaging in devotion to Krishna alone, all of one's duties will be fulfilled."

(*Chaitanya Charitāmṛta* 2.22.62)

Such faith is based in an understanding of Krishna's factual position as the very root of all existence:

yathā taror mūla-niṣecanena
tṛpyanti tat-skandha-bhujopaśākhāḥ
prāṇopahārāc ca yathendriyāṇāṁ
tathaiva sarvārhaṇam acyutejyā

"As a tree's trunk, branches, twigs, and leaves are nourished by watering its roots, and as all the senses are satisfied by giving food to the stomach, so simi-

larly, all living beings are served by worshiping the infallible Supreme Person."
(*Śrīmad Bhāgavatam* 4.31.14)

This means that by worshiping the Supreme Lord, all other gods and objects of worship are automatically served. If the Lord is pleased, the entire universe is pleased—*tasmiṁs tuṣṭe jagat tuṣṭam prīṇīte prīṇitaṁ jagat*. A person who has this kind of faith is eligible to engage in devotional service.

As stated in the *Bhāgavatam* (11.20.9), until one's faith has been awakened by listening to discussions of devotional subjects, one will continue to have a taste for works and knowledge. This preliminary kind of faith is called scriptural or doctrinal faith. Bhaktivinoda Ṭhākura writes the following in his *Āmnāya Sutra*:

śraddhā tv anyopāya-varjaṁ
bhakty-unmukhī-citta-vṛtti-viśeṣaḥ
sā ca śaraṇāpatti-lakṣaṇā

"*Śraddhā*, faith, is a particular mental attitude directed toward devotion that rejects all other means of spiritual achievement. It is characterized by the process of surrender (*śaraṇāpatti*)."

Until one has this kind of faith, there is no chance that one will get a taste for listening to the *Bhāgavatam* and other scriptures of its type. So this faith is the seed of the creeper of devotion. After wandering throughout the universes, the fortunate *jīva* who has accumulated a stock of the appropriate merit gets the seed of devotion, faith, by the mercy of Krishna and the spiritual master.

After wandering throughout the universes, the fortunate jiva who has accumulated a stock of the appropriate merit gets the seed of devotion, faith, by the mercy of Krishna and the spiritual master.

Planting the Seed

The seed of faith is planted in the soil of the heart. Devotional activities such as hearing the topics of Krishna from sadhus and then repeating them are the water that irrigates this seed, which soon sprouts in the form of the creeper of devotion. The creeper then grows and grows until it crosses the Virajā River, pierces through the Brahmaloka to the spiritual sky, and then goes on to Goloka Vrindavan where it gives forth the divine, delightful fruits of *prema*.

mālī hañā kare sei bīja āropaṇa
śravaṇa-kīrtana-jale karaye secana
upajiyā bāṛe latā brahmāṇḍa bhedi jāya
virajā brahma-loka bhedi para-vyoma pāya
tabe jāya tad-upari goloka-vṛndāvana
kṛṣṇa-caraṇa-kalpa-vṛkṣe kare ārohaṇa

"The *jīva* then takes the role of a gardener, plants the seed of faith in the heart and waters it with the acts of hearing and chanting. The creeper sprouts and starts to grow until it penetrates the coverings of the universe, crosses the Virajā River, passes through the Brahmaloka until it reaches the spiritual sky. From there, it continues to grow until it reaches Goloka Vrindavan where it winds around the desire tree of Krishna's lotus feet." (*Chaitanya Charitāmṛta* 2.19.152-154)

If by some great fortune, a certain living entity develops faith in Krishna, that jiva begins to associate with devotees.

Krishnadāsa Kavirāja Gosvāmī, foremost of Śrī Rūpa Gosvāmī's followers, has also taken up Śrī Rūpa's description of the gradual process that leads to *prema-bhakti*, devotion in pure love:

kona bhāgye kona jīvera śraddhā jadi haya
tabe sei jīva sādhu-saṅga je karaya
sādhu-saṅga haite haya śravaṇa-kīrtana
sādhana-bhaktye haya sarvānartha-nivartana
anartha-nivṛtti haile bhaktye niṣṭhā haya
niṣṭhā haite śravaṇādye ruci upajaya
ruci haite bhaktye haya āsakti pracura
āsakti haite citte janme kṛṣṇe prīty-aṅkura
sei bhāva gāḍha haile dhare prema-nāma
sei premā prayojana sarvānanda-dhāma

> "If by some great good fortune one develops faith in Krishna, that *jīva* begins to associate with devotees. As a result of associating with devotees, one takes up practical devotional service beginning with hearing and chanting. Such practical devotional service frees one from all unwanted material contamination and that leads to constancy. When one has *niṣṭhā*, or firmness in one's practice, then a real taste develops for hearing and chanting and the other devotional practices. The next step is the awakening of a deep attachment and from that attachment the first manifestations of love finally appear in the heart like the sprouting tree. These first ecstatic manifestations are called *bhāva*, which intensify to become love of Godhead or *prema*, the ultimate goal of life and the reservoir of all pleasure." (*Chaitanya Charitāmṛta* 2.23.9-13)

The fruits of devotion are nectarean, that is, supremely delightful in their essence. Once one has tasted that fruit, one feels fully satisfied. All sadness, bewilderment, fear and longing are removed forever from one's heart and a strong distaste for all desires for sense gratification, liberation or mystic powers is awakened. Hatred, jealousy, enviousness, and the tendency to criticize others no longer find a place within the heart. Then one is not tempted by the satisfactions of sex, riches or power and remains constantly fixed in the culture of Krishna consciousness through hearing, chanting, and remembering. One has no other duty but activities executed for the pleasure of the Lord. Other than the knowledge related to developing Krishna consciousness—*sambandha, abhidheya* and *prayojana-tattvas*—one has no interest in accumulating any other knowledge. Such a person never thinks that any yogic practice has precedence over Bhakti yoga.

A living being can become eligible for this treasure of devotion only through the grace of Krishna's internal, joy-bestowing energy. One who has been lucky enough to associate with a devotee blessed by the *hlādinī-śakti* inherits this treasure. This is why association with Krishna's devotees is said to be the root cause of devotion to Krishna. Just like a person who wishes to make money must come into the association of rich people, a person seeking the wealth of devotion must enter into the association of people who are rich in devotion. Then one must accept instruction and strictly following such guidance they enter a life of devotion.

Chapter IV

Serve the Lord's Devotees

When in Prayaga, Lord Chaitanya Mahāprabhu met Rūpa Gosvāmī and instructed him in the process of devotional service. In the course of their conversations, which are recorded in the *Chaitanya Charitāmṛta*, Mahāprabhu told Rūpa Gosvāmī just how rare a pure devotee is. The Lord said that the unlimited living entities can be divided into two categories, the eternally liberated and the eternally conditioned. The conditioned entities are further divided into those that can move and those that cannot. Those whose consciousness is more covered, such as trees, are the non-moving creatures, while the moving beings include birds, aquatics and land animals, all of which have more developed consciousness.

"Out of many millions of such philosophers, one may actually achieve liberation; but it is very difficult to find a pure devotee of Lord Krishna even amongst many millions of liberated persons"

Of all the land creatures, only a small proportion are humans. Among them, the Mlecchas, Pulindas, and Śabaras are outside the pale of civilized society, which includes only those who follow the Vedic principles. Half of those who follow the Vedas simply give lip service to the scriptures while in fact they live irreligious and sinful lives. Further, of those who follow the Vedic principles, most are engaged in fruitive ritual activity. One out of many such fruitive workers may become a philosopher. Among the many millions of such philosophers, one may actually achieve liberation; but it is very difficult to find a pure devotee of Lord Krishna even amongst many millions of liberated persons.

Up to and including the liberated person, everyone is bound by desire, either gross or subtle. Those who are engaged in fruitive activity are bound by a desire for material enjoyment (*bhukti*), whether here in this life or after death in heaven. Those who are attached to the quest for knowledge are bound by a desire for liberation, while the yogis are bound by the desire for spiritual powers. As long as there are desires for sensual enjoyment, salvation or spiritual perfections in the heart, one will be disturbed. One who is engaged in devotional service to Krishna stops desiring the satisfaction of his own senses and seeks only the pleasure of his Lord. For this reason, the devotee alone truly knows peace.

kṛṣṇa-bhakta niṣkāma ataeva śānta
bhukti-mukti-siddhi-kāmī sakali aśānta

"Because a devotee of Lord Krishna is desireless, he is peaceful. Fruitive workers desire material enjoyment, *jñānīs* desire liberation, and yogis desire material opulence; therefore they are all lusty and cannot be peaceful."
(*Chaitanya Charitāmṛta* 2.19.149)

'Without the association and service of a perfected devotee of the Lord, the person Bhagavata, no aspect of devotional service can be exercised properly'

muktānām api siddhānāṁ
nārāyaṇa-parāyaṇaḥ
sudurlabhaḥ praśāntātmā
koṭiṣv api mahā-mune

"Of all liberated and perfected beings, O great sage, one who is devoted to Nārāyaṇa is most rare. He alone amongst countless millions has found divine peace." (*Śrīmad Bhāgavatam* 6.14.5)

TADĪYA—"THOSE CONNECTED TO THE LORD"

Those special beings who have come into intimate contact with the Lord are known as *tadīya,* "His own." Vrindavan Dāsa Ṭhākura has written in his *Chaitanya Bhāgavata*:

bhāgavata tulasī gaṅgāya bhakta-jane
caturdhā vigraha kṛṣṇa ei cāri sane
jīva-nyāsa karile śrī-mūrti pūjā haya
janma-mātra e cāri īśvara vede kaya

"The Supreme Lord is always associated with the four following things: the book *Bhāgavata*, Tulasi, the Ganges, and the devotees. The deity form of the Lord becomes worshipable after it has been consecrated ritually and the Lord's presence has been invoked. Scripture says that these four things, however, are innately divine." (*Chaitanya Bhāgavata* 2.21.81-82)

The book *Bhāgavata*, the person *Bhāgavata*, Tulasī, and the Ganges are all considered to be manifestations of the Lord Himself because of their intimate connection with Him. They are called His *prakāśa-vigraha.* The deity form is not considered worshipable until the *prāṇa-pratiṣṭhā* ritual has been performed. These four *prakāśa-vigrahas*, however, are considered to be naturally worshipable; there is no need for any kind of ritual in order to elevate them to that status. They are all spiritual and due to their natural connection to the Lord, are considered to be in a relationship to us as masters to servants. They are always to be considered distinct from the material nature and never looked upon as potential objects of sense enjoyment.

Krishnadāsa Kavirāja Gosvāmī expresses the same idea in *Chaitanya Charitāmṛta*:

tadīya tulasī vaiṣṇava mathurā bhāgavata
ei cārira sevā haya kṛṣṇera abhimata

"The word *tadīya* refers to those things or persons which are connected to the Lord: Tulasī, Krishna's devotees, the land of Mathurā, and the *Śrīmad*

Bhāgavatam. Krishna is pleased when one renders service to any of these four things." (*Chaitanya Charitāmṛta* 2.22.121)

This last couplet is found in the *Chaitanya Charitāmṛta* in the context of an enumeration of 64 elements of devotional service in practice. Of these sixty-four devotional practices, five are considered to be most important.

sādhu-saṅga nāma-kīrtana bhāgavata-śravaṇa
mathurā-vāsa śrī-mūrtira śraddhāya sevana

"One should associate with devotees, chant the Holy Name of the Lord, hear *Śrīmad Bhāgavatam*, reside at Mathurā, and worship the deity with faith and veneration." (*Chaitanya Charitāmṛta* 2.22.214)

These five limbs of devotional service are considered to be the best of all because even a slight performance of them awakens love for Krishna. Whether a person executes only one or many of these processes of devotional service, love for Krishna can quickly manifest. (*Chaitanya Charitāmṛta* 2.22.214) Clearly, there is a close relationship between these five most potent devotional activities and the concept of *tadīya*, or things related to the Lord.

What needs to be particularly emphasized is that service to the Vaishnavas cannot be separated from any aspect of devotional service. Thus Śrīla Narottama dāsa Ṭhākura sings, *chāṛiyā vaiṣṇava-sevā nistāra pāyeche kebā*—"Who has ever attained supreme beatitude without serving the Vaishnavas?" (*Prema-bhakti-candrikā*) Without the association and service of a perfected devotee of the Lord, the person *Bhāgavata*, no aspect of devotional service can be exercised properly.

"The book Bhagavata, the person Bhagavata, Tulasi, and the Ganges are all considered to be manifestations of the Lord Himself"

Furthermore, as Śrī Chaitanya Mahāprabhu taught Sanātana Gosvāmī, association with devotees is important at all stages of one's devotional life.

kṛṣṇa-bhakti-janma-mūla haya sādhu-saṅga
kṛṣṇa-prema janme teṅho punaḥ mukhya aṅga

"The root cause of devotional service to Krishna is association with advanced devotees. And when one's love for Krishna awakens, the association with devotees becomes the chief element in one's devotional service."
(*Chaitanya Charitāmṛta* 2.22.83)

Devotion to Krishna is the fruit of associating with devotees. When that devotion attains its most mature state and is transformed into pure love for the Lord, then associating with devotees continues to be the essential expression of such love.

THE SPECIAL STATUS OF THE VAISHNAVAS

In two verses from *Pādmottara-khaṇḍa*, Mahādeva emphasized the glory of worshiping *tadīyas* to Pārvatī:

ārādhanānāṁ sarveṣāṁ
viṣṇor ārādhanaṁ param

tasmāt parataraṁ devi
tadīyānāṁ samarcanam

"Of all types of worship, worship of Lord Vishnu is best. Even better than the worship of Lord Vishnu is the worship of those things which are connected to Him." (*Bhakti-rasāmṛta-sindhu* 1.2.214, *Hari-bhakti-vilāsa* 10.361)

arcayitvā tu govindaṁ
tadīyān nārcayet tu yaḥ
na sa bhāgavato jñeyaḥ
kevalaṁ dāmbhikaḥ smṛtaḥ

"One who worships Govinda without worshiping those who are connected to Him cannot be considered a true devotee. In fact, he is nothing more than a hypocrite." (*Hari-bhakti-vilāsa* 10.362)

"The Lord does not accept the service of one who has no affection for Tulasi and the other things described as tadiya and who simply tries to show affection for Him alone"

The Lord does not accept the service of one who has no affection for Tulasī and the other things described as *tadīya*, and who simply tries to show affection for Him alone. The devotees are so dear to Lord Govinda that He subordinates Himself to them. He is therefore easily won over by anyone who shows love and respect for them. Indeed, He says that anyone who claims to be a devotee is not truly His devotee. It is only the person who acts as a devotee of His devotees who can make such a claim:

ye me bhakta-janāḥ pārtha
na me bhaktāś ca te janāḥ
mad-bhaktānāṁ ca ye bhaktās
te me bhaktatamā matāḥ

"O Arjuna, those who claim to be My devotees are actually not My devotees. I consider only those who are the servants of My devotees to factually be My devotees." (*Ādi Purana*, quoted in *Bhakti-rasāmṛta-sindhu* 1.2.218, *Hari-bhakti-vilāsa* 10.133, and *Chaitanya Charitāmṛta* 2.11.28)

Uddhava is one of the foremost devotees of the Lord. When Uddhava approached Krishna in order to learn about the discipline of yoga, the Lord delivered the instructions known as the *Uddhava-gīta*, which have been preserved in the eleventh canto of the *Bhāgavatam*. Amongst the characteristics of a pure devotee given there, the Lord said,

ādaraḥ paricaryāyāṁ
sarvāṅgair abhivandanam
mad-bhakta-pūjābhyadhikā
sarva-bhūteṣu man-matiḥ

mad-artheṣv aṅga-ceṣṭā ca
vacasā mad-guṇeraṇam
mayy arpaṇaṁ ca manasaḥ
sarva-kāma-vivarjanam

"My devotees take great care in rendering service to Me, offering obeisances to Me through the use of all their bodily limbs and faculties. They consider the worship of other devotees to be even more important than My worship; they see My presence in all living beings. They engage their bodies in working for Me; they use the power of speech for glorifying My qualities. They offer up the activity of their mind to Me and they give up all material desires."

(*Śrīmad Bhāgavatam* 11.19.21-22)

Vrindavan Dāsa Ṭhākura confirms the third line of the first verse, *mad-bhakta-pūjābhyadhikā*, as follows:

āmāra bhaktera pūjā āmā haite baṛa
sei prabhu vede bhāgavate kaila daṛha

"The Lord has forcefully declared in the Vedas and the *Bhāgavatam*: 'Worshiping or serving My devotee is even greater than worshiping Me.' "

(*Chaitanya Bhāgavata* 1.1.8)

The Three Levels of Devotees

Rāmānanda Basu and his father Satyarāja Khān were exemplary householders from the village of Kulīnagrāma, amongst Mahāprabhu's dearest followers. Once, they came to see the Lord in Purī and asked Him about a householder devotee's duties. Mahāprabhu answered them in detail, advising all householders everywhere that they have three principal duties: serving the deity form of Krishna, chanting the Holy Names and serving the Vaishnavas.

On hearing this, Satyarāja Khān began to think as follows: "Service to the deity and chanting the Holy Names are both fairly straightforward and can be easily executed according to the spiritual master's instructions. If one is unable to recognize a Vaishnava, however, the instruction to serve them will not be easily carried out." He thus asked the Lord how to recognize a Vaishnava—who is a real Vaishnava and what are his characteristics?

Tulasi puja

Over the next three years, Mahāprabhu answered this question by first of all describing the lower category of Vaishnava, the *kaniṣṭha,* then the *madhyama* and finally, the highest class of devotee, the *uttama-adhikārī*. The first year, he said,

prabhu kahe jāṅra mukhe śuni eka-bāra
kṛṣṇa-nāma sei pūjya śreṣṭha sabākāra
eka kṛṣṇa-nāme kare sarva-pāpa kṣaya
nava-vidhā bhakti pūrṇa nāma haite haya
dīkṣā-puraścaryā-vidhi apekṣā nā kare
jihvā-sparśe ā-caṇḍāla sabāre uddhāre
anuṣaṅga-phale kare saṁsārera kṣaya
citta ākarṣiyā karāya kṛṣṇe premodaya

"If I hear someone chant Krishna's Holy Name just once, I consider him to be worshipable and the best of all humans. A single repetition of Krishna's holy name destroys all the consequences of a sinful life. All the nine processes of devotional service are completed simply by chanting the Holy Name. With the Holy Name, one does not have to undergo initiation or the *puraścaryā* observances as with other mantras. The Name delivers even a person in the lowest ranks of human society as soon as one chants it. Secondarily, the Holy Name dissolves one's entanglement in material activities; it attracts the mind and awakens one's love for Krishna." (*Chaitanya Charitāmṛta* 2.15.106-109)

"One who chants the name of Krishna should be recognized as a Vaishnava and you should offer all respects to him"

ataeva jāṅra mukhe eka kṛṣṇa-nāma
sei ta vaiṣṇava kariha tāṅhāra sammāna

Śrī Chaitanya Mahāprabhu then concluded, "Therefore one who chants the name of Krishna should be recognized as a Vaishnava and you should offer all respects to him." (*Chaitanya Charitāmṛta* 2.15.111)

Bhaktivinoda Ṭhākura has provided some clarification of this broad instruction given by Mahāprabhu: "There are many people who have taken initiation in the Vaishnava mantra but continue to be under the sway of the Māyāvāda philosophy due to their ignorance of Vaishnava doctrine. A devotee who chants the Holy Name without offenses will not be contaminated by such faults. A person who has simply been initiated is called a *Vaiṣṇava-prāya*, or 'almost a Vaishnava.' One who has chanted the Holy Name even once without offenses is a pure devotee, even though he may be on the lowest platform. A householder should serve devotees who are at least of this caliber." (*Amṛta-pravāha-bhāṣya*, 2.15.111)

THE CHARACTERISTICS OF THE MORE ADVANCED DEVOTEES

A year later, the Kulīnagrāma residents returned to Purī and asked the same questions of the Lord. This time He said:

prabhu kahe vaiṣṇava-sevā nāma-saṅkīrtana
dui kara śīghra pābe śrī-kṛṣṇa-caraṇa

"You should both serve the Vaishnavas and chant the holy name of Krishna. If you do these two things, you will quickly attain the shelter of Krishna's lotus feet." (*Chaitanya Charitāmṛta* 2.16.70)

Satyarāja Khān once again asked how to recognize a Vaishnava. This time, Mahāprabhu told him about the devotee at the middle stage of progress, the *madhyama adhikārī*.

kṛṣṇa-nāma nirantara jāṅhāra vadane
sei vaiṣṇava-śreṣṭha bhaja tāṅhāra caraṇe

"A person who is always chanting the holy name of the Lord is to be considered a first-class Vaishnava. Worship his lotus feet."

(*Chaitanya Charitāmṛta* 2.16.72)

The third year, again, Satyarāja once again asked the same question and this time, Mahāprabhu responded by describing the characteristics of the most advanced Vaishnava, the *uttama-adhikārī*, or *mahā-bhāgavata*:

jāṅhāra darśane mukhe āise kṛṣṇa-nāma
tāṅhāre jāniha tumi vaiṣṇava-pradhāna

"One whose very sight brings the name of Krishna to your lips should be recognized as the best of all Vaishnavas." (*Chaitanya Charitāmṛta* 2.16.74)

These three degrees of Vaishnava are also sometimes called progressively *vaiṣṇava*, *vaiṣṇavatara*, and *vaiṣṇavatama*: basic, superior, and superlative types of devotee. Mahāprabhu thus stressed the householder devotee's duty to respect and serve these three types of Vaishnava. Bhaktivinoda Ṭhākura elaborates by saying, "One has no need of serving a Vaishnava who may have undergone formal initiation but who has never once chanted the Holy Name offenselessly. One should still act as his well-wisher and offer him kindness as a guest, however." (*Amṛta-pravāha-bhāṣya*, 2.16.71)

The Qualities of a Devotee

There are many descriptions of the qualities of a devotee in the *Bhāgavata* and other Vaishnava scriptures. In fact, the devotee is the reservoir of all virtue. Śrī Śukadeva said to Mahārāja Parīkṣit:

yasyāsti bhaktir bhagavaty akiñcanā
sarvair guṇais tatra samāsate surāḥ
harāv abhaktasya kuto mahad-guṇā
mano-rathenāsati dhāvato bahiḥ

"For those who have devotion for the Supreme Lord without any desire for any personal goal, all the demigods come and invest them with their qualities. As for the nondevotees, where are their virtues? Led by personal desires, they are always superficially running about in the impermanent existence. Therefore it is impossible for them to be truly virtuous." (*Śrīmad Bhāgavatam* 5.18.12)

Gadādhara Pundit Gosvāmī's disciple, Ananta Ācārya, was such an infinitely virtuous devotee. His dear disciple was Haridāsa Pundit, who directed the service of Govindajī at the Yogapīṭha in Vrindavan. Krishnadāsa Kavirāja Gosvāmī described the qualities of this Haridāsa in the *Chaitanya Charitāmṛta*:

sevāra adhyakṣa śrī-paṇḍita haridāsa
tāṅra yaśaḥ-guṇa sarva-jagate prakāśa
suśīla sahiṣṇu śānta vadānya gambhīra
madhura-vacana madhura-ceṣṭā mahā-dhīra
sabāra sammāna-kartā karena sabāra hita
kauṭilya-mātsarya-hiṁsā nā jāne tāṅra cita
kṛṣṇera ye sādhāraṇa sad-guṇa pañcāśa
se saba guṇera tāṅra śarīre nivāsa

"One whose very sight brings the name of Krishna to your lips should be recognized as the best of all Vaishnavas"

"The chief *pūjārī* at the Govindajī temple was Haridāsa Pundit. His reputation as a virtuous man spread throughout the world. He was polite, tolerant, peaceful, generous, grave, sweet in his words and endeavors, as well as sober. He was respectful to everyone and acted for the welfare of all. His heart was free from duplicity, envy, and malice. The fifty ordinary qualities of Lord Krishna had all taken residence in his body."

(*Chaitanya Charitāmṛta* 1.8.24-27)

Elsewhere, Mahāprabhu Himself gave the following discourse on the subject of the devotee's qualities to Sanātana Gosvāmī:

Govindaji Temple, Vrindavan

sarva mahā-guṇa-gaṇa vaiṣṇava-śarīre
kṛṣṇa-bhakte kṛṣṇera guṇa sakali sañcāre
sei saba guṇa haya vaiṣṇava-lakṣaṇa
saba kahā nā jāya kari dig-daraśana
kṛpālu akṛta-droha satya-sāra sama
nidoṣa vadānya mṛdu śuci akiñcana
sarvopakāraka śānta kṛṣṇaika-śaraṇa
akāma anīha sthira vijita-ṣaḍ-guṇa
mita-bhuk apramatta mānada amānī
gambhīra karuṇa maitra kavi dakṣa maunī

"All the great virtues manifest in a Vaishnava's body, for it is said that all of Krishna's virtues are transferred to His devotee. These transcendental qualities are the characteristics of pure Vaishnavas, and though they cannot be described fully, I shall try to give some indication of them. Devotees are compassionate; they never deliberately creates enmity; they are truthful in words and deeds and without prejudice; they are blameless, magnanimous, mild, clean, and uninterested in material possessions or ambition. Engaged in welfare work for everyone, they are peaceful; they have taken complete shelter of Krishna and are uninfluenced by lust. They are harmless, steady, and have overcome the six cardinal sins—lust, anger, greed, envy, illusion, and jealousy. They eat only as much as required, and are not inebriated. Devotees are respectful, and without false prestige; they are grave, compassionate, friendly, poetic, expert, and silent." (*Chaitanya Charitāmṛta* 2.22.75, 77-80)

The qualities described in the above verses are the symptoms or distinguishing characteristics of the pure, saintly devotee. Of them, the essential characteristic is *kṛṣṇaika-śaraṇa*: he has taken complete shelter of Krishna. The other twenty-five qualities are contingent on the first.

Essential and Secondary Virtues

In the *Bhāgavatam*, Kapiladeva recounted to his mother Devahūti, the symptomatic virtues of a devotee:

titikṣavaḥ kāruṇikāḥ
suhṛdaḥ sarva-dehinām
ajāta-śatravaḥ śāntāḥ
sādhavaḥ sādhu-bhūṣaṇāḥ

"Saintly persons who are tolerant, merciful and friendly to all creatures, who do not make enemies and are peaceful, are jewels amongst the pious."
(*Śrīmad Bhāgavatam* 3.25.21)

The qualities listed in this verse are characteristics of the devotee; such qualities are contingent on the essential virtue of being completely surrendered to Krishna. They are known as the *taṭastha-lakṣaṇa.* In the next two verses Kapiladeva goes on to describe the essential characteristics, or *svarūpa-lakṣaṇa,* of the devotee.

mayy ananyena bhāvena
bhaktiṁ kurvanti ye dṛḍhām
mat-kṛte tyakta-karmāṇas
tyakta-svajana-bāndhavāḥ

"With their emotions fixed exclusively in Me, these sadhus engage in staunch devotional service to Me. For My sake they have renounced all activities as well as their family relationships and friendships." (*Śrīmad Bhāgavatam* 3.25.22)

mad-āśrayāḥ kathā mṛṣṭāḥ
śṛṇvanti kathayanti ca
tapanti vividhās tāpā
naitān mad-gata-cetasaḥ

"Taking shelter of Me, they engage in constantly hearing and chanting about Me. The various kinds of material miseries do not affect them because they are always filled with thoughts of My pastimes and activities."
(*Śrīmad Bhāgavatam* 3.25.23)

ta ete sādhavaḥ sādhvi
sarva-saṅga-vivarjitāḥ
saṅgas teṣv atha te prārthyaḥ
saṅga-doṣa-harā hi te

"O virtuous lady! Sadhus such as these are free from all attachment. You should pray for the association of such saintly persons, for that will counteract the pernicious effects of contact with unholy persons." (*Śrīmad Bhāgavatam* 3.25.24)

"All the great virtues manifest in a Vaishnava's body, for it is said that all of Krishna's virtues are transferred to His devotee"

In a relationship of increasing affection, as one listens to Krishna *kathā* from the mouths of the saintly devotees and the spiritual master, one is enriched by their grace and goes on to free himself from the grips of illusion and attain pure devotion to Krishna.

More Characteristics of the Devotee

The following verses which give the qualifications of the holy person are found in the *Bhāgavata,* wherein the Lord explains to Uddhava the story of King Aila and his attachment to the Apsarā Urvaśī:

santo'napekṣā mac-cittāḥ
praśāntāḥ sama-darśinaḥ

nirmamā nirahaṅkārā
nirdvandvā niṣparigrahaḥ

"The holy are desireless and peaceful; they treat everyone equally. They claim nothing as their own; they are without ego. They are unaffected by dualities like hot and cold, and are uninterested in others' possessions. Above all, their minds are always fixed on Me." (*Śrīmad Bhāgavatam* 11.26.27)

teṣu nityaṁ mahābhāga
mahābhāgeṣu mat-kathāḥ
sambhavanti hi tā nṛṇāṁ
juṣatāṁ prapunanty agham

"O most fortunate one! Like you, these fortunate saintly persons are constantly engaged in discussing Me. Any person who listens to what they say is purified of his or her sins." (*Śrīmad Bhāgavatam* 11.26.28)

tā ye śṛṇvanti gāyanti
hy anumodanti cādṛtāḥ
mat-parāḥ śraddadhānāś ca
bhaktiṁ vindanti te mayi

"Those who listen to, sing, or simply appreciate or honor such topics, become devoted to Me and develop faith and devotion to Me."
(*Śrīmad Bhāgavatam* 11.26.29)

Factually speaking, just as a boat is the salvation of a person drowning in the sea, so the saintly devotees are the salvation of the poor souls who are sinking in the ocean of material existence. Krishna says,

annaṁ hi prāṇināṁ prāṇa
ārtānāṁ śaraṇaṁ tv aham
dharmo vittaṁ nṛṇāṁ pretya
santo'rvāg bibhyato'raṇam

"Food is life for all beings; I am the refuge of the distressed; a person's religious acts are the only wealth he can take with him after dying; and the saintly persons are the salvation of anyone who fears material existence."
(*Śrīmad Bhāgavatam* 11.26.33)

santo diśanti cakṣūṁṣi
bahir arkaḥ samutthitaḥ
devatā bāndhavāḥ santaḥ
santa ātmāham eva ca

"The saintly bestow inner vision on humanity in the way that the sun lights up the external universe upon rising. They are verily gods, they are the truest friends; they are one's very self, indeed, they are My very self."
(*Śrīmad Bhāgavatam* 11.26.34)

Our worshipable spiritual master, Śrīla Prabhupāda Bhaktisiddhānta Sarasvatī Ṭhākura, has elaborated on this last verse in his *Bhāgavata-vivṛti*: "The saintly are comparable to the sun. Their words are like the light which gives the power of sight to the conditioned soul's inner eye of knowledge, thus destroying the darkness of ignorance into which he has fallen. The truly holy are those who have taken to the path of devotion. Non-devotees can neither be considered saintly nor one's truest friends. Those who see the world either as a source of enjoyment to be exploited or as something fearful which must be rejected, as well as those who have desires other than for the pleasure of the Lord, are all situated at a great distance from Him. Only those fully committed to the path of devotion have the expertise to overcome dualities and distinctions."

The Benefits of Associating with the Saintly

What are the benefits of associating with the saintly? The compassion of the saintly—the guru and the pure devotees—results principally in the dissipation of one's bad habits and the development of pure bhakti.

kṛṣṇa-bhakti-janma-mūla haya sādhu-saṅga
kṛṣṇa-prema janme teṅho punaḥ mukhya aṅga

"The root cause of devotional service to Lord Krishna is association with advanced devotees. Even after one's dormant love for Krishna has awakened, association with such devotees remains one's primary devotional activity." (*Chaitanya Charitāmṛta* 2.22.80)

Puja to the Lord

mahat-kṛpā vinā kona karme bhakti naya
kṛṣṇa-bhakti dūre rahu, saṁsāra nahe kṣaya

"Without the favor of a great devotee, no activity qualifies as devotion. Not only is one unable to attain pure devotion to Krishna, but one cannot even be freed from the bondage of material existence."
(*Chaitanya Charitāmṛta* 2.22.51)

There are numerous verses in the *Bhāgavatam* which similarly glorify the association of devotees:

rahūgaṇaitat tapasā na yāti
na cejyayā nirvapaṇād gṛhād vā
na cchandasā naiva jalāgni-sūryair
vinā mahat-pāda-rajo-bhiṣekam

"O Rahūgaṇa, one cannot realize the Absolute Truth unless one smears one's entire body with the dust of the lotus feet of great devotees. Such realization cannot come from penances and austerities, performing sacrifice, renunciation of family life, or undergoing severe penances such as keeping oneself submerged in water in winter or surrounding oneself by fire and the scorching heat of the sun in summer." (*Śrīmad Bhāgavatam* 5.12.12)

naiṣāṁ matis tāvad urukramāṅghriṁ
spṛśaty anarthāpagamo yad-arthaḥ
mahīyasāṁ pāda-rajo-bhiṣekaṁ
niṣkiñcanānāṁ na vṛṇīta yāvat

> "Unless they smear upon their bodies the dust of the lotus feet of a Vaishnava who is completely freed from material contamination, persons who are very inclined toward materialistic life can never purify themselves and approach the feet of the glorious Lord." (*Śrīmad Bhāgavatam* 7.5.32)

"A person who is attempting to advance in the discipline of bhakti must be especially careful about the type of person to whom he renders service"

Pious people, or sadhus on the *karma* and *jñāna* paths, are not to be defined as *tadīya*, "people or things related to the Lord." Thus, those who are attempting to advance in the discipline of bhakti must be especially careful about the type of person to whom they render service. Otherwise, one will not master the discipline and attain its goal—perfection in pure devotion and love for Krishna.

AVOIDING OFFENSES TO THE VAISHNAVAS

The *Hari-bhakti-vilāsa* quotes the *Agni Purana* about the results of showing disdain to a devotee decorated with the symbols of Vishnu. The verse is spoken by a brahmin lamenting the death of his son by the arrow of Lord Rāmacandra's father, King Daśaratha:

śilā-buddhiḥ kṛtā kiṁ vā
pratimāyāṁ harer mayā
kiṁ mayā pathi dṛṣṭasya
viṣṇu-bhaktasya karhicit
tan-mudrāṅkita-dehasya
cetasā nādaraḥ kṛtaḥ
yena karma-vipākena
putra-śoko mamedṛśaḥ

> "Did I once think the deity form of the Lord to be nothing more than a piece of stone? Did I once see a devotee of Vishnu on the road and feel disrespect for him because his body was covered with the Lord's symbols? Is it as a reaction to these sins that I am now lamenting the death of my son?"
> (*Hari-bhakti-vilāsa* 15.41)

This incident is described in the *Rāmāyaṇa*. Lord Rāmacandra's father King Daśaratha was an archer of great talent who was able to pierce an animal target just by hearing the sound it made, without having to see it. On one occasion, he went to the forest to hunt. In the same forest, a brahmin boy named Śravaṇa had gone to the river to fetch water for his parents, both of whom were blind. While Śravaṇa was drawing water, Daśaratha heard the sound and, thinking that it was an elephant drinking, shot an arrow in that direction. His aim was true and the unfortunate child was mortally wounded. As the boy was in his final throes, he painfully managed to tell Daśaratha about his thirsty parents and asked him to bring them the water that he had been unable to provide.

The King took the waterpot and stood silently in front of Śravaṇa's father and mother. The blind father said, "My child, why has it taken you so long to fetch water today? Why are you saying nothing?" Daśaratha heard the fear and anxiety in the blind brahmin's voice and told him what had happened in great sorrow. "O sage, my name is Daśaratha. I mistook your son for an animal and killed him."

As soon as the blind sage heard the tragic news, he fainted. After some time, when he had regained consciousness, he began to lament his loss. It was at this moment that he began to speculate on possible reasons for his son's death.

The *Padma Purana* also warns against seeing the Vaishnava as an ordinary human being:

"One who thinks the guru is an ordinary man, who disrespects a Vaishnava of the infallible Lord's own entourage, thinking that he belongs to a certain caste or creed, or who thinks of the Lord's or the devotee's *caraṇāmṛta,* which purifies all the faults of the Age of Kali, to be ordinary water is taken to be a resident of hell."

It is further written in the *Skanda Purana,*

nindāṁ kurvanti ye mūḍhā
vaiṣṇavānāṁ mahātmanām
patanti pitṛbhiḥ sārdhaṁ
mahā-raurava-saṁjñite

hanti nindati vai dveṣṭi
vaiṣṇavān nābhinandati
krudhyate yāti no harṣaṁ
darśane patanāni ṣaṭ

"Those fools who criticize the great souls who are devotees of Vishnu fall down into the hell known as Mahāraurava along with their ancestors. Six types of behavior result in falldown: killing a Vaishnava, blaspheming one, feeling inimical toward one, not following the etiquette by standing up to greet one, or getting angry with one. It is even a source of falldown to not take pleasure in seeing a Vaishnava." (*Hari-bhakti-vilāsa* 10.311-2)

Deity of Sri Balarama

Furthermore, it is said that even hearing the criticism of Vaishnavas results in falldown.

nindāṁ bhagavataḥ śṛṇvan
tat-parasya janasya vā
tato nāpaiti yaḥ so'pi
yāty adhaḥ sukṛtā cyutaḥ

"Anyone who upon hearing blasphemy of the Lord or those who have dedicated their lives to Him, does not leave the scene immediately, falls down and loses all the merit he had previously earned."
(*Śrīmad Bhāgavatam* 10.74.40; *Hari-bhakti-vilāsa* 10.316)

The Devotee is the Channel of the Lord's Mercy

When Śrī Chaitanya Mahāprabhu observed the affection and esteem in which King Pratāparudra held his associate Rāmānanda Rāya, He gave an indication of his intention to be merciful to the king by saying,

prabhu kahe tumi kṛṣṇa-bhakata-pradhāna
tomāke je prīti kare sei bhāgyavān
tomāte je eta prīti ha-ila rājāra
ei guṇe kṛṣṇa tāṅre karibe aṅgīkāra

"My dear Rāmānanda Rāya, you are the foremost of all the devotees of Krishna; therefore whoever loves you is certainly a very fortunate person. Because the King has shown so much love for you, Lord Krishna will certainly accept him."
(*Chaitanya Charitāmṛta* 2.11.26)

"Those fools who criticize the great souls who are devotees of Vishnu fall down into the hell known as Maharaurava"

Śrīla Saccidānanda Bhaktivinoda Ṭhākura taught how a devotee should pray for the association of advanced Vaishnavas, how we should fall at their feet and, crying, tell them of our miseries of being burned in the fire of material life as a result of our disinterest in the service of the Lord. The devotees are oceans of mercy and their only distress is to see the suffering of the conditioned souls. When they are aware of our suffering and intercede on our behalf to the Supreme Lord, He will act mercifully towards us, knowing us to be under the care of those in His own entourage. The mercy of the Supreme Lord is received through the medium of His devotees.

The Supreme Lord's potency of compassion manifests in the great Vaishnava or in the body of the spiritual master devotee of Krishna. Because the devotees hold Krishna in their hearts, they can bestow Him on anyone who takes shelter of them without duplicity. There is no alternative method to finding Krishna other than fully accepting the shelter of a devotee who has completely given himself to the Supreme Lord. This is why Krishnadāsa Kavirāja Gosvāmī described Raghunātha dāsa's uncle Kālidāsa's fervent dedication to the remnants of Vaishnavas' foodstuffs with such approval.

vaiṣṇavera śeṣa-bhakṣaṇera eteka mahimā
kālidāse pāoyāila prabhura kṛpā-sīmā
tāte vaiṣṇavera jhuṭā khāo chāṛi ghṛṇā-lāja
jāhā haite pāibā nija vāñchita saba kāja
kṛṣṇera ucchiṣṭa haya mahā-prasāda nāma
bhakta-śeṣa haile mahā-mahā-prasādākhyāna
bhakta-pada-dhūli āra bhakta-pada-jala
bhakta-bhukta-avaśeṣa tina mahā-bala
ei tina-sevā haite kṛṣṇa-premā haya
punaḥ punaḥ sarva-śāstre phukāriyā kaya
tāte bāra bāra kahi śuna bhakta-gaṇa
viśvāsa kariyā kara e-tina sevana
tina haite kṛṣṇa-nāma-premera ullāsa
kṛṣṇera prasāda tāte sākṣī kālidāsa

"This is the extent of the glories of the remnants of the devotees' foodstuffs: through dedication to them, Kālidāsa was able to attain Śrī Chaitanya Mahāprabhu's lotus feet. Therefore, set aside your shame and disgust and eat the Vaishnavas' remnants, for by so doing you will be able to fulfill all your desires. The remnants of Krishna's food are called *mahā-prasāda*, but the remnants of the devotees are given the name *mahā-mahā-prasāda*. The dust of the devotees' feet, the water that has washed their feet, and the remnants of their food are three very powerful aids to spiritual practice. All revealed scriptures loudly declare again and again that one can attain the supreme goal of ecstatic love for Krishna through the use of these three substances. So, my dear devotees, please listen to me for I insist on this point: keep faith in these three substances and render service to them with complete faith. Through these three substances you will taste the joy of sacred love, which is found in the holy name of Krishna, and you will win Krishna's pleasure. This has been proved by the experience of Kālidāsa."

(*Chaitanya Charitāmṛta* 3.16.58-63)

Chaitanya Mahaprabhu and Nityananda Prabhu

Bhaktivinoda Ṭhākura also sang:

kabe śrī-caitanya more karibena dayā
kabe āmi pāiba vaiṣṇavera pada-chāyā
gala-vastra kṛtāñjali vaiṣṇava-nikaṭe
dante tṛṇa dhari dāṅṛāiba niṣkapaṭe
kāṅdiyā kāṅdiyā jānāiba duḥkha grāma
saṁsāra anala hate māgiba viśrāma
śuniyā āmāra kathā vaiṣṇava ṭhākura
āmā lāgi kṛṣṇe āvedibena pracura
vaiṣṇavera āvedane kṛṣna dayāmaya
mo-hena pāmara prati habena sadaya

"When will Śrī Chaitanya Mahāprabhu be merciful to me? When will I find shelter in the shade of a Vaishnava's lotus feet? I will approach the saint with a cloth around my neck in humility, my hands folded and with straw between my teeth. In this way I will stand before him and bare my soul to him. Crying, I will tell him of my suffering and beg him to release me from the fire of materialistic life. When he hears my story, the most merciful Vaishnava will intercede on my behalf to the Supreme Lord Krishna. Even though I am most unworthy and insignificant, Krishna will be compassionate towards me when He hears the Vaishnava's prayers on my behalf." (*Kalyāṇa-kalpataru*)

"The devotees are oceans of mercy and their only distress is to see the suffering of the conditioned souls"

vaiṣṇava ṭhākura dayāra sāgara e-dāse karuṇā kari
diyā pada-chāyā śodhaha āmāre tomāra caraṇa dhari
kṛṣṇa se tomāra kṛṣṇa dite pāra tomāra śakati āche
āmi ta kāṅgāla kṛṣṇa kṛṣṇa bali dhāi tava pāche pāche

"O venerable Vaishnava, ocean of compassion, be merciful to me, your servant. I beg of you to give me shelter at your feet and purify me. Since Krishna is yours, it is within your power to give Him to others. I am helpless and so, calling out the names of Krishna, I follow you wherever you go." (*Śaraṇāgati*)

Without the mercy of the spiritual master one cannot receive the mercy of the Vaishnavas. And without the mercy of both the spiritual master and the Vaishnavas, there is no hope of receiving the Supreme Lord's mercy. The spiritual master gives us the power to recognize the real devotees and separate them from those who simply pretend to be devotees. Without this discrimination it is easy to fall under the thrall of bad association and be misled from the path of pure devotion. No one will be able to point us in the direction of

"Without the mercy of the spiritual master one cannot receive the mercy of the Vaishnavas. And without the mercy of both the spiritual master and the Vaishnavas, there is no hope of receiving the Supreme Lord's mercy"

genuine devotional association other than a genuine spiritual master possessing all the qualifications described in scripture: he must be fully conversant in the scriptural truths and enriched by direct realization of the Supreme Truth, on the highest levels of the path of Bhakti yoga and free from the pushing and pulling of the material modes. The guidance necessary to achieve perfection is certainly not within the capacity of so-called gurus who have no real knowledge of Vaishnava doctrine, who are indifferent to the path of chanting the Holy Name instituted by Mahāprabhu Himself, who commit offenses to the Holy Name, or who are contaminated by the unholy association of non-devotees or those engaged in illicit sexual relations.

The blackness of coal cannot be changed by all the water contained in the lakes and oceans of the world; it can only be transformed by fire. In the same way, it is only by the blazing fire of divine instructions from the *sad-guru* that one can be purified of material contamination. Only then can one be freed from the clutches of the witch of material illusion.

CHAPTER V

AVOIDING BAD ASSOCIATION

As we have seen from the extensive descriptions above, all auspiciousness comes to one who has the good fortune of encountering and relishing the company of the saintly. By the same token, the completely opposite effect can take place if one has contact with those who are impious or unholy. Therefore, the conduct of a Vaishnava is based primarily on these two principles: the acceptance of saintly company and the rejection of the company of the unholy.

The association of devotees is a positive, direct expression of Vaishnava conduct. Similarly, an indirect or negative expression of Vaishnava conduct is the avoidance of non-devotional association. Much emphasis has been given in the scriptures to this prohibition, and an aspiring devotee should give it special attention.

asat-saṅga-tyāga ei vaiṣṇava ācāra
strī-saṅgī eka asādhu kṛṣṇābhakta āra

"The rejection of unholy company is the essence of Vaishnava behavior. The unholy are divided into those who are attached to sex life and those who are against the principles of devotion to Krishna." (*Chaitanya Charitāmṛta* 2.22.87)

The same principle is stated in the *Bhāgavatam*:

tato duḥsaṅgam utsṛjya
satsu sajjeta buddhimān
santa evāsya chindanti
mano-vyāsaṅgam uktibhiḥ

"An intelligent person should therefore abandon all bad association and stay in the company of devotees. Only such holy persons can cut through our

"All auspiciousness comes to one who has the good fortune of encountering and relishing the company of the saintly"

unhealthy mental attachments through the use of their powerful words."
(*Śrīmad Bhāgavatam* 11.26.26)

Thus one must be extremely careful in the selection of the company he keeps. In the *Bhakti-rasāmṛta-sindhu*, while discussing the need to seek out like-minded association, Rūpa Gosvāmī quotes the following verse from *Hari-bhakti-sudhodaya* (8.51). In this verse, Hiraṇyakaśipu tells Prahlāda:

yasya yat-saṅgatiḥ puṁso
maṇivat syāt sa tad-guṇaḥ
sva-kula-rddhyai tato dhīmān
sva-yūthān eva saṁśrayet

"Like a mirror, a person takes on the qualities of those with whom he comes in contact. One who is intelligent should therefore seek the company of those who have the same ideals in order to develop their good qualities in himself."
(*Bhakti-rasāmṛta-sindhu* 1.2.229)

"Like a mirror, a person takes on the qualities of those with whom he comes in contact. One who is intelligent should therefore seek the company of those who have the same ideals in order to develop their good qualities in himself"

The great authorities have thus always warned us to avoid bad company.

PHILOSOPHERS, YOGIS AND FRUITIVE WORKERS

The *Kātyāyana-saṁhitā* shows the extent to which a devotee abhors the association of non-devotees:

varaṁ huta-vaha-jvālā-
pañjarāntar-vyavasthitiḥ
na śauri-cintā-vimukha-
jana-saṁvāsa-vaiśasam

"Better to be locked in a cage surrounded by burning flames than to suffer in the association of those who dislike thinking of Krishna."
(*Hari-bhakti-vilāsa* 10.295, *Chaitanya Charitāmṛta* 2.22.91)

The point is that if you must suffer great hardship from physical pain or imprisonment, you should accept it rather than place your spiritual life in danger by associating with non-devotees.

The most worshipable Gosvāmīs have also stated:

mādrākṣīḥ kṣīṇa-puṇyān kvacid api
bhagavad-bhakti-hīnān manuṣyān

"Never look upon those men who are bereft of devotion to the Lord and whose merit has thus dwindled to nothingness." (*Chaitanya Charitāmṛta* 2.22.92)

There are several kinds of non-devotee, but primarily the word *abhakta* refers to (1) the fruitive worker who seeks sense gratification, (2) the philosopher who seeks liberation, and (3) the yogi who seeks mystic powers. Narottama dāsa Ṭhākura has summarized the viewpoint of the devotee in his *Prema-bhakti-candrikā*:

karmī jñānī michā-bhakta nā habe tāya anurakta
śuddha-bhajanete kara mana
vraja-janera jei mata tāhe habe anugata
ei se parama-tattva dhana

"Don't be attached to the fruitive worker, the philosopher, and the hypocritical devotee, but fix your mind in pure *bhajana*. Follow the understanding of the residents of Vraja, for this is the invaluable supreme truth."

durlabha janama hena nāhi bhaja hari kena
ki lāgiyā mara bhava-bandhe
chāṛa anya kriyā-karma nāhi dekha veda-dharma
bhakti kara kṛṣṇa-pada-dvandve

"This human life is a rare attainment, so why don't you use it to worship Lord Hari? Why are you just waiting to die in bondage? Put aside all other tasks and forget about the Vedic religion. Just engage in devotion to Krishna's lotus feet."

karma-kāṇḍa jñāna-kāṇḍa kevala biṣera bhāṇḍa
amṛta baliyā jebā khāya
nānā yoni sadā phire kadarya bhakṣaṇa kare
tāra janma adhaḥpāte jāya

"The sections of the Veda dealing with fruitive activities and spiritual knowledge are reservoirs of poison. Anyone who drinks from them, thinking they contain the nectar of the gods, is doomed to repeated births in various species, where they will eat the unspeakable. Such a person's life is one of degradation."

jñāna karma kare loka nāhi jāne bhakti-yoga
nānā mate haiyā ajñāna
tāra kathā nāhi śuni paramārtha tattva jāni
prema-bhakti bhakta-gaṇa-prāṇa

"People practice philosophical speculation and the fruitive activities of the scriptures, but they do not know the process of bhakti for linking with the Supreme Lord. They subscribe to many different philosophical schools, but are fundamentally ignorant of the truth. I do not listen to them when they speak for I know the ultimate truth: the life of the devotee is loving devotion to the Lord."

"The life of the devotee is loving devotion to the Lord"

Two Kinds of Unholy Persons: the Womanizer and the Impersonalist

The unholy are classed in two fundamental categories: the sensualist or womanizer, and the non-devotee, atheist, or impersonalist. Thus Mahāprabhu said,

niṣkiñcanaṣya bhagavad-bhajanonmukhasya
pāraṁ paraṁ jigamiṣor bhava-sāgarasya
sandarśanaṁ viṣayiṇām atha yoṣitāṁ ca
hā hanta hanta viṣa-bhakṣaṇato'py asādhu

"Alas, the sight of materialistic persons or women is even more harmful than

drinking poison for one who is renounced, inclined towards the worship of the Supreme Lord and desiring to cross over the ocean of material suffering, ."
(*Chaitanya-candrodaya Nāṭaka* 8.23, *Chaitanya Charitāmṛta* 2.11.8)

Our most worshipable Śrīla Prabhupāda has discussed this priciple in general terms in his *Anubhāṣya*: "The unique principle of conduct for the Vaishnava is the rejection of non-Vaishnava association. The non-Vaishnava refers to two types of persons: one is the licentious person and the other is the nondevotee. The licentious are of two types: legally married individuals who are overly attached to the company of their spouses or those attached to illicit sexual activity. The first of these is legitimate according to the arrangements of the *varṇāśrama-dharma* system, while the other is engaged in illegitimate sexual activity which is disruptive to the *varṇāśrama* system, and results in sinful reactions and hellish births. Anyone engaged in sinful activities within the material world is absolutely unworthy of the Vaishnava name. The three goals of human life, *dharma, artha,* and *kāma*, are all tied up with the non-Vaishnava behavior centered on sexual enjoyment.

"The fourth goal of life, *mokṣa*, has no basis in sexual enjoyment, but because those seeking liberation are Māyāvādīs—those who deny a personal conception of God—they are even worse than those addicted to sexual pleasures and are thus considered non-Vaishnavas. They are to be avoided. The company of both the Māyāvādī who rejects everything as illusion (including the Supreme Person's name, form and activities) and the *māyā-vilāsī* who takes pleasure in the illusory world, has a negative effect on one's development of Vaishnava qualities and attainment of pure devotional service. The Māyāvādī seeker of liberation rejects material enjoyments in order to enjoy salvation and to make a show of his personal superiority. The womanizer is representative of all hedonists. What they have in common is their self-centered effort to seek the satisfaction of their own senses. Goals other than Krishna dominate their actions. Their lives are full of self-deception and thus they cannot be accepted as servants of Krishna." (*Anubhāṣya* to *Chaitanya Charitāmṛta* 2.22.87)

"Don't be attached to the fruitive worker, the philosopher, and the hypocritical devotee, but fix your mind in pure bhajana. Follow the understanding of the residents of Vraja, for this is the invaluable supreme truth"

In the third canto of the *Bhāgavatam*, Kapiladeva describes in more detail to his mother, Devahūti, the negative effects of associating with the licentious:

satyaṁ śaucaṁ dayā maunaṁ
buddhir hrīḥ śrīr yaśaḥ kṣamā
śamo damo bhagaś ceti
yat-saṅgād yāti saṅkṣayam

teṣv aśānteṣu mūḍheṣu
khaṇḍitātmasv asādhuṣu
saṅgaṁ na kuryāc chocyeṣu
yoṣit-krīḍā-mṛgeṣu ca

na tathāsya bhaven moho
bandhaś cānya-prasaṅgataḥ
yoṣit-saṅgād yathā puṁso
yathā tat-saṅgi-saṅgataḥ

"At all costs, one should avoid association with those lamentable creatures who have become the playthings of the opposite sex. They are lacking in peace, are constantly bewildered, and their concept of self is fragmented. Indeed there is no enchantment more powerful, no bondage for one more sure than that which comes through the association of the opposite sex and through the association of the sensualist. By keeping such company, one loses the qualities of truthfulness, cleanliness, mercy, gravity, intelligence, modesty, beauty, reputation, forgiveness, control of the mind and senses, and good fortune."

(*Śrīmad Bhāgavatam* 3.31.33-35)

Kapiladeva goes on with his criticism of the sensualist and concludes by saying,

yopayāti śanair māyā
yoṣid deva-vinirmitā
tām īkṣetātmano mṛtyuṁ
tṛṇaiḥ kūpam ivāvṛtam

"Maya, in the form of woman created by the Lord, slowly approaches a man in the guise of offering him service, but he must see her as the death of the soul, as dangerous as a blind well covered with grass." (*Śrīmad Bhāgavatam* 3.31.40)

"One thing that is particularly noticeable in Mahaprabhu's teachings is His disapproval of the Mayavada, or monistic philosophy"

The Māyāvādī

The Supreme Lord Śrī Krishna Himself took on the mood of a devotee and appeared in this world as Śrī Gaurāṅga Mahāprabhu. During His life on this earth, Mahāprabhu set the standard for the conduct of a saintly spiritual master. One thing that is particularly noticeable in Mahāprabhu's teachings is His disapproval of the Māyāvāda, or monistic philosophy.

When Mahāprabhu was traveling through northern India, He stopped for a few days in Benares. There He heard about the great Māyāvādī sannyasi Prakāśānanda Sarasvatī from a Maharashtrian brahmin. The Lord made the following comments:

prabhu kahe māyāvādī kṛṣṇe aparādhī
brahma ātmā caitanya kahe niravadhi
ataeva tāra mukhe nā āise kṛṣṇa-nāma
kṛṣṇa-nāma kṛṣṇa-svarūpa duita samāna
nāma vigraha svarūpa tina eka-rūpa
tine bheda nāhi tina cid-ānanda-rūpa
deha-dehīra, nāma-nāmīra kṛṣṇe nāhi bheda
jīvera dharma nāma-deha-svarūpe vibheda

"Māyāvādī impersonalists are offenders to Krishna. They constantly repeat words like Brahman, atman, and *caitanya*. As a result, they are unable to utter Krishna's holy name. Krishna's name and His essence are the same. Krishna's name, His form and His essential being are all one. They are spiritual and there is no distinction to be made between them. In Krishna, there is no difference between body and soul, nor between the signified and signifier as is the case with the *jīva,* in whom all these distinctions are present."

(*Chaitanya Charitāmṛta* 2.17.129-132)

Other verses in the *Chaitanya Charitāmṛta* confirm that because the Māyāvādīs are inimical to the concept of eternal service to Krishna, they are incapable of chanting the pure name of the Lord.

ataeva kṛṣṇa-nāma nā āise tāra mukhe
māyāvādi-gaṇa jāte mahā bahir-mukhe

"The holy name of Krishna does not come from the mouths of the Māyāvādīs, for they are completely opposed to the Lord." (*Chaitanya Charitāmṛta* 2.17.143)

"Mahaprabhu appeared in five forms as the Panca-tattva, in order to inundate the world with love of God"

Mahāprabhu appeared in five forms as the Pañca-tattva, in order to inundate the world with love of God. Only the Māyāvādī philosophers were able to somehow escape and avoid being affected.

māyāvādī karma-niṣṭha kutārkika-gaṇa
nindaka pāṣaṇḍī jata paṛuwā adhama
sei saba mahādakṣa dhāñā palāila
sei vanyā tā-sabāre chuṅite nārila

The Pancha-tattva.

"The Māyāvādīs, fruitive workers, the argumentative, blasphemers, atheists, and inferior students were very expert in avoiding the flood of *prema*. They ran away and so it could not touch them." (*Chaitanya Charitāmṛta* 1.7.29-30)

THE DANGER OF HEARING MĀYĀVĀDA COMMENTARIES

The *Vedanta Sutras* were written by Vyāsadeva in order to explain the philosophy of pure devotional service, but in the Māyāvādī interpretation of the sutras, the Lord's eternal transcendental form is denied. Furthermore, this interpretation eliminates the eternal distinction between the individual and the supreme souls, effectively negating the existence of an eternal relationship of service between the infinitesimal individual soul and the Supreme Lord. Service to the Lord is in fact the eternal constitutional activity of the soul, so anyone who hears the Māyāvāda philosophy compromises his true self-understanding. Losing the sense of devotion to the Lord, he becomes lost to himself and, in effect, ruined. Therefore, it is said,

jīvera nistāra lāgi sūtra kaila vyāsa
māyāvādi-bhāṣya śunile haya sarva-nāśa

"Vyāsadeva wrote the *Vedanta Sutra*s for the salvation of the living entities, but if they hear the interpretation of the Māyāvādīs, they will go to ruin." (*Chaitanya Charitāmṛta* 2.6.169)

Svarūpa Dāmodara Gosvāmī's good friend, Bhagavān Ācārya, had a younger brother, Gopāla Bhaṭṭācārya, who had studied Vedanta in Benares. When Gopāla came to visit him in Purī, Bhagavān Ācārya repeatedly asked Svarūpa Dāmodara to hear his brother explain the *Vedanta Sutras*. Svarūpa Dāmodara was not eager to do so and explained his objections by saying:

buddhi-bhraṣṭa haila tomāra gopālera saṅge
māyāvāda śunibāre upajila raṅge
vaiṣṇava hañā jebā śārīraka-bhāṣya śune
sevya-sevaka-bhāva chāḍi āpanāre īśvara māne
mahā-bhāgavata jei kṛṣṇa prāṇa-dhana jāra
māyāvāda-śravaṇe citta avaśya phire tāṅra

"You have lost your intelligence by keeping Gopāla's company, so now you have developed a fancy to hear Māyāvāda philosophy. When a Vaishnava listens to Śaṅkara's *Śārīraka-bhāṣya* (the Māyāvāda commentary upon *Vedanta Sutra*), he gives up making a distinction between master and servant and considers himself the Supreme Lord. Hearing the Māyāvāda philosophy will unfailingly change the consciousness of even a *mahā-bhāgavata* devotee whose life and soul is Krishna."

In spite of Svarūpa Dāmodara's protest, Bhagavān Ācārya continued to defend his desire. He said, "We have given our life and soul to Krishna's lotus feet. Śaṅkara's commentary will not be able to change our minds."

"Service to the Lord is in fact the eternal constitutional activity of the soul, so anyone who hears the Mayavada philosophy compromises his true self-understanding"

svarūpa kahe tathāpi māyāvāda śravaṇe
cit brahma māyā mithyā ei mātra śune
jīvā jñāna-kalpita īśvare sakala-i ajñāna
yāhāra śravaṇe bhaktera phāṭe mana-prāṇa

Svarūpa Dāmodara replied, "Even so, in the Māyāvāda philosophy, we only hear about how Brahman is pure consciousness and that the universe of maya is false. We also hear that the independent consciousness of the individual *jīva* is just imagination and that all is ignorance, even in the Supreme Lord. When a devotee hears such things, his heart bursts with pain."

Bhagavān Ācārya felt greatly ashamed and fearful. He said nothing, but the next day, he asked Gopāla Bhaṭṭācārya to return home to Bengal. (*Chaitanya Charitāmṛta* 3.2.94-100)

THE LORD'S FORM AND POTENCIES ARE ETERNAL

Vrindavan dāsa Ṭhākura also writes in the *Chaitanya Bhāgavata* that Mahāprabhu made the following criticism of the Māyāvāda philosophy to Murāri Gupta:

hasta-pada-mukha mora nāhika locana
ei mata vede more kare viḍambana
kāśīte paṛāya beṭā prakāśānanda
sei beṭā mora aṅga kare khaṇḍa khaṇḍa
bākhānaye veda mora vigraha nā māne
sarva aṅga haila kuṣṭha tabu nāhi jāne
sarva-yajña-maya mora je aṅga pavitra
aja-bhava-ādi gāya jāhāra caritra
puṇya pavitratā pāya je aṅga paraśe
tāhā mithyā bale beṭā kemana sāhase

śunaha murāri gupta kahi mata sāra
veda guhya kahi ei tomāra gocara
āmi yajña-varāha sakala veda-sāra
āmi se karinu pūrve pṛthivī uddhāra
saṅkīrtana ārambhe mohāra avatāra
bhakta jana lāgi duṣṭa karimu saṁhāra
sevakera droha muñi sahite nā pāroṅ
putra jadi haya mora tathāpi saṁhāroṅ

"The Vedic scriptures describe Me as being without hands or feet, with no face or eyes. In this way they make a mockery of Me. In Kāśī, there is a fool named Prakāśānanda who is teaching this doctrine. He too cuts My body into little pieces. He teaches the Vedic scriptures, but he does not accept the truth of My eternal form. As a result of his offences, his body has been covered with leprosy, but still he refuses to understand. My body is eternally pure and the embodiment of all the Vedic sacrifices; Brahmā and Shiva glorify My activities. Whoever touches My body gains spiritual merit and becomes purified of sin, but this insolent fool thinks that it is illusory. Listen, Murāri, and I will tell you the confidential essence of the Vedic teaching. I am the incarnation Yajña-varāha, the cream of the Vedic literature who previously lifted up the world. Now I have come in this form to preach the *saṅkīrtana* movement. For the sake of the devotees, I will destroy the wicked. I am unable to tolerate those who act as the enemies of My devotees; even if He is My own son, I will destroy him.

(*Chaitanya Bhāgavata* 2.3.36-44)

"In the Mayavada philosophy, we hear...that all is ignorance, even the Supreme Lord. When a devotee hears such things, his heart bursts with pain"

The Vedic scriptures have used words like *nirākāra* ("formless") and *nirviśeṣa* ("undifferentiated, without attributes") in order to negate the presence of material form, activities, and attributes in the Supreme Lord. But in turn, they go on to reveal the truth of the Lord's eternal form and attributes, His appearance and pastimes in this world. In fact, because the Lord is omnipotent, no one can deny His eternal form. The same scriptures that negate the form and qualities of the Supreme on the one hand go on to later approve the Lord's form and attributes. Therefore, if one examines the scriptures in detail he will become convinced that the doctrine of the Lord's transcendental form and attributes takes precedence.

īśvarera śrī-vigraha sac-cid-ānandākāra
se-vigrahe kaha sattva-guṇera vikāra
śrī-vigraha je nā māne sei ta pāṣaṇḍī
adṛśya aspṛśya sei haya yama-daṇḍī

"The transcendental form of the Supreme Lord is complete in eternity, cognizance and bliss. You, however, say that this form is a product of the material quality of goodness. Whoever denies the Lord's transcendental form is certainly an atheist. One should neither see nor touch such a person who will be punished by the lord of death." (*Chaitanya Charitāmṛta* 2.6.166-167)

sarvaiśvarya-paripūrṇa svayaṁ bhagavān
tāṅre nirākāra kari karaha vyākhyāna
nirviśeṣa tāṅre kahe yei śruti-gaṇa
prākṛta niṣedhi kare aprākṛta sthāpana

"The Supreme Lord Himself is complete in all divine majesty, but you describe him as formless. Those scriptures which say that He is impersonal are simply condemning a material understanding of His form and attributes and go on to say that His form and attributes are transcendental and free of mundane characteristics." (*Chaitanya Charitāmṛta* 2.6.140-141)

"If one examines the scriptures in detail one will become convinced that the doctrine of the Lord's transcendental form and attributes takes precedence"

Krishnadāsa Kavirāja quotes a verse from the *Hāyaśīrṣa-pañcarātra* which substantially says the same thing:

yā yā śrutir jalpati nirviśeṣaṁ
sā sābhidhatte sa-viśeṣam eva
vicāra-yoge sati hanta tāsāṁ
prāyo balīyaḥ sa-viśeṣam eva

"Those *Upanishads* which describe the Absolute Truth as formless and impersonal go on to prove in the end that He is a person. Upon close analysis, it can be seen that though both the personal and impersonal descriptions of the Supreme are valid, the personal conception ultimately predominates in these scriptures." (*Chaitanya-candrodaya-nāṭaka,* 6.67)

The *Taittirīya Upanishad* (3.1) uses the ablative, instrumental and locative cases to indicate three kinds of attributes present in the Supreme Person.

yato vā imāni bhūtāni jāyante
yena jātāni jīvanti yat prayanty
abhisaṁviśanti tad brahma tad vijijñāsasva

"Brahman is that from which all these living entities are born, by Brahman they live, and after death, they enter into Brahman. That is what you must know." (*Taittirīya Upanishad* 3.1)

The words *bahu syām* ("I become many") which are found in both the *Chāndogya Upanishad* (6.2.3) and the *Taittirīya Upanishads* indicate that the Supreme Lord had the desire to expand His energies in creation. The words *sa aikṣata* ("He glanced over creation") found in the *Aitareya Upanishad* indicate that the Supreme Lord had a desire to create and that He extended His powers over the material nature. As such, His existence prior to creation is clearly being emphasized.

The word *brahman* is repeatedly mentioned throughout the *Upanishads*. The *Śrīmad Bhāgavatam* is said to be the essence of the Vedanta (*sarva-vedānta-sāraṁ hi—Śrīmad Bhāgavatam* 12.13.12). There, Krishna is named as the complete manifestation of Brahman:

aho bhāgyam aho bhāgyaṁ
nanda-gopa-vrajaukasām
yan-mitraṁ paramānandaṁ
pūrṇaṁ brahma sanātanam

"How fortunate! How fortunate are the residents of Nanda's cowherd community! They have made the eternal, supreme and complete form of bliss, the complete Brahman, their friend and relative." (*Śrīmad Bhāgavatam* 10.14.32)

A number of verses in the *Upanishads* state that the Supreme Truth has no material hands or feet; in the next breath, however, they affirm that He moves everywhere. Here is an example of such a verse from the *Śvetāśvatara Upanishad* :

"How fortunate! How fortunate are the residents of Nanda's cowherd community! They have made the eternal, supreme and complete form of bliss, the complete Brahman, their friend and relative"

apāṇi-pādo javano grahītā
paśyaty acakṣuḥ sa śṛṇoty akarṇaḥ
sa vetti vedyaṁ na ca tasyāsti vettā
tam āhur agryaṁ puruṣaṁ mahāntam

"He has no hands and no feet, yet He runs and takes hold of all things. Though He has no eyes, He sees. He has no ears, but He hears. He knows everything that is to be known, but no one knows Him. He is called the original great person." (*Śvetāśvatara Upanishad* 3.19)

The Māyāvādīs reject the direct meaning of such *Śruti* texts and establish that the Supreme Truth is impersonal on the basis of an indirect interpretation. This does not change the actual personal meaning of these texts. The factual understanding of Brahman is the Supreme Lord Bhagavān, full of six opulences and possessing a form of spiritual bliss. Scriptures which say that He is formless are simply stating that He has no material form. The Māyāvādīs further say that He is inactive even though He is always engaged in delightful, transcendental pastimes.

na tasya kāryaṁ karaṇaṁ ca vidyate
na tat-samaś cābhyadhikaṁ ca dṛśyate
parāsya śaktir vividhaiva śrūyate
svābhāvikī jñāna-bala-kriyā ca

Sri Krishna and his cowherd friends

"He has neither activities nor senses. No one is equal or superior to Him can be found. He possesses a natural superior energy which manifests variously as knowledge, strength and action." (*Śvetāśvatara Upanishad* 6.8)

The purport of this verse is that the Supreme Lord has no material activities. This is because He has no material form consisting of hands, feet or other working senses. Despite not having material senses, He is engaged in the work of His divine diversions. Though situated in His divine abode beyond all material anxiety, He is all-pervading. No one is the Lord's equal, what to speak of being superior to him. He is *asamordhva.* The Supreme Lord's transcendental potencies are natural to Him. These natural potencies are of three kinds: *jñāna-śakti,* or the power of knowledge; *bala-śakti,* or the power of strength; and *kriyā-śakti*, the power of action. These potencies are *parā* or primary. These energies are also known by the following names: (1) *cit-śakti,* or *saṁvit-śakti*, (2) *sat-śakti,* or *sandhinī-śakti*, and (3) *ānanda-śakti,* or *hlādinī-śakti*.

The Māyāvādīs, however, take a lot of trouble to prove that Krishna has no potencies even though this verse clearly states that He naturally possesses them intrinsically. The Supreme Lord's energies are further subdivided into three: His internal or spiritual potency, His external potency of maya, and the marginal energy consisting of the living entities.

The essence of the combined ecstatic and conscious elements of the spiritual potency is bhakti. When this is given to the living entity and he wholeheartedly adopts it, he can break free of the coverings of the material or external energy and enter into the divine ecstatic consciousness of pure love for Krishna. This great achievement is the consequence of association with pure devotees: he then becomes fixed in the conduct standardized by such saintly persons.

Ṭhākura Bhaktivinoda's Prayer

The eternally liberated associate of Śrī Chaitanya Mahāprabhu Śrī Śrīla Bhaktivinoda Ṭhākura has written the following song in his *Śaraṇāgati*:

viṣaya-vimūḍha āra māyāvādī jana
bhakti-śūnya duṅhe prāṇa dhare akāraṇa
ei dui saṅga nātha nā haya āmāra
prārthanā kariye āmi caraṇe tomāra
se duwera madhye viṣayī tabe bhāla
māyāvādī-saṅga nāhi māgi kona kāla
viṣayī-hṛdaya jabe sādhu-saṅga pāya
anāyāse labhe bhakti bhaktera kṛpāya
māyāvāda doṣa jāra hṛdaya paśila
kutarke hṛdaya tāra vajra-sama bhela
bhaktira svarūpa āra viṣaya āśraya
māyāvādī anitya boliyā saba kaya
dhik tāra kṛṣṇa-sevā śravaṇa-kīrtana
kṛṣṇa aṅge vajra hāne tāhāra stavana
māyāvāda sama bhakti pratikūla nāi
ataeva māyāvāda saṅga nāhi cāi
bhakativinoda māyāvāda dūra kari
vaiṣṇava-saṅgete baise nāmāśraya dhari

"Both those who are bewildered by the promise of sense enjoyment and Māyāvādī impersonalists are devoid of devotion. Their lives have no purpose. I pray, O Lord, that I never be subjected to their association. Of the two, however, I would rather be with a sensualist than with a Māyāvādī, to whose company I hope I will never be subjected. A sensualist may be transformed by the association of a devotee whose mercy can easily turn him to a life of devotion. On the other hand, once the impersonalist contamination has touched someone's heart, it becomes as hard as stone with all manner of false argument. The Māyāvādī considers devotion itself, the devotee and the object of devotion all to be temporary manifestations of the material world. I curse his so-called service to Krishna, his hearing of the *Bhāgavatam* and chanting of the Holy Names. His prayers to Krishna are like thunderbolts on the Lord's body. There is nothing more harmful to devotion than Māyāvāda, therefore I do not wish to ever be with people who subscribe to that philosophy. Bhaktivinoda hereby rejects the Māyāvāda philosophy and takes shelter of the Holy Names in the association of devotees." (*Śaraṇāgati*, 27)

"Those who have other desires and are trapped in the company of non-devotees, may chant for thousands of lifetimes without ever attaining the goal of love for Krishna"

The result of bad association is that one does not get free of material desire. When one's mind is overcome with the elation and disappointment resulting from attachment to the sense objects, how can something as pure as Krishna *prema* find a place there? Or, as Krishnadāsa Kavirāja Gosvāmī writes:

bhukti-mukti-ādi vāñchā jadi mane haya
sādhana karile prema utpanna nā haya

"If desires for sense enjoyment and liberation find a place in a devotee's heart, all his practice of devotional activities will not result in love for Krishna."
(*Chaitanya Charitāmṛta* 2.19.175)

Amongst the various practices of devotional service, the chanting of the Holy Names has pride of place. Those who have other desires and are trapped in the company of non-devotees, however, may chant for thousands of lifetimes without ever attaining the goal of love for Krishna. Therefore, Jagadānanda Pundit wrote,

asādhu-saṅgete bhāi nāma nāhi haya
nāmākṣara bāhirāya baṭe nāma kabhu naya
kabhu nāmābhāsa sadā haya nāma aparādha
e saba jānibe bhāi kṛṣṇa-bhaktir bādha
jadi karibe kṛṣṇa-nāma sādhu-saṅga kara
bhukti-mukti-siddhi-vāñchā dūre parihara

"O brother! You cannot chant the Holy Name in the association of non-devotees. The sounds of the Holy Name may come out of your mouth, but it will not really be the Name. It will sometimes be the Name's reflection (*nāmābhāsa*) and sometimes offensive chanting (*nāmāparādha*), but brother, you should know that in either case, this kind of chanting interferes with the attainment of pure devotion to Krishna. If you want to chant the Holy Names, then associate with devotees and keep desires for sense enjoyment, liberation, and yogic powers at a distance." (*Prema-vivarta*, 7)

daśa-aparādha tyaja māna-apamāna
anāsaktye viṣaya bhuñja āra laha kṛṣṇa-nāma
kṛṣṇa-bhaktira anukūla saba karaha svīkāra
kṛṣṇa-bhaktira pratikūla saba kara parihāra
jñāna-yoga-ceṣṭā chāṛa āra karma-saṅga
markaṭa-vairāgya tyaja jāte deha-raṅga
kṛṣṇa āmāra pāle rākhe jāna sarva-kāla
ātma-nivedana dainye ghucāo jañjāla
sādhu pāowā kaṣṭa baṛa jīvera jāniyā
sādhu-bhakta rūpe kṛṣṇa āila nadīyā
gorāpada āśraya karaha buddhimān
gorā bai sādhu-guru āche kebā āna

"An intelligent person takes shelter of Mahaprabhu's lotus feet, for such a person knows that other than Mahaprabhu, there is no true saint or spiritual master"

"Give up the ten offenses to the Holy Name as well as worrying about receiving respect or criticism. Consume what you need without attachment and always chant the Holy Name. Accept everything which favors devotion to Krishna and reject everything which interferes with its practice. Abandon any efforts for liberation or mystic power as well as devotion mixed with karma. Above all, give up the false renunciation of the monkeys, in which bodily consciousness and attachment to sense gratification dwell. Remain strong in the knowledge that Krishna is always taking care of you. Offer yourself to Krishna completely and, in humility, become free from all entanglements. It is very difficult for an ordinary person to find the association of genuine saintly persons. Krishna Himself knows this and so He kindly came to Nadiyā in the form of a saintly devotee. An intelligent person takes shelter of Mahāprabhu's lotus feet, for such a person knows that other than Mahāprabhu, there is no true saint or spiritual master."

Chaitanya Mahaprabhu reveals His Sadbhuja form

The only way to be free of bad association is thus by replacing it with the good:

sādhu saṅga kṛpā kiṁ vā kṛṣṇera kṛpāya
kāmādi-duḥsaṅga chāṛi śuddha-bhakti pāya

"Either through the benediction of devotional association or through the mercy of Krishna Himself, one becomes free of the bad association resulting from lust, anger, and greed, and attains pure devotional service."

(*Chaitanya Charitāmṛta* 2.24.97)

sat-saṅgān mukta-duḥsaṅgo
hātuṁ notsahate budhaḥ
kīrtyamānaṁ yaśo yasya
sakṛd ākarṇya rocanam

"Once freed from bad association by keeping the company of the saintly, an intelligent person becomes reluctant to give up listening to the glories of the Lord, which are so pleasing, even if only heard once."

(*Śrīmad Bhāgavatam* 1.10.11)

Thus the *Bhāgavatam* advises:

tato duḥsaṅgam utsṛjya
satsu sajjeta buddhimān
santa evāsya chindanti
mano-vyāsaṅgam uktibhiḥ

"An intelligent person should therefore abandon all bad association and hold fast to the company of devotees. Such saints are the only ones who, through their instructions, can cut through our unhealthy mental attachments."

(*Śrīmad Bhāgavatam* 11.26.26)

One has to be attentive in avoiding the association of opposite sex and non-devotees. But if one remains in good company, the dangers of the world disappear. Thus, Narottama dāsa sings in his *Prema-bhakti-candrikā*: "What can lust, anger and greed do to the practitioner who has the association of saintly persons?"

GOVINDA, LOVER OF THE COWS

Chapter VI

Taking Shelter of Krishna

Out of compassion for the living beings, Śrī Chaitanya Mahāprabhu appeared in the holy city of Nabadwip in the land of Gauḍa, or Bengal. Accompanied by His associates, He came to distribute the very rare ecstatic love of God as experienced by the residents of Vraja. In order to do so He first taught the process of surrender, for it is only through taking shelter of Krishna, also known as *śaraṇāgati*, that one can attain this ecstatic love. The Supreme Lord makes the devotee who has taken shelter of Him the inheritor of this treasure of love.

In his hymns to the Supreme Lord, the elephant Gajendra sang the following stanza:

ekāntino yasya na kañcanārthaṁ
vāñchanti ye vai bhagavat-prapannāḥ
aty-adbhutaṁ tac-caritaṁ sumaṅgalaṁ
gāyanta ānanda-samudra-magnāḥ

> "Unalloyed devotees, who have fully surrendered to the Lord, have no desire for anything other than to serve Him. Merged into an ocean of transcendental bliss, they are always singing the glories of His most wonderful personality and activities."
> (*Śrīmad Bhāgavatam* 8.3.20)

The devotees who have surrendered to the Lord are fully self-satisfied by the great wealth which comes to them through this surrender. The happiness they feel is higher than the joy felt by any other person. Their hearts are never disturbed by any sense of insufficiency.

The devotees who have surrendered to the Lord are fully self-satisfied by the great wealth which comes to them through this surrender.

When we are deficient in this process of self-surrender, we turn to sense enjoyment, liberation, or mystic success for satisfaction. In search of such temporary appeasements, we end up wandering from place to place, from birth to birth, simply accumulating calamity and misfortune.

THE SIX ASPECTS OF ŚARAṆĀGATI

Out of compassion for the fallen jivas, Sri Krishna Chaitanya appeared in this world with all of His eternal associates and His eternal abode. Wishing to bestow on them that most rare gift of love for Himself, He taught saranagati, the process that is the life of the devotees —taking shelter of the Lord

The first song in Bhaktivinoda Ṭhākura's *Śaraṇāgati* is the following:

śrī kṛṣṇa caitanya prabhu jīve dayā kari
sva-parṣada svīya dhāma saha avatari
atyanta durlabha prema karibāre dāna
śikhāya śaraṇāgati bhakatera prāṇa
dainya, ātma-nivedana, goptṛtve varaṇa
avaśya rakṣibe kṛṣṇa viśvāsa pālana
bhakti-anukūla mātra kāryera svīkāra
bhakti-pratikūla-bhāva varjanāṅgīkāra
ṣaḍ-aṅga śaraṇāgati haibe jāṅhāra
tāṅhāra prārthanā śune śrī-nanda-kumāra
rūpa sanātana pade dante tṛṇa kari
bhakativinoda paṛe dui pada dhari
kāṅdiyā kāṅdiyā bale āmi ta adhama
śikhāye śaraṇāgati karahe uttama

"Out of compassion for the fallen *jīvas*, Śrī Krishna Chaitanya appeared in this world with all of His eternal associates and His eternal abode. Wishing to bestow on them that most rare gift of love for Himself, He taught *śaraṇāgati*, the process that is the life of the devotees—taking shelter of the Lord. Humility; self-surrender; accepting Krishna as your protector; belief that Krishna will save you in all circumstances; undertaking only activities conducive to developing love for Krishna, and rejecting everything which is detrimental to that end: these are the six elements of taking shelter. Krishna, the son of Nanda, listens to the prayers of anyone who takes shelter of him in this way. I fall down at the feet of Rūpa and Sanātana and take hold of them in all humility. Crying, I call out, saying, 'I am most fallen. Please teach me how to take shelter of Krishna so that I can perfect my human life.'"

Bhaktivinoda Ṭhākura's song is based on a verse from the *Vaiṣṇava-tantra,* which Jīva Gosvāmī quotes in his *Bhakti-sandarbha* (236). The six elements of taking shelter are described there as follows:

ānukūlyasya saṅkalpaḥ
prātikūlyasya varjanam
rakṣiṣyatīti viśvāso
goptṛtve varaṇaṁ tathā
ātma-nikṣepa-kārpaṇye
ṣaḍ-vidhā śaraṇāgatiḥ

"Accepting that which is favorable, rejecting the unfavorable, believing that Krishna will save me, accepting Krishna as one's maintainer, self-surrender and humility are the six types of *śaraṇāgati*." (*Chaitanya Charitāmṛta* 2.22.97)

Śrīla Bhaktivinoda Ṭhākura has elaborated on these processes in his *Amṛta-pravāha-bhāṣya*: "(1) 'Accepting that which is favorable' means that which is favorable to developing one's devotion to Krishna. (2) 'Rejecting the unfavorable' means one must vow, 'I renounce any activity which does not lead to Krishna.' (3) 'Believing that Krishna will save me' means believing that Krishna alone is my savior. In other words, one should think, 'I do not believe knowledge of Brahman will save me from death, but Krishna will definitely be merciful and deliver me.' (4) 'Accepting Krishna as one's maintainer' means one thinks: 'I do not believe that the deities presiding over the different sacrifices or religious performances deliver the results of these acts, nor do they maintain me. It is rather Krishna alone who takes care of me and not any other man or god.' (5) 'Self-surrender' means to think, 'My wishes are not independent. I am completely subordinate to the will of Krishna.' (6) 'Humility' means to think of oneself as very lowly."

Accepting that which is favorable, rejecting the unfavorable, believing that Krishna will save me, accepting Krishna as one's maintainer, self-surrender and humility are the six types of saranagati.

The Supreme Lord loves those devotees who have taken shelter of Him. He listens to their prayers and awards them the gift of *vraja-prema*.

TAKING SHELTER IN BODY, MIND, AND WORDS

The following verse from the *Hari-bhakti-vilāsa* (11.677) further elaborated on the sixfold process of taking shelter in body, mind, and words. Jīva Gosvāmī also quotes this verse in *Bhakti-sandarbha*:

tavāsmīti vadan vācā
tathaiva manasā vidan
tat-sthānam āśritas tanvā
modate śaraṇāgataḥ

"With one's body, one who has taken shelter of the Lord resides in the holy place where Krishna performed His pastimes. With his words, he says, "O Lord, I am Yours," while with the mind, devotees know himself to belong to the Lord. In this way, he enjoys spiritual bliss."

(Also quoted in *Chaitanya Charitāmṛta* 2.22.98)

The devotee who takes shelter by completely surrendering to Krishna is considered by the Lord to be equal to Himself, that is, most dear.

śaraṇa lañā kare kṛṣṇe ātma-samarpaṇa
kṛṣṇa tāṅre kare tat-kāle ātma-sama

"As soon as a devotee has taken shelter of Krishna and surrendered to Him, Krishna makes him equal to Himself." (*Chaitanya Charitāmṛta* 2.22.99)

This is corroborated by a statement made by Krishna Himself to His dear associate and disciple, Uddhava:

martyo yadā tyakta-samasta-karmā
niveditātmā vicikīrṣito me
tadāmṛtatvaṁ pratipadyamāno
mayātma-bhūyāya ca kalpate vai

"When the living entity who is subjected to birth and death gives up all his works and completely surrenders himself to Me, engaging in activities according to My desire, then he attains immortality by My grace, becoming equal to Myself in spiritual quality and thus able to enjoy the divine rapture of life in the spiritual world in My association."

(*Śrīmad Bhāgavatam* 11.29.32, *Chaitanya Charitāmṛta* 3.4.193)

The devotee who has taken refuge in the Lord is so dear to Him that He considers Him to be as close as His own body.

Śrīla Prabhupāda Bhaktisiddhānta Sarasvatī Ṭhākura has elaborated on this verse as follows: "The knowledge of the living entity who is subject to death is limited to that which is perceived by the senses. When he gives up fruitive activities and mental speculation to simply surrender himself to the Lord, then he no longer knows any insufficiency because he attains the Lord. Due to serving the Lord of Vaikuṇṭha, he himself takes on the qualities of Vaikuṇṭha. This means that the *kuṇṭha* nature, that is, the illusory material nature, no longer has any hold over him."

In the above verse, the words *ātma-bhūyāya kalpate* can also be interpreted to mean that such a person obtains opulences equal to those of the Lord Himself. But however one interprets these words, they should never be taken to mean oneness in the monistic sense. The devotee who has taken refuge in the Lord is so dear to Him that He considers Him to be as close as His own body.

Every time a devotee pays his obeisances to the Lord, he engages in an act of self-surrender. The Sanskrit word *namaḥ,* which appears in *namaskāra* and in many mantras, has been explained in the *Padma Purana, Uttara-khaṇḍa.*

ahaṅkṛtir makāraḥ syān
nakāras tan-niṣedhakaḥ
tasmāt tu namasā kṣetri-
svātantryaṁ pratiṣidhyate

bhagavat-paratantro'sau
tadāyattātma-jīvanaḥ
tasmāt sva-sāmarthya-vidhiṁ
tyajet sarvam aśeṣataḥ

īśvarasya tu sāmarthyāt
nālabhyaṁ tasya vidyate
tasmin nyasta-bharaḥ śete
tat-karmaiva samācaret

"False ego is represented by the syllable *ma*; the word *na* negates it. The word '*namaḥ*' therefore indicates that the embodied being has no independent existence. He is always dependent on the Supreme Lord and his life is in every way confined within Him. He therefore should completely give up any illusion he has of his own independent capacity to do anything. Through the Lord's power, there is nothing that he cannot achieve. Knowing this, he surrenders responsibility for his own existence to the Lord and simply engages in His service."

(*Bhakti-sandarbha* 236)

THE LORD IS THE ONLY REFUGE

When Devakī saw that Krishna had taken birth as her own son, she glorified Him as follows:

martyo mṛtyu-vyāla-bhītaḥ palāyan
lokān sarvān nirbhayaṁ nādhyagacchat
tvat-pādābjaṁ prāpya yadṛcchayādya
susthaḥ śete mṛtyur asmād apaiti

> "We living beings are subject to death and are thus constantly afraid of being swallowed up by the great serpent of death. We flee wherever we can within this world, but nowhere can we find freedom from danger. O Lord, through some great fortune we have come to Your lotus feet. Now we can finally rest in peace and happiness, for Death himself flees in fear of You."
> (*Śrīmad Bhāgavatam* 10.3.27)

In fact, there is no reliable refuge anywhere in the universe for the living beings other than the lotus feet of the Lord, for they are fearless, free from all lamentation, and full of the nectar of immortality. The Lord Himself repeatedly states that He delivers His devotees from all distress when they take shelter of Him. He alone is the *jīva*'s protector and maintainer. Thus the Lord's following utterance, taken from the *Brahma Purana*:

tvāṁ prapanno'smi śaraṇaṁ
deva-devaṁ janārdanam
iti yaḥ śaraṇaṁ prāptas
taṁ kleśād uddharāmy aham

> "I deliver anyone who takes refuge in Me with these words: 'O Lord of lords, O Janārdana! I surrender to You, my only shelter.'"
> (*Hari-bhakti-vilāsa* 11.654, *Bhakti-sandarbha* 236)

Śrīla Bhaktivinoda Ṭhākura has written many songs demonstrating the principles of taking shelter, not only in his collection titled *Śaraṇāgati*, but also in *Kalyāṇa-kalpa-taru*, *Gītāvalī*, and *Gītā-mālā*. These and the songs of Narottama dāsa recorded in *Prārthanā* and *Prema-bhakti-candrikā* should be memorized by the devotees. Anyone who enters into the spirit of these songs will make quick progress on the path of bhakti.

There is no reliable refuge anywhere in the universe for the living beings other than the lotus feet of the Lord, for they are fearless, free from all lamentation, and full of the nectar of immortality.

"I HAVE SURRENDERED MYSELF TO YOUR LOTUS FEET"

ātma-nivedana tuwā pade kari
hainu parama sukhī
duḥkha dūre gela cintā nā rahila
caudike ānanda dekhi

aśoka abhaya amṛta ādhāra
tomāra caraṇa-dvaya
tāhāte ekhana viśrāma labhiyā
chāṛinu bhavera bhaya

"I have surrendered myself to Your lotus feet
and have become supremely joyful.
All my miseries have left me
and I have no more worries.
All I see is joy in every direction.
Your lotus feet are free from lamentation,
and there is no fear, no death;
they are the reservoir of ambrosia.
Now that I have found repose there,
I have no more fear of material existence."
(*Śaraṇāgati*, 16)

"I Have Finally Understood, O Lord"

ekhana bujhinu prabho tomāra caraṇa
aśoka-abhayāmṛta pūrṇa sarva-kṣaṇa
sakala chāṛiyā tuwā caraṇa-kamale
paṛiyāchi āmi nātha tava pada-tale
tava pāda padma nātha rakṣibe āmāre
āra rakṣā-kartā nāhi e bhava-saṁsāre
āmi tava nitya-dāsa jāninu e-bāra
āmāra pālana-bhāra ekhana tomāra
baṛa duḥkha pāiyāchi svatantra jīvane
saba duḥkha dūre gela o pada varaṇe

My life of so-called independence gave me so much misery, but now that I have taken shelter of Your feet, all these miseries have disappeared.

"I have finally understood, O Lord, that Your feet are full of the ambrosia of immortality, joy, and fearlessness. I have now given up everything to fall down and take shelter of Your lotus feet, my Lord. Your lotus feet, O Lord, will protect me. Nothing else in this world can give me the same protection. Now I know myself to be Your eternal servant, so the responsibility for my maintenance is Yours. My life of so-called independence gave me so much misery, but now that I have taken shelter of Your feet, all these miseries have disappeared."
(*Śaraṇāgati*, 21)

"I am Your Dog and You are My Master"

sarvasva tomāra caraṇa saṁpiyā
paṛechi tomāra ghare
tumi ta ṭhākura tomāra kukura
baliyā jānaha more

bāṅdhiyā nikaṭe āmāre pālibe
rahiba tomāra dvāre
pratīpa janere āsite nā diba
rākhiba gaṛera pāre

tava nija-jana prasāda seviyā
ucchiṣṭa rākhibe jāhā
āmāra bhojana parama ānande
prati dine habe tāhā

basiyā śuiyā tomāra caraṇa
cintiba satata āmi
nācite nācite nikaṭe jāiba
jakhana ḍākibe tumi

nijere poṣaṇa kabhu nā bhāviba
rahiba bhāvera bhare
bhakativinoda tomāre pālaka
baliyā varaṇa kare

"I have surrendered everything to Your lotus feet and have thrown myself down at Your door. I ask You to recognize that I am Your dog and you are my master.

"You will tie me up nearby and take care of me. I will remain near your doorway and chase away thieves and other dangerous people, keeping them on the other side of the moat.

"Every day, I will joyfully eat only the leftovers of the devotees who have eaten Your *prasāda.*

"Whether sitting or lying down, I will only think of Your lotus feet. Whenever You call, I will go dancing toward You.

"I will never think of my own needs or maintenance, but will remain blissfully in the joy of my feelings for You. Bhaktivinoda officially accepts you as his protector." (*Śaraṇāgati*, 19)

Anyone who wishes to make progress on this path should study the subject of *śaraṇāgati*. One who has not taken shelter of Krishna, but takes up the *rāga-mārga* only out of a desire for profit, adoration and prestige is a shameless pretender. It is not long before he is attacked by all kinds of *anarthas*. It is true that the path of *vidhi-bhakti* cannot give *vraja-prema*, but we must follow the path shown by the spiritual masters in the disciplic succession. They have made it abundantly clear that it is through devotion to the chanting of the Holy Name that our capacity to practice *rāgānugā-bhakti* is developed. The process of chanting the Holy Name is like the ceremony which gives life to the deity form of the Lord. The life of the devotee is the process of taking shelter. This life is bestowed on the devotee by the Holy Name.

Chapter VII

The Guru and Initiation

From the previous chapters, it is clear that it is of paramount importance to come into contact with the Vaishnavas and, in particular, with a pure devotee spiritual master who can instruct one on the path of spiritual life.

We have also seen that one must have accumulated many lifetimes of pious acts before he can get the good fortune of associating with a pure devotee. When Vidura's doubts had been erased by listening to Maitreya Muni's explanations of the Supreme Lord, he said in gratitude:

durāpā hy alpa-tapasaḥ
sevā vaikuṇṭha-vartmasu
yatropagīyate nityaṁ
deva-devo janārdanaḥ

> "Someone who has made few sacrifices and accumulated little merit can never win service to the great souls travelling the path to the Lord's abode of Vaikuṇṭha. The travellers on that path are constantly engaged in glorifying Him who is the God of gods and controller of all living entities."
> (*Śrīmad Bhāgavatam* 3.7.20)

Without such merit, one cannot have faith in the manifestation of the guru, nor can one even recognize him.

mahā-prasāde govinde
nāma-brahmaṇi vaiṣṇave
svalpa-puṇyavatāṁ rājan
viśvāso naiva jāyate

"Those who have little merit, O king, never develop faith in the Lord's *mahā-prasāda*, Govinda Himself, the Holy Name (*nāma-brahma*), and the Vaishnavas."
(*Skanda Purana*)

Jīva Gosvāmī confirms this, at the beginning of his *Bhakti-sandarbha,* with a quote from the *Brahma-vaivarta Purana*:

yāvat pāpais tu malinaṁ
hṛdayaṁ tāvad eva hi
na śāstre satya-buddhiḥ syāt
sad-buddhiḥ sad-gurau tathā

"As long as one's heart is contaminated by sin, one will not see the truth given in the scriptures"

"As long as our hearts are contaminated by sin, we will not see the truth given in the scriptures. In other words, we will not develop faith in the theistic conclusions of the scripture, nor will we recognize the divine authority of the spiritual master. we will take gifts to a misleader, a guru whose instructions will lead us along the road that takes us away from Goloka-Vaikuṇṭha, and surrender to him."

SURRENDERING TO THE GURU

Krishna states in the *Bhagavad-gītā:*

tad viddhi praṇipātena
paripraśnena sevayā
upadekṣyanti te jñānaṁ
jñāninas tattva-darśinaḥ

"Learn the truth through surrender, submissive inquiry, and service. The self-realised soul, who has seen the truth, will enlighten you." (*Gītā* 4.34)

In the *Muṇḍaka Upanishad*, there is a famous verse which states the importance of surrendering to a spiritual master.

tad-vijñānārthaṁ sa gurum evābhigacchet
samit-pāṇiḥ śrotriyaṁ brahma-niṣṭham

"In order to realize the truth, one should take gifts in hand and approach a spiritual master who is learned and fixed in Brahman."

The word *samidh* ("gifts") used here literally means wood for the sacrificial fire, but it is taken to have an extended meaning which includes all three elements of surrender mentioned in the *Gītā*: obeisances, submissive inquiry, and service. The disciple approaches the spiritual master with these three kinds of gifts. The spiritual master, for his part, must have the requisite knowledge and determined faith in the Supreme Truth to be able to remove all of the disciple's doubts. The essential characteristic of the spiritual master, then, is that he possesses knowledge of the three categories: *sambandha, abhidheya,* and *prayojana*. This is why the *Chaitanya Charitāmṛta* says: "One who knows the truth about Krishna is qualified to be guru" (*jei kṛṣṇa-tattva-vettā sei guru haya*).

Thus one should fall at the feet of the spiritual master in the same way as Sanātana Gosvāmī fell at Lord Chaitanya's feet and asked Him questions which, in the *Gītā* verse 4.34, are called *paripraśna*:

ke āmi kene āmāya jāre tāpa-traya
ihā nāhi jāni āmi kemane hita haya

"Who am I? And why do the threefold miseries of material life continually cause me suffering? I do not know the answers to these questions, nor do I know what is ultimately beneficial for me." (*Chaitanya Charitāmṛta* 2.20.102)

The disciple should then serve the guru in such a way that the guru will be pleased. When such a submissive and service-minded devotee asks questions about spiritual life, the spiritual master will reveal to him the truths which he himself has realized.

There are many other examples in the scripture of surrender, submissive inquiry and service. Once, the king of Videha, Nimi, fortuitously came upon the nine great devotees known as the Yogīndras who had gathered in his sacrificial arena. Overjoyed to see them, he offered them the worship appropriate to their station and said,

durlabho mānuṣo deho
dehināṁ kṣaṇa-bhaṅguraḥ
tatrāpi durlabhaṁ manye
vaikuṇṭha-priya-darśanam

ata ātyantikaṁ kṣemaṁ
pṛcchāmo bhavato'naghāḥ
saṁsāre'smin kṣaṇārdho'pi
sat-saṅgaḥ śevadhir nṝṇām

"Birth in a human body is a very rare achievement for the embodied soul, but I hold that for one having such a short-lived human body, it is even rarer fortune to see a devotee who is dear to the Lord of Vaikuṇṭha. In this world, even a moment's association with saintly persons like yourselves is the greatest treasure in human life. Therefore, I take this opportunity to ask you sinless souls, what is the ultimate good?" (*Śrīmad Bhāgavatam* 11.2.29-30)

"When such a submissive and service-minded devotee asks questions about spiritual life, the spiritual master will reveal to him the truths which he himself has realized"

Only sinless, highly realized devotees like the Nava Yogīndra are capable of answering King Nimi's submissive inquiry about the ultimate good (*ātyantika-kṣema*). They had delved into the scriptures and extracted their essential teachings; with great faith and belief, they had applied these teachings in their own lives which are now dedicated to the instruction of others. These are the characteristics of a genuine *ācārya* according to the definition given in the *Vāyu Purana*:

ācinoti yaḥ śāstrārtham
ācāre sthāpayaty api

svayam ācarate yasmād
ācāryas tena kīrtitaḥ

"The *ācārya* is thus called because he has studied and understood the meaning of the scripture, he establishes this meaning in the behavior of others, and himself practices what he preaches." (*Manu Saṁhitā*)

As Krishnadāsa says of Mahāprabhu: *āpani ācari jīvere śikhāya*—He taught the world by behaving like an exemplary devotee Himself.

HOW TO PAY OBEISANCES TO THE GURU

The way to pay obeisances to the guru has been described in the *Hari-bhakti-vilāsa*:

dorbhyāṁ pādbhyāṁ ca jānubhyām
urasā śirasā dṛśā
manasā vacasā ceti
praṇāmo'ṣṭāṅga īritaḥ

jānubhyām caiva bāhubhyāṁ
śirasā vacasā dhiyā
pañcāṅgakaḥ praṇāmaḥ syāt
pūjāsu pravarāv imau

Srila Bhakti Promode Puri Maharaja offering obeisances to the deities

"The *aṣṭāṅga-praṇāma*, or prostrated obeisance, is performed with the following eight parts of the body: the arms, legs, knees, chest, and head, as well as the eyes, mind, and speech. One should perform the *pañcāṅga-praṇāma*, or the five-part obeisance, with the knees, the arms, head, words and intelligence. Thus these are the two kinds of obeisances which are performed in the course of one's puja." (*Hari-bhakti-vilāsa* 8.162-163)

"The acarya is thus called because he has studied and understood the meaning of the scripture, he establishes this meaning in the behavior of others, and himself practices what he preaches"

Sanātana Gosvāmī explains these verses in his commentary: "Obeisances are performed with eyes slightly closed, the hands touching the Lord's feet, with head lowered, and mind meditating on paying obeisances to the Lord. One should pray with words like, 'Lord, be pleased with me.' Indeed, the meaning of paying one's obeisances to the guru, the Vaishnavas, and the Supreme Lord, is to say to them, 'I am surrendering my body to you.'"

If one does not pray to become worthy to give one's body, mind and soul to the spiritual master when paying obeisances then it becomes no more than a physical exercise like pushups. Surely this is not the real purpose of performing prostrations, or *daṇḍavats*, to the guru.

THE NECESSITY OF TAKING INITIATION

There are two kinds of spiritual master: the instructing spiritual master or *śikṣā-guru* and the initiating spiritual master. Initiation is necessary for anyone who wants to take up the discipline of devotional *sādhanā*—especially deity worship.

Keśava Ācārya wrote a great deal about *dīkṣā* in his *Krama-dīpikā*. The Vaishnava *smṛti*, *Hari-bhakti-vilāsa*, explains initiation in accordance with his descriptions. There it is said,

"Without being initiated, no one has the right to engage in deity worship."
(*Hari-bhakti-vilāsa* 2.2)

vinā dīkṣāṁ hi pūjāyāṁ
nādhikāro'sti karhicit

For this reason, the various *Āgamas*, or scriptures in the *Pāñcarātra* tradition, state that initiation is a necessary (*nitya*) element of the devotional path:

Srila Bhaktivinode Thakur, the pioneer of the Gaudiya Tradition

dvijānām anupetānāṁ
svakarmādhyayanādiṣu
yathādhikāro nāstīha
syāc copanayanād anu

tathātrādīkṣitānāṁ tu
mantra-devārcanādiṣu
nādhikāro 'sty ataḥ kuryād
ātmānaṁ śiva-saṁstutam

"Just as one born in a brahmin family who has not received the sacred thread is ineligible for the performance of Vedic rituals or the study of the Vedic literature, a person who has not received Vaishnava initiation has no authority to chant the mantra or to worship the deity form of the Lord. Therefore one should take initiation, by which he will become praised by even Lord Shiva." (*Hari-bhakti-vilāsa* 2.3-4, *Bhakti-sandarbha* 283)

In the conversation between Nārada and Brahmā described in the *Kārttika-māhātmya* of the *Skanda Purana*, the following text is found:

te narāḥ paśavo loke
kiṁ teṣāṁ jīvane phalam
yair na labdhā harer dīkṣā
nārcito vā janārdanaḥ

"Those human beings who have not been initiated into the service of Lord Hari and have never worshiped Him are comparable to animals. What is the value of their lives?" (*Hari-bhakti-vilāsa* 2.5)

The following verse, found both in the same *Skanda Purana*, in the conversation between Rukmāṅgada and Mohinī, as well as in the *Vishnu-yāmala*, confirms the necessity of taking initiation:

adīkṣitasya vāmoru
kṛtaṁ sarvaṁ nirarthakam
paśu-yonim avāpnoti
dīkṣā-virahito janaḥ

"Everything done by an uninitiated person is meaningless. One who is not properly initiated will be reborn as an animal." (*Hari-bhakti-vilāsa* 2.6)

In his commentary to these verses in the *Hari-bhakti-vilāsa*, Sanātana Gosvāmī writes the following: "The words *śiva-saṁstutaṁ* refer to initiation, indicating that anyone who takes initiation becomes a Vaishnava and an object of praise to the best of all Vaishnavas, Shiva himself. This is a result of the supremacy of the worship of Vishnu over even that of Shiva. There is a verse which states: 'Anyone who eats without having first offered his food to the Śālagrāma-śilā will for aeons be repeatedly born as a worm in the stool of outcastes and other lower human beings.' Verses such as this indicate that worship of the deity is absolutely necessary, and since one cannot engage in such deity worship without having first been initiated, they also establish the absolute necessity of initiation. Since worship of the Śālagrāma-śilā is given the most prominent place amongst the various types of service performed to the Lord, all other types of devotional activities are being indicated by extension. In other words, initiation is necessary to become eligible for all devotional practices. The necessity of initiation is further supported by Brahmā's statement, 'Those human beings who have not been initiated into the service of Lord Hari and have never worshiped Him are comparable to animals.' This verse indicates that without first being initiated, one cannot possibly engage in worship of the deity."[1]

Mahadeva Shiva

It may be asked that since there are descriptions in the scriptures of the great benefits to be derived from even the negligent worship of deities such as Śālagrāma-śilā, then what need is there of taking shelter of a spiritual master and being initiated by him? But the fact is that one will not derive full benefit from his puja if he ignores the established etiquette of worshiping the guru before worshiping the deity.

ato guruṁ praṇamyaivaṁ
sarvasvaṁ vinivedya ca
gṛhṇīyād vaiṣṇavaṁ mantraṁ
dīkṣā-pūrvaṁ vidhānataḥ

"Therefore, everyone should surrender to a bonafide spiritual master and, after offering him everything–body, mind and property–should take the Vishnu mantra from him according to the appropriate rites of initiation."

(*Hari-bhakti-vilāsa* 2.10)

"Through the grace of Krishna, a devotee who has received initiation possesses a divine body and is thus able to engage in the Lord's service"

The Transformation of the Disciple by Initiation

In the *Chaitanya Charitāmṛta*, Krishnadāsa Kavirāja Gosvāmī has explained the transformative effects of initiation:

dīkṣā-kāle bhakta kare ātma-samarpaṇa
sei-kāle kṛṣṇa tāre kare ātma-sama
sei deha kare tāra cid-ānanda-maya
aprākṛta-dehe tāṅra caraṇa bhajaya

"At the time of initiation, when a devotee surrenders to the spiritual master, Krishna makes him equal to Himself. He transforms the devotee's body into spiritual substance; the devotee then worships the Lord in that spiritualized body."

(*Chaitanya Charitāmṛta* 3.4.192-3)

When the living being who has taken to the devotional path first surrenders himself to the lotus feet of his spiritual master, then Krishna accepts him as one of His very own. He frees him from the bondage of bodily identity and gives him an experience of his eternal spiritual nature. With this divine knowledge, the devotee takes a spiritual body appropriate for the transcendental service of the Lord. This is the inner mystery of initiation.

"When the living being who has taken to the devotional path first surrenders himself to the lotus feet of his spiritual master, then Krishna accepts him as one of His very own"

To the extent that one is able to grasp the concept of surrender to the spiritual master, one will have clear realization of the spiritual truth. By Krishna's mercy, one will become fully conscious of their divine relationship with the Lord and as one realizes one's own transcendental identity, by this great good fortune, they become eligible for the Lord's direct service. Through the grace of Krishna, a devotee who has received initiation possesses a divine body and is thus able to engage in the Lord's service. Unfortunately, materialistic persons are not able to recognize this transformation and consider the devotee's activities to be on the same level as any other bodily activity. This conception of the guru or Vaishnava's body as material is a great offense. Mahāprabhu Himself stated this:

prabhu kahe vaiṣṇava-deha prākṛta kabhu naya
aprākṛta deha bhaktera cid-ānanda-maya

> "The body of a devotee is never material. It is transcendental, full of spiritual bliss." (*Chaitanya Charitāmṛta* 3.4.191)

The *Tattva-sāgara* also gives further details about this transformative power of the initiation process:

yathā kāñcanatāṁ yāti
kāṁsyaṁ rasa-vidhānataḥ
tathā dīkṣā-vidhānena
dvijatvaṁ jāyate nṛṇām

> "Just as bell metal turns into gold when touched by mercury; a person becomes twice-born through the process of initiation." (*Hari-bhakti-vilāsa* 2.12)

Sri Sri Radha and Krishna

Sanātana comments that the word *nṛṇām* here refers to every human being of any race or caste and that being twice-born (*dvijatva*) means *vipratā* or brahminhood.

Alchemists were said to know a process by which they could produce gold by mixing mercury with bell metal (an alloy of copper and tin). Anybody might go around calling himself an alchemist, deceiving some ignorant people and cheating them of their money, but that does not make one any less ignorant of this process and incapable of executing it. We may say the same of initiation: though the above verse indicates that through *dīkṣā* an ordinary person gains the qualities of a brahmin, when a so-called guru makes a mere show of initiating without the appropriate knowledge or expertise, no good can be expected to come of it. If one has not oneself come to possess the advanced spiritual understanding, that is, if one has not come to be a knower of Krishna as the supreme truth (*kṛṣṇa-tattva-vettā*) and has not become free of sinful activity as a consequence of that knowledge, and still takes the responsibility of giving out initiation, then the result is the same as that of a blind person leading other blind persons into a ditch.

"Some persons call themselves guru when they do not have the gravity necessary for the task"

The Qualifications of the Disciple and the Spiritual Master

In view of the great importance and the responsibility involved in giving and taking initiation, it is regrettable that in most circumstances both disciple and guru are unqualified for their role and the value of the sacrament is lost. Some persons call themselves guru when they do not have the gravity necessary for the task. They merely play the role of a bonafide spiritual master out of insolence. Similarly, a disciple in name only will pretend to have the humility of a spiritual seeker. These two types of persons find each other out and use each other for material gratifications such as wealth, fame, and prestige. The reciprocation between them is restricted to these fleeting gains, rather than anything of true value. They may dress the part; they may even engage in the worship of the deity and in the study of the scriptures, but all of these activities are superficial and lack internal substance. Therefore, Bhaktisiddhānta Sarasvatī Prabhupāda has written in his poem, "Who is a Vaishnava?" *(Vaiṣṇava ke?)*—

śrī dayita-dāsa kīrtanete āśa
kara uccaiḥsvare harināma rava
prāṇa āche jāra, sei hetu pracāra
prāṇa-hīna jata kṛṣṇa-gāthā śava

> "O mind! This humble servant of Radha and Krishna, Vārṣabhānavī-dayita dāsa, placing his hopes in *kīrtana*, loudly sings the names of Lord Hari! Those who have spiritual life in abundance preach the Lord's message. Whatever is spoken about Krishna without the life of realization resembles nothing more than a cadaver."

"If one is not revived by the process of surrender, then in whatever preaching activity he engages, he will be just like an actor"

Bhaktivinoda Ṭhākura also states in his book of songs, *Śaraṇāgati,* that the life of a devotee is the process of surrender that was taught by Śrī Chaitanya Mahāprabhu: *śikhān śaraṇāgati bhakatera prāṇa*. This surrender consists of six different attitudes, all of which must be executed with complete sincerity. If persons are not revived by the process of surrender, then in whatever preaching activity they engage in, they will be just like actors playing a role on the stage. If the preaching of religious principles is carried out in this way, is it not to be expected that their preachers will become a laughing stock? For this reason, one who has not the weight of spiritual realization should not blacken the glorious seat intended for the supremely munificent guru.

A person whose heart is full of the desires for materialistic sense gratification ahould not make a pretense of being a genuine seeker of spiritual truth simply as a way of extracting some ulterior benefit from the spiritual path. If such falsehood permeates both the spiritual master and the disciple, then it cannot be expected that either of them attain anything approximating the ultimate good.

Our most worshipable Śrīla Prabhupāda wrote:

kanaka-kamini pratiṣṭhā-bāghinī
chāṛiyache jāre sei to vaiṣṇava

sei anāsakta sei śuddha-bhakta
saṁsār tathā pāy parābhava

"One who has been abandoned by the tigress of money, beautiful women, and fame is truly a Vaishnava. Such a soul alone is truly detached; such a soul is a pure devotee. The illusory creation of repeated birth and death is defeated before him." (From *Vaiṣṇava ke?*)

Krishna Himself says that it takes great effort to come to the point of being able to worship Him properly, in other words, to come to the position of being able to initiate others in the act of worshiping Him:

yeṣāṁ tv anta-gataṁ pāpaṁ
janānāṁ puṇya-karmaṇām
te dvandva-moha-nirmuktā
bhajante māṁ dṛḍha-vratāḥ

"But those persons of virtuous deeds, in whom sinfulness has been eradicated, worship Me with great steadfastness in their vows, free from the bewilderment of sensual life." (*Gītā* 7.28)

The sum and substance is that one who is blinded by ignorance may play the role of a guru but will not be able to remove another's blindness of ignorance. The *Skanda Purana* gives the following etymology of the word *guru*:

gu-śabdas tv andhakārasya
ru-śabdas tan-nivārakaḥ
andhakāra-nirodhitvād
gurur ity abhidhīyate

"The syllable '*gu*' refers to the darkness of ignorance; the syllable '*ru*' means that which impedes it. Thus the guru is so named because he eradicates the darkness of ignorance in others."

How then can one who is covered by ignorance give divine, transcendental, spiritual knowledge consisting of metaphysical knowledge of God and creation, the process of devotional service, and the goal of love of God? Rather, unqualified persons who falsely present themselves as spiritual masters are engaged in bringing about ruin on themselves and the world. The relation between a spiritual master and his disciple is something of great significance. It is a great responsibility—indeed, it is a matter of life and death. Yet, out of their greed for gain, prestige, and adoration, there are still irresponsible people who treat it as lightly as a child's game.

"When my devotional creeper crosses the spiritual worlds to enter the divine abodes of Krishna—Dvaraka, Mathura, and finally the most beautiful dhama, Vrindavan—my guru winds it around the desire tree of Krishna's lotus feet, giving me the chance to taste the delicious fruits of love of God which ripen on it"

THE DIVINE CHARACTER OF THE GURU

I should see my guru as a great personality, the only helmsman who can navigate across the immeasurable ocean of material suffering and take me to the other side. It is he who plants the seed of devotion in my heart and then sprinkles it with the water of the divine sounds of Krishna's name and scriptural knowledge. The seed then germinates and grows until finally it traverses the Virajā River which forms the border between this world and the next. When my devotional creeper crosses the spiritual worlds to enter the divine abodes of Krishna—Dvārakā, Mathurā, and finally the most beautiful *dhāma*, Vrindavan—my guru winds it around the desire tree of Krishna's lotus feet, giving me the chance to taste the delicious fruits of love of God which ripen on it. The guru is my only true friend in this world and the next. He is thus my only worshipable divinity and if I foolishly think of him as an ordinary human being, it is certain that all my chanting of mantras, my worship of the deity, indeed, all my spiritual activities will be fruitless like oblations of clarified butter on the ashes of the sacrificial fire.

Lord Narasimha, who slays the demons of material desires

Lord Śrī Krishna Himself said to His dear associate Uddhava:

ācāryaṁ māṁ vijānīyān
nāvamanyeta karhicit
na martya-buddhyāsūyeta
sarva-deva-mayo guruḥ

"A disciple should consider the teacher to be My very self and never disrespect him in any way. One should not envy him, thinking him to be an ordinary man, for he is the sum total of all the demigods."
(*Śrīmad Bhāgavatam* 11.17.27)

One should not think of the mantra, the *mantra-devatā,* and the guru as being distinct from each other. The most sinful people think that the spiritual master is an ordinary human being like them. If someone commits offenses and angers the Supreme Lord, the spiritual master can intercede with the Lord on behalf of his disciple. On the other hand, if the spiritual master becomes angry with his disciple, Krishna will not even turn around to look at the offender. Nor should one think that other gods and deities can offer respite to such an offender. Therefore one should take great care to satisfy the spiritual master.

"One should not think of the mantra, the mantra-devata, and the guru as being distinct from each other. The most sinful people think that the spiritual master is an ordinary human being like them"

"Whatever words are uttered by the spiritual master should be considered equal to the Vedic revelation. Anyone who disbelieves his words or derides his directions has no possibility of achieving any kind of auspiciousness."

Compared to the act of surrendering to the spiritual master, performing pilgrimage, austerities, muttering prayers and mantras, meditation and concentration, following of rules and regulations and keeping vows, taking bath and giving in charity are all ineffective for self-purification. On the other hand, service to the guru's lotus feet, in other words, the effort to please him, is the essence of a disciple's spiritual practice. Even if one's life is at risk, they should not abandon the spiritual master's directives. One should be willing to give up his life in the service of the spiritual master.

Though one should certainly make an effort to understand the preceptor's words, a disciple should never criticize them nor try to demonstrate an absence of logic in them. One who knows the secret of satisfying Krishna and is constantly engaged in the life of devotion should not be considered less of a guru if he lacks knowledge of grammar or logic. In this regard, a disciple has no authority to judge the guru's actions.

On the other hand, if the disciples have any question about their own service, there is no fault if they were to humbly submit it to the guru's judgement with the intention of accepting his verdict. If one tries to prove that he is more intelligent than the spiritual master, his downfall is inevitable. There is a Bengali saying: *ati buddhi galāy daṛi*—"One who is too smart for his own good ends up with a noose around his neck.

Disciples should be ready to sacrifice their independence to carry out the guru's orders, providing personal service wholeheartedly even when the guru does not ask for it. The disciples prove their devotion to the spiritual master by giving him water, food or bath-water. They should be prepared to render service to the guru at every minute; and when engaged in such service, they should never give quarter to service offenses like laziness or inattention. Rather, they should fix their mind on the satisfaction of the guru's senses. Torpor, distraction, indifference and negligence are equally considered to be offenses to the Holy Name.

"Even if one's life is at risk, they should not abandon the spiritual master's directives"

One must always recall the instructions of Krishnadāsa Kavirāja Gosvāmī as heard from the lips of the spiritual master.

guru vaiṣṇava bhagavān tinera smaraṇa
tinera smaraṇe haya vighna-vināśana
anāyāse haya nija vāñchita pūraṇa

> "I meditate on the guru, the Vaishnavas, and the Lord. By remembering them, all obstacles are destroyed and one quickly attains the fulfillment of his desires."
> (*Chaitanya Charitāmṛta* 1.1.20-21)

This is the instruction of the great authorities.

THE GURU'S MERCY

If an aspirant for pure devotion meditates on the guru, is conscious of him and is fixed in his service, then whether he or she is physically near to the spiritual master or far away, there is no chance of being troubled by the enemies of lust and anger. And if they do come near, then all the *sādhaka* has to do is call out loudly to the spiritual master for help and he will certainly protect him or her.

"If one tries to prove that one is more intelligent than the spiritual master, his downfall is inevitable"

One who has received the guru's mercy will automatically find good association. A serious aspirant for spiritual perfection should not waste any time in useless activities. For one who is a beginner in devotional life, however, a life of worship in a secluded place is not recommended as it is fraught with danger. At this stage, he should remain constantly in the presence of the spiritual master or in the company of those who have received the spiritual master's mercy and take up the spiritual master's service under their direction. Otherwise, lust and anger will see devotees sitting alone and unprotected and will attack him or her without their even realizing it. One should always remember the following words of a *mahājana*:

māyāre kariyā jaya chāṛāno nā jāya
sādhu kṛpā binā āra nāhika upāya

"On one's own, it is impossible to conquer Maya and leave her behind. There is no means to do it other than through the grace of the saints."

Without the permission and blessings of the spiritual master, no disciple should go to visit the homes of past friends or even one's own family members or engage in conversation with them. One must at all costs avoid the association of women, the association of those who are attached to women, or the association of non-devotees who think that fruitive activities or learning are the highest objective in life. The disciple should always seek that which is helpful to his spiritual life and reject that which is detrimental to it. In all matters, large or small, he should take the spiritual master's advice. He should not take up any work without his approval.

"One who has received the guru's mercy will automatically find good association"

The Lord's external energy takes many forms in order to deceive us, constantly lurking about waiting for the opportunity to mislead us. She weakens the minds of even very learned, intelligent and powerful people, making them disinterested in service to the Lord. The spiritual master has taken up Śrī Chaitanya Mahāprabhu's mission and is begging all of us to chant Krishna's name, to worship Krishna, and to learn about Krishna. He tells us to keep our goal fixed in our sights and to chant 100,000 names daily without fail. We must bow down and humbly accept his directions, giving our lives to carry them out.

The spiritual master is preaching Lord Chaitanya's message everywhere. He says:

jāre dekha tāre kaha kṛṣṇa-upadeśa
āmāra ājñāya guru hañā tāra ei deśa

> "Teach everyone you see this message of devotion to Krishna. On My command, become a guru and deliver this land." (*Chaitanya Charitāmṛta* 2.7.128)

The essence of this instruction is that one should practice the principles taught by the guru and to preach them in the mentality of service to him, and not that one puts on airs and pretends to be a spiritual master.

THE DISCIPLE'S ATTITUDE

Every intelligent disciple should think that the entire universe's well-being depends on his character and strict adherence to spiritual life. They should take the welfare of the entire world as his own personal responsibility. Therefore, before criticizing the activities of others, he makes sure that his own example of devotional practice is maintained without any blemish. If he does so, then not only does he benefit, but truly everyone throughout the world will also profit.

The disciple thinks as follows: "I have taken shelter of the guru and been initiated by him. I have now embarked on the road to pure devotion. If my behavior is faulty, then people will not stop at criticizing only me, but will also find fault with my spiritual master, my worshipable deity, the devotional path, the entire Vaishnava *sampradāya*, the previous *ācāryas*, even religion itself. They will disparage the scriptures, the great authorities who wrote them, and everyone who follows their injunctions. In the end, they will criticize belief in God itself and all doctrines leading to a higher, transcendental goal in life. They will even condemn my father and mother and their families. As a result, I will have become blameworthy before all these people and end up in a hellish existence for many births with nothing to say in my defense.

"If a true devotee takes birth in any family, whatever its social status, then that entire family is purified by his presence. His mother's life is successful. His home and the land of his birth is glorious. His ancestors in heaven dance in joy that a devotee has taken birth amongst their descendants and out of the expectation that they will receive oblations of *mahā-prasāda* and the Lord's *caraṇāmṛta* to bring them good fortune. If I fall from the standard of behavior expected of a saintly person and Vaishnava, then immediately all the generations of my family will fall into hell. Can I fall down in this way and become the shame and misfortune of my entire family? Just as a drop of ink on a white cloth is clearly visible, the misbehavior of a person who has taken to the religious life stands out and attracts the criticisms of all."

Even so, one should not stick to the spiritual life simply out of fear of being criticized. Devotion to the Lord is the natural activity of the soul. If one takes up the path of such devotion according to the scriptural injunctions, not only is his personal welfare assured, but that of everyone in the world.

Initiation is the Transmission of Divine Knowledge

Śrīla Sanātana Gosvāmī further explains *dīkṣā* as the transmission of divine knowledge. The following verse is from the *Vishnu-yāmala*:

divyaṁ jñānaṁ yato dadyāt
kuryāt pāpasya saṅkṣayam
tasmād dīkṣeti sā proktā
deśikais tattva-kovidaiḥ

"Those who are expert in the study of the revealed scriptures consider *dīkṣā* to be the process which gives one transcendental knowledge and causes the destruction of all sinful reactions." (*Hari-bhakti-vilāsa* 2.9)

The spiritual master gives his disciple knowledge of 10 basic tenets of spiritual knowledge, the *daśa-mūla,* consisting of the authoritative source of knowledge (*pramāṇa*)—the Vedic scriptures and the *ācāryas* in the disciplic succession—and the nine *prameyas*, the nine elements which are proved by this authority. These include seven aspects of relationships (*sambandha*), namely Krishna Himself; Krishna's energies; Krishna's divine mood (*rasa*); the soul, its bondage and its liberation; the inconceivable oneness and difference of the Lord and the individual soul; the *abhidheya,* bhakti, and the *prayojana,* love of God. The one who bestows the divine grace of this knowledge on his disciple is the supreme benefactor—the spiritual master.

Because the spiritual master recognizes the capacity of the disciple to take up either the *vaidhī* or *rāgānugā* devotional paths, he is a knower of the science of Krishna. This is the defining characteristic of the divine preceptor.

kibā vipra kibā nyāsī śūdra kene naya
jei kṛṣṇa tattva vettā sei guru haya

"Whether one belongs to the brahmin, *śūdra* or any other caste, or to the *sannyāsa* or any other *āśrama*, if he knows the science of Krishna, he is qualified to be a guru." (*Chaitanya Charitāmṛta* 2.8.128)

The disciple approaches such a preceptor with humility, honest inquiry, and a spirit of service and learns the divine knowledge of *sambandha, abhidheya,* and *prayojana.* Then the disciple takes up the path of worship, for one who worships is exalted, whereas a nondevotee is lowly and insignificant—*jei bhaje sei baṛa, abhakta hīna chāra* (*Chaitanya Charitāmṛta* 3.4.67). Just learning a few impressive and knowledgeable-sounding verses by heart and becoming a platform lecturer and giving speeches is not adequate for obtaining the Lord's mercy. The proof of one's realization or spiritual experience is his *bhajana.* It is not enough to be able to explain the offenses to the Holy Name (*nāmāparādha*), its reflection (*nāmābhāsa*), and the full manifestation of its glories; one has to give up offenses and chant the Holy Names in a pure devotional attitude and taste their sweetness for oneself. Then only will the Lord in the form of His own name be pleased and destroy all obstacles to the practitioner's spiritual life and, ultimately, bestow love of God on him.

Krishna speaks the Gita to His friend and devotee, Arjuna, on the battlefield

The Bhāgavata religion (*bhāgavata-dharma*) consists of all the instructions the Lord Himself gave to His own students such as Arjuna and Uddhava. This religion is the process by which even the most ignorant and unlearned person can easily attain direct contact with the Lord. One should consider the spiritual master to be one's worshipable deity and take instruction from him in the Bhāgavata Dharma. Then one should engage in a life of devotion, cultivating consciousness of the Lord according to the guru's direction.

guru-mukha-padma-vākya cittete kariyā aikya
āra nā kariha mane āśā
śrī guru caraṇe rati, ei se uttama gati
je prasāde pūre sarva āśā

"Fix your mind on the words emanating from the lotus mouth of the spiritual master. Place your hopes in nothing else. Affection for the guru's lotus feet is the ultimate goal, for by his mercy all of one's aspirations are realized."
(Narottama dāsa, *Prema-bhakti-candrikā*)

The blessings of the guru result in liberation from all obstacles arising out of one's own impurities and the hope for the intimate service of Their Lordships Radha and Mādhava comes to fruition and one's life becomes successful. Once the disciples have received the 32-syllable *Mahā-mantra* and *Pāñcarātrika* initiation in the 18-syllable mantra, they still have many things to learn from the spiritual master. The various aspects of devotional practice which must be learned from the guru are explained in more detail in the next chapter.

"The proof of one's realization or spiritual experience is his bhajana"

If one has no devotion for the spiritual master, who is a form of the Lord—His *prakāśa-vigraha*—or for the pure devotees who are fixed up in divine attachment for the Lord, then there is no way that he can fathom the vast ocean of the scriptures and discover their essential teachings. This is stated in the *Śvetāśvatara Upanishad* (6.23):

yasya deve parā bhaktir
yathā deve tathā gurau
tasyaite kathitā hy arthāḥ
prakāśante mahātmanaḥ

"Only unto those great souls who have implicit faith in both the Lord and the spiritual master, who is His manifestation and non-different from Him, are all the imports of Vedic knowledge automatically revealed."

Chapter VIII

Duties of an Initiated Disciple

Anyone who has taken shelter of and initiation from a genuine Vaishnava guru automatically garners the right to serve the Lord's deity form. Indeed, the *Pañcarātra* scriptures (also known as *Āgamas*) say that if one does not do so, he incurs fault:

labdhvā mantraṁ tu yo nityaṁ
nārcayen mantra-devatām
sarva-karma-phalaṁ tasyā-
niṣṭaṁ yacchati devatā

"If one has been initiated and does not regularly worship his mantra's deity, then the deity sees to it that all his projects fail." (*Hari-bhakti-vilāsa* 3.3)

It must be remembered, however, that without the appropriate conduct, or *sad-ācāra,* one cannot engage in the worship of the deity. Therefore the moral conduct appropriate to a Vaishnava is absolutely necessary to one's spiritual advancement. The definition of *sad-ācāra* is found in the *Vishnu Purana* (3.11.3):

"The moral conduct appropriate to a Vaishnava is absolutely necessary to one's spiritual advancement"

sādhavaḥ kṣīṇa-doṣās tu
sac-chabdaḥ sādhu-vācakaḥ
teṣām ācaraṇaṁ yat tu
sad-ācāraḥ sa ucyate

"The sadhu is one whose faults have been eliminated. The word *sat* refers to the sadhu. The behavior of the sadhus is therefore known as *sad-ācāra.*"
(*Hari-bhakti-vilāsa* 3.8)

It is further stated in the *Bhaviṣyottara Purana,*

ācāra-prabhavo dharmaḥ
santaś cācāra-lakṣaṇāḥ
sādhūnāṁ ca yathā vṛttaṁ
sa sad-ācāra iṣyate

ācāra eva dharmasya
mūlaṁ rājan kulasya ca
ācārād vicyuto jantur
na kulīno na dhārmikaḥ

> "The essence of all instructions is to always remember the spiritual master, the Vaishnavas, and the Supreme Lord, and the essence of all prohibitions is to never forget them"

"*Dharma* (religion) is based in conduct. Saintly persons are also recognized by their conduct. Thus the activities of the saintly are given the name *sad-ācāra*. Duty and nobility are rooted in conduct, O king! He who does not maintain standards of conduct is neither noble nor righteous."

(*Hari-bhakti-vilāsa* 3.15-16)

Sad-ācāra comprises all aspects of an initiated devotee's behavior, from broad matters of the regulative principles to one's daily routine, from rising in the *brahma-muhūrta* period until he takes rest at night. They also include various regular duties related to specific days such as Ekādaśīs and feast days. All of these things have been described in such religious lawbooks as the *Hari-bhakti-vilāsa*.

Hari-bhakti-vilāsa, however, gives far more regulation than is possible for anyone to follow. The disciple should therefore seek specific instruction from the spiritual master about what exactly he must or must not do. The essence of all instructions, however, should be kept in mind. That essence is to always remember the spiritual master, the Vaishnavas, and the Supreme Lord, and the essence of all prohibitions is to never forget them. Whatever injunctions and prohibitions are found in the scripture are merely variations on this theme.

> "One should chant one's mantra understanding that there is no distinction between the initiating spiritual master, the mantra given by the guru, and the deity of that mantra"

INSTRUCTIONS OF THE SPIRITUAL MASTER TO THE STUDENT PREPARING TO TAKE INITIATION

The second chapter of the *Hari-bhakti-vilāsa* discusses the process of initiation. Upon being initiated, the disciple should immediately chant the mantra 108 times.

One should chant one's mantra understanding that there is no distinction between the initiating spiritual master, the mantra given by the guru, and the deity of that mantra. After doing so, the disciple should take instruction from the spiritual master in the various activities which go with knowledge of the mantra, such as the *nyāsas, dhyānas*, and other aspects of devotional ritual.

The general duties of the initiated disciple are called *samaya* in Sanskrit, or "agreement." The *Hari-bhakti-vilāsa* gives two lists of *samayas*. The first (which contains twelve rules) comes from the *Pañcarātra* literature, and the second contains 104 prescriptions and prohibitions from the *Vishnu-yāmala*. Here I will comment on some items of devotional service. Others have been explained elsewhere in this book in greater detail.

Keeping the Mantra Secret

(1) The *Nārada-pañcarātra* list begins with the following instruction:

sva-mantro nopadeṣṭavyo
vaktavyaś ca na saṁsadi
gopanīyaṁ tathā śāstraṁ
rakṣaṇīyaṁ śarīravat

"The guru tells the disciple not to instruct anyone in the mantra publicly, nor reveal his mantra in a public assembly. One should always keep the mantra and the scriptures containing confidential material like the *Śrīmad Bhāgavatam* and details about puja secret—protecting them as he would his own body."
(*Hari-bhakti-vilāsa* 2.136)

Elsewhere in *Hari-bhakti-vilāsa* (2.146), another verse is quoted from the *Sammohana-tantra* which also says that one should keep his *iṣṭa-devatā*, his guru and his mantra secret. It also says that he should also keep his japa-mala hidden which is why Gauḍīya Vaishnavas always keep their japa beads hidden from view in a cloth bag.

gopayed devatām iṣṭāṁ
gopayed gurum ātmanaḥ
gopayec ca nijaṁ mantraṁ
gopayen nija-mālikām

However, some people incorrectly interpret the words *sva-mantro nopadeṣṭavyaḥ* to mean that the guru should not initiate any disciple in the same mantra that he has received from his guru. If this is the case, then what does the guru do at the time of giving mantra to his disciple—make one to measure by cutting a word here and adding another there according to his whims? Would this not disrupt the mantra, interfering with its already perfect form? There are so many mantras, each with a fixed number of syllables, such as the four-, six-, eight-, 10-, 12-, 18-, or 32-syllable mantras. Did the guru receive them from his predecessor gurus in a transformed state? And even if he did, does he have the right to transform it again before whispering it into his disciple's ear? If so, the original, genuine article would soon get lost forever amidst all the transformed and disfigured mantras!

The mantra is said to be the Paraṁ Brahman's sound incarnation. If that is the case, then who has the authority or power to change it or reduce it in size? Will not any guru who gives or a disciple who accepts such a disfigured mantra have to suffer the consequences of his offensive action by entering a hellish state after death?

Is this actually the rule which is applied at initiation? I have personally seen a handwritten mantra given by a so-called guru from a Gosvāmī family to his disciples, in which he deliberately made spelling mistakes and left out entire words. When I saw it, I realized that the guru had likely been trying to follow this misconceived understanding of the

"One should always keep the mantra and the scriptures containing confidential material like the Srimad Bhagavatam and details about puja secret—protecting them as he would his own body"

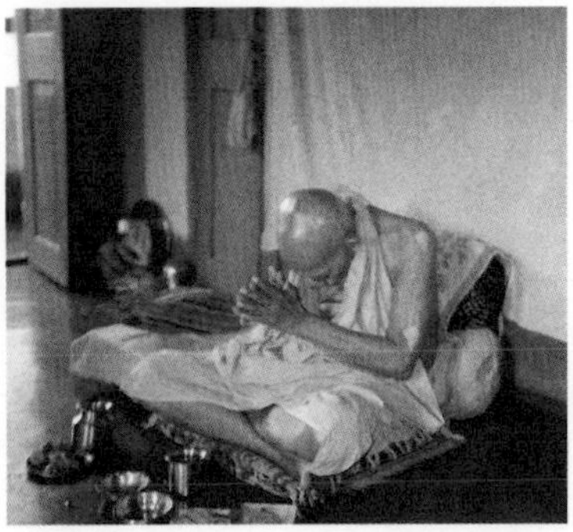

Swami B.P. Puri Maharaja performs his daily ritual of sandhya —chanting of sacred mantras

above verse and at the same time trying to keep his disciple under his influence by giving him an incomplete mantra.

Another incorrect interpretation of the above verse is given as follows: Some say that if you have received the 18-syllable mantra from your spiritual master, that is your own mantra, or *sva-mantra.* You are, in this understanding, not to instruct your disciple in this mantra, but to give him another, such as the 10-syllable mantra. My question is, how is the principle of disciplic succession maintained in this case? Should a spiritual master not initiate his disciple in the same mantra that he has received from his guru? If he has himself been initiated in the 18-syllable mantra, what gives him the right to innovate by giving the 10-syllable mantra to his own disciple? How then has he maintained the principle of adherence to the path of spiritual life set out by the previous teachers in the disciplic succession? The very principle of the *paramparā* will lose its integrity if this distorted concept of initiation is followed.

We have to look more closely at the grammar of the verse *sva-mantro nopadeṣṭavyo vaktavyaś ca na saṁsadi.* Since the negative particle *na* appears twice in this line, some people divide it into two separate parts, *sva-mantro nopadeṣṭavyo* and *ca saṁsadi na vaktavyaḥ*. The first part then means "one should not instruct his disciple in his own mantra, i.e., the mantra which he himself has received from his guru." In fact, we should take the word *saṁsadi*, "in the assembly," or, "in public," to be read with both verbs in the verse. Thus, we arrive at the idea that "one should not instruct his disciple in his mantra in public, nor should he speak it aloud in public." The intelligent reader can judge whether this interpretation of the verse is more logical or closer to the original intention of the author than that of the caste Gosvāmīs.

There is another school of thought according to which *śūdras* should be given a different mantra than upper-caste Vaishnavas. Rather than giving them a mantra with *praṇava* (*oṁ*) and the word *svāhā*, the gurus of this school give a mantra with another seed syllable and the word *namaḥ*. Sometimes they give a mantra without any seed syllable at all, simply attaching the word *namaḥ*. We wonder whether these kinds of gurus are trying to free themselves from any possibility of contamination which may come from taking disciples from the lower caste. But does anyone have the right to disfigure or transform the mantra according to his or her whim? Is there not something offensive about taking something which is a complete whole and cutting it up into bits?

Since Sanātana Gosvāmī Prabhu has not commented on this particular verse, we have explained it according to the teachings and example of our own revered spiritual master.

Other Instructions from the Nārada-pañcarātra

To return to the other samayas:

(2)

vaiṣṇavānāṁ parā bhaktir
ācāryāṇāṁ viśeṣataḥ
pūjanaṁ ca yathā-śakti
tān āpannāṁś ca pālayet

"The disciple should be devoted to all the Vaishnavas, but in particular to the

> *ācāryas*. He should perform puja to them according to his ability, and protect them if they are ever in danger. In other words, the disciple should make all efforts to serve the Vaishnavas, using his life energy, wealth, intelligence, and words."
> (*Hari-bhakti-vilāsa* 2.137)

(3) When taking the flowers and other waste materials from the temple, the disciple should carry them on his head. They should be disposed of into running water and never be allowed to touch the ground. One should always be careful not to show any disrespect for these things as they have been sanctified by use in the temple and are considered *prasāda*.

(4) The disciple should consider his worshipable deity, Vishnu, to be present in the moon and the sun, in the cow, in the Aśvattha tree, and in fire, as well as within the body of the guru and the brahmins.

"The disciple should consider his worshipable deity, Vishnu, to be present in the moon and the sun, in the cow, in the Asvattha tree, and in fire, as well as within the body of the guru and the brahmins"

(5) The disciple should never remain in a place where he knows that his spiritual master has been blasphemed. He should immediately fix his mind on the Supreme Lord and leave the scene. It is very dangerous to listen to the criticism of one's own guru. Scripture says: "O Nārada! Never listen to someone who has blasphemed the spiritual master, the Supreme Lord, or the scriptures. Never live in the same place with such a person, nor indulge in conversation with him."

(6) The disciple should remember his *iṣṭa-mantra* especially when walking, about to leave on a trip, giving in charity, early in the morning, and whenever away from home.

(7) If the disciple has a wondrous divine vision, either in dreams or in a waking state, he should not reveal it to anyone other than the guru.

In another *Pañcarātra* text, it is said that (8) the disciple should not eat fish or meat; (9) he should not eat from a plate made of bell metal, or leaves of the holy fig tree; (10) he should not spit or blow his nose in the temple room; (11) he should not enter the inner sanctum of the deities with any kind of footwear on.

Keeping the Ekādaśī Vow

In the same text it is said that the disciple (12) should not eat on Ekādaśī, either in the waxing or waning phases of the moon. He should perform a special puja on Ekādaśī and keep vigil on that night. This is stated in *Hari-bhakti-vilāsa* (2.147)—*jāgaraṁ niśi kurvīta viśeṣāc cārcayed vibhum*. In this verse, the word *viśeṣāt* has been explained in Sanātana's commentary as follows: *viśeṣād iti anya-tithibhyo viśeṣeṇa ekādaśyāṁ tatrāpi viśeṣato jāgaraṇe'rcayed ity arthaḥ*. That is, "On Ekādaśī one should keep vigil in a way that is not done on other nights. While maintaining this vigil, one should perform special worship of the deity."

There are, in fact injunctions for the vigil to the effect that in each of the three-hour periods or *prahāras* of the night, one should engage in special worship activities such as puja, making food offerings, performing *ārātrika*, reading loudly from scriptures, and chanting the Holy Names and other hymns congregationally.

Injunctions from the Vishnu-yāmala

In another *Pañcarātra Āgama* named the *Vishnu-yāmala*, it is said that even before receiving the mantra from the guru, the disciple must agree to follow 104 rules. It is stated that the spiritual master must attentively examine a prospective disciple for at least a year and explain these 104 rules and regulations to him. Of these, there are 52 injunctions, given as follows:

(1) to rise during the *brahma-muhūrta*;
(2) to wake the deity of Mahāviṣṇu;
(3) to perform the light ceremony, *maṅgalārātrika,* to the deity with musical instruments;
(4) to take a morning bath according to the rules;
(5) to put on a pair of pure and new garments, i.e., an upper and lower garment;[1] [One may wonder how someone who is engaged in daily worship of the deity can possibly procure new clothes every single day. Perhaps some very rich persons can afford to do so, but this is not possible for everyone. So this injunction should be understood to mean that one's garments should daily be washed in pure water.];

Temple of Lord Jaganath in Puri dhama

(6) to worship one's personal deity [Sanātana Gosvāmī says that this means offering water while one is taking one's bath, and does not refer to the temple deity worship, which is enjoined separately.];
(7) to make the tilak markings on the forehead with *gopīcandana* or some other pure clay or earth, such as that from Radha Kund or the base of a *tulasī* plant;
(8) using *gopīcandana* to daily decorate the body with the five weapons of Lord Vishnu, namely the conch, discus, mace, sword, and bow; [this custom is not followed by the Gauḍīya Vaishnavas who simply mark twelve parts of the body with tilak];
(9) to take *caraṇāmṛta*, the water which has washed the deity;
(10) to wear necklaces made of *tulasī* and precious metals or jewels; [Gauḍīya Vaishnavas simply wear a few strands of *tulasī* beads around the neck];
(11) to remove the leftover flowers from the deity of Vishnu and His altar;
(12) to smear the deity's used sandalwood on the body as *prasāda*;
(13) to worship one's personal deity in the Śālagrāma-śilā or the image;
(14) to eat Lord Vishnu's *tulasī* remnants or to place them on the head as a decoration;
(15) to pick *tulasī* leaves according to the regulations;
(16) to perform the *Pāñcarātrikī* meditation on the mantra three times a day according to the regulations;
(17) to tie one's *śikhā* at the beginning of worship or the performance of *sandhyā*;
(18) to make one's offerings (*tarpaṇa*) to the forefathers with Lord Vishnu's *caraṇāmṛta*;
(19) to serve the deity (if one has the ability), in a manner befitting a king;
(20) to perform the regular (*nitya-kriyā*) and occasional (*naimittika-kriyā*) rites only when they do not go against the principles of devotion to Vishnu. [*Nitya-kriyā* are rites such as bathing and chanting one's mantras, etc., while the

naimittika-kriyā are rites of passage, such as making offerings to the ancestors (*śrāddha, tarpaṇa*), etc.]

(21) to perform before *sandhyā* and puja, the *bhūta-śuddhi* ("self-purification") and *nyāsas*;[2]

(22) to offer fresh seasonal fruits and flowers to the Lord.

The Offerings of the Devotee and Non-devotee

Devotees consider pure love of God to be the ultimate goal of life. Fruitive workers consider the ability to execute their prescribed duties, wealth, and sense gratification to be the goals of life, or *puruṣārthas*. These are the grosser purposes which motivate their actions. On a more subtle level, philosophers are interested in the goal of liberation. Devotees, however, consider that in all these cases, there is either a gross or subtle desire for satisfying the personal senses. Thus they remain as far away as possible from the association of those who have these four types of selfish desire. Such persons may make a pretense of worshiping the deity of Nārāyaṇa despite their selfish motivations, but when they come with *prasāda*, the devotees are reluctant to accept it from them as they are afraid it will have negative effects on their pure attitude of devotion. The Lord Himself is eager to accept the offerings of a pure devotee, but is completely indifferent to the offerings of a superficial devotee who has no interest other than his own sense gratification. There is a verse from *Chaitanya Charitāmṛta* which supports this idea:

bhaktera dravya prabhu kāṛi kāṛi khāya
abhaktera dravya prabhu ulaṭi nā cāya

"The Lord snatches the food from a devotee and eats it; He does not even turn to look at the food of a nondevotee."

The Lord took great pleasure in such ordinary food offerings such as the broken rice of the great devotee, Vidura's wife, the four handfuls of flat rice brought by Sudāmā Vipra, the devotee Śrīdhara's banana flowers and banana tree cores, and the coconut water of Rāghava Pundit. On the other hand, the high-priced confections of the non-devotees such as Duryodhana held no attraction for Him.

Then again, though the Lord has no interest in the offerings of non-devotees, He has a merciful attitude to the simple or those ignorant of spiritual truths. Though He does not immediately accept their worship, He guides them into the association of devotees. Through the association of pure devotees, these innocent persons (*bāliśa*) soon become conscious of Vaishnava theology. Then they become fortunate enough to take shelter of a spiritual master and learn the secrets of worshiping the Supreme Lord. Krishna Himself states in the *Bhagavad-gītā*:

patraṁ puṣpaṁ phalaṁ toyaṁ
yo me bhaktyā prayacchati
tad ahaṁ bhakty-upahṛtam
aśnāmi prayatātmanaḥ

"If someone with a pure heart offers Me a leaf, a fruit, a flower or some water with devotion, I gladly accept his gift of love." (*Gītā* 9.26)

"The worshipers of other demigods go to great pains to make offerings to Me made up of wonderful ingredients, but since their faith is momentary, I do not accept them. The reason is that they feel under some compulsion to make these offerings and are not truly sincere."

The Lord in His deity form not only accepts the affectionate offerings of His exclusive devotees, He sometimes goes so far as to actually eat them. According to the commentators, the words *prayatātmanaḥ* in the above verse is interpreted to mean "one whose body and mind are pure." They go on to paraphrase the Lord's words as follows, "I therefore do not accept the offerings of someone whose body is impure, in other words, women who are having their monthly period and others are not to make such offerings" (*apavitra-śarīratve sati nāśnāmīti rajasvalādayo vyāvṛttāḥ*).

Srila Bhakti Promode Puri Maharaja offering obeisances to the dieties

(23) to regularly worship the *tulasī* plant;
(24) to regularly worship the *Śrīmad Bhāgavatam*;
(25) to worship Vishnu three times a day—in the morning, at midday, and in the evening;
(26) to daily hear the *Śrīmad Bhāgavatam* and other scriptures such as the *Puranas*;
(27) to wear the clothes which have been worn by the deity;
(28) to accept pious works as the order of the Lord Himself and to perform them in a spirit of service, thinking, "I am being engaged according to Your will" (*yathā niyukto'smi tathā karomi*);
(29) to accept the orders of the spiritual master;
(30) to believe in the words of the spiritual master;
(31) to decorate oneself with one's own mudras (*sva-mudrā-racanam*).

THE VAISHNAVA SYMBOLS

Sanātana Gosvāmī explains in his commentary that "one's own" means those which are related to one's personal object of worship as designated by the mantra. But he does not explain the word mudra, which has several different meanings. In the Berhampore edition of the *Hari-bhakti-vilāsa*, this word is explained as "the tilak, etc., which pertain to one's own *sampradāya*." Worshipers of Lakṣmī-Nārāyaṇa and other devotees of the Lord's majestic features not only mark their bodies with the weapons of the Lord (as in number 8 above), but also place other markings representing the Fish incarnation, the Tortoise incarnation, etc. These markings, which are often stamped on the body, are also called mudra. Sometimes *tapta-mudrā* or permanent markings of this sort are branded on the body by Vaishnavas of the Madhva or Rāmānuja schools. This is a custom that is not followed by the Gauḍīya Vaishnavas.

An extended description of these markings is given in the fifteenth chapter of the *Hari-bhakti-vilāsa*. There it is said:

"On the twelfth day of the waxing moon in the month of Āṣāḍha (June-July), when Lord Hari is about to go to sleep, an initiated Vaishnava should break his Ekādaśī fast and then brand the symbols (*tapta-mudrā*) of Vishnu on his body."(*Hari-bhakti-vilāsa* 15.24)

This marking of the body is compared to a faithful wife's wearing the signs of marriage such as conchshell bracelets. The verse mentions that Lord Hari is about to take rest. In fact, the preceding day is the Śayana Ekādaśī which marks the beginning of the Cāturmāsya period during which Lord Vishnu is said to be sleeping. Dvādaśi is sometimes said to be an extension of Ekādaśī, thus this kind of statement is permissible. In some circumstances, one may have the *tapta-mudrā* done on the Ekādaśī day itself. The same injunction is also given for Pārśva Ekādaśī (which marks the halfway point in the Cāturmāsya when Vishnu is said to turn over in His sleep) and Utthāna Ekādaśī (at the end of the four month period, when Vishnu rises).

Hari-bhakti-vilāsa (15.52) goes on to describe the symbols, which are also called Vishnu's five weapons (*pañcāyudha*) and where on the body they should be branded. Vishnu's club named Kaumudakī goes on the forehead; on the head, Vishnu's bow and quiver; over the heart goes Vishnu's sword named Nandaka; brahmins should place His discus Sudarśana on the right arm, His conch on the left.

Though these three days are set aside for the marking of the symbols of Vishnu with a red-hot iron, on all other occasions Vaishnavas use *gopīcandana* clay to make such marks. Thus it is said, "The intelligent person daily marks himself with the symbols such as the discus with *gopīcandana*. On Śayana Ekādaśī and other specific dates, one brands these symbols on the body." (*Hari-bhakti-vilāsa* 4.116)

In this same chapter of the *Hari-bhakti-vilāsa*, a section of the *Gautamīya-tantra* is quoted, giving the regulations for the use of *gopīcandana* for marking the body with Vishnu's symbols: "One should place the discus on the right arm, the conchshell on both the left and the right; the mace on the left, and below the mace, another discus. Above the conchshell on both arms one should stamp the lotus. The sword goes on the chest and the bow along with the quiver go on the head. Every Vaishnava should first wear the five weapons of Vishnu; then he should stamp the symbol of the Fish incarnation on the right hand and the Tortoise on the left." It is also said, "A brahmin should place Sudarśana-cakra, the Fish and lotus on his right arm, the conch, lotus, and mace on the left arm." (*Hari-bhakti-vilāsa* 4.110-113)

Sanātana writes in his commentary to verse 111 that, in fact, one can place any of the mudras on any part of the body as he wishes. This is further confirmed by the *Hari-bhakti-vilāsa* which states: "Alternatively, following the traditions of his own *sampradāya*'s *ācāryas,* one can place the conch, discus, and other markings on any part of the body he likes, adding out of devotion the specific markings which signify his personal deity." (*Hari-bhakti-vilāsa* 4.114)

Scripture says that the person whose body is decorated with markings representing the Lord's conch, etc., can never be invaded by sin. These symbols act as a shield, or *kavaca*, for the Vaishnava.

For those in our disciplic succession (Sanātana specifies in his commentary) these symbols are the flute, etc., which recall Śrī Krishna. In the next verse (*Hari-bhakti-vilāsa* 4.115), it is said that some people place the discus and the conchshell together (*cakra-śaṅkhau ca dhāryete saṁmiśrāv eva kaiścana*). Sanātana explains: "There can be no fault in wearing the sign of Krishna's conch, for it is the Lord's eternal associate and one of the foremost of His devotees. It is said that on one occasion the wife of a brahmin miscarried on hearing its sound. The brahmin was angry and cursed the conch to take birth as a demon. It was during this particular birth as the son of the demon Pañcajanya that it received the name Pāñcajanya. Because of this demonic connection, certain Vaishnavas place the sign of the conch separately."

The *Hari-bhakti-vilāsa* (4.117) states that alternatively one should stamp the body, either with the names of the Lord or with the entire mantras such as that of eight syllables (*oṁ nārāyaṇāya namaḥ*) or that of five syllables (*klīṁ kṛṣṇāya svāhā*); (*mudrā vā bhagavan-nāmnāṅkitā vāṣṭākṣarādibhiḥ*).

In our disciplic succession, some Vaishnavas who worship in the *madhura-rasa* stamp the names of Gaura, the Hare Krishna mantra, or the Lord's footprints on their chest, arms or elsewhere. The purpose of such a custom is to help one to remember the Lord. This is also the fundamental intention behind placing the tilak on twelve parts of the body and placing *tulasī* beads around the neck. All Vaishnavas in the Gauḍīya school are obliged to follow at least this custom.

The *Hari-bhakti-vilāsa* continues with a quote from the *Nāradīya Purana*: "Vaishnavas can be recognized by the *tulasī* or lotus-seed necklace they wear, the vertical marks of *gopī-candana* or sandalwood on their foreheads, and the signs of the conchshell and discus on their shoulders. Such Vaishnavas quickly purify the world." (*Hari-bhakti-vilāsa* 4.123)

The subsequent verse is similar in spirit: "I am the servant of one whose arms are marked with the symbols of Vishnu, whose power of speech is constantly used in glorifying the names of the Supreme Person, who wears the vertical tilak lines on his forehead, and a necklace of lotus seeds." (*Hari-bhakti-vilāsa* 4.124)

We should recognize that it has been said previously that even though someone may wear the symbols which are reminders of the Supreme Lord, if he acts in ways which go against the principles of devotion as outlined in the scriptures, even participating in sinful activities, then one should not consider him worthy of association. He should, however, be offered respect due to his having the external signs of a Vaishnava.

In the *Brahma Purana* it is said, "Anyone who does not offer respect to someone who is marked with the symbols of Krishna will lose the accumulated merit of 12 years of pious acts." (*Hari-bhakti-vilāsa* 4.98)

In the *Padma Purana*, the following statement is made about branding the symbols on the body: "One should purify himself by looking at the sun if he should ever see the face of an inferior human being who blasphemes a devotee tattooed with the symbols of Vishnu, such as the discus." (*Hari-bhakti-vilāsa* 15.40)

The hand signs made at certain times in the course of worship, which are also known as mudras, are not being indicated here in this injunction. These mudras have names such as *āvāhanī* (used when calling the deity), *sthāpinī* (when seating him), *sannidhāpanī* (placing him closer), *dhenu* ("the cow"), *matsya* ("the fish"), *kūrma* ("the tortoise"), *śaṅkha* ("the conch"), *cakra* ("the discus"), *gadā* ("the mace"), *padma* ("the lotus"), etc. In particular, there are sixteen such hand movements which are used at each stage of worship with sixteen elements (*ṣoḍaśopacāra*).

(32) to sing devotional songs;
(33) to dance for the deity;[3]
(34) to make auspicious sounds by blowing a conch to remind one of the Lord;
(35) to put on dramatic performances of the Lord's pastimes;
(36) to perform fire sacrifices according to the scriptural regulations;
(37) to make food offerings to the deity;
(38) to invite saintly persons and devotees into one's own home;
(39) to perform puja;
(40) to take the remnants of food offered to the deities and to the Vaishnavas;
(41) to take the remnants of *pān* offered to the deity; [Gauḍīya Vaishnavas have taken on the mood of Rādhārāṇī in Her separation from Krishna after He has left for Mathurā. In this spirit of separation, they are constantly seeking their Lord, praying, "Where is the lord of my life, the player of the flute?" In this mood of *vipralambha,* which was the example set by Śrī Chaitanya Mahāprabhu Himself, Gauḍīya Vaishnavas do not put *pān* into their mouths or swallow it, even though it is offered to Radha and Govinda as an element of their pastimes of union. Rather they place it on their heads in respect. One may offer *tāmbūla* to Śrī Chaitanya Mahāprabhu in the awareness that He is the combined incarnation of both Radha and Krishna, but should not take and eat it afterwards, only offering it respect and worship as the remnants of the deity. The reason for this is that *tāmbūla* is considered to be an aphrodisiac. Śrīmatī Rādhārāṇī, the daughter of King Vṛṣabhānu, is the incarnation of the highest aspect of divine emotion or *mahābhāva.* She is the beloved of Krishna, the foremost of His lovers, and totally absorbed in Him; She enchants Him who bewilders even Cupid himself. She offers *pān* to Krishna in order to please Him by increasing His transcendental desire for love. Her only motivation in this is to please His senses. However, if someone pretends to accept *prasādī pān* without this kind of pure motivation, simply in order to increase one's capacity to please his own senses, this cannot be approved by those who seek to achieve pure devotional service. Beginners on the path of devotional practice are filled with contaminations and should not enter areas which lie outside their realm of competence. They may pretend to be honoring *prasāda*; but the result, however, will be that their hidden desires for sense enjoyment will be awakened and they will become sensualists. For this reason, Gauḍīya Vaishnavas do not eat *prasādī pān*, but venerate it by holding it to their heads. Of course, other kinds of *prasādī* foodstuffs can be eaten. But even there, Śrīla Krishnadāsa Kavirāja Gosvāmī has warned that:

jihvāra lālase jebā iti uti dhāya
śiśnodara-parāyaṇa kṛṣṇa nāhi pāya

"Someone who runs back and forth out of a desire to please his tongue becomes attached to his belly and genitals and does not attain Krishna."
(*Chaitanya Charitāmṛta* 3.6.227)]

(42) to associate with Vaishnavas [There are many scriptural quotes which illustrate the importance of such association, and these have been discussed in an

earlier chapter];
(43) to inquire into particular aspects of duty, i.e., religious duties connected with devotional service;
(44) to follow the particular fasting rules governing the three days from Daśamī to Dvādaśī [According to *Hari-bhakti-vilāsa*, on Daśamī and Dvādaśi, one should eat only once at midday, taking *haviṣyānna*, a gruel without salt or spices. On Ekādaśī, one should fast without taking even water. Alternatively one can take *anukalpa*, a token amount of non-grain *prasāda*. One should be fixed in faithfully keeping one's vows on these three days, as long as one is in good health.][4];
(45) to observe the Vaishnava feasts and holy days and go on pilgrimages [Sanātana Gosvāmī comments that feasts and holy days include Janmāṣṭamī, etc., while pilgrimage refers to visiting temples, etc. By extension, this injunction refers to making *tulasī* and flower gardens, etc.];
(46) to observe the eight special days [The eight special days (*vāsarāṣṭakam*) are the eight great Dvādaśis—Unmīlanī, Vyañjulī, Trispṛśā, Pakṣavardhinī, Jayā, Vijayā, Jayantī, Pāpanāśinī];
(47) to make the appropriate offerings of foodstuffs and service to the deity according to each season, if possible, in the royal style [Sanātana gives the example of the swing festival in the spring as a type of service appropriate to that season];
(48) to follow all the special Vaishnava observances;
(49) to think of the spiritual master as God; [There are many verses which should be studied in connection with this idea. Some of them are:

sākṣād-dharitvena samasta-śāstrair
uktas tathā bhāvyata eva sadbhiḥ
kintu prabhor yaḥ priya eva tasya
vande guroḥ śrī-caraṇāravindam

"I worship the lotus feet of my spiritual master, who is said by all scriptures to be Lord Hari Himself, and is indeed thought of that way by all the saints. But this identity is due to his being very dear to the Lord."
(Viśvanātha Cakravartī's *Gurvaṣṭakam*, 7)

mukunda-preṣṭhatve smara param ajasraṁ nanu manaḥ

"O mind! Think of the guru as the one who is most dear to Mukunda."
(Raghunātha dāsa's *Manaḥśikṣā*, 2)

ācāryaṁ māṁ vijānīyān
nāvamanyeta karhicit
na martya-buddhyāsūyeta
sarva-deva-mayo guruḥ

"Know the guru to be My very self and never disdain him. Never think of him as an ordinary man, for the guru is the sum total of all the demigods."
(*Śrīmad Bhāgavatam* 11.17.27)];

(50) to take care of the *tulasī* plant and daily collect her leaves;
(51) to serve the deity and guru by putting them to rest with foot massages and a proper bed to sleep on, etc.;
(52) at the time of going to bed to remember Rāma and His entourage, for it is said,

rāmaṁ skandaṁ hanumantaṁ
vainateyaṁ vṛkodaram
śayane yaḥ smaren nityaṁ
duḥsvapnas tasya naśyati

"One who remembers Rāma, Skanda, Hanumān, Garuḍa or Bhīma before going to bed will never have nightmares." (*Hari-bhakti-vilāsa* 11.155);

The Prohibitions from the Vishnu-yāmala

These are the fifty-two rules which an initiated disciple is expected to follow. There are also fifty-two prohibitions listed in the same *Vishnu-yāmala*. An initiated disciple is forbidden:

(53) to sleep at dusk or dawn;
(54) to go to the toilet without cleansing himself afterward with earth;
(55) to perform *ācamana* while standing;
(56) to sit on the guru's seat;
(57) to sit before the spiritual master with his legs spread out;
(58) to step across the spiritual master's shadow;
(59) to miss his morning bath as long as he is in good health—if ill, he should take bath mentally and then put on clean clothes;
(60) to miss performing his daily worship of the deity—unless he is incapable;
(61) to forget to awaken the deity and the spiritual master and to greet them in the morning;
(62) to make a display of his learning before the spiritual master;
(63) to sit on his hams before the spiritual master;[5]
(64) to put tilak on without uttering the proper formula;
(65) to do *ācamana* without uttering the proper formula;
(66) to wear a blue cloth;
(67) to make friendship with non-devotees [As Narottama writes in *Prema-bhakti-candrikā*: *karmī jñānī michā bhakta nā habe tāhe anurakta*—"Do not place your affections in fruitive workers, impersonal philosophers, and false devotees"];
(68) to read texts which do not teach devotional service;
(69) to be attached to trivial matters and pleasures;
(70) to eat meat or drink alcoholic beverages;
(71) to take other intoxicating substances;
(72) to eat red lentils (*masura*) and other foods in the mode of ignorance such as burnt rice, etc.;
(73) to eat *śāka, tumbī,* or *kalañja,* etc.; [*Śāka* here refers to certain kinds of

Sri Garuda

leaves which adversely affect the eyesight, or bodily strength, in short any kind of vegetable that is bad for the health. Of course there are many other kinds of leaves such as *paṭola-śāka*, *vāstūka* or *betho śāka*, *nalitā* (spinach prepared from the leaves of the hemp plant) and other kinds of spinach which are allowed. *Vāstūka* spinach was particularly dear to Śrī Chaitanya Mahāprabhu. We follow Bhaktivinoda Ṭhākura in daily singing:

gaura priya śāka sevane jīvana sārthaka māni

"I consider my life perfect when I eat the spinach which was so dear to Gaura."

śuktā śākādi bhāji nālitā kuṣmāṇḍa

"Yaśodā serves *śuktā*, various kinds of spinach, deep fried vegetables, jute spinach, and pumpkin."

Tumbī is also called *alāmbu* and is commonly known in Bengali as *lāu*, in English, "bottle-gourd." What is being forbidden here are certain kinds of gourds such as the round *tumba,* the white *lāu*, and the bitter gourd, and not every kind of pumpkin or squash. Mahāprabhu was particularly fond of a preparation made from *lāu* and milk. On the evening before taking *sannyāsa*, he ate the *lāu* brought by His devotee Śrīdhara, which was cooked with milk by His mother, Śacī.

The definition of *kalañja* is found in the Sanskrit dictionary *Śabda-kalpa-druma* as follows: *viṣāstra-hata-mṛga-pakṣiṇau*—"an animal or bird struck with a poison weapon, or the flesh of such a creature."[6] It is also described as being dried meat. The words *na kalañjaṁ bhakṣayet* ("do not eat *kalañja*") are also found in the *Upanishads*. Other scriptures also state that eating dried meat, having sexual relations with a woman older than oneself, the rays of the early morning sun, curds made with milk just given by the cow, sexual activity, and sleeping after sunrise all to vitiate the life energy. In the Tretā and Dvāparā Yugas, *kṣatriyas* were permitted to eat the meat of animals which they had hunted themselves. In the Kali Yuga, however, there are several types of behavior known as the *kali-varjya* which are not permitted. These are five in number: the performance of the horse sacrifice (*aśvamedha-yajña*), the cow-sacrifice (*go-medha yajña*), the renunciation of works (*karma-sannyāsa*), making offerings of meat to the forefathers, and the custom of having one's younger brother sire offspring to maintain the family lineage (*Chaitanya Charitāmṛta* 1.18.64).

aśvamedhaṁ gavālambhaṁ
sannyāsaṁ palapaitṛkam
devareṇa sutotpattiṁ
kalau pañca vivarjayet

The word "etc." in the original verse describing this rule is said by Sanātana Gosvāmī to mean eggplant. In the eighth chapter of *Hari-bhakti-vilāsa*, verses 64-65, there is another list of forbidden foods which includes things such as onions and garlic.

(74) to take foodstuff offered by a nondevotee;
(75) to follow any special observances related to gods other than Vishnu;

(76) to chant any formula other than mantras of Vishnu;
(77) to engage in any kind of black magic rites such as *māraṇa* (meant to kill someone), *uccāṭana* (meant to cause someone distress), or *vaśīkaraṇa* (to bring someone under one's thrall);
(78) to worship the deity with inferior ingredients when he is capable of doing better;
(79) to allow himself to be overcome by emotions such as grief;
(80) to observe Ekādaśī when it overlaps with Daśamī;
(81) to differentiate between the Ekādaśī of the waxing fortnight and that of the waning fortnight; [in other words, fasting should be discarded on either Ekādaśī should be observed without making any distinction.]
(82) to engage in illegal business practices or to gamble;
(83) to eat fruits and such on a fast day if he is capable of fasting completely;
(84) to perform the *śrāddha* ceremony on Ekādaśī;
(85) to sleep during the day on Dvādaśi;
(86) to pick *tulasī* leaves on Dvādaśi;
(87) to avoid bathing Vishnu on Dvādaśi;
(88) to perform the *śrāddha* ceremony with something other than Vishnu's *prasāda*;
(89) to perform *vṛddhi-śrāddha* (an offering to the progenitors on any prosperous occasion such as the birth of a son, etc.) without *tulasī* leaves;
(90) to perform a *śrāddha* ceremony with a non-Vaishnava priest [to which Sanātana adds, "where there are no Vaishnavas present, or where something other than Vishnu's *prasāda* is used to make the oblations"];
(91) to use other water to purify himself with *ācamana* after having drunk *caraṇāmṛta*;
(92) to worship the Lord while sitting on a wooden seat [One may do so as long as he is not sitting directly on the wood, i.e., on a piece of cloth spread over the wood.];
(93) to engage in useless conversation while performing the deity's worship or puja;
(94) to worship with the oleander[7] and other poisonous flowers like the milkweed (*calotropis gigantea*);
(95) to use iron implements in worship;
(96) to wear horizontal tilak like the Śaivites;
(97) to use any impure or unwashed item in worshiping the deity, or to worship with an unattentive mind;
(98) to pay obeisances with only one hand or to circumambulate only one time;
(99) to offer the deity leftover foodstuffs or foodstuffs which have been contaminated by the touch of leftovers;
(100) to chant the mantra without counting the number of times one does so [The mantra being referred to here is the one which has a seed syllable and contains the word *svāhā* or *namaḥ* and has been given by the spiritual master. The regulation is that one should always chant the mantra a fixed number of times daily. This does not apply to the *Mahā-mantra* (Hare Krishna) which can either be chanted on beads according to a fixed number or aloud without counting.];
(101) to reveal his mantra to anyone;
(102) due to engaging in some sinful act, to miss the principal occasions for the performance of devotional acts, or
(103) to engage in the performance of religious acts at times other than prescribed;

(104) to show reluctance to take Vishnu *prasāda*.

THE INITIATION CEREMONY

All Vaishnavas should be careful to avoid engaging in any of these prohibited acts. Before giving initiation, the guru should instruct a prospective disciple in these fifty-two prescriptions and fifty-two prohibitions. The disciple should accept each one of these injunctions by saying *bāḍham,* or "I accept." When the disciple has agreed to do everything, the guru should make him perform the ceremony of the lights and then worship the deity. When he has done so, the guru can whisper the mantra into his right ear.

aṅgīkāre kṛte bāḍhaṁ
tan-nīrājana-pūrvakam
deva-pūjāṁ kārayitvā
dakṣa-karṇe mantraṁ japet

> "After being so initiated, the disciple, now completely fulfilled, should rise and then prostrate himself before the spiritual master, placing his head on the guru's feet for as long as he is permitted. Then asking him for his blessings, the disciple should give the guru gifts to the limit of his capacity."
>
> (*Hari-bhakti-vilāsa* 2.179)

After worshiping his spiritual master, he should go on to worship the other Vaishnavas according to his capacity and then feed them all. After receiving the blessings of the guru and the Vaishnavas, he should take their permission and then sit down himself and eat along with his family and friends. The fortunate person who follows this scriptural procedure for initiation will certainly live a long and blessed life, fulfilling all his dreams.

All the paraphernalia, such as a waterpot which has been used in performing the initiation rituals, should be respectfully offered to the spiritual master as gifts (*dakṣiṇā*), even if he does not request they be given him. The guru will likely ask for nothing more of his student than that he honor his teachings. Nevertheless, the disciple should not demonstrate miserliness, but rather present the guru with appropriate gifts of land, cows, clothing, gold, or whatever is within his power. He should also seek to satisfy the guru's wife and children with presents such as gold ornaments. However, if a poor disciple can do nothing more than offer himself with heartfelt sincerity, the spiritual master will be content.

Scholars of the scriptures have given the name *dīkṣā* to the process by which a living entity gains divine knowledge and, abandoning the happiness that comes from the pushing and pulling of temporal sense objects, enters into the search for eternal devotion to Lord Krishna. The secondary result of this process is that all his tendencies to sin are completely eliminated. The spiritual master's real satisfaction comes from seeing the disciple's sincere effort to engage in devotional service without any aspiration to worldly enjoyments, liberation or yogic powers. This attitude is called the *jñāna-sandeśa-dakṣiṇā*, or "the gift of the sincere search for knowledge." False teachers seek service, fame, wealth, and other gains from their disciples, while a real guru is happy simply to see his disciple's increasing desire for worshiping the Lord.

"The spiritual master's real satisfaction comes from seeing the disciple's sincere effort to engage in devotional service without any aspiration to worldly enjoyments, liberation or yogic powers. This attitude is called the jnana-sandesa-daksina, or 'the gift of the sincere search for knowledge'"

After giving the mantra to his disciple, the spiritual master should himself chant it 1,008 times in order to preserve his own ability to experience the mantra's power (*sāṣṭaṁ sahasraṁ tan-mantraṁ sva-śakty-akṣataye japet—Hari-bhakti-vilāsa* 2.181).

Chapter IX

Diksa Mantra and the Holy Name

On Sunday, the third of December, 1967, an intriguing news item appeared in the *Ananda Bazar Patrika*, an important Calcutta newspaper. The headline read, "Miracles Still Happening Today." The story had been sent in on the previous day by a staff reporter from Alipore Dwar, who wrote:

"The youngest son of Kulup Chandra Das of the Chekmari area of Madari Hat was bitten by a snake. Many ayurvedic doctors and exorcists were called in to no avail. Finally an allopathic doctor came and declared the poisoned child to be dead. Even so, his parents wanted to see if there was some last chance at saving their son. They had heard of a small community of exorcists, or *ojhās,* who lived near the village of Bogribari Hat, located between Phalakata and Jateshwar, and who apparently knew how to cure snakebites.

"One of these *ojhās* came to Chekmari and, after chanting a spell over three small shells, sent them off to find the snake that had bitten the child. Under the effects of the spell, the snake came out of its hiding place and slithered into Kulup Das' home. The three shells over which the *ojhā* had recited his incantation over were stuck to the snake's head, back and tail.

"For an entire day and night, the snake sucked the poison out of the body of Kulup Das's son from the same spot where it had bitten him. Then suddenly, the child's body rose from the dead. Thousands of people witnessed this event."

The reporter did not mention when all this took place, but this is not the only incident of its kind. The amazing power of such mantras or spells can still be seen today working in various different areas of life. In my home village of Ganganandapur in Jessore district, there was a leather worker named Haripada Muchi who was a very good *ojhā* who also knew how to cure snakebites by incantations of this sort. He once told me, "Unless one has complete faith in the guru and the mantra he has given, he will never directly experience its potency."

There are numerous spells that work against ghostly possession or snakebite. Even though these spells may be in a vulgar dialect and call on the power of some lower god, they are still seen to be remarkably effective. If such mantras are seen to produce results, then we should inquire into the reason why the powerful mantras of six, eight, 10, 12, 18, or 32 syllables, sanctified by the presence of the seed syllable and the words of surrender (*svāhā* or *namaḥ*) do not reveal their innate potencies, even when they have come down in a pure disciplic succession. Perhaps we should consider the leather worker from Ganganandapur's insight, for he has clearly divined the reason for our failure.

The Potency of Vishnu-mantras

The Supreme Lord's *śaktyāveśa* avatar Vedavyāsa hinted at the same thing many centuries ago in his *Padma Purana*:

arcye viṣṇau śilā-dhīr guruṣu nara-matir
vaiṣṇave jāti-buddhir
viṣnor vā vaiṣṇavānāṁ kali-mala-mathane
pāda-tīrthe 'mbu-buddhiḥ
śrī-viṣṇor nāmni mantre sakala-kaluṣa-he
śabda-sāmānya-buddhir
viṣṇau sarveśvareśe tad-itara-sama-dhīr
yasya vā nārakī saḥ

Swami B.P. Puri Maharaja giving mantra dikṣa

"One who thinks the deity in the temple to be made of wood or stone; who thinks of the spiritual master in the disciplic succession as an ordinary man; who thinks a Vaishnava of the infallible Lord's own clan belongs to a certain caste or creed; who thinks of *caraṇāmṛta* or Ganges water as ordinary water; who considers the mantra composed of the names of the Lord, which destroys all sins, to be a set of ordinary words; or who considers the Supreme Lord of all lords, Vishnu, to be equal to an ordinary human being—is taken to be a resident of hell."

Any mantra which reveals the sweetness of the Supreme Lord as manifest in Vrindavan is to be considered superior because this form is superior to all other forms of the Lord, such as the one He reveals in Dvārakā. The 18-syllable mantra named *sammohana* is precisely such a mantra; indeed, it is considered to be the king of all mantras. The *Hari-bhakti-vilāsa* has cited many scriptures, including the *Gopāla-tāpinī Upanishad*, the *Trailokya-sammohana-tantra*, and the *Sanat-kumāra-kalpa*, all of which attest to the superexcellence of this mantra.

The *Bhāgavata* states that all the different portions and plenary portions of the Lord emanate from Krishna, who is the Supreme Lord Himself. Therefore, just as Krishna is clearly the Supreme Person above all the other manifestations of the Godhead, so too is His mantra supreme above all other mantras. Since Krishna's *līlā* in Vrindavan, with its qualities of sweetness and munificence, is superior to the Lord's other pastimes, the mantra that contains that *līlā* and reveals it, namely the 18-syllable mantra, is supreme among them all.

In the *Trailokya-sammohana-tantra*, Mahādeva himself glorifies this mantra to his consort

Bhagavatī Devī:

yathā cintāmaṇiḥ śreṣṭho yathā gauś ca yathā satī
yathā dvijo yathā gaṅgā tathāsau mantra uttamaḥ
yathāvad akhila-śreṣṭhaṁ yathā śāstraṁ tu vaiṣṇavam
yathā susaṁskṛtā vāṇī tathāsau mantra uttamaḥ
ato mayā sureśāni pratyahaṁ japyate manuḥ
naitena sadṛśaḥ kaścid jagaty asmin caracare

"Just as the philosopher's stone is the best of all jewels, just as the cow is the best of all beasts, just as Satī is the best among women, just as the brahmin is the best of human beings, and just as the Ganges is the best among rivers, so too is this mantra the best of all mantras. Just as the Vaishnava scriptures are the best among all spiritual teachings, and just as Sanskrit is supreme among languages, so too is this the best of all mantras. Therefore, O queen of the goddesses, I daily chant this mantra. There is nothing like it in the entire universe."
(*Hari-bhakti-vilāsa* 1.185-6)

The *Hari-bhakti-vilāsa* also quotes the *Sanat-kumāra-kalpa*, which says, "By the grace of this mantra, Indra easily attained his position as king of the demigods. Due to his bad luck, Indra was cursed by Durvāsā, but again, through the power of this mantra, he was reinstated to his position." (*Hari-bhakti-vilāsa* 1.190-1)

It is so powerful that it does not depend on *puraścaraṇa* or any other kind of customary ritual performance to enhance it. Simply by reciting the mantra, one can attain the desired result.

"Any mantra that reveals the Supreme Lord in His aspect of sweetness as manifest in Vrindavan is considered superior because that form is superior to all other forms of the Lord"

bahunā kim ihoktena puraścaraṇa-sādhanaiḥ
vināpi japa-mātreṇa labhate sarvam īpsitam

"What is the use of all these instructions? Simply by chanting this mantra, even without the strict restrictions of the *puraścaraṇa vrata*, one can obtain everything one wishes."
(*Sanat-kumāra-kalpa*, quoted in *Hari-bhakti-vilāsa* 1.192)

Puraścaraṇa

Ordinarily, there are various purifying procedures (*saṁskāras*) that are prescribed before an initiation in order to purify the mantra and fully invest it with power. According to *Hari-bhakti-vilāsa*, these are ten in number: *janana, jīvana, tāḍana, rodhana, abhiṣeka, vimalīkaraṇa, āpyāyana, tarpaṇa, dīpana* and *gopana*.[1] However, Krishna mantras in general are so powerful that there is no necessity for these *saṁskāras*: *balitvāt kṛṣṇa-mantrāṇāṁ saṁskārāpekṣaṇaṁ na hi* (*Hari-bhakti-vilāsa* 1.235).

Even though such *saṁskāras* are deemed unnecessary, the *Hari-bhakti-vilāsa* does give an extensive description of the *puraścaraṇa* observance in its seventeenth chapter, or *vilāsa*. *Puraścaraṇa* is defined as follows in the *Agastya-saṁhitā:*

pūjā traikālikī nityaṁ
japas tarpaṇam eva ca

homa brāhmaṇa-bhuktiś ca
puraścaraṇam ucyate

"There are five aspects to the *puraścaraṇa* observance: puja three times a day, constant chanting of japa, oblations of water, daily fire sacrifice and feeding the brahmins." (*Hari-bhakti-vilāsa* 17.11)

According to these directions, one should surrender to the guru, to Gaurāṅga, and to Radha-Krishna, performing a puja with the 16 ingredients. Then, taking the permission of the spiritual master, at the auspicious moment, one should start reciting the mantra. There is a specific mantra that the devotee should utter as a commitment to completing the vow:

adyāṣṭādaśākṣara-saṁmohana-mantrasya siddhi-kāma iyat-sāṅkhya-japa-tad-daśāṁśāmukadravyaka-homa-tad-daśāṁśāṁśāmuka-tarpaṇa-tad-daśāṁśa-brāhmaṇa-bhojanātmaka-puraścaraṇaṁ kariṣye.[2]

"Starting today, I will perform a *puraścaraṇa* for the sake of achieving perfection in the 18-syllabled *Sammohana-mantra*. Each day, I will chant a specified number of mantras. I will offer one tenth that many oblations of (object to be specified) into the fire sacrifice. I will perform one tenth that many oblations of holy water and will feed one tenth that number of brahmins."

In other words, if one decides to chant the mantra 20,000 times, 2,000 oblations into the sacrificial fire must be offered, 200 oblations of water made and 20 brahmins fed. To perform such an elaborate ceremony in full consciousness is not easily accomplished by people in this day and age, whose minds are flickering. In view of this, the *Hari-bhakti-vilāsa* has provided a shorter version of the *puraścaraṇa* based on the faithful service to the guru. This section of the *Hari-bhakti-vilāsa* is reproduced here for the special attention of the *sādhaka*.

THE SHORTER VERSION OF PURAŚCARAṆA

tato mantra-prasiddhy-arthaṁ
guruṁ sampūjya toṣayet
evaṁ ca mantra-siddhiḥ syāt
devatā ca prasīdati

"In order to achieve the perfection of the mantra one should satisfy the guru with appropriate acts of worship. By so doing, not only will one achieve the goal of perfecting the mantra, but the deity will also be pleased with him." (*Hari-bhakti-vilāsa* 17.238)

"In order to achieve the perfection of the mantra one should satisfy the guru with appropriate acts of worship. By so doing, not only will one achieve the goal of perfecting the mantra, but the deity will also be pleased with him"

athavā devatā-rūpaṁ
guruṁ dhyātvā pratoṣayet
tasya cchāyānusārī syād
bhakti-yuktena cetasā
guru-mūlam idaṁ sarvaṁ
tasmān nityaṁ guruṁ bhajet

puraścaraṇa-hīno'pi
mantrī siddhyen na saṁśayaḥ

"Alternatively, one should satisfy the guru by meditating on him as the form of the deity. One should think of oneself as devotedly following the guru like a shadow. One should constantly worship the guru, who is the basis of all of one's spiritual activities. Even if one does not perform the *puraścaraṇa* one can attain perfection in chanting the mantra through service to the guru. Of this there can be no doubt."

yathā siddha-rasa-sparśāt
tāmraṁ bhavati kāñcanam
sannidhānād guror eva
śiṣyo viṣṇumayo bhavet

For as it is said, "Just as copper becomes gold through the touch of specially treated mercury, so the disciple takes on the qualities of Vishnu through the association of his guru." (*Hari-bhakti-vilāsa* 17.241-243)

In his commentary on *Hari-bhakti-vilāsa* 17.241, Sanātana Gosvāmī further states, "Simply through the grace of the spiritual master, the perfection of *puraścaraṇa* can be achieved." (*kevala-śrī-guru-prasādenaiva puraścaraṇa-siddhiḥ syāt*).

According to the *Hari-bhakti-vilāsa*, one should chant the mantra after worshiping the deity with puja three times a day. Failing that, one should do it twice a day, or at least once. If the *sādhaka* lives in the same village as the guru he should go daily to pay homage to him. One should always associate with devotees, etc."

yasya deve ca mantre ca
gurau triṣv api niścalā
na vyavacchidyate buddhis
tasya siddhir adūrataḥ

mantrātmā devatā jñeyā
devatā guru-rūpiṇī
teṣāṁ bhedo na kartavyo
yadīcched iṣṭam ātmanaḥ

"One is not far from perfection if his intelligence is fixed unwaveringly in the deity, the mantra and the guru. The soul of the mantra is the deity. The deity is manifest in the form of the guru. One should not make a distinction between these three if he wishes to obtain the heart's desire."

(*Hari-bhakti-vilāsa* 17.65-66)

In the seventh canto of the *Śrīmad Bhāgavatam* it is similarly stated that one obtains the grace of the Lord through faithful and devoted service to the guru. Krishna said the same thing to His friend Sudāmā Vipra:

nāham ijyā-prajātibhyāṁ
tapasopaśamena ca

"Just as copper becomes gold through the touch of specially treated mercury, so the disciple takes on the qualities of Vishnu through the association of his guru"

tuṣyeyaṁ sarva-bhūtātmā
guru-śuśrūṣayā yathā

"I, the soul of all beings, am not as pleased by the performance of the prescribed duties of the four *āśramas* (i.e., sacrifices, service to the family, austerities and renunciation) as I am by service to the guru."

(*Śrīmad Bhāgavatam* 10.80.34)

Sri Radha

Even though we have obtained such a powerful mantra from Śrī Gurudeva, due to our lack of steadfastness and our inability to receive the mercy of the spiritual master, we are not able to perceive the great potency that lies dormant within the mantra. We saw from the newspaper story earlier in this chapter that even a non-brahmin who did not follow the fundamental regulative principles of spiritual life was still able to recite a mantra with such potency that the three shells attacked a snake's body and brought it out of a dense jungle, forcing it to return to the house where it had bitten a child and then made it counteract its own bite. Should then those who have received the mantra in a pure disciplic succession be unable to perceive the power which lies within it? Of course not.

Devotion has the power to attract Śrī Krishna Himself. By the grace of Krishna's internal potency, Śrīmatī Rādhārāṇī, one can expect to receive the grace of the goddess of devotion. Through the grace of the guru, who is non-different from Śrīmatī Rādhārāṇī, one can directly experience the Lord's statement: "through devotion alone one can know Me" (*bhaktyāham ekayā grāhyaḥ, bhaktyā mām abhijānāti*).

"Through the grace of the guru, who is non-different from Srimati Radharani, one can directly experience the Lord's statement: through devotion alone one can know Me"

The Distinction between the Mantra and the Holy Name

In His instructions to Prakāśānanda Sarasvatī, Mahāprabhu made the following distinction between the mantra (the initiation mantra) and the Holy Name (also called the *Mahā-mantra*):

kṛṣṇa-mantra haite habe saṁsāra-mocana
kṛṣṇa-nāma haite pābe kṛṣṇera caraṇa

"By chanting the Krishna mantra one will be liberated from material existence. And by chanting Krishna's name, one will attain His lotus feet."

(*Chaitanya Charitāmṛta* 1.7.73)

This world is based on the principle of accepting and rejecting sense objects. One who fixes his mind on the mantra is liberated from such entanglement. Then, by chanting the Holy Names in *saṅkīrtana*, one obtains direct service to the Lord's lotus feet.

kṛṣṇa-nāma-mahā-mantrera ei ta svabhāva
je jape tāra kṛṣṇe upajaya bhāva

"The nature of the *Mahā-mantra* of Krishna's names is such that whoever chants it develops feeling for Krishna." (*Chaitanya Charitāmṛta* 1.7.83) *kṛṣṇa-nāmera phala premā sarva-śāstre kaya*

"All scriptures say that the fruit of chanting the Holy Names is to develop love for Krishna." (*Chaitanya Charitāmṛta* 1.7.86)

The Lord Himself stated that all perfections will come by the grace of the Holy Name (*ihā haite sarva siddhi haibe sabāra*). But most importantly, the fifth and ultimate goal of human life, love for Krishna, arises from the chanting of the Lord's names:

kṛṣṇa-viṣayaka prema parama puruṣārtha
jāra āge tṛṇa-tulya cāri puruṣārtha
pañcama puruṣārtha premānandāmṛta-sindhu
mokṣādi ānanda jāra nahe eka bindu

"Love for Krishna is the supreme goal of human life, or *puruṣārtha*. The other four goals of life are insignificant in comparison to it. This fifth goal of life, *prema*, is like an ocean of ecstatic nectar. In comparison, the joys derived from dharma, *artha*, *kāma*, and *mokṣa* are nothing more than a drop of water."
(*Chaitanya Charitāmṛta* 1.7.84-5)

All these quotations from the scriptures show that the ultimate achievement of the devotee who takes shelter of the Holy Name is love for Krishna, or *prema*. "In their heart of hearts, saintly persons constantly behold the inconceivably beautiful blackish form of the son of Yaśodā, Krishna, and His inconceivable innumerable attributes, with the eye of devotion tinged with the salve of love."[3]

"In their heart of hearts, saintly persons constantly behold the inconceivably beautiful blackish form of the son of Yasoda, Krishna, and His inconceivable innumerable attributes, with the eye of devotion tinged with the salve of love"

The Pañcarātra and Bhāgavata Approaches to Devotional Service

The Supreme Lord, the son of the king of Vraja, is influenced only by the love of a devotee, whose sole desire is to bring pleasure to His transcendental senses. However, due to the very fact that people possess material bodies, they are generally engaged in sinful activities and their minds are disturbed. In the *Pāñcarātrika* school, importance has been given to deity worship, preceded by initiation in the mantra, in order to diminish these characteristics. However, the ultimate goal of pure devotion is described in the same fashion both in the *Pañcarātra* literature and the *Bhāgavatam*. Thus, on the one hand, in the *Bhakti-rasāmṛta-sindhu,* the essence of the *Bhāgavatam* is summarized in the following way by Rūpa Gosvāmī:

anyābhilāṣitā-śūnyaṁ
jñāna-karmādy-anāvṛtam
ānukūlyena kṛṣṇānu-
śīlanaṁ bhaktir uttamā

"The highest category of devotion, bhakti, is defined as the culture of a favorable attitude toward Krishna, devoid of all material desires and without any adulteration by monistic philosophy or fruitive action."
(*Bhakti-rasāmṛta-sindhu* 1.1.11, *Chaitanya Charitāmṛta* 2.19.167)

This is translated by Krishnadāsa Kavirāja Gosvāmī as follows:

anya-vāñchā anya-pūjā chāṛi jñāna karma
ānukūlye sarvendriye kṛṣṇānuśīlana

> "A devotee must engage all the senses in the cultivation of favorable Krishna consciousness. He must give up all other desires, the worship of other gods, the cultivation of monistic knowledge and fruitive activities."
> (*Chaitanya Charitāmṛta* 2.19.168)

"The highest category of devotion, bhakti, is defined as culturing a favorable attitude toward Krishna, that is devoid of all material desires"

But Rūpa goes on to support this definition of bhakti with a verse from the *Nārada-pañcarātra:*

sarvopādhi-vinirmuktaṁ
tat-paratvena nirmalam
hṛṣīkeṇa hṛṣīkeśa-
sevanaṁ bhaktir ucyate

> "Bhakti is defined as the engagement of the senses in the service of the proprietor of the senses. This service is to be free from any contamination from indentification with the body, and pure through being exclusively fixed on Me."
> (*Bhakti-rasāmṛta-sindhu* 1.1.12; *Chaitanya Charitāmṛta* 2.19.170)

Here the primary characteristic of devotion is the engagement of the senses in the service of the Lord of the senses. This devotion has two characteristics that are considered secondary, that is, dependent on its proper execution. The first is that it should be free from any *upādhi,* or identification with selfish bodily interests. The second is that it will be purified due to being absolutely fixed on Him alone. Thus the two definitions are parallel to one another. From this practice of the *abhidheya* of bhakti, one arrives at the ultimate goal—the *prayojana*—of *prema.*

ei śuddha-bhakti ihā haite premā haya
pañcarātre bhāgavate ei lakṣaṇa kaya

> "These activities are called *śuddha-bhakti*, pure devotional service. In the rendering of such pure devotional service, one's original love for Krishna develops in due course of time. Its characteristics have been described in the *Pañcarātras* and *Śrīmad Bhāgavatam.*" (*Chaitanya Charitāmṛta* 2.19.169)

Thus, though the characteristics of pure devotional service are identical according to both those on the *Pañcarātra* and *Bhāgavata* paths, each path exhibits some differences in its most prominent practices. The chanting of the mantra and deity worship are associated with the *Pāñcarātrika* system and the Dvāparā Yuga, while the chanting of the Holy Names is an ecstatic practice associated with the *Bhāgavata*s and is particularly appropriate in the age of Kali. This is confirmed by Madhvācārya in the following verse found in his commentary on the *Maṇḍūkya Upanishad*:

dvāparīyair janair viṣṇuḥ
pañcarātraiś ca kevalam
kalau tu nāma-mātreṇa
pūjyate bhagavān hariḥ

"The Supreme Lord Vishnu was worshiped according to the *Pāñcarātrika* method alone in the Dvāparā; in the age of Kali, He is worshiped exclusively by the Holy Name."

The Importance of Chanting the Holy Names

There are many verses in the *Bhāgavatam* that attest to the preeminence of the three principal devotional activities of hearing, chanting, and remembering:

tasmād ekena manasā
bhagavān sātvatāṁ patiḥ
śrotavyaḥ kīrtitavyaś ca
dhyeyaḥ pūjyaś ca nityadā

"Therefore, one should constantly hear about, glorify, meditate on, and worship the Supreme Lord, the protector of the devotees, with single-minded concentration." (1.12.14)

tasmāt sarvātmanā rājan
hariḥ sarvatra sarvadā
śrotavyaḥ kīrtitavyaś ca
smartavyo bhagavān nṛṇām

"Therefore, O King, wherever one may be, the Supreme Lord Hari should always be spoken about, glorified and remembered with full concentration." (2.2.36)

tasmād bhārata sarvātmā
bhagavān īśvaro hariḥ
śrotavyaḥ kīrtitavyaś ca
smartavyaś cecchatābhayam

"O scion of the Bharata dynasty! One who desires fearlessness should hear about, glorify and also remember the Supreme Lord Hari, the soul of all beings and supreme controller, for He alone steals away all one's miseries." (2.1.5)

"In the rendering of such pure devotional service, one's original love for Krishna is developed in due course of time"

In the final analysis however, despite the emphasis on these three types of devotional activity, *kīrtana,* glorifying the Lord or chanting His names, is singled out as supreme by the *Bhāgavatam*:

etan nirvidyamānānām
icchatām akuto-bhayam
yogināṁ nṛpa nirṇītaṁ
harer nāmānukīrtanam

"O King, it has been ascertained that for those yogis who are indifferent to material pleasures and who desire complete fearlessness, the best path is constant chanting of the holy name of the Lord." (2.2.36)

nāma-saṅkīrtanaṁ yasya
sarva-pāpa-praṇāśanaṁ

praṇāmo duḥkha-śamanas
taṁ namāmi hariṁ param

"I bow down to the Supreme Lord Hari, the chanting of whose name results in the destruction of all sin, and by paying homage to whom, all miseries are quieted."
(12.13.23)

Śrī Chaitanya Mahāprabhu also confirmed these statements from the *Bhāgavatam* in His own words:

"Of these nine processes of devotional service, the most important is the chanting of the Lord's holy name"

bhajanera madhye śreṣṭha nava-vidhā bhakti
kṛṣṇa-prema, kṛṣṇa dite dhare mahā-śakti
tāra madhye sarva-śreṣṭha nāma-saṅkīrtana
niraparādhe laile nāma pāya prema-dhana

"Of the many ways of executing devotional service, there are nine varieties that are considered to be the best, for they possess a great capacity to deliver love for Krishna and thus Krishna Himself. Of these nine processes of devotional service, the most important is the chanting of the Lord's holy name, for in chanting offenselessly, one will obtain the treasure of love for the Lord."
(*Chaitanya Charitāmṛta* 3.4.70-1)

eka kṛṣṇa-nāme kare sarva-pāpa kṣaya
nava-vidhā bhakti pūrṇa nāma haite haya

"Simply by chanting the holy name of Krishna, one is relieved from all the reactions of a sinful life. One can complete the nine processes of devotional service simply by chanting the Holy Name." (*Chaitanya Charitāmṛta* 2.15.107)

In the twelfth chapter of the *Bhagavad-gītā*, it is said that remembering, contemplating and meditating on the Lord are dependent on inner purification and therefore not easily perfected by ordinary people. On the other hand, since *saṅkīrtana* is an activity executed by the external senses, it is within the grasp of anyone, even the disturbed human beings of this age of Kali.

The sixth canto of the *Śrīmad Bhāgavatam*, states that bhakti, or devotional service, is primarily executed in the form of *saṅkīrtana*:

etāvān eva loke 'smin
puṁsāṁ dharmaḥ parah smṛtaḥ
bhakti-yogo bhagavati
tan-nāma-grahaṇādibhiḥ

"Therefore, the supreme religious activity for people in this world is devotional service to the Lord, performed by such acts as repeating His divine names."
(6.3.22)

The definition of *kīrtana* has been given in the *Bhakti-rasāmṛta-sindhu* (1.2.145) as "the audible glorification of the Lord's names, attributes, and activities, etc." (*nāma-līlā-*

guṇādīnām uccair bhāṣaṇaṁ tu kīrtanam). Even so, the best type of *kīrtana*, also spoken of in the *Bhāgavatam* and taught by the Gosvāmīs like Śrī Sanātana, Śrī Rūpa, and Śrī Jīva, is the chanting of the Holy Name. This is the religious principle of the age of Kali as promulgated by the incarnation of Krishna, Śrī Chaitanya Mahāprabhu.

THE CHANTING OF THE HOLY NAMES IS THE RELIGIOUS PROCESS FOR THIS AGE

Mahāprabhu and all His associates clearly stated that among all the devotional practices, the chanting of the Holy Names is the most important. *Harināma-saṅkīrtana* has nothing other than love for Krishna as its goal, or intended result. Religiosity, material prosperity, sense enjoyment and liberation are not to be sought through the chanting of the Holy Name. In the age of Kali, the Holy Name is the essence of all religious activity and the essence of all mantras. There are many statements in the scriptures that support this idea:

nāma vinā kali-kāle nāhi āra dharma
sarva-mantra-sāra nāma ei śāstra marma

"In the age of Kali, there is no religious activity other than the chanting of the Holy Names. The Holy Name is the essence of all mantras."
(*Chaitanya Charitāmṛta* 1.7.74)

"The Holy Name is the essence of all mantras"

A number of verses from the last book of the *Śrīmad Bhāgavatam* also emphasize the chanting of the Holy Names in the age of Kali.

kaler doṣa-nidhe rājann
asti hy eko mahān guṇaḥ
kīrtanād eva kṛṣṇasya
mukta-saṅgaḥ paraṁ vrajet

"O king! The age of Kali is an ocean of faults, but it contains one great virtue: simply by chanting the names of Krishna one becomes liberated and goes to the supreme abode." (*Śrīmad Bhāgavatam* 12.3.51)

kṛte yad dhyāyato viṣṇuṁ
tretāyāṁ yajato makhaiḥ
dvāpare paricaryāyāṁ
kalau tadd hari-kīrtanāt

"That which is achieved in the Satya Yuga by meditation on Vishnu, in the Tretā-yuga by performing fire sacrifices, and in Dvāparā Yuga by deity worship, is attained in Kali Yuga by chanting the name and glories of Hari." (SB 12.3.52)

Sri Krishna Chaitanya, the Golden Avatar

Nārada Muni, the seer of the gods, clearly stated that, in the age of Kali, there is no other means of attaining perfection:

harer nāma harer nāma
harer nāmaiva kevalam
kalau nāsty eva nāsty eva
nāsty eva gatir anyathā

"In this age of quarrel and hypocrisy the only means of deliverance is the chanting of the Holy Names of the Lord. There is no other way, there is no other way, there is no other way." (*Bṛhan-nāradīya Purana*, *Chaitanya Charitāmṛta* 1.7.76)

Mahāprabhu Himself explained this verse to Prakāśānanda Sarasvatī:

> "The age of Kali is an ocean of faults, but it contains one great virtue: simply by chanting the names of Krishna one becomes liberated and goes to the supreme abode"

kali-kāle nāma-rūpe kṛṣṇa-avatāra
nāma haite haya sarva-jagat-nistāra
dārḍhya lāgi harer nāma-ukti tina-vāra
jaḍa loka bujhāite punaḥ eva-kāra
kevala-śabde punarapi niścaya-karaṇa
jñāna-yoga-tapa-karma-ādi nivāraṇa
anyathā je māne tāra nāhika nistāra
nāhi nāhi nāhi e tina eva-kāra

"In this Age of Kali, Krishna has incarnated in the form of His Holy Name, the Hare Krishna *Mahā-mantra*. The whole world will be delivered through the grace of the Holy Name. In order to vigorously affirm this, Nārada's verse repeats the words *harer nāma* three times. Then, just to make it clear for the really dull, it stresses those words with the word *eva* ['certainly']. This assertion is further strengthened by the use of the word *kevala* ['alone'] which prohibits all other processes, such as cultivation of knowledge, practice of mystic yoga, and performance of austerities and fruitive activities. Then, to make sure it is clear that one who disregards this teaching will not achieve salvation, the words 'there is no other way' are repeated thrice."

(*Chaitanya Charitāmṛta* 1.17.22-5)

The importance of the *Mahā-mantra* for the age of Kali has also been emphasized in the *Kali-santarana Upanishad*:

hare krishna hare krishna
krishna krishna hare hare
hare rāma hare rāma
rāma rāma hare hare

iti ṣoḍaśakaṁ nāmnāṁ
kali-kalmaṣa-nāśanam
nātaḥ parataropāyaḥ
sarva-vedeṣu dṛśyate

"The 16 names of the *Mahā-mantra* destroy the pollution of this age of Kali. Throughout the entire body of Vedic literature one cannot find a more sublime means of spiritual religion."

Mahāprabhu Appeared to Preach the Chanting of the Holy Names

avatari caitanya kaila dharma-pracāraṇa
kali-kāle dharma kṛṣṇa-nāma-saṅkīrtana

saṅkīrtana-yajñe tāṅre kare ārādhana
sei ta sumedhā āra kali-hata-jana

"Śrī Chaitanya Mahāprabhu descended to preach religious principles. In the age of Kali, the only religious principle is the chanting of the holy names of Lord Krishna. Anyone who worships the Lord by the sacrifice of the Holy Name is most intelligent. As for the rest, they have been defeated by the spirit of the age of quarrel." (*Chaitanya Charitāmṛta* 2.11.98-9)

The significance of Mahāprabhu's appearance to teach the Holy Names is furthermore underlined by the *Śrīmad Bhāgavatam*:

kṛṣṇa-varṇaṁ tviṣākṛṣṇaṁ
sāṅgopāṅgāstra-pārṣadam
yajñaiḥ saṅkīrtana-prāyair
yajanti hi su-medhasaḥ

Mahaprabhu's divine sankirtana

"In the Age of Kali, the golden Lord, upon whose lips the name of Krishna always remains, appears in the company of His expansions, portions, weapons and associates. Those who are very intelligent will worship him through the sacrifice of congregational glorification *(saṅkīrtana-yajña).*" (*Śrīmad Bhāgavatam* 11.5.32)

Mahāprabhu had the further purpose of bestowing the most elevated and effulgent kind of spiritual experience to all the world. One day, as He was thinking how the living beings of the world could be made eligible to enter this experience, He put His arms around Svarūpa Dāmodara and Rāmānanda Rāya, His closest companions, and said in great jubilation:

harṣe prabhu kahena śuna svarūpa-rāma-rāya
nāma-saṅkīrtana kalau parama upāya
saṅkīrtana-yajñe kalau kṛṣṇa-ārādhana
sei ta sumedhā pāya kṛṣṇera caraṇa
nāma-saṅkīrtana haite sarvānartha-nāśa
sarva-śubhodaya, kṛṣṇa-premera ullāsa

"Simply by chanting the holy name of Lord Krishna, one can be freed from all undesirable habits"

"My dear Svarūpa Dāmodara and Rāmānanda Rāya, know from Me that chanting of the Holy Names is the most feasible means of salvation in this age of Kali. In this age, the process of worshiping Krishna is to perform sacrifice by chanting the holy name of the Lord. One who does so is certainly very intelligent, attaining shelter at the lotus feet of Krishna. Simply by chanting the holy name of Lord Krishna, one can be freed from all undesirable habits. This is the means of awakening all good fortune and initiating the flow of waves of love for Krishna." (*Chaitanya Charitāmṛta* 3.20.8-9,11)

From this statement we can easily understand that the Lord invested some special powers in the chanting of His holy names in this fortunate age of Kali. This special power is its capacity to awaken affectionate attachment, or *rāga*, for the Lord. Therefore, this is the best process by which one can develop *rāga-bhakti*, or devotional service in spontaneous affection.

Ways of Chanting

The scriptures ordinarily describe three styles of chanting mantras: the *vācika*, or vocal chanting; the *upāṁśu*, chanting in a whisper such that it can only be heard by oneself; the *mānasa,* in which one chants mentally. Each of these is said to be superior to the one which precedes it. Nevertheless, a mantra is *japya*, uttered or recited silently, only when one tries to fulfill the obligation of chanting it a certain number of times. Generally, we don't encounter scriptural injunctions that direct us to chant a mantra while keeping track of the number of times it is chanted. In the case of the *Mahā-mantra,* this particular distinction is not made either. One can chant both within the constraints of a vow to chant a certain daily amount or outside of such constraints. There are no restrictions in this matter, just as there are none concerning the appropriate times of day to chant, or the state of one's purification. Mahāprabhu Himself says as much in His *Śikṣāṣṭaka*: *niyamitaḥ smaraṇe na kālaḥ*.

ki bhojane ki śayane kibā jāgaraṇe
aharniśa cinta kṛṣṇa balaha vadane

> "Think of Krishna and utter His names both day and night, whether you are eating, lying down or engaged in waking activities."

sarva kṣaṇa bala ithe vidhi nāhi āra

> "The only rule is to chant the Holy Name always. There is no other requirement."

"The only rule is to chant the Holy Name always"

Elsewhere it is said,

na deśa-niyamas tatra na kāla-niyamas tathā
nocchiṣṭādau nimeṣo'sti śrī-harer nāmni lubdhaka

> "O hunter! There are no rules governing the time or place where one may chant the holy name of the Lord. Nor is it necessary for one to be in a state of ritual purity. One can chant even if one's hands or mouth are unwashed after eating, sleeping, or going to the toilet."

We must remember the 16 names and 32 syllables of the Hare Krishna mantra are called the *Mahā-mantra* and they are especially powerful.

kṛṣṇa-nāma mahā-mantrera ei ta svabhāva
jei jape tāra kṛṣṇe upajaye bhāva

> "This is the nature of the *Mahā-mantra* consisting of Krishna's names. Whoever recites it develops ecstatic feeling for Krishna." (*Chaitanya Charitāmṛta* 1.7.83)

In the *Anubhāṣya* to this verse, Śrīla Prabhupāda Bhaktisiddhānta Sarasvatī Ṭhākura has written the following:

"Some foolish people do not understand that the formula consisting of 16 names and 32 syllables is the *Mahā-mantra*. Taking it to be another ordinary mantra that should be uttered silently or mentally, they artificially claim it should not be chanted aloud or sung. Those who have attained love for Krishna engage in loud chanting of these names in the company of other devotees. Through such singing of the *Mahā-mantra*, everyone in the world is initiated in the Holy Name. Anyone who sings the Names aloud will simultaneously hear and remember the Name. Because Krishna and His name are not different from each other, a tendency to serve the Lord will awaken in anyone who recites His names in *japa*. Someone who has attained the stage of *bhāva* is no longer polluted by the contaminations resulting from bondage in ignorance. Their personal relationship with the Lord has been awakened within them and therefore they relish the combination of ingredients that go into the composition of divine mellows, or *rasa*. As this stage of ecstatic feeling, or *bhāva*, intensifies, it becomes *prema*. The 16 names and 32-syllable formula consisting of Krishna's names is the most potent; all the other mantras listed in the *Pañcarātra* literature are considered to be less effective. The holy names of the Lord are known as the *Mahā-mantra*."

"The only rule is to chant the Holy Name always. There is no other requirement"

dīkṣā puraścaryā vidhi apekṣā nā kare
jihvā sparśe ācaṇḍāle sabāre uddhāre

"All perfections come from the Holy Name. It does not require initiation or the observance of *puraścaraṇa*. As soon as it touches the tongue of even the lowest class of humankind, it immediately delivers them."

(*Chaitanya Charitāmṛta* 2.15.108)

All these statements show that the *Mahā-mantra* of the Holy Names is more powerful than any other mantra, including the 18-syllable Gopāla mantra. One who has initiation in the mantra is given the right to practice the *vidhi-mārga*, whereas someone who chants the *Mahā-mantra*, whether initiated or not, is given the qualifications for all situations in life. In particular, a practitioner of the *rāgānugā* path quickly attains his desired goal in Vraja by taking shelter of the worship of the Holy Name. For one on the *vidhi-mārga* or *arcanā-mārga*, the ecstatic mood of Vraja is vague and distant. Spiritual practices on the *vidhi-mārga* have no power to bestow this mood. *Vidhi-mārge vraja-bhāva pāite nāhi śakti.*

If the Name is so Powerful, Then Why do We Need Initiation?

Jīva Gosvāmī responds to the question of why the mantra and initiation are necessary if the Holy Name has such purificatory power. The following paragraph is found in his *Bhakti-sandarbha* (285):

"Now you may say, 'The mantra itself consists of names of the Lord. Added to that are words indicating submission, such as *namaḥ* or *svāhā*, etc., through which Nārada and other seers have endowed the mantra with some special potency by the desire of the Lord. Furthermore they are capable of awakening a specific personal relationship with the Lord. [Of all these constituents] of the mantra, the names of the Lord alone are capable of independently giving its reciter the supreme goal of life [i.e., *prema*]. Thus we find that in the mantra there is an even greater power than can be found in the Name. In view of all these considerations, why then is there any necessity for initiation?'

"The answer is as follows: there is no fundamental necessity for initiation. Nevertheless, because people are generally by nature caught up in bad habits and are unable to concentrate due to bodily associations, etc., the great seers such as Nārada and others have on occasion established some fundamental regulations here and there calling for the performance of worship of the deity (*arcana-mārga*) in order to reduce such bad habits and lack of concentration. For this reason, the scriptures call for the performance of penances as an atonement for the non-performance of such deity worship. Where neither of these faults (bodily and mental aberrations) are prominent, there is no need for initiation."[4]

"When a submissive disciple approaches the spiritual master with questions and a service mentality, the guru awards initiation into the mantra which contains within it the divine knowledge of a specific relationship with Krishna"

Śrīla Prabhupāda further clarifies this distinction by writing the following: "The conditioned soul absolutely must achieve perfection in the mantra in order to rid himself of his material ego and his tendency for sense gratification. The word *namaḥ* is interpreted as follows: *ma* means *ahaṅkāra*; *na* negates this egoism. Through perfecting the chanting of the mantra (*mantra-siddhi*) one gains direct experience of the transcendent reality. Thus Śrī Rūpa Gosvāmī sings in his *Nāmāṣṭakam*, addressing the Holy Name as follows: *ayi mukta-kulair upāsyamānam*—"O Holy Name! You are worshiped by the liberated souls.'" (*Anubhāṣya* 1.7.72-4)

The Mantra brings Purification—the Holy Name brings Ecstatic Love

We have already seen that Mahāprabhu gave instructions about the Holy Name and the mantra to the Māyāvādī sannyasi, Prakāśānanda Sarasvatī, when in Kāśī. Prakāśānanda criticized the Lord, saying that chanting the Holy Name was not a suitable activity for a person in the renounced order of life. In response, the Lord said:

prabhu kahe śuna śrīpāda ihāra kāraṇa
guru more mūrkha dekhi karila śāsana
mūrkha tumi, tomāra nāhika vedāntādhikāra
kṛṣṇa-mantra japa sadā ei mantra-sāra
kṛṣṇa-mantra haite habe saṁsāra-mocana
kṛṣṇa-nāma haite pābe kṛṣṇera caraṇa
nāma vinu kali-kāle nāhi āra dharma
sarva-mantra-sāra nāma ei śāstra-marma

> "Venerable sir, please hear from me the reason why I chant. My spiritual master considered me a fool and therefore chastised me. 'You are a fool,' he said, 'and have no qualification to study Vedanta philosophy. Go and chant the Krishna mantra constantly, for it is the essence of all mantras. By chanting the Krishna mantra one will be liberated from material existence. And by chanting Krishna's name, one will attain His lotus feet. In the age of Kali, there is no religious activity other than the chanting of the Holy Names. The Holy Name is the essence of all mantras.'" (*Chaitanya Charitāmṛta* 1.7.71-74)

The sum and substance of these statements is the following: When a submissive disciple approaches the spiritual master with questions and a service mentality, the guru awards initiation into the mantra which contains within it the divine knowledge of a specific relationship with Krishna. From that moment, having received the divine mercy of the guru, the disciple starts to cast off all absorption in anything that distracts him from devotional life. The disciple engages in Krishna's service and as affection for the Lord develops, becomes inclined to call out His names. Through this practice he reaches fulfillment in pure love for the Lord's lotus feet. Our most worshipable Śrīla Prabhupāda

Bhaktisiddhānta Sarasvatī Ṭhākura has summarized this process in his *Anubhāṣya* to *Chaitanya Charitāmṛta* 1.7.73 as follows:

"Through chanting the Krishna mantra, the *jīva* begins to have experience of the supramundane realm. He begins to give less precedence to external sense perception and material attachment. Then taking shelter in one of the five relationships, he begins to relish the divine mellows through the combination of all the ingredients that go into their composition: the *vibhāvas, anubhāvas, vyabhicāri-bhāvas,* and *sāttvikas*. The heart, which has been purified through the influence of divine exultation, becomes illuminated in pure goodness. In such a state, the living being can experience the object of worship. This process is completely distinct from the enjoyments of the *jīva*'s gross or subtle coverings.

"The Name and the One who is Named are not distinct entities. This is the divine knowledge (*divya-jñāna*) that is achieved through initiation. One who is actually situated in the regular practice of spiritual life, with the intention of having this realization, attains direct service to Krishna. In this state, he loses interest in the grammatical formalism of the mantra, with its *bīja* mantra (*oṁ, klīṁ*, etc.), dative case endings (*-āya, -ave, āyai, -ābhyāṁ, -ebhyaḥ*, etc.) and words indicating relationships (*svāhā, namaḥ*, etc.). Rather, he favors a direct expression of this relationship with the Lord by calling out to Him in the vocative case. This takes place naturally in the heart that has been illuminated by the mode of pure goodness.[5] In this state, the devotee gains the ability to unrestrictedly serve the Holy Name in the vocative form. All scriptures and all mantras which contain *divya-jñāna* liberate the *jīva* completely and then engage that soul directly in the service of the Lord."

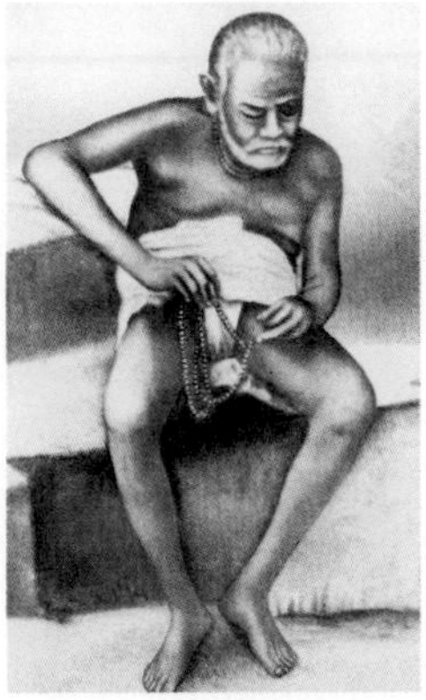

Jagannatha das Babaji Maharaja, the guru of Bhaktivinode Thakur

In his comments on the subsequent verse, Sarasvatī Ṭhākura continues:

"The Name and the Named are not different from one another. Therefore, just as Lord Krishna is the absolute reality, liberated, the embodiment of pure consciousness, a transcendental philosopher's stone, so too is His name. Only through the worship of the Holy Name (*nāma-bhajana*) can both one's gross and subtle misidentifications both be destroyed. The Vaikuṇṭha name alone can save the living being from absorption in thoughts of material sense gratification. Because it is powerful enough to do this, it is called the *mantra-sāra,* the essence of all mantras. Every material thing has its name, form, attributes, characteristics, and functions, all of which are subject to arguments and experimental knowledge. The same is not true for the Vaikuṇṭha name; the name, form, attributes and associates of the Lord are all situated in nonduality."

"Through chanting the Krishna mantra, the jiva begins to have experience of the supramundane realm"

THE GLORIES OF THE HOLY NAMES

The chanting of the Holy Names, *harināma-saṅkīrtana,* is designated as the religious principle of the age of Kali in the Vedas (*oṁ āsya jānanto nāma cid vivaktan mahas te viṣṇo sumatiṁ bhajāmahe*), the *Upanishads* (*Kali-santarana)*, the *Smṛtis* (*Bhagavad-gītā)*, the *Śrīmad Bhāgavatam* and other lesser *Puranas*, as well as in histories such as *Mahābhārata*. Even so, Śrī Chaitanya Mahāprabhu descended in this age to show by His own example that the loud chanting and singing of this great mantra stands above all other religious activities. Furthermore, in His *Śikṣāṣṭaka*, He proclaimed the glorious victory of *harināma-saṅkīrtana* in a booming voice. He also taught the same through His *Nāmācārya*, Śrīla

Haridāsa Ṭhākura, who unfailingly chanted 300,000 names out loud every single day. After being flogged in 22 market places on the order of the governor of Ambikā Kalna, Haridāsa showed his allegiance to the Holy Name when he said:

khaṇḍa khaṇḍa deha mora jāya yadi prāṇa
tathāpiha vadane nā chāṛi harināma

"Though my body may be torn to bits and my life may leave it, even then I will never give up chanting the Holy Names." (*Chaitanya Bhāgavata* 1.14.135)

Mahāprabhu's other dear associates showed similar allegiance to the Holy Name. When we consider the way in which the Lord and His devotees have revealed the power of the *Mahā-mantra*, we must be thrilled with joy and astonishment.

Then why are we so unfortunate? Why do we not immediately receive the fruits of chanting? The reason is clear: we are offenders to the Holy Name.

nāmaikaṁ yasya vāci smaraṇa-patha-gataṁ
śrotra-mūlaṁ gataṁ vā
śuddhaṁ vāśuddha-varṇaṁ vyavahita-rahitaṁ
tārayaty eva satyam
tac ced deha-draviṇa-janatā-
lobha-pāṣaṇḍa-madhye
nikṣiptaṁ syān na phala-janakaṁ
śīghram evātra vipra

"The Vaikuntha name alone can save the living being from absorption in thoughts of material sense gratification"

"Should someone utter the holy name of the Lord even once, or should he merely remember it or hear it in passing, it will certainly deliver him from material bondage, whether it is correctly or incorrectly pronounced, properly joined, or vibrated in separate parts. O brahmin, if one uses the Holy Name for the benefit of the material body, for material wealth and followers, or under the influence of greed or atheism—in other words, if one utters the name with offenses—such chanting will not produce the desired result with the same rapidity."
(*Padma Purana*, *Hari-bhakti-vilāsa* 11.527, *Chaitanya Charitāmṛta* 3.3.60)

Even so, if we continue to chant diligently, inasmuch as our offensiveness is eliminated, we will be able to experience its benefits, love for Krishna. By chanting the mantra received in initiation one will minimize his material attachments and his taste for chanting the Holy Names will increase. By chanting the Holy Name—by its grace—one will experience the awakening of love for Krishna.

Bhaktivinoda Ṭhākura has written in his song, "*Kṛṣṇa-nāma dhare kata bala?*" (*Śaraṇāgati*)

īṣat vikaśi punaḥ dekhāya nija-rūpa-guṇa
citta hari laya kṛṣṇa pāśa
pūrṇa vikaśita hañā vraje more jāya lañā
dekhāya nija svarūpa vilāsa

"When the Name is even slightly revealed, it shows me my own spiritual form

> and characteristics. It steals my mind and takes it to Krishna's side. When the Name is fully revealed, it takes me directly to Vraja, where it shows me my personal role in the eternal pastimes."

By the grace of the Holy Name, we too will come to a state where we will say with Chaitanya Mahāprabhu:

kibā mantra dile gosāñi kibā tāra bala
japite japite mantra karila pāgala

> "What mantra have you given me, O gurudeva! What powers does it possess? As I chant this mantra, I feel that it is turning me into a madman."
> (*Chaitanya Charitāmṛta* 1.7.81)

When we come to this point, we will begin to understand the power of the Holy Name.

"Though my body may be torn to bits and my life may leave it, even then I will never give up chanting the Holy Names"

Chapter X

Expertise in Bhajana

Śrīla Rūpa Gosvāmī has described devotion as very rare (*durlabhā*). With the following verse he illustrates just how difficult it is to attain pure bhakti.

sādhanaughair anāsaṅgair
alabhyā sucirād api
hariṇā cāśv adeyeti
dvidhā sā syāt sudurlabhā

> "Bhakti is very difficult to attain for two reasons. First, without genuine attachment to Krishna one cannot attain devotional perfection even if he performs large amounts of devotional activities. The other reason is that Krishna does not easily give it to the aspirant." (*Bhakti-rasāmṛta-sindhu* 1.1.35)

An important word in this verse is *anāsaṅga*, "without attachment." The word *āsaṅga* is explained by Jīva Gosvāmī as "expertise in devotional practice, characterized by direct engagement." The devotional activities referred to in this verse include all the practices, especially the five most potent: associating with compassionate devotees in the same mood and who are more advanced than oneself; chanting the Holy Name, listening to the *Bhāgavatam*; living in Mathurā or the holy *dhāma*; and serving the deity form of the Lord with faith. Even if one engages in these powerful devotional activities, if he is without the necessary expertise, he will not attain their true fruit, *prema*. And even if one should perform devotional service with the required expertise, Krishna does not give *prema* until that devotee has become extremely attached to the goal of the practice (*yāvat phala-bhūte bhakti-yoge gāḍhāsaktir na jāyate tāvan na dadātīty arthaḥ*).

Jīva Gosvāmī's definition of *āsaṅga* as expertise in devotional practice characterized by direct engagement is significant. If someone is engaged in devotional service while seeking goals such as heavenly sense enjoyment, he cannot be considered expert. Fruitive work, philosophical speculation or yoga are of no help in realizing the goal of love for Krishna either. For this reason, Rūpa Gosvāmī has given a comprehensive definition of bhakti as the cultivation of Krishna consciousness coupled with an effort to please Him. This culture must not be mixed with the abovementioned practices, or motivated by any other objectives.

Choosing the Right Kind of Practice

Since the first characteristic of expertise in *bhajana* is direct engagement in appropriate devotional activities (*sākṣāt tad-bhajane pravṛttiḥ*), it is necessary to judge which are the most effective. There are a large number of verses in the *Bhāgavatam*[1] that specifically mention a variety of devotional practices—hearing, chanting, and remembering—but in the final analysis, the chanting of the Holy Names is considered to be the most powerful. This is supported by the following text from the *Bhāgavatam*:

"Kirtana is defined as the audible recitation of Krishna's name, pastimes, and attributes. Of these, nama-kirtanam, chanting of the Holy Names, is supreme"

etan nirvidyamānānām
icchatām akuto-bhayam
yogināṁ nṛpa nirṇītaṁ
harer nāmānukīrtanam

> "O King, it has been ascertained that for those yogis who are indifferent to material pleasures and who desire complete fearlessness, the best path is constant chanting of the Holy Name of the Lord." (*Śrīmad Bhāgavatam* 2.1.11)

In the *Sārārtha-darśinī*, Viśvanātha gives the following extensive commentary:

"Śukadeva recites this verse in response to the following anticipated question: 'It is clear throughout the *Bhāgavatam* that devotion is the only process for attaining the Supreme. But does it specify any devotional practice which stands out above all others in the way that an emperor stands above his vassals?'

"According to the verse *tasmād bhārata* [*Śrīmad Bhāgavatam* 2.1.5] hearing, chanting, and remembering are the three primary aspects of devotional practice. Now this verse makes it clear that, of these three, chanting or *kīrtana,* is foremost. *Kīrtana* is defined as the audible recitation of Krishna's name, pastimes, attributes, etc. Of these, *nāma-kīrtanam*, chanting of the Holy Names, is supreme.

"In this verse, the word *anu-kīrtanam* is used. This can be interpreted in two ways: either as chanting those names of the Lord which correspond to one's own devotional mood, or simply as uninterrupted chanting of the Names. By saying 'it has been ascertained,' (*nirṇītam*) Śukadeva is not claiming personal authority, but that of the previous *ācāryas*. Thus there is no need to cite any other proofs.

"Śukadeva goes on to further describe the nature of the chanting of the Holy Name by saying *akuto-bhayam* ('complete fearlessness'). Not only is there no fear of considerations of purity of time and place, but no objection from the infidels (*mlecchas*) who normally object to deity worship and certain other aspects of devotional service.[2]

"Next, Śuka uses the word *nirvidyamānānām* ('indifferent') to indicate that there is no more beneficial activity for either those in the beginning stages of devotional service or those on the perfected stage. *Nirvidyamānānām* refers to those who are indifferent to all desires up to and including the desire for liberation. On the other hand, *icchatām* ('those who desire') indicates that all desires are fulfilled by chanting the Holy Name. As the saying goes, 'Go to the hub'; anyone who goes to the center can easily go in any direction; so too, the chanting of the Holy Name is like the root activity which leads to the fulfillment of all desires.

"Another understanding of this verse is that the chanting of the Holy Names is suitable for anyone; *nirvidyamānānām* refers to the exclusive devotees; *icchatāṁ* refers to all those who desire heavenly pleasures or liberation; while *yoginām* refers to the self-satisfied *ātmārāmas*. No matter who they are, the chanting of the Holy Name bestows on each of them the results they seek."[3]

Expertise is Desireless Devotion

This idea that expertise in devotion is measured by one's freedom from desire is supported by the *Bhāgavatam*, where it is said;

akāmaḥ sarva-kāmo vā
mokṣa-kāma udāra-dhīḥ
tīvreṇa bhakti-yogena
yajeta puruṣaṁ param

> "All people of expansive intelligence should worship the Supreme Person by the process of intense Bhakti yoga, whether they are pure devotees without any personal desire, or whether they are filled with all kinds of desires, or seek liberation."
> (*Śrīmad Bhāgavatam* 2.3.10)

In his commentary to this verse, Viśvanātha elaborates on some of the words used in it. "The words *udāra-dhī* mean 'truly intelligent.' In other words, the sign of true intelligence is to make the Supreme Lord the object of one's devotion, whether he has all kinds of material desires or no desires at all. The absence of such devotion is a sign of low intelligence. The word *tīvreṇa* ('intense') means unmixed by other activities such as *jñāna* or *karma*. Bhakti when unmixed in this way is intense in the way sunlight is in a cloudless sky."

"Those who do not possess expansive intelligence, the narrow-minded, are not able to take up intense devotional service"

Those who do not possess expansive intelligence, the narrow-minded, are not able to take up intense devotional service. However, because of the purifying nature of devotional service, it is also a sign of good intelligence to take up bhakti even if one isn't pure.

buddhimān-arthe yadi vicāra-jña haya
nija-kāma lāgiha tabe kṛṣṇere bhajaya
bhakti binu kona sādhana dite nāre phala
saba phala deya bhakti svatantra prabala
ajā-gala-stana-nyāya anya sādhana
ataeva hari bhaje buddhimān jana

"The meaning of 'intelligent' is to have good judgement. It is a sign of good judgement to engage in devotional service, even if one has desires for sense gratification or liberation. This is because no other processes can yield its promised results unless supplemented by bhakti. Bhakti, however, is so strong and independent that it can give all results on its own. Other practices are unable to independently yield their results any more than the nipples on the neck of a she-goat can give milk. Knowing this, an intelligent person worships Krishna exclusively." (*Chaitanya Charitāmṛta* 2.24.91-93)

"You Must be a Lakṣeśvara, a Millionaire!"

Deity of Mahaprabhu in Vrindavan

The next aspect of devotional expertise in chanting is in the amount that one chants. Whenever invited to dine, Mahāprabhu took the opportunity of revealing His desire to have His devotees chant the Holy Names. Upon being asked, He would laugh and say, "First become a *lakṣa-pati* or millionaire. I only eat at the houses of millionaires." When they heard this, the brahmins who had tendered the invitation became puzzled and worried. They made some remarks of praise and then one of them made this submission to the Lord: "Sir, none of us even has a thousand rupees to his name, what to speak of a lakh (hundred thousand) rupees. But if you don't accept my invitation, then my whole existence as a householder has been a waste and is better off going up in flames."

The Lord answered, "Do you know what I mean by a *lakṣa-pati*? I mean someone who chants a hundred thousand names of the Lord every single day. To Me, such a person is a true millionaire. I only take meals at the house of such a person and I never eat anywhere else."

When the brahmins heard the Lord's statement, they no longer worried. Indeed they became joyful. They said, "Thank you, Lord. We will chant a hundred thousand names every day. Please come and eat at our house. We are so fortunate that you teach us in this way."

"Devotion is life's real treasure. Anyone who possesses these riches is treated with respect in the society of devotees, even if he is materially poor"

So from that day on, all the brahmins chanted a lakh of names in the hope that the Lord would accept their invitation. The Lord of Vaikuṇṭha engaged people in the performance of Bhakti yoga while Himself relishing the ocean of devotion. Lord Śrī Krishna Chaitanya descended to this earth to preach Bhakti yoga; thus He never greeted anyone without inquiring about their spiritual progress." (*Chaitanya Bhāgavata* 3.9.116-127)

Here we see just how Mahāprabhu both practiced and taught the process of Bhakti yoga, chiefly as expressed through the chanting of the Holy Names. Mahāprabhu's avatar had this purpose. Other than devotion, He had no subject of inquiry—*bhakti vinā jijñāsā nā kare prabhu āra.*

prabhu bale je janera kṛṣṇa-bahkti āche
kuśala maṅgala tāra nitya thāke pāche

The Lord said, "Whoever has devotion for Krishna is followed everywhere by good fortune and happiness." (*Chaitanya Bhāgavata* 3.9.128)

One who is engaged in the practice of devotion has all good fortune. Without such devotion, even an emperor is unfortunate. Devotion is life's real treasure. Anyone who possesses these riches is treated with respect in the society of devotees, even if he is materially poor.

Our most worshipable spiritual master, Śrīla Bhaktisiddhānta Sarasvatī Prabhupāda, commented on the above verses as follows: "Lord Gaurasundara says that the Supreme Lord [in His deity form] is truly served in a home where someone chants 100,000 Names every single day. The Lord accepts the food offerings made to Him by such a devotee. However, the Lord does not bless a disciple by accepting his offerings if he does not chant a lakh of Names a day. Every single devotee must daily chant a lakh of Names; if he does not, then he will soon become attached to various sense objects and become incapable of serving the Lord. For this reason, everyone who has taken up residence at the Chaitanya Math makes it a rule to chant a lakh of Holy Names every day. If not, the deity of Gaurasundara will not accept the offerings made to Him." (*Gauḍīya-bhāṣya*, 3.9.121)

He further writes: "Chaitanya Mahāprabhu's followers do not converse with non-devotees. One should not make friendship with those who are engaged in talking about fruitive activities, philosophy, or other desires. Fallen conditioned souls, those who do not daily chant a lakh of *Harināma*, are affected by growing material desires. The presence of such desires results in an incapacity to serve Lord Gaurasundara. The standard in the Gauḍīya school of devotion is *lakṣeśvara*. The fallen, unable to accept this standard, engage in other kinds of practices in the name of *bhajana*. Such activities are all deception and of no real benefit to the practitioner."(*Gauḍīya-bhāṣya*, 3.9.127)

"Srila Bhaktivinoda Thakura had previously observed a vow of chanting a billion Holy Names (three complete years of chanting three lakh a day) and had given Srila Prabhupada the japa-mala with which he had performed this feat"

In the book *Sarasvatī-jaya-śrī*,[4] the following account is given of the example set by Śrīla Prabhupāda himself: "While living at Mayapura, Śrīla Prabhupāda took a vow to observe the strictest rules of austerity and to chant three lakh of *Harināma* every single day. Oṁ Vishnupāda Śrīla Bhaktivinoda Ṭhākura had previously observed a vow of chanting a billion Holy Names (three complete years of chanting three lakh a day) and had given Śrīla Prabhupāda the japa-mala with which he had performed this feat. Śrīla Prabhupāda used this mala to fulfill his own vow of chanting a billion names. Up to the present day, Śrīla Prabhupāda still uses this same japa-mala. Śrīla Prabhupāda did not approve of those who whimsically changed their japa beads."

Our worshipable Śrīla Prabhupāda set the example of concentrated devotional service in the same way that Mahāprabhu did, knowing that without teaching by example spreading these doctrines is impossible. We, who claim to be the servant of His servants, pray to Lord Gaurasundara and to all the spiritual masters who represent him (beginning with Śrī Svarūpa Dāmodara and Rūpa Gosvāmī), for nothing more than the ability to follow this example so that we too can become expert in the matter of worship; that is, chanting the Holy Name without offenses.

Expertise in Bhajana Means Offenseless Chanting

Mahāprabhu stated that the nine processes of devotional service have great power to bestow upon one love for Krishna. Of these nine, the chanting of the Holy Name is most powerful of all—but it must be chanted without offenses. Śrīla Bhaktivinoda Ṭhākura therefore states in his *Harināma-cintāmaṇi* that expertise in *bhajana* means chanting the Holy Name without offenses:

aparādha nāhi chāṛi nāma jadi laya
sahasra-sādhane tāra bhakti nāhi haya
jñāne mukti karme bhukti jñānī karmī jane
sudurlabhā kṛṣṇa bhakti nirmala sādhane
bhukti-mukti śukti-sama bhakti muktā-phala
jīvera mahimā bhakti-prāpti sunirmala
sādhane naipuṇya-yoge atyalpa sādhane
bhakti-latā prema-phala dena bhakta-jane
daśa aparādha chāṛi nāmera grahaṇa
ihāi naipuṇya haya sādhane bhajana

"If one's practice is done expertly, there is no necessity for engaging in great amounts of practice. The creeper of devotional service will grow and give the fruits of love to the devotee"

"If someone chants the Holy Name without giving up offenses, then he may perform outstanding feats of devotion without developing love for Krishna. The fruitive workers and monist philosophers seek sense gratification and liberation. Devotion to Krishna is only attainable through engagement in pure devotional practices and is thus very rare. Sense gratification and liberation are like the mother of pearl which is worthless, while bhakti is a pearl, a jewel of great value.

"The glory of the living entity comes from the attainment of pure devotion. If one's practice is done expertly, there is no necessity in engaging in great amounts of practice. The creeper of devotional service will grow and give the fruits of love to the devotee. So give up the ten offenses and chant the Holy Name. This is the expertise which gives power to your devotional practice." (*Hari-nāma-cintāmaṇi*, 13)

Krishnadāsa Kavirāja Gosvāmī also states in the *Chaitanya Charitāmṛta* that, if one commits offenses, one may chant the Holy Name or listen to Krishna *kathā* for many lifetimes without obtaining the result of pure devotional service.

bahu janma kare jadi śravaṇa kīrtana
tabu ta nā pāya kṛṣṇa-pade prema-dhana

Śrīla Bhaktivinoda Ṭhākura comments on this verse in the following way: "A person who commits the ten types of offenses to the Holy Name may hear and chant for many lifetimes without attaining love for Krishna."(*Amṛta-pravāha-bhāṣya* 1.8.16)

Śrīla Prabhupāda elaborates: "One who engages in hearing and chanting without taking shelter of Lord Gaurasundara Mahāprabhu may do so for many lifetimes without achieving the treasure of love for Krishna. Those who follow Mahāprabhu's instruction to chant while thinking themselves lower than the straw in the street, as tolerant as a tree, with a respectful and modest attitude towards others, quickly become free of the ten offenses and attain their reward of ecstatic love."

kṛṣṇa-nāma kare aparādhera vicāra
kṛṣṇa balile aparādhīra nā haya vikāra

"One must take offenses into consideration when chanting the holy name of Krishna. Therefore one who commits offenses does not experience ecstatic transformations even while chanting." (*Chaitanya Charitāmṛta* 1.8.24)

The Ten Offenses to the Holy Name

In his *Anubhāṣya* to the above verse, Śrīla Prabhupāda quotes the following verses from the *Padma Purana,* summarizing the ten offenses to the Holy Name.

satāṁ nindā nāmnaḥ paramam
aparādhaṁ vitanute
yataḥ khyātiṁ yātaṁ katham u
sahate tad-vigarhām

(1) The first and greatest offense is to blaspheme devotees who, through their attachment to the Holy Name, spread its glories throughout the world. How will the Lord who is manifest in the Holy Name ever tolerate such blasphemous activities?

śivasya śrī-viṣṇor ya iha
guṇa-nāmādi-sakalaṁ
dhiyā bhinnaṁ paśyet sa khalu
hari-nāmāhita-karaḥ

(2) Anyone who considers the all-auspicious name, form, qualities, and pastimes of Lord Vishnu to to be distinct from His person in the way that material signifiers are different from the signified object, is acting in a way displeasing to the Holy Name.

Anyone who considers demigods such as Lord Shiva to be independent, or nondifferent from Lord Vishnu, thinking such demigods' names, qualities, forms or pastimes to be equal to Vishnu's, is committing the second offense to the Holy Name.

"One who engages in hearing and chanting without taking shelter of Lord Gaurasundara Mahaprabhu may do so for many lifetimes without achieving the treasure of love for Krishna"

guror avajñā śruti-śāstra-nindanam
tathārtha-vādo hari-nāmni kalpanam

(3) The third offense, called *guror avajñā,* is to consider the spiritual master, who knows the truth of the Holy Name, to be an ordinary man of the world and so to be envious of him.

(4) The fourth offense (*śruti-śāstra-nindā*) is to blaspheme the scriptures such as the Vedas and the Vaishnava Puraṇas.

(5) The fifth offense (*artha-vāda*) is to consider the glory of the Holy Name an exaggeration.

(6) The sixth offense is to consider the glories of the holy name of the Lord to be imaginary.

nāmno balād yasya hi pāpa-buddhir
na vidyate tasya yamair hi śuddhiḥ

(7) One who thinks that he may commit sins on the strength of the Hare Krishna mantra's power to overcome all sinful reactions is such a great offender that he cannot be purified by any amount of regulative activities, meditation, withdrawal of the senses from their objects, concentration, or other yoga practices.

dharma-vrata-tyāga-hutādi-sarva-
śubha-kriyā-sāmyam api pramādaḥ

(8) The eighth offense is to erroneously think that chanting the Holy Name is in any way equal to other kinds of religious activity, vow of renunciation, sacrificial ritual or auspicious mundane performance.

aśraddadhāne vimukhe 'py aśṛṇvati
yaś copadeśaḥ śiva-nāmāparādhaḥ

(9) The ninth offense is to preach the glories of the most auspicious Holy Name to someone who has no faith, who is uninterested, or who is not listening.

śrute 'pi nāma-māhātmye
yaḥ prīti-rahito naraḥ
ahaṁ-mamādi-paramo
nāmni so 'py aparādha-kṛt

(10) One who has heard the glories of the Lord's holy name but develops no appreciation for it and continues to be absorbed in thinking of himself and his possessions is also an offender to the Holy Name.

"To worship Mahaprabhu, the combined form of Radha and Krishna, means to accept His leadership and that of His intimate associates like Svarupa Damodara and the six Gosvamis"

THE MERCIFUL NAMES OF GAURA-NITĀI

In chanting the holy name of Krishna, there is therefore, a consideration of offenses. An offender may chant lakhs and lakhs of Names without ever achieving the fruit of the chanting, the wealth of ecstatic love. Different rules apply, however, to the chanting of the names of Gaura-Nitāi:

caitanya-nityānande nāhi e-saba vicāra
nāma laite prema dena bahe aśrudhāra

"But all these considerations do not exist in the chanting of the names of Lord Chaitanya and Nityānanda. As soon as anyone chants their names, he is awarded the ecstasies of love, and tears flow from his eyes."
(*Chaitanya Charitāmṛta* 1.8.31)

The *Prākṛta-sahajiyā* school of Tāntrikas interpret this verse in an unauthorized way. They think that they can commit offenses on the strength of this statement without any attempt at restraint. The fact is that the founders of the *saṅkīrtana* movement, Lord

Chaitanya and Nityānanda, would never tolerate any offensive behavior. They possess unlimited qualities, foremost among which are Their generosity and munificence. A living being, even if still in a state of contamination, will be purified by taking shelter of them. By Their mercy, one will understand the nature of Their divine form and expansions. Gradually, They mercifully teach expertise in chanting by freeing one from the offenses to the Holy Name. This leads to the experience of love of God.

"To chant this Maha-mantra without offenses demonstrates real expertise in the worship of the Lord"

Śrīla Prabhupāda explains further, "Krishna's name and Gaura's name are both identical with the person they signify. If after reading the above discussion one thinks the name of Krishna less powerful or limited, then he should be recognized as suffering the effects of ignorance. Nevertheless, in terms of attaining the ultimate goal of life, the names of Gaura-Nitāi have a greater benefit for the conditioned soul. Gaura-Nityānanda are magnanimous, and within this magnanimity sweetness can be found. Krishna's magnanimity is felt only by the liberated, the perfected, and surrendered souls. By contrast, the flood of Gaura-Nityānanda's compassion flows even over those who are contaminated by materialistic desires and offenses, delivering them from these contaminants. Such persons can then attain to Krishna's lotus feet."

Samadhi of Sri Raghunath dasa Goswami

This does not mean, however, that one abandons the worship of Radha and Krishna to exclusively worship Mahāprabhu. Such is not the meaning of worshiping Mahāprabhu. To worship Mahāprabhu, the combined form of Radha and Krishna, means to accept his leadership and that of His intimate associates like Svarūpa Dāmodara, the Gosvāmīs (Rūpa, Raghunātha) and others. Rāmānanda Rāya revealed Mahāprabhu's desire:

śreṣṭha upāsya yugala rādhā-kṛṣṇa nāma

> "The best of all objects of worship is the Divine Couple named Radha and Krishna." (*Chaitanya Charitāmṛta* 2.8.256)

Read otherwise, this can be understood to mean, "The best of all objects of worship are the names of the Divine Couple, Radha and Krishna, in other words, the Hare Krishna *Mahā-mantra.*" To chant this *Mahā-mantra* without offenses demonstrates real expertise in the worship of the Lord.

Chapter XI

Listening to the Bhagavata

The word *maṭha* includes the ideas of a student hostel, an educational establishment, and a temple, or place of worship. The Sanskrit verb root *maṭh* means "to dwell, to reside." Thus, the word is defined in the following way: *maṭhanti vasanti yatra paramārtha-śikṣārthinaḥ*—"A *maṭha* is a place where those desiring to learn about the ultimate spiritual truth reside." Though the presence of a deity and temple is also implied in the term, the *maṭha*'s primary purpose is the dissemination of knowledge of the categories of *sambandha, abhidheya* and *prayojana* to those who serve that deity. There is furthermore an implied obligation to distribute this knowledge to those living outside the *maṭha*'s confines, for their welfare.

Through contact with the tiny spiritual spark, the mind and intelligence maintain a semblance of consciousness. The eternal function of this spiritual spark or soul is to be attracted to the all-attractive, infinite consciousness of the Supreme Soul. On the other hand, the eternal function of the all-attractive Supreme Soul is to pull all the infinitesimal individual souls towards Him and to give them a place at His feet where they can get a taste of everlasting, infinite, supreme joy. Though the *jīva*, the spiritual spark, is eternal, until it comes into contact with the eternal, infinite and supremely joyful substance it will never find satisfaction in the passing pleasures derived from limited and temporary substances.

The word *kṛṣi* refers to the all-attractive state of being, while *ṇa* means the supreme bliss. When these two are combined, one gets the name of the Supreme Brahman, Krishna. Out of His affection for His lost eternal servants, Krishna calls out to them anxiously like a cow who has lost her calf. He cries out, *mām ekaṁ śaraṇaṁ vraja*—"Take shelter of Me alone." Unfortunately, however, the living beings are so enthralled by the Lord's external energy that they pay Him no notice. They do not know that there is no other way of overcoming the powerful enchantments of maya other than by surrendering to Him. As Krishna Himself says in the *Gītā* (7.14):

daivī hy eṣā guṇamayī
mama māyā duratyayā
mām eva ye prapadyante
māyām etāṁ taranti te

"There is a great and unavoidable need for places like mathas where those who have taken up an exemplary lifestyle devoted to the Supreme Lord can live, associate, and study the divine knowledge of devotional service"

"The external energy consisting of the three qualities is divinely empowered and thus impossible to conquer. Whoever surrenders to Me, however, can cross over this maya."

The eternal constitutional position of the spirit soul is service to the Lord. Because he has forgotten this service, he now has to be buffeted by all kinds of distresses and evils in this world of matter. A life bereft of service offers no hope for true satisfaction. Despite the great treasure of love for Krishna, the *jīva* whose vision is obscured by ignorance pursues so many inferior, meaningless, worthless affairs, all of which are temporary and lifeless. Rather than discovering friendship with other living beings, he becomes entangled in competitive and envious relationships with them.

Having fallen into the blind well of ignorance, the *jīvas* fail to recognize that their only real welfare lies with the Supreme Lord. In competition for the objects which they falsely think are beneficial to them, they create terrible tragedies such as wars which threaten to engulf the entire world like great blazing fires. The fire which leads to the universal destruction, Durjayaliṅga, results from Rudra's anger upon seeing the general indifference of humanity to the service of the Lord.

Hearing the Bhagavatam from the Lord's dear devotees

The meaning of ignorance is lack of knowledge about that entity from whom we have come, by whose mercy our existence is maintained, and in whom we will have our final and supreme resting place after the destruction of this body. This ignorance (*ajñāna,* or *avidyā*) is the source of all our troubles. It is by the higher knowledge of devotion to Krishna that such ignorance is to be overcome. The *Bhāgavatam* says: *sā vidyā tan-matir yayā,* "That alone is knowledge by which one's mind becomes fixed on Him." Therefore, we must acknowledge the great and unavoidable necessity for *maṭhas* where those who have taken up an exemplary lifestyle devoted to the Supreme Lord can live, associate, and study the divine knowledge of devotional service.

THE AUTHORITY OF THE BHĀGAVATAM

Since the mind and body are composed of dull and temporary matter, their nature, or essential activities, are similarly temporary. By contrast, the soul is eternal and spiritual and its nature, or essential activities, are similarly eternal. The essential activity, or *dharma,* of the soul has been established by the Supreme Lord Himself. None of the gods, seers, *siddhas*, demons, humans, Yakṣas, Rākṣasas, Gandharvas, Kinnaras, Vidyādharas, or Cāraṇas know the inner secret of this natural function of the soul. It is a mystery which has been mercifully revealed by the Lord only to Brahmā, Nārada, Śambhu, the four Kumāras, Lord Kapiladeva, Svāyambhuva Manu, Prahlāda, Janaka, Bhīṣma, Bali, Śukadeva, and Yamarāja. These twelve *mahājanas*, or great authorities, thus know the most secret, pure, and inscrutable *Bhāgavata-dharma.* Despite the inaccessibility of this divine knowledge, one can get a taste of it through the mercy of these devotees and the

Lord Himself. To be able to relish this divine nectar is certainly a matter of great fortune.

The natural activity of the soul, or *Bhāgavata-dharma*, is identical with the yoga of devotion, which consists primarily of *harināma-saṅkīrtana*. This activity has been identified in all the scriptures as the supreme religion of for all beings. One should look particularly at the story of Ajāmila in the sixth canto of the *Bhāgavatam*, where this has been described in full.

The Supreme Lord lies beyond the purview of the material senses. He is thus known as Adhokṣaja. The supreme religion is causeless devotion to Him. Such devotion should be free from any ulterior motive such as personal sense enjoyment, liberation or mystical perfections, and uninterrupted by other types of activities such as *karma* and *jñāna*. This is also stated in the first canto, second chapter of the *Śrīmad Bhāgavatam*.

"The mahajanas are great devotees in whom the Bhagavatam's teachings are incarnate"

When Dharmarāja disguised himself as a heron and asked questions of Yudhiṣṭhira, one of the questions was about the truth of religion. The eldest Pāṇḍava responded:

dharmasya tattvaṁ nihitaṁ guhāyāṁ
mahā-jano yena gataḥ sa panthāḥ

> "It is very difficult to understand the secret of religion, but one who follows in the footsteps of the great authorities, or *mahājanas*, will be successful."
> (*Mahābhārata, Vana-parva* 313.117)

The *mahājanas* are great devotees in whom the *Bhāgavatam*'s teachings are incarnate. Thus anyone who wishes to understand the doctrines of the *Bhāgavata* religion must absolutely follow in the footsteps of those great authorities like Śuka and Vyāsa. The father of the creation, Brahmā, received the essential *Bhāgavata* doctrines in a condensed form of four essential verses directly from the Lord Himself. The seer of the gods, Nārada, subsequently heard it from him. Vyāsadeva then heard the *Bhāgavata* from Nārada Muni. Śukadeva received the teachings from Vyāsa and Parīkṣit from Śuka. Ugraśravā Sūta listened to the *Bhāgavatam* as it was spoken by Śuka to Parīkṣit and then went on to recount the entire *Purana* to the sages at Naimiṣāraṇya led by Śaunaka. From this history we can note the dissemination of the *Bhāgavatam*'s teachings.

In our age, the golden avatar and purifier of the Kali Yuga, Gaurahari, and His associates accepted the *Bhāgavatam* as the king of all literature, the best of all scriptures, and the genuine commentary on the Vedanta. Mahāprabhu thus called the *Bhāgavatam* the most authoritative source of knowledge about the Supreme Brahman. In view of this, it is evidently the duty of those who live in the *maṭha* to study and teach this great scripture.

Hearing the Bhāgavatam is a Devotional Activity

The *Bhāgavatam* discards all false or incomplete understandings of religion. Therefore, the *Bhāgavata* itself states:

śrīmad-bhāgavataṁ purāṇam amalaṁ yad vaiṣṇavānāṁ priyaṁ
yasmin pāramahaṁsyam ekam amalaṁ jñānaṁ paraṁ gīyate
tatra jñāna-virāga-bhakti-sahitaṁ naiṣkarmyam āviṣkṛtaṁ
tac chṛṇvan supaṭhan vicāraṇa-paro bhaktyā vimucyen naraḥ

"The beautiful *Bhāgavatam* is the spotless Purana, the scripture most dear to the Vaishnavas. The supreme knowledge which is the unique wealth of the *paramahaṁsas* is glorified therein. One who reads it will discover the liberation which comes from knowledge, renunciation, and devotion. A human being who hears and studies the *Bhāgavatam* and then discusses and meditates on what he has heard and studied will, by this devotional act alone, be liberated." (*Śrīmad Bhāgavatam* 12.13.18)

Narada Muni

Of course, it should be understood that the *Bhāgavatam* reveals more than just the means for attaining liberation; it also shows how to attain the ultimate liberated platform of *prema-bhakti*.

The Bhāgavatam—Commentary on Gayatri and Vedanta

When discussing the devotional act of hearing, Jīva Gosvāmī indicates that its topmost manifestation comes from listening to the *Śrīmad Bhāgavatam* as spoken by Śuka, and realized by Vyāsa in the highest reaches of his trance, and as transmitted by Śaunaka to the 60,000 seers at Naimiṣāraṇya. In his *Tattva-sandarbha,* Jīva quotes the *Garuḍa Purana,* which calls the *Bhāgavata* "the meaning of the *Vedanta Sutra*, the explanation of the purpose of the *Mahābhārata*, a commentary on the Gayatri Mantra, and an elaboration of the Vedas themselves."

artho'yaṁ brahma-sūtrāṇāṁ
bhāratārtha-vinirṇayaḥ
gāyatrī-bhāṣya-rūpo'sau
vedārtha-paribṛṁhitaḥ

"The seed of the desire tree of the Vedic literature is the syllable om, also known as pranava"

In the twenty-fifth chapter of the *Madhya-līlā* in the *Chaitanya Charitāmṛta*, Prakāśānanda Sarasvatī asked to hear the primary purport of the Vedanta from the Lord. Mahāprabhu elaborated on the glories of the *Bhāgavatam*, reiterating that the *Bhāgavatam* is the natural commentary on the *Vedanta Sutras*.

The seed of the desire tree of the Vedic literature is the syllable om, also known as *praṇava*. This seed germinates and becomes a seedling, the Gayatri Mantra, which is called the Mother of the Veda and is said to explain the *praṇava*. The fruit of the Vedic desire tree is the *Bhāgavatam* in its compact form of four verses—the *Catuḥślokī Bhāgavatam*. This essential *Bhāgavatam* was taught to Brahmā by the Supreme Lord Himself. Brahmā then expanded on these few verses and taught it to his son Nārada. Nārada again repeated the same teaching to Vyāsa, who upon hearing it, realized:

ei artha āmāra sūtrera vyākhyānurūpa
bhāgavata kariba sūtrera bhāṣya-svarūpa

"This teaching is an explanation of the sutras that I have written. I shall now write the *Bhāgavatam* on the basis of this teaching and that will be my own full commentary on the *Brahma Sutra*." (*Chaitanya Charitāmṛta* 2.25.95)

According to this statement, it is clear that the *Bhāgavata* is the crowning glory of the Vedic literature. Krishna Dvaipāyana Vyāsa churned all the *Upanishads* to extract the cream of its knowledge and then composed the *Śrīmad Bhāgavatam* as the only commentary which is true to the word of the *Vedanta Sutras*. This means that the knowledge of *sambandha, abhidheya* and *prayojana* that is found throughout the Vedic literature is summarized in essence in the four verses of the *Catuḥślokī Bhāgavatam* and expanded on in greater detail throughout the 18,000 verses of the *Śrīmad Bhāgavatam*.

There are 11 principal *Upanishads: Īśa, Kena, Kaṭha, Praśna, Muṇḍaka, Māṇḍūkya, Aittareya, Taittarīya, Chāndogya, Bṛhadāraṇyaka* and *Śvetāśvatara*. Vyāsa based the *Vedanta Sutras* on the essential teachings found in these texts. Many of the verses of the *Upanishads* are directly explained in the *Bhāgavatam*, such as the *Īśopaniṣad* verse (*īśāvāsyam idaṁ sarvam*), which is elaborated on at *Śrīmad Bhāgavatam* 8.1.10. The very first verse of the *Śrīmad Bhāgavatam* explains the first sutra of the Vedanta, *janmādy asya yataḥ*. That same verse also includes an explanation of the Gayatri Mantra. Thus Mahāprabhu states:

> "Krishna Dvaipayana Vyasa churned all the Upanishads to extract the cream of its knowledge and then composed the Srimad Bhagavatam as the only commentary which is true to the word of the Vedanta Sutras"

gāyatrīra arthe ei grantha-ārambhana
satyaṁ paraṁ sambandha dhīmahi sādhana-prayojana

> "The first verse of this book gives an explanation of the Gayatri Mantra. The *sambandha-tattva* is hinted at in the words *satyaṁ paraṁ* ('the supreme truth') and the word *dhīmahi* ('we meditate upon') indicates the *abhidheya* of devotional practice and the *prayojana*, love for Krishna."
> (*Chaitanya Charitāmṛta* 2.25.140)

In his *Anubhāṣya* to this verse, our most worshipable spiritual master Prabhupāda Bhaktisiddhānta Sarasvatī Ṭhākura elucidates as follows: "The very first verse of the *Bhāgavatam* is an explanation of the Gayatri Mantra. The supreme truth refers to the *sambandha*. The effort to meditate is an indication of the practice of devotional service, which is the *abhidheya*. That which is achieved by the practice of devotional service, the *prayojana*, is perfected meditation, or *prema-bhakti*."

Krishnadāsa Kavirāja Gosvāmī also confirms that the *Mahābhārata* and its explanation, the *Śrīmad Bhāgavatam* are the two primary scriptures in this age. These two scriptures state that the Lord appears as an avatar in the Age of Kali. This is his conclusion:

bhāgavata-bhārata dui śāstrera pradhāna
sei dui kahe kalite sākṣāt-avatāra

> "*Śrīmad Bhāgavatam* and the *Mahābhārata* are the two most important Vedic scriptures, and both reveal that the Lord appears Himself as an incarnation in the Age of Kali." (*Chaitanya Charitāmṛta* 2.6.97-8)

MAHĀPRABHU'S TEACHINGS ABOUT THE BHĀGAVATAM

Krishnadāsa Kavirāja Gosvāmī summarizes the personal teachings of Śrī Chaitanya Mahāprabhu as follows:

kṛṣṇa-tattva bhakti-tattva prema-tattva sāra
bhāva-tattva rasa-tattva līlā-tattva āra
śrī-bhāgavata-tattva-rasa karilā pracāre
kṛṣṇa-tulya bhāgavata jānāilā saṁsāre

"Śrī Chaitanya Mahāprabhu personally preached Krishna's doctrines, devotional service, love of Godhead, emotional ecstasy, sacred rapture, and the Lord's pastimes. All these nectarean doctrines are found in the *Śrīmad Bhāgavatam*. Thus Mahāprabhu taught the entire world that the *Śrīmad Bhāgavatam* and the Supreme Lord Śrī Krishna are identical." (*Chaitanya Charitāmṛta* 2.25.258-9)

The Lord also mentions the *Bhāgavatam* when He lists the 64 kinds of devotional service in practice. There, the idea of serving things which are related to the Lord (*tadīya*) is explained as follows:

"Mahaprabhu taught the entire world that the Srimad Bhagavatam and the Supreme Lord Sri Krishna are identical"

tadīya tulasī vaiṣṇava mathurā bhāgavata
ei cārira sevā haya kṛṣṇera abhimata

"'Things related to the Lord' include the *tulasī* plant, Krishna's devotees, His abode in Mathurā, and the *Śrīmad Bhāgavatam*. Krishna is very eager to see everyone render the appropriate service to these four."
(*Chaitanya Charitāmṛta* 2.22.121)

Hearing the *Śrīmad Bhāgavatam* is also included among the five principal acts of devotional service.

sādhu-saṅga nāma-kīrtana bhāgavata-śravaṇa
mathurā-vāsa śrī-mūrtira śraddhāya sevana
sakala-sādhana-śreṣṭha ei pañca aṅga
kṛṣṇa-prema janmāya ei pāṅcera alpa saṅga
eka aṅga sādhe keha sādhe bahu aṅga
niṣṭhā haile upajaya premera taraṅga

"One should associate with devotees, chant the holy name of the Lord, hear *Śrīmad Bhāgavatam*, reside at Mathurā, and worship the deity with faith and veneration. These five limbs of devotional service are the best of all. Even a slight performance of these five awakens love for Krishna. Whether a person executes only one or many of these processes of devotional service, the waves of love of Godhead will well up as a result of his fixed determination, or *niṣṭhā*."
(*Chaitanya Charitāmṛta* 2.22.214-5, 219)

After hearing Śrī Chaitanya explain the *ātmārāma* verse from the *Bhāgavatam* in 61 different ways, Sanātana was so amazed that he fell at the Lord's feet and began to praise Him as follows:

sākṣāt īśvara tumi vrajendra-nandana
tomāra niśvāse sarva-veda-pravartana
tumi vaktā bhāgavatera tumi jāna artha
tomā vinā anya jānite nāhika samartha

"My dear Lord, You are the Supreme Lord Krishna Himself, the son of Mahārāja Nanda. All the Vedic literatures are manifested with Your exhalation. You are the original speaker of the *Śrīmad Bhāgavatam* and You alone know its true meaning. Other than You, no one can grasp it completely."
(*Chaitanya Charitāmṛta* 2.24.309-310)

To this, Mahāprabhu answered,

prabhu kahe kene kara āmāra stavana
bhāgavatera svarūpa kene nā kara vicāraṇa
kṛṣṇa-tulya bhāgavata vibhu sarvāśraya
prati-śloke prati-akṣare nānā artha kaya
praśnottare bhāgavate kariyāche nirdhāra
jāṅhāra śravaṇe loke lāge camatkāra

"Why are you glorifying Me? Why do you not try to understand the transcendental position of the *Śrīmad Bhāgavatam*? Like Krishna, *Śrīmad Bhāgavatam* is the infinite shelter of everything. There are multiple meanings in each and every verse, in each and every syllable of this scripture. The *Śrīmad Bhāgavatam* establishes its conclusions in the form of questions and answers and those who hear them are amazed." (*Chaitanya Charitāmṛta* 2.24.311-313)

Mahāprabhu's Devotees' Love for the Bhāgavatam

Mahāprabhu's associates also showed great affection for the *Bhāgavatam*. Even before leaving his position in Shāh Hussain's court to join Mahāprabhu, Śrīla Sanātana Gosvāmī stayed at home and took up the study of the *Bhāgavatam* in the company of 20 or 30 scholars.

lobhī kāyastha-gaṇa rāja-kārya kare
āpane sva-gṛhe kare śāstrera vicāre
bhaṭṭācārya paṇḍita biśa triśa lañā
bhāgavata vicāra karena sabhāte vasiyā

"While he himself remained at home and discussed revealed scriptures, Sanātana's ambitious clerical and secretarial staff performed all of his government duties. In the meantime, he called together an assembly of 20 or 30 learned brahmin scholars and discussed the *Bhāgavatam* with them."
(*Chaitanya Charitāmṛta* 2.19.16-17)

"You must study the Srimad Bhagavatam and constantly chant Krishna's names. If you do so, Lord Krishna will very soon bestow his mercy upon you"

Mahāprabhu's dear associate, Raghunātha Bhaṭṭa, had a great reputation as a speaker on the *Bhāgavatam*. When in Purī, the Lord told him:

āmāra ājñāya raghunātha jāha vṛndāvane
tāhāṅ jāñā raha rūpa-sanātana-sthāne
bhāgavata paṛa sadā laha kṛṣṇa-nāma
acire karibena kṛpā kṛṣṇa bhagavān"

"My dear Raghunātha, follow My instructions and go to Vrindavan. Once there, place yourself under the care of Rūpa and Sanātana Gosvāmīs. You must study the *Śrīmad Bhāgavatam* and constantly chant Krishna's names. If you do so, Lord Krishna will very soon bestow His mercy upon you."
(*Chaitanya Charitāmṛta* 2.14.120-1)

prabhura ṭhāñi ājñā lañā gelā vṛndāvane
āśraya karilā āsi rūpa-sanātane

rūpa-gosāñira sabhāya karena bhāgavata-paṭhana
bhāgavata parite preme āulāya tāṅra mana

"Raghunātha Bhaṭṭa then took permission from Śrī Chaitanya Mahāprabhu and departed for Vrindavan. When he arrived there, he took shelter of Rūpa and Sanātana Gosvāmīs. Whenever Raghunātha Bhaṭṭa recited *Śrīmad Bhāgavatam* and gave discourses on it in Rūpa and Sanātana's assembly, he would be overwhelmed with ecstatic love for Krishna."

(*Chaitanya Charitāmṛta* 2.14.125-6)

Hear the Bhāgavatam in the Association of Devotees

Saraswati, goddess of learning

Rūpa Gosvāmī also writes in his *Bhakti-rasāmṛta-sindhu* that one should relish the topics of the *Śrīmad Bhāgavatam* in the association of *rasikas—śrīmad-bhāgavatārthānām āsvādo rasikaiḥ saha* (*Bhakti-rasāmṛta-sindhu* 1.2.91). By this, Rūpa means that one should seek the company of devotees who know the transcendental meaning of the *Bhāgavatam*, who understand pure devotional mellows and who are expert in the art of rendering devotional service. They should have the same kinds of aspirations as oneself and should preferably be more advanced than oneself. It is in the association of such people that one can relish the *Śrīmad Bhāgavatam*.

On the other hand, the deeper meaning of the *Bhāgavatam* will not be understood if one studies it in the company of well-educated persons who have no interest in the devotional path, even though they may be expert in grammar or etymology, or connoisseurs of mundane poetry and literature. If they are attached to the company of women or absorbed in their mundane household affairs, so much the worse. Other types of persons from whom one should not hear the *Bhāgavatam* are impersonalists who reject the eternal character of service to the Lord and His devotees, offenders to the Holy Name, people who use the trappings of the renounced life to make a living, or those who are professional distributors of mantra initiation. One cannot learn the inner meaning of the scripture meant for *paramahaṁsas* on the highest platform of spiritual realization by approaching those who make a living by reciting the *Bhāgavatam* while seeking the gratification of their material senses and remaining attached to mundane sense objects.

None of the above-mentioned persons has any qualification to comprehend the purport of that great scripture. The *Śrutis* and *Śmṛtis* have given their verdict on how this comprehension can be achieved:

yasya deve parā bhaktir
yathā deve tathā gurau
tasyaite kathitā hy arthāḥ
prakāśante mahātmanaḥ

"Only unto those great souls who have implicit faith in both the Lord and the spiritual master, who is the Lord's manifestation and not different from him, are all the imports of Vedic knowledge automatically revealed."

(*Śvetāśvatara Upanishad* 6.23)

In other words, only such a person be revealed a deeper understanding of the scriptures such as the *Śrīmad Bhāgavatam*.

bhaktyā bhāgavataṁ grāhyaṁ
na buddhyā na ca ṭīkayā.

"A person can understand the *Śrīmad Bhāgavatam* through devotion; not simply by exercising his intelligence, or simply through studying the commentaries." (*Chaitanya Charitāmṛta* 2.24.314)

Vrindavan dāsa Ṭhākura has also written:

bhāgavata bujhi hena jāra āche jñāna
se nā jāne kabhu bhāgavatera pramāṇa

"Anyone who thinks that he has understood the meaning of the *Śrīmad Bhāgavatam* will never truly be able to know its significance." (*Chaitanya Bhāgavata* 2.21.24)

Without single-minded commitment to the pleasure of the Supreme Lord Krishna and His devotees, it is indeed impossible to understand the meaning of the *Bhāgavatam* through mundane scholarship or simply by mental gymnastics. And even if one should understand something, to bring this understanding to fruition would be impossible without faithful and determined chanting of the Holy Names, purely and without offenses, following in the footsteps of the spiritual master and other exemplary devotees. When one develops a taste for the Holy Name, his study of the *Bhāgavatam* bears fruit. Anyone who studies the *Bhāgavatam* with a view to showing off his brilliance and learning, or to make a comfortable living, or to gain wealth, fame or status, is simply wasting his valuable time.

"Anyone who thinks that he has understood the meaning of the Srimad Bhagavatam will never truly be able to know its significance"

Thus Svarūpa Dāmodara Gosvāmī advised the brahmin from East Bengal:

jāha bhāgavata paṛa vaiṣṇavera sthāne
ekānta āśraya kara caitanya-caraṇe
caitanyera bhakta-gaṇera nitya kara saṅga
tabe ta jānibā siddhānta-samudra-taraṅga

"Go and study the *Bhāgavatam* with a Vaishnava. Take exclusive shelter of Chaitanya Mahāprabhu's lotus feet. Always associate with Chaitanya Mahāprabhu's devotees. If you do all these things, you will be able to plunge into the ocean of His divine teachings." (*Chaitanya Charitāmṛta* 3.5.131-32)

The Importance of Siddhānta

Someone may object that there is no need of studying scriptures in order to establish the correct spiritual doctrine, that simply engaging in devotional service itself is sufficient to attain perfection. Krishnadāsa Kavirāja Gosvāmī responds to this possible objection by saying that through a correct understanding of doctrine one's taste for rendering service increases:

siddhānta baliyā citte nā kara alasa
ihā ha-ite kṛṣṇe lāge sudṛḍha mānasa

caitanya-mahimā jāni e saba siddhānte
citta dṛḍha hañā lāge mahimā-jñāna haite

"Do not be lazy and avoid discussing these doctrines, for such discussions strengthen the mind's attachment to Śrī Krishna. I know Śrī Chaitanya's glories through my study of all these teachings and have become strong and fixed in attachment to Him through the knowledge of His greatness."
(*Chaitanya Charitāmṛta* 1.2.117-8)

"When one develops a taste for the Holy Name, his study of the Bhagavatam bears fruit"

Svarūpa Dāmodara also said:

rasābhāsa haya jadi siddhānta-virodha
sahite nā pāre prabhu mane haya krodha

"If any statement contains perverted reflections of the transcendental aesthetic or goes against the doctrines of the *Bhāgavatam*, Mahāprabhu finds it intolerable and becomes angry." (*Chaitanya Charitāmṛta* 3.5.97)

The Six Goswamis

jadbā-tadbā kavira vākye haya rasābhāsa
siddhānta-viruddha śunite nā haya ullāsa
rasa rasābhāsa jāra nāhika vicāra
bhakti-siddhānta-sindhu nāhi pāya pāra

"Some poets think they can write anything that pleases them. In their writings there is usually an incorrect presentation of the divine loving relationships. There is no pleasure in hearing words which are contrary to the scriptural conclusions. Anyone who cannot distinguish between the genuine sacred aesthetic and its reflection will never be able to cross the ocean of scriptural conclusions which lead to devotional service." (*Chaitanya Charitāmṛta* 3.5.102-3)

Only Listening to the Bhāgavatam with Full Attention Will Produce Results

Even after an aspirant to spiritual life has attained the company of devotees and hears the *Bhāgavatam* in their association, he must still be careful to hear it in the proper manner. Otherwise he will not get the full result of this powerful devotional activity.

The instructive tale of Gokarṇa is found in the section of *Padma Purana* known as "The Glories of the *Śrīmad Bhāgavatam*" (*Bhāgavata-māhātmya*). Gokarṇa was the adopted son of the brahmin Ātmadeva and his wife Dhundhulī. Dhundhulī and her husband also raised her sister's child Dhundhukārī, who unfortunately was very wicked. Because of his sinful life, when Dhundhukārī died he became a ghost and haunted his family's village. Out of compassion for his stepbrother, Gokarṇa recited the entire 12 cantos of the *Bhāgavatam* over a period of seven days and, when it was over, Dhundhukārī was liberated from his ghostly body. Where he had previously been invisible, he suddenly appeared before the entire assembly of devotees in a wonderful form, described in the *Bhāgavata-māhātmya* as follows:

divya-rūpa-dharo jātas tulasī-dāma-maṇḍitaḥ
pītavāsā ghana-śyāmo mukuṭī kuṇḍalānvitaḥ

"Dhundhukārī manifested before them in a marvellous, beautiful deep blue-colored form, garlanded with *tulasī* leaves and wearing a yellow cloth, a jewelled crown, and earrings." (*Bhāgavata-māhātmya* 5.51)

Dhundhukārī prostrated himself before his stepbrother and thanked him sincerely for having recited the entire *Bhāgavatam* for his benefit. As he was himself energetically glorifying the seven-day recital of the *Bhāgavatam*, a marvellous celestial carriage, attended by residents of the Vaikuṇṭha world, descended into the midst of the assembly, brightening the surroundings with their effulgence. Before the eyes of the amazed spectators, Dhundhukārī boarded the lustrous carriage. Before leaving, however, Gokarṇa asked the denizens of Vaikuṇṭha the following important question:

atraiva bahavaḥ santi
śrotāro mama nirmalāḥ
ānītāni vimānāni
na teṣāṁ yugapat kutaḥ

śravaṇaṁ samabhāgena
sarveṣām iha dṛśyate
phala-bhedaḥ kuto jātaḥ
prabruvantu hari-priyāḥ

"There were many people in the audience who were purified by listening to the *Bhāgavatam* recital. Why then were celestial carriages not brought for all of them? I observed them all participating equally in the act of hearing. Please explain, O beloved of Hari, why there is a difference in the results they have gotten?" (*Bhāgavata-māhātmya* 5.69-70)

The associates of the Lord answered by speaking the following verses:

śravaṇasya vibhedena
phala-bhedo'tra saṁsthitaḥ
śravaṇaṁ tu kṛtaṁ sarvair
na tathā mananaṁ kṛtam
phala-bhedas tato jāto
bhajanād api mānada

"The difference in results comes of the differences in the quality of their hearing. Everyone present, it is true, listened to the *Bhāgavatam*, but not everyone reflected on what they had heard. The difference in results came from this, as well as from the quality of their worship, O respectful one."
(*Bhāgavata-māhātmya* 5.71)

sapta-rātram upasyaiva
pretena śravaṇaṁ kṛtam
mananādi tathā tena
sthira-citte kṛtaṁ bhṛśam

adṛḍhaṁ ca hataṁ jñānaṁ
pramādena hataṁ śrutam

sandigdho hi hato mantro
vyagra-citto hato japaḥ

avaiṣṇavo hato deśo
hataṁ śrāddham apātrakam
hatam aśrotriye dānam
anācāraṁ hataṁ kulam

viśvāso guru-vākyeṣu
svasmin dīnatve-bhāvanā
mano-doṣa-jayaś caiva
kathāyāṁ niścalā matiḥ

evam ādi kṛtaṁ cet syāt
tadā vai śravaṇe phalam
punaḥ śravānte sarveṣāṁ
vaikuṇṭhe vasatir dhruvam

gokarṇa tava govindo
golokaṁ dāsyati svayam

"In order to obtain the fruits of hearing the Bhagavatam, one should have faith in the words of the spiritual master and an attitude of humility about his own worth"

"The ghost listened for seven days, but each night he worshiped the Lord, during which time he reflected with concentration on what he had heard. Knowledge which is unstable is lost, as is the learning of someone who has been inattentive. Japa done without concentration or hearing advice which comes from a doubtful source are both wasted. A land without Vaishnavas is worthless, as is the offering of oblations by a person without qualifications, charity given to an unlearned person, and a family which has no ethical principles. In order to obtain the fruits of hearing the *Bhāgavatam,* one should have faith in the words of the spiritual master and an attitude of humility about his own worth; he should be victorious over the flaws of the mind and have unswerving concentration on the topics he is hearing.

"When all these people hear the *Bhāgavatam* a second time, they too will gain eternal residence in Vaikuṇṭha, of this there is no doubt. As for you, Gokarṇa, Govinda will personally take you to Goloka, the abode of the cows"

(*Bhāgavata-māhātmya* 5.72-77)

After thus speaking to Gokarṇa, the associates of Lord Hari began to loudly sing the Lord's names, ascending to Vaikuṇṭha with the transformed Dhundhukārī.

In the following month of Śrāvaṇa, Gokarṇa undertook a second *Bhāgavata-saptāha*. The same audience was again present, but this time they listened more carefully than they had previously. At the end of the week, there was the most wonderful epiphany. Śrī Hari Himself descended into the assembly, surrounded by innumerable associates in innumerable celestial carriages. The sounds of prayer and glorification resounded in every direction. Even Lord Hari Himself added to the auspicious cacophony by blowing the conch Pāñcajanya, which He always holds in His hand. The Lord then embraced Gokarṇa tightly, transforming the devotee who took the dark form of a Vaikuṇṭha resident with four arms, yellow silk dress, and jewelled crown and earrings. Instantly, everyone in the assembly was similarly transformed. Even other creatures and lower-caste residents of the village were also transformed into divine beings and, as a result of Gokarṇa's mercy, were given places in the celestial carriages and taken to the transcendental abode sought after by the great yogis. The Lord of the cows, Gopāla, took His dearmost devotee Gokarṇa, with Him to His own abode of Goloka.

One may perform penances for many lifetimes and not obtain residence in Goloka-Vaikuṇṭha—the fruit of listening to the *Bhāgavatam* for a single week. Just as all the citizens of Ayodhyā were taken by Rāmacandra to Sāketa in Vaikuṇṭha, by the Lord's mercy, anyone who listens to the *Bhāgavatam* will be taken to His transcendental abode, for the mercy of Śrī Krishna is present in the account of His pastimes found therein. One who recites the *Bhāgavatam* as well as those who listen to it will have the great fortune of obtaining this divine reward.

The Importance of Reflection

The second verse of the *Śrīmad Bhāgavatam*'s *maṅgalācaraṇa* (auspicious invocation) serves as the *vastu-nirdeśa*, or indication of the book's subject matter. There it is said, *īśvaraḥ sadyo hṛdy avarudhyate'tra kṛtibhiḥ śuśruṣubhis tat-kṣaṇāt*: "The Lord described in the *Bhāgavatam* appears in the pure heart of the pious listener and remains there from the moment he starts to listen to its recital." On the other hand, as the commentator explains, *akṛtibhis tu bahu-vilambane*—the impious may listen to the *Bhāgavatam* for a long time without ever obtaining the same result.

Krishna states in the *Bhagavad-gītā*:

mayy eva mana ādhatsva
mayi buddhiṁ niveśaya
nivasiṣyasi mayy eva
ata ūrdhvaṁ na saṁśayaḥ

"Just fix your mind upon Me alone; engage all your intelligence in Me. Thus, without a doubt you will reside in Me forever, even after death." (*Gītā* 12.8)

In this interpretation of this verse, Viśvanātha Cakravartī writes: "Just fix your mind by always remembering and meditating on Me, the black and beautiful cowherd boy dressed in yellow silks and garlanded with forest flowers. Engage your intelligence, your power of discrimination, in Me; in other words, reflect on Me. By reflection (*manana*), I mean studying the various words of the scripture which encourage and induce you to meditate on Me. Then you will reside in Me, by which I mean that you will dwell with Me in My abode."[1]

The word *manana* means to reflect on the subjects which one has heard or read about, along with their meaning. Without this kind of reflection, hearing alone is incomplete and ineffective.

yad-anudhyāsinā yuktāḥ
karma-granthi-nibandhanam

chindanti kovidās tasya
ko na kuryāt kathā-ratim

"Those who are expert cut through the binding knots of reactionary work with the sword of constant meditation on the Lord. Who then will not adore the discussion of His topics?" (*Śrīmad Bhāgavatam* 1.2.15)

"One should study the Bhagavatam constantly, approaching it with single-minded devotion. As he does so, the Lord Himself becomes imprisoned in his heart"

The above verse from the *Bhāgavatam* compares the constant meditation on the Lord to a sword with which one can cut through the entanglement of activities arising out of false ego, and their results. This means that such constant remembrance destroys one's tendency to egocentric sense enjoyment. Constant remembrance (*anudhyāna*) means reflecting on the topics after (*anu*) one has heard them from the mouths of the guru and the Vaishnavas. This again confirms that simply hearing or studying scriptures without reflecting on what one has read cannot possibly bring the desired results.

Devotion is Needed to Understand the Bhāgavatam

The *Śrīmad Bhāgavatam* is the essence of all scriptures and the emperor of all literature. The *Bhakti-rasāmṛta-sindhu, Chaitanya Charitāmṛta, Ṣaṭ-sandarbha, Bṛhad-bhāgavatāmṛta, Bṛhad-vaiṣṇava-toṣaṇī, Laghu-vaiṣṇava-toṣaṇī, Bhāvārtha-dīpikā, Sārārtha-darśinī,* and other works are explanations of the *Bhāgavatam*. One should study this literature through the disciplic succession by humbly submitting to a spiritual master, asking appropriate questions and maintaining a service attitude. Insight into the practice of devotional service, by which one makes real progress in worshiping the Lord, cannot result without such an approach.

Gopal Bhatta Goswami

As stated before, the *Bhāgavatam* can be understood only by devotion and not by the exercise of intelligence or by the study of many commentaries (*bhaktyā bhāgavataṁ grāhyaṁ na buddhyā na ca ṭīkayā*). No amount of mundane speculation or scholarship can help one understand the divine mood of the *Bhāgavatam*. One has to take shelter of the process of devotional service as taught by the pure devotees of the Lord; this is the only way one will be able to enter into its mysteries. One should study the *Bhāgavatam* constantly, approaching it with single-minded devotion. As he does so, the Lord Himself becomes imprisoned in his heart.

The devotee's heart is filled with the pure desire to bring pleasure to Krishna's senses alone; thus, it is the Lord's favored resting place. Thus Narottama dāsa Ṭhākura has sung:

bhaktera hṛdaye govindera satata viśrāma
govinda kahena mama bhakta se parāṇa

"Govinda constantly remains in the heart of His devotee. He says, 'My devotee is My life.'" (*Prārthanā*)

The conclusion is a serious aspirant of pure devotion needs to take shelter of a *maṭha* where he can cultivate knowledge of the devotional scriptures in the association of pure devotees.

Chapter XII

Controlling the Mind

In the *Vedanta-sāra*[1] it is written that the inner self (*antaḥkaraṇa*) is composed of mind, intelligence, ego, and *citta* (*mano buddhir ahaṁkāraś cittaṁ kāraṇam antaram*). Intellect (*buddhi*) is the aspect of the internal self (*antaḥkaraṇa*) that establishes certainty, while the mind (*manas*) is the aspect of the internal self whose function is to accept and reject.

The word *citta* is the past passive participle of the verb root *cit*, which means "to know," or "to be conscious." Thus, *citta* is that aspect of the internal organ by which one becomes conscious of oneself, or that by which awareness develops. It is thus synonymous with mind, as stated by Sāyana in his commentary to *Ṛgveda* (1.163.11): "Your *citta* is like the gliding wind," (*tava cittaṁ vāta iva dhrajīmānaḥ*).

In Sanskrit, there are numerous words used as synonyms for "mind" (*manas*), including *citta, cetas, hṛt, hṛdaya* ("heart"), *svānta* ("inner self"), *anaṅgaka* ("limbless"), and sometimes, *aṅga* ("limb").

The word *manas* is defined as follows: "The mind is that by which things are perceived or recognized (*manute budhyate'neneti manaḥ*)." It is one of the elements of the subtle body, or *liṅga-śarīra*. This subtle body has 17 different elements: the five knowledge-gathering senses, the five working senses, the five airs, mind, and intelligence.

The *Vedanta-sāra* also gives the following definition of the mind (*manas*):

mano nāma saṅkalpa-vikalpātmikā'ntaḥkaraṇa-vṛttiḥ
manas tu jñānedriyaiḥ sahitaṁ sat mano-maya-kośo bhavati

> "The mind is the function of the internal self dealing with decision (*saṅkalpa*) and indecision (*vikalpa*). Along with the knowledge-gathering senses (*jñānendriya*), it forms the sheath of mind (*mano-maya-kośa*)." (*Vedanta-sāra* 62,68)

The mind is considered to be one of the working senses, and one of the knowledge-gathering senses. Because it depends on the eyes and other knowledge-gathering senses (sight, hearing, touch, taste, and smell), it is considered to be one of them. On the other hand, because it is the director of the other working senses (speech, hands, feet, reproductive organs, and excretory organs), it can be also listed among these.

The senses of knowledge (such as sight) pick up general impressions of external objects, and the mind then supplies particulars. Thus the mind is called *saṅkalpātmaka*, which means the act of choosing or deciding (*vivecanā*). In other words, the mind is constantly sifting through the data it receives through the senses, accepting or rejecting what it gathers.

One of the many transformations of the mode of goodness (*sattva-guṇa*) is the mind. Nature's first transformation or manifestation is the Mahat-tattva. In the *Sāṅkhya-kārikā* it is stated that mind arises out of the Mahat-tattva (*mahad-ākhyaṁ ādyaṁ kāryaṁ tan-manaḥ*)(1.71).

THE MIND ACCORDING TO LORD KAPILADEVA

In the third canto of the *Śrīmad Bhāgavatam*, Lord Kapiladeva instructs his mother Devahūti in the theistic Sāṅkhya philosophy. Some of His teachings about the mind are in many respects similar to the description given in the *Sāṅkhya-kārikā*. Kapila teaches that the mind is one of the four functions of the inner self, or *antaḥkaraṇa*. These four functions are known as *citta* ("contaminated consciousness"), *ahaṅkāra* (ego), *buddhi* (intelligence), and *manas* (mind). According to Lord Kapila, the Mahat-tattva manifests within the body as the four-fold inner organ, first as the contaminated consciousness, then as the ego, then intelligence, and finally as the mind (*Śrīmad Bhāgavatam* 3.26.14).

For the sake of purifying these elements, the four deities of the Caturvyūha accept the position of presiding over them. Vāsudeva is thus the *adhiṣṭhātṛ-devatā*, or presiding deity of *citta*, Saṅkarṣaṇa of *ahaṅkāra*, Pradyumna of *buddhi*, and Aniruddha of *manas*. On the material level, the following deities preside over the same subtle elements: Vishnu, Rudra, Brahmā, and Candra. (See also *Śrīmad Bhāgavatam* 3.26.21, commentary of Viśvanātha Cakravartī Thākura).

According to the Sāṅkhya system, there are five great elements (*mahā-bhūta*): air, earth, water, fire, and ether, which evolve into the five sense objects: odor, flavor, sight, touch, and sound. These are followed by five corresponding senses of knowledge namely, smell, taste, vision, feeling, and hearing, and the five working senses: speech, hands, feet, excretory organs, and reproductive organs.

The sum of the four subtle senses of the internal self (ego, mind, intelligence, and consciousness) is 24 elements, or *tattvas*. To these, time (*kāla*) is sometimes added, bringing the total to 25. A further calculation then adds the individual living entity, the *jīva*, nature itself (*prakṛti*), and the Supersoul (the *puruṣa*), as further elements, their total amounting to 28.

The twenty-fifth element, time, indicates the Supreme Person's action that sets material nature (as yet undifferentiated by the actions of the three modes) into motion. The word *kāla* itself is derived from the verb root *kal*, which means "to impel," or "to incite." It is said that time is the might of God. The same aspect of the Supreme Lord that, out of His own potency, acts as the Supersoul, dwelling in the heart of every sentient creature, is fully present externally, ruling over the 24 elements of the material creation in the form of time.

Outside the perception of the individual souls with their minute awareness, the Supreme Lord's prowess, in the form of time, sets the three modes of material nature in action. At that moment, He places the individual souls into material nature. This process is explained by the Lord Himself in the *Bhagavad-gītā* where He states:

mama yonir mahad brahma
tasmin garbhaṁ dadāmy aham
sambhavaḥ sarva-bhūtānāṁ
tato bhavati bhārata

> "The total material nature, also known as Brahman, is impregnated by Me, with the living beings; thus I make their embodied existence possible." (*Gītā* 14.3)

After being impregnated by the Lord, the material energy brings forth the Mahat-tattva in an effulgent golden form. This Mahat-tattva then undergoes various transformations caused by the effects of the three modes of nature namely, purity (*sattva*), passion (*rajas*), and darkness (*tamas*), and as a result of these transformations, three corresponding types of ego endowed with acting capacity come into being. Mind is a by-product of ego in the mode of goodness, the ten senses are the by-products of ego in the mode of passion, the five sense objects and the five gross elements are the products of the ego in the mode of darkness. The second of the Puruṣas, Saṅkarṣaṇa, who is also known as Anantadeva, is said by scholars to be the cause of the mind, the senses, and the five primary elements. (See also *Śrīmad Bhāgavatam* 3.26.23-25)

The mind is the by-product of the action of ego in the mode of goodness on the Mahat-tattva. The mind's function is to accept and reject. The operation of this function results in desire. Intelligence (*buddhi*) is a by-product of the *rājasika* ego; in its elemental form, intelligence is the recognition of things (*dravya-sphuraṇa-vijñānam*) and as such it acts as an aid to the senses (*indriyāṇām anugrahaḥ*).

When the aspect of material ego in the mode of darkness is set into motion by the Lord's prowess in the form of time, the five sense objects (odor, flavor, sight, touch, and sound) come into being. From these, the five great elements devolve. The universe, in its entire microcosmic and macrocosmic manifestations, is the result of the interactions of all these elements. However, if the Supreme Soul was not present within everything at creation, nothing would be created and nothing maintained.

The material body is known as the field, and the living entity who dwells within the body is called the knower of the field. The Supreme Lord, however, is omniscient and omnipotent, the knower of all fields in every one of the infinity of universes. Thus, if one does not establish a relationship with Him, there is no possibility of any true self-purification taking place.

The Mind, the Self, and the Supreme Self

The mind should not be mistaken for the self. The spiritual being, or soul, should not be misidentified with the mind. While the soul is a spark of the conscious spiritual energy , the mind merely reflects this consciousness. The mind depends on the presence of the *jīva* soul in order to function; it has no independent existence. We can speak about "my mind," but we never hear anyone saying, "I am the mind." The self is the observer and the mind is the observed. Therefore the self should be understood as categorically different from the mind.

"The soul is composed of consciousness, the mind of unconscious matter. Consciousness is self-illuminating, while matter has no power to illuminate"

The soul is composed of consciousness, the mind of unconscious matter. Consciousness is self-illuminating, while matter has no power to illuminate. The logicians say, "The soul becomes connected to the mind, the mind to the senses, the senses to the sense object. Therefore, it is through this process that knowledge is acquired" (*ātmā manasā yuñjāte mana indriyeṇa, indriyaṁ viṣayeṇa, tasmād adhyakṣa ity-ukta-diśā jñānaṁ jāyate—Nyāya-darśana).*

Without consciousness as their support, the senses cannot acquire knowledge of any sense object. Therefore, the soul itself acts as the director, first coming into contact with the mind, which then acts through the senses to contact the sense objects. Thus, through the mind, the self not only gains knowledge but also experiences material happiness and distress. Without the mind, the self would be unaware of sensual happiness or distress. Thus, the *Nyāya-vrtti* states: "The mind is the sense which is capable of comprehending happiness and distress" (*sukhādy-upalabdhi-sādhanaṁ indriyaṁ manaḥ).*

By contrast, in the *Bhagavad-gīta* (2.24) Krishna says that the *jīva* soul is everlasting, capable of migrating in all species, fixed, immovable, and beginningless (*nityaḥ sarva-gataḥ sthānur acalo'yaṁ sanātanaḥ*). The soul is unborn, forever changeless, free from decay, and free from the sixfold transformations of matter; it is not killed when the body is killed (*Gītā* 2.20: *ajo nityaḥ śāśvato'yaṁ purāṇo na hanyate hanyamāne śarīre*).

This individual self or soul is also eternally related with the Supreme Soul, the Paramātmā. There are many, many verses in the *Bhagavad-gītā* that distinguish the individual soul from his eternal master, the Supreme Lord. The Lord Himself says: "I am the primeval origin of all the celestial beings and great sages." (*Gītā* 10.2—*aham ādir hi devānāṁ maharṣīṇāṁ ca sarvaśaḥ*; "He who knows Me to be birthless, the origin of everything, and the Supreme Lord of all beings..." (*yo māṁ ajam anādiṁ ca vetti loka-maheśvaram—Gītā* 10.3); "I am the root cause of all things and everything comes from Me." (*ahaṁ sarvasya prabhavo mattaḥ sarvaṁ pravartate—Gītā* 10.8); "I alone am the cause of generation of the whole world, and the cause of its dissolution as well" (*ahaṁ kṛtsnasya jagataḥ prabhavaṁ pralayas tathā—Gītā* 7.6); "I am the father of this universe, the mother, the bestower of the fruits of all actions, the forefather, and the object of all knowledge" (*pitāham asya jagato mātā dhātā pitāmahaḥ—Gītā* 9.17).

mattaḥ parataraṁ nānyat
kiñcid asti dhanañjaya
mayi sarvam idaṁ protaṁ
sūtre maṇi-gaṇā iva

"O Arjuna! There is nothing superior to Me. Like gems strung on a thread, this entire creation depends on Me." (*Gītā* 7.7)

gatir bhartā prabhuḥ sākṣī
nivāsaḥ śaraṇaṁ suhṛt
prabhavaḥ pralayaḥ sthānaṁ
nidhānaṁ bījam avyayam

"And certainly I am everyone's goal, maintainer, controller, witness, refuge, guardian, and unconditional well-wisher. I am creation, dissolution, and sustenance. I am the reservoir and the seed, the eternal Supreme Person." (*Gītā* 9.18)

Arjuna also responded by confirming the statements of the Lord:

paraṁ brahma paraṁ dhāma
pavitraṁ paramaṁ bhavān
puruṣaṁ śāśvataṁ divyam
ādidevam ajaṁ vibhum

āhus tvām ṛṣayaḥ sarve
devarṣir nārada tathā
asito devalo vyāsaḥ
svayaṁ caiva bravīṣi me

Temple of Tota Gopinath, Jagannatha Puri

"O Lord, You are the Supreme Absolute Truth, the supreme shelter, and the supreme savior. All the prominent sages such as Devarṣi Nārada, Asita, Devala and Vyāsa have described You as the self-illuminating, self-manifest eternal Supreme Person, the foundation of almighty majesty, and the origin from whose divine play everything emanates—and now You are personally declaring this to me." (*Gītā* 10.12-13)

svayam evātmanātmānaṁ
vettha tvaṁ puruṣottama
bhūta-bhāvana bhūteśa
devadeva jagatpate

"O Supreme Person, O universal father, O Lord of all beings, Lord of all gods, Lord of the universe! You alone can truly know Yourself through Your own divine cognizant potency." (*Gītā* 10.15)

Following the conclusions of the *Upanishads* the *Bhagavad-gītā* further states:

nityo nityānāṁ cetanaś cetanānām
eko bahūnāṁ vidadhāti kāmān
ye ātmastham anupaśyanti dhīrās
teṣāṁ śāntiḥ śāśvatī netareṣām

"There is a single Supreme Eternal Being among all eternal beings; a single supremely conscious entity among all conscious entities. He is the one who fulfills the desires of the many. Sages who constantly meditate upon Him, seated on His throne, shall attain everlasting perfection; others shall not." (*Kaṭha 2.2.13 and Śvet* 6.13)

The distinction between the Supreme and individual souls is further clarified in the two following verses from the *Muṇḍaka* (3.1.1-2) and *Śvetāśvatara Upanishads* (4.6-7):

dvā suparṇā sayujā sakhāyā
samānaṁ vṛkṣaṁ pariṣasvajāte
tayor anyaḥ pippalaṁ svādv atty
anaśnann anyo 'bhicākaśīti

samāne vṛkṣe puruṣo nimagno
'nīśayā śocati muhyamānaḥ
juṣṭaṁ yadā paśyaty anyam īśam
asya mahimānam eti vīta-śokaḥ

"Two fair-plumed friends sit in the same tree. One eats the tree's sweet berries while the other only observes. In the same way, in the tree of the body, the individual soul sits bewildered, constantly and helplessly grieving. When he wisely turns to his friend (who is always served by the devotees), looking upon Him as his Lord, he gives up his suffering and realizes his glorious birthright."

The loving relationship between the Supreme Soul and the individual soul is also eternal. Thus Krishna, the supreme knower of the Veda, the ultimate object of Vedic knowledge, and the original author of the Vedanta, lovingly spoke His most confidential teachings and the essence of all religion to His dear friend Arjuna as follows:

"The Lord is so affectionate to His exclusive devotees that He voluntarily takes responsibility for their bodily maintenance, taking care of their families as well"

man-manā bhava mad-bhakto
mad-yājī māṁ namaskuru
mām evaiṣyasi satyaṁ te
pratijāne priyo'si me

"Always think of Me, worship Me by engaging in the devotional services of hearing and chanting, serve Me in My deity form, offer your very being unto Me, and you will surely reach Me. This is My sincere promise to you because you are My dear friend." (*Gītā* 18.65)

sarva-dharmān parityājya
mām ekaṁ śaraṇaṁ vraja
ahaṁ tvāṁ sarva-pāpebhyo
mokṣayiṣyāmi mā śucaḥ

"Abandoning all religious observances related to the *varṇāśrama* system, giving up the worship of all demigods related to those religious activities, surrender exclusively unto Me. You need have no fear of any ill effects resulting from not performing the permanent and periodical duties enjoined in the Vedic literature, even though these were ultimately dictated by Me. I will liberate you from any sins or impediments resulting from such neglect; do not despair. I hereby promise that anyone who surrenders to Me is freed from sin, is liberated from the cycle of repeated birth and death, and receives all that is needed to attain Me." (*Gītā* 18.66)

Elsewhere in the *Gītā,* Krishna makes a similar promise:

ananyāś cintayanto māṁ
ye janāḥ paryupāsate
teṣāṁ nityābhiyuktānāṁ
yoga-kṣemaṁ vahāmy aham

> "I personally assume the whole responsibility of acquiring and protecting the necessities of My fully dependent devotees. They are always absorbed in thought of Me alone and worship Me exclusively; they want nothing but to be united with Me forever." (9.22)

The Lord is so affectionate to His exclusive devotees that He voluntarily takes responsibility for their bodily maintenance, taking care of their families as well. He also protects the devotee's *bhajana* as well by eliminating all obstacles to its practice. Then He grants the devotees the perfection of that *bhajana* (which is the treasure of love for Himself) and protects that love. Such is the true extent of the Lord's statement, *yoga-kṣemaṁ vahāmy aham.*

"All religious activities have control of the mind as their aim, for concentration of the mind is the supreme goal of yoga."

The Mind as Friend and as Enemy of the Self

In the first part of the Lord's above-mentioned instruction, He says, *man-manā bhava*: "Absorb your mind in Me." However, in the process of attaining the treasure of love, the mind acts not only as friend but also as enemy. The *Bhāgavata* clearly states that unless one controls one's mind, perfection is impossible.

dānaṁ svadharmo niyamo yamaś ca
śrutaṁ ca karmāṇi ca sad-vratāni
sarve mano-nigraha-lakṣaṇāntāḥ
paro hi yogo manasaḥ samādhiḥ

> "All religious activities such as charity, execution of one's duties, observance of rules and regulations, study of scripture, sacrifices, and penances, all have the control of the mind as their aim, for concentration of the mind is the supreme goal of yoga." (*Śrīmad Bhāgavatam* 11.23.45)

One must begin the conquest of the mind by practicing that which Krishna calls "the austerity of the mind." In the *Bhagavad-gītā* (17.16) this practice is explained by Krishna as follows:

manaḥ-prasādaḥ saumyatvaṁ
maunam ātma-vinigrahaḥ
bhāva-saṁśuddhir ity etat
tapo mānasam ucyate

> "Austerity of the mind comprises serenity, simplicity, moderation in speech, self-control by withdrawing from the sense objects, and purity of being through renunciation of deceptive behavior."

Of these, self-control through withdrawal from the sense objects is of great significance. Indeed, Krishna states that no one becomes a yogi without giving up desire for sense gratification. (*Gītā* 6.2: *na hy asannyasta-saṅkalpo yogī bhavati kaścana*). Unless one has uprooted gross as well as subtle desires, and renunciations of all kinds, including the desires for sense enjoyment, heavenly pleasures, liberation and mystic powers, one cannot be considered a yogi.

"As soon as the mind is absorbed in devotion to the Lord, it becomes truly pure and holy and a true friend to the self"

"Only one who has given up all incentive of desire can be said to have ascended to yoga" (*Gītā* 6.4: *sarva-saṅkalpa-saṁnyāsī yogārūḍhas tadocyate*). In other words, when a pure-hearted *jīva* gives up the desire and abhorrence of sense enjoyments, keeping only the desire to serve Krishna for the satisfaction of His senses, can he be elevated to the topmost rung of the yoga ladder.

For this reason, the Lord says:

uddhared ātmanātmānaṁ
nātmānam avasādayet
ātmaiva hy ātmano bandhur
ātmaiva ripur ātmanaḥ

bandhur ātmātmanas tasya
yenaivātmanā jitaḥ
anātmanas tu śatrutve
vartetātmaiva śatruvat

> "The aspiring yogi should lift himself from the blind well of material life by freeing the mind from attachment to the sense objects. He should not debase it by attachments to the material world. According to different circumstances, the mind is either the friend of the self, or its enemy. That *jīva* who has conquered the mind can consider his mind a friend. But the mind is the enemy of one who has not conquered it." (*Gītā* 6.5-6)

With the following words Lord Kapiladeva instructs his mother Devahūti:

cetaḥ khalv asya bandhāya
muktaye cātmano matam
guṇeṣu saktaṁ bandhāya
rataṁ vā puṁsi muktaye

> "My dear mother, the mind alone is the cause of the *jīva's* bondage as well as the *jīva's* liberation. When the mind is attached to the senses (sight, hearing, smell, taste and touch) and the sense objects (form, sound, odor, flavor, and feeling), the living entity enters into bondage. When the same mind is attached to the Supreme Person, he is liberated." (*Śrīmad Bhāgavatam* 3.25.15)

Krishna explains the same thing more directly to Uddhava:

viṣayān dhyāyataś cittaṁ
viṣayeṣv anuṣajjate

mām anusmarataś cittaṁ
mayy eva pravilīyate

"The mind which dwells on sense objects becomes attached to sense objects. The mind which constantly remembers Me becomes absorbed in Me."
(Śrīmad Bhāgavatam 11.14.27)

It is thus evident that as soon as the mind is absorbed in devotion to the Lord, it becomes truly pure and holy and a true friend to the.

Five Stages of Mind Control According to Yoga Sutras

The great sage Patañjali, the author of the *Yoga Sutra*, has written that the meaning of yoga is to stop the activities of the mind (*yogaś citta-vṛtti-nirodhaḥ,* 1.2). It is impossible to achieve yoga unless one first controls the activities of the mind. Yoga psychology describes five basic states of mind—*kṣipta* (disturbed), *mūḍha* (bewildered), *vikṣipta* (distracted), *ekāgra* (concentrated), and *niruddha* (controlled).

(1) When the mind is unsteady and flickering, it is said to be disturbed (*kṣipta*). When one desires things other than Krishna, the mind finds it impossible to remain fixed exclusively on Him. Rather, it flitters from one subject to another, wishing first for some sense object and then for another. In this way it remains unsteady.

(2) The mind may be confused about what to do or not to do, and as a result one is overcome with desire, anger or other manifestations of the mode of passion; or sleep, drowsiness and laziness or other manifestations of the mode of ignorance. This is called the bewildered state of the mind.

(3) The state of being disturbed (*kṣiptāvasthā*) described above, and the distracted state (*vikṣipta*) are quite similar in many respects. However, a difference between them is that from time to time, in the *vikṣipta* state, there are occasional moments of calm and steadiness even within the general overall picture of inability to concentrate.

(4) When the mind becomes fixed on some external or internal object, and thus becomes as steady as a flame in a windless room; when it has overcome the modes of ignorance and passion and is situated in goodness, it develops the power of single-minded concentration, which is called *ekāgratā*.

(5) In the stage of concentration, *ekāgratā*, the mind is still dependent on something external to itself, but in the fully controlled state (*niruddha*), there is no longer dependency. The mind regains its causal nature and remains inactive as though it had achieved its purpose and had no need of further action. Like a burnt thread, it shows the lines of its previous characteristics, but is not negatively affected by them. In this controlled state, the self is fixed in its true nature. At other times, the self identifies with the activities of the mind and thus takes on various identities.

Devotional scriptures tell us that the *jīva*'s eternal nature (as Krishna's marginal energy) is to be the servant of the Lord. As one of His energies the *jīvas* are simultaneously one and different from Him (*jīvera svarūpa haya nitya kṛṣṇa-dāsa kṛṣṇa-taṭastha śakti bhedāb-*

heda-prakāśa). When situated in this natural constitutional position, the mind has no function other than to seek out Krishna. The living entity is then constantly engaged in the culture of Krishna consciousness and the mind then acts as his friend.

THE ACTUAL PURPOSE OF THE MENTAL FUNCTION

In his teachings to Maitreyī, Yajñavalkya describes four practices which lead to control of the mind: "The atman is to be seen, to be listened to, to be reflected on, and to be contemplated" (*ātmā vā are draṣṭavyaḥ śrotavyo mantavyo nididhyāsitavyaḥ—Bṛhad-āraṇyaka Upanishad*, 4.5.6).

From this statement it is understood that the first duty of the mind is to seek out the Supreme Self. One should therefore use the mind to seek out Vāsudeva, the mind's own titulary deity, and never other sense objects. As instructed to Maitreyī, one should look at and listen to things related to Krishna, then reflect on and contemplate those things, as well as Krishna Himself. Not following these instructions will cause one to miss the actual purpose of mental functions. In such an instance, the mind becomes the principal enemy of the soul.

"The first step in controlling the mind is to listen to the Bhagavatam with strong faith in the guru, attentiveness and care, concentration and patience. If there is inattention and carelessness, the true fruit of hearing will not be achieved"

If one wishes to know the Supreme Truth, it is absolutely essential that one take shelter of a spiritual master and hear from him. The spiritual master is non-different from the Supreme Truth; a manifest expansion, or *prakāśa-vigraha,* of that Truth. Thus he can show the truth—Lord Krishna's lotus feet—to his surrendered disciple. He shows the disciple the means by which the vision of the Lord can be attained. Therefore one should first prostrate himself before the guru and then submissively ask him about the nature of the self, the nature of God, the goal of life and the means of attaining it, and the nature of maya, or the forces which oppose the attaining of spiritual understanding.

The disciple should approach the spiritual master in a spirit of service. It is imperative that the disciple listen submissively to the directions given by the spiritual master, then, by reflection, follow up such hearing. The word *manana* means reflection, or assiduous meditation on the subject matter that has been heard from the spiritual master. It also means determination, i.e., the power to determine the nature of things. Vijñāna Bhikṣu writes in his works on Sāṅkhya philosophy that the self should be heard in accordance with the words of the revealed literature, and should be reflected on according to their proofs and arguments (*śrotavyaḥ śruti-vākyebhyo mantavyaś copapattibhiḥ*). By this process, one comes to determine the true meaning of the words registered in the scriptures.

The *Gāyatrī-tantra* (1.4) states:

mananāt pāpatas trāti mananāt svargam aśnute
mananāt mokṣam āpnoti caturvargamayo bhavet

> "One is delivered from sin through reflection. One enjoys heaven through reflection. One attains liberation and all the goals of human life through reflection."

A pure devotee will naturally engage in the kind of reflection that results in pure devotional service. The importance of reflecting on what one has heard is specifically connected with the importance of listening to the *Bhāgavata*. We saw in a previous chapter how Dhundhulī was taken by a group of divine beings to the Vaikuṇṭha planets after hearing Gokarṇa recite the entire *Bhāgavatam* for over a seven-day period. Other people in the audience were not similarly rewarded because they had not reflected deeply on what they heard. The ghost Dhundhulī fasted each day for the entire week and listened to Gokarṇa with great concentration and faith. Just as importantly, throughout the night he contemplated the subject matter of the day's recital. Thus he was rewarded with the attainment of the full results of listening to the *Bhāgavata*. Accordingly, the *Bhāgavatam* states, *sadyo hṛdy avarudhyate'tra kṛtibhiḥ śuśrūṣubhis tat-kṣaṇāt* (*Śrīmad Bhāgavatam* 1.1.2): "The Lord becomes bound up in the heart of the pious devotees the very moment they desire to hear about Him."

"The Lord becomes bound up in the heart of the pious devotees the very moment they desire to hear about Him"

Therefore the first step in controlling the mind is to listen to the *Bhāgavatam* with strong faith in the guru, attentiveness and care, concentration and patience. If there is inattention and carelessness, the true fruit of hearing will not be achieved.

Abhyāsa-yoga

The fourth function of the mind described by Yajñavalkya to Maitreyī is *nididhyāsana*, or "profound and repeated meditation." In his commentaries on *Bhagavad-gītā's* twelfth chapter, Viśvanātha Cakravartī writes that bhakti is of two types; it is performed 1) by dedicating the inner senses to the Lord, and 2) by dedicating the external senses to Him, i.e., by engaging in unlimited devotional activities like hearing and chanting about the Lord's attributes, pastimes, name, and form as well as praying to Him; glorifying Him; and engaging in such practices as worshiping His deity form, cleaning the temple, and picking flowers for His service, this last practice being accessible to everyone.

Temple at Imlitala, Vrindavan

Bhakti performed by the internal senses is of three kinds: remembering the Lord (*smaraṇa*), reflecting on Him (*manana*) and—for those who are attached to the Lord but unable to remember Him uninterruptedly—practicing control of the mind (*abhyāsa*). All three of these mental disciplines of the devotional path are more difficult for one lacking pure will, than for those who are intelligent and free from an offensive mentality. Reflection is better than external practices; but constant and direct remembrance is superior to reflection. One engaged in external devotional practices should still make added efforts to meditate on the Lord, for external practices are meant to remind one of the Lord and from there lead to reflection, which once achieved, allows for one's easy engagement in constant meditation.

In the following instructions given in the *Bhagavad-gītā*, Krishna emphasizes the importance of the mental aspect of devotional service:

mayy eva mana ādhatsva
mayi buddhiṁ niveśaya
nivasiṣyasi mayy eva
ata ūrdhvaṁ na saṁśayaḥ

"Dedicate your mind exclusively to Me, O Arjuna. Fix your intelligence in Me, and

as a result, you will definitely reside with Me after death. Of this there is no doubt."
(*Gītā* 12.8)

In his *Sārārtha-darśinī* commentary to this verse, Viśvanātha writes: "When Krishna says *mayy eva*, the emphatic participle *eva* prohibits us from meditating on the impersonal aspect of the Lord. When He says 'upon Me' (*mayi*), He refers to His beautiful blackish form dressed in yellow silk and garlanded with forest flowers. The words *mana ādhatsva*, 'dedicate your mind,' an instruction to constantly remember Him. To fix one's intelligence in Him means to use one's powers of discrimination in understanding Him, in other words, to reflect (*manana*) on Him. Such reflection means to study the words of scripture that help awaken the tendency to meditate on Him (*tac ca mananaṁ dhyāna-pratipādaka-śāstra-vākyānuśīlanaṁ*). In following these instructions one comes to live with the Lord in His abode; of this there can be no doubt."

"Repeatedly bringing the mind back from wherever it wanders and fixing it on the form of the Lord is called practice; and that alone is the yogic discipline"

In the following verse, the Lord states:

atha cittaṁ samādhātuṁ
na śaknoṣi mayi sthiram
abhyāsa-yogena tato
mām icchāptuṁ dhanañjaya

"O Dhanañjaya, if you cannot establish your mind in Me with firm faith, alternatively try to reach Me by the practice (*abhyāsa-yogena*) of repeated meditation on Me."
(*Gītā* 12.9)

In regard to the words *abhyāsa-yogena*, Viśvanātha makes the following comments: "Repeatedly bringing the mind back from wherever it wanders and fixing it on the form of the Lord is called practice; and that alone is the yogic discipline" (*anyatrānyatra-gatam api manaḥ punaḥ punaḥ pratyāhṛtya mad-rūpa eva sthāpanam abhyāsaḥ sa eva yogaḥ*).

In the *Gītā's* sixth chapter Krishna explains the practice of yoga meditation to Arjuna. Still bewildered, Arjuna submitted the following question: "Lord, You tell Me to control my mind with the help of the powers of discrimination, or intelligence, but I find that the mind is so powerful that it confuses even my powers of intelligence. I think it easier to capture the wind than to control the mind—it is too difficult for me." In answer, Krishna assured Arjuna that, through repeated practice (*abhyāsena*) and renunciation (*vairāgyena*) it is possible to conquer the restless mind.

Viśvanātha comments on this verse as follows: "Although fickle and exceedingly difficult to control, the mind should be engaged in the constant discipline of cultivation of consciousness of the Supreme Lord (*sad-gurūpadiṣṭa-prakāreṇa parameśvara-dhyāna-yogasya muhur anuśīlanena*), and renunciation and detachment from the sense objects (*viṣayeṣv anāsaṅgena*) by the means and practices given by the spiritual master. This has been confirmed by no less an authority than Patañjalī, who states in his *Yoga Sutras* (1.12): "Practice and detachment are the means by which to still the mind (*abhyāsa-vairāgyā bhyāṁ tan-nirodhaḥ*)."

Conquering the Mind with Higher Intelligence

The process of degradation of the mind is described in the *Bhagavad-gītā* (2.62-63) as follows: First the mind comes in contact with the sense objects and begins to intensely desire to enjoy them. This desire for enjoyment is called lust, from which anger arises. Anger leads to bewilderment; loss of ability to discriminate between proper and improper action. This bewilderment leads to forgetfulness of one's true good as described in scripture. Such forgetfulness leads to the destruction of one's resolute intelligence (*vyavasāyātmikā buddhi*). Finally, the *jīva* falls into the blind well of material existence.

In the *Gītā* (16.2), Krishna names lust, anger, and greed as the three doors leading to hell, and advises the *jīva*s to be particularly on guard against them. In the *Gita's* third chapter, Krishna instructs Arjuna on how to overcome lust and anger. There, Arjuna asks Krishna, "By what is one impelled to sinful acts, even unwillingly, as if engaged by force?"

The Lord answers: "Lust, which is born of the mind and develops out of the mode of passion, causes the living being to engage in sinful activity. Lust is the overriding impulse to engage in sense activities; it causes one to engage in sinful acts and then turns into anger: when one's desires for sense gratification are unsatisfied, lust takes on the characteristics of the mode of ignorance and becomes anger.

"Lust and anger together are the savage and all-devouring foes of the living being. If one is unable to deal with these fearsome enemies, there is no question of one engaging in devotional service to the Lord, or even being worthy to be called a 'human being.' Such a person is inevitably destined to go to the lower, hellish destinations.

"Lust takes up residence in the mind, intelligence, and the senses. Therefore, O Arjuna, in order to overcome this sinful enemy which destroys knowledge and understanding, your first duty is to control your senses. The learned say the senses are superior to the sense objects; mind is stronger than the senses; intelligence is still stronger than the mind; and the soul is even more powerful than the intelligence. Thus the *jīvātmā* can conquer over lust by controlling the senses. Understanding himself to be transcendental to even the intelligence, the *jīvātmā* must realize his position beyond matter, his spiritual nature. With this knowledge, the *jīvātma* steadies the mind and finally destroys his otherwise unconquerable enemy, lust." (*Gītā* 3.37-43)

"Practice and detachment are the means by which to calm the mind"

In his extended translation of the last of the verses in this section of the *Gītā*, Bhaktivinoda Ṭhākura writes,"In this way, being fully aware of your own transcendental spiritual nature, stop thinking of yourself in terms of the material nature, whether with or without attributes. Thus in full knowledge of your own superiority as a pure servant of the Lord, still the unconquerable mind by the power of the spiritual energy and gradually win it over."

Narottama dāsa holds that the association of devotees is essential for one who wants to conquer lust, anger, and greed. He sings, "What can lust and anger do to the practitioner who takes shelter of saintly association?" (*kibā se karite pāra kāma-krodha sādhakere, jadi haya sādhu-janāra saṅga*). Jagadānanda Pundit similarly writes in his *Prema-vivarta*, "All I want is to chant the Holy Name in the company of devotees. I need nothing else to conquer over the cycle of repeated births and deaths" (*sādhu-saṅge kṛṣṇa-nāma ei mātra cāi, saṁsāra jinite āra kono vastu nāi*).

Having attained this invaluable human form of life, we must not become the servants of lust and anger and be beaten by the brooms and sticks of *māyā*. We must do everything within our power to save ourselves from lust and anger. We should have faith that, on seeing our genuine efforts to become good and holy persons, to have unflagging determination in offering heartfelt prayers at the feet of the spiritual master, the Vaishnavas, and the Lord, surely the Lord will come to our aid. On the other hand, if we allow ourselves to float along the stream of sensual desire, ignoring the instructions of the scriptures, the spiritual master, and the saintly, how then can we expect our lives to amount to anything?

In the *Gītā* (2.41), Krishna states that the resolute intellect (*vyavasāyātmikā buddhi*) is directed to a single goal, while those whose intelligence is irresolute are led by their desires and imagination along unlimited paths leading in different directions. On the devotional path, the intelligence is resolute and has only one purpose.

Viśvanātha has paraphrased the words of a devotee possessed of such resolute purpose, "My guru has instructed me to worship the Lord by chanting about Him, by remembering Him and serving His lotus feet. This is my spiritual practice; the goal I must achieve, and my life's nourishment. Whether I reach perfection or remain imperfect, this is the one thing I can never give up. It is my duty; the object of my desire, for even in my dreams I wish for nothing else. Whether it brings me happiness or distress, whether it brings ruin upon me and my family, I do not care."

"My guru has instructed me to worship the Lord by chanting about Him, by remembering Him and serving His lotus feet. This is my spiritual practice; the goal I must achieve, and my life's nourishment"

Viśvanātha cites this example as the kind of resolute determination only possible when one is engaged in devotion beyond all self-deception. Such single-minded determination is not possible in any path of spiritual life other than bhakti, whether it be *karma-yoga, jñāna-yoga*, or any other. Instructing Uddhava to have this kind of strong faith and will power in the execution of devotional service, the Lord says, "Be faithful and worship Me with firm conviction" (*Śrīmad Bhāgavatam* 10.20.28).

A Combination of Divine Grace and Effort

In the *Gītā* (7.14), the Lord tells us that other than by surrendering to Him, there is no alternative way of overcoming His divine energy made of the three qualities of goodness, passion, and ignorance. The mind is easily distracted and flickering, but the Lord is the controlling deity of the mind and He Himself attracts all minds.

kṛṣir bhū-vācakaḥ śabdo ṇaś ca nirvṛti-vācakaḥ
tayor aikyaṁ paraṁ brahma kṛṣṇa ity abhidhīyate

> "The verb root *kṛṣ* refers to the action of attracting, while the suffix *ṇa* means 'supreme joy' The Supreme Brahman has been given the name Krishna because He embodies the combination of these two meanings."

How then can any of us find a place at the Lord's lotus feet if He Himself does not drag us there?

Mother Yaśodā once became angry with baby Krishna and decided to punish Him by tying Him to a mortar. To her chagrin, she found that the rope was always two inches too short. After making repeated efforts and failing each time, Krishna finally became merciful to her and allowed Himself to be tied up. Viśvanātha Cakravartī explains the symbolism of

Krishna bound by a rope as follows: "Two things are necessary before the Lord can be bound by a devotee: 1) the devotee must put great effort into his worship; and 2) there must be mercy on the part of the Lord upon seeing such efforts (*bhakta-niṣṭhā bhajanot-thā śrāntis tad-darśanotthā sva-niṣṭhā kṛpā ceti dvābhyām eva bhagavān baddhaḥ*). This mercy of the Lord is the most powerful of His energies" (*Sārārtha-darśinī*, 10.9.18). Without the combination of the devotee's effort and the Lord's mercy, the rope that binds Him will always be two inches short.

"The mind is easily distracted and flickering, but the Lord is the controlling deity of the mind and He Himself attracts all minds"

The Lord again speaks of the effort (*yatna*) required to attain Him in verse 9.14 of the *Gītā* (*yatantaś ca dṛḍha-vratāḥ*). In his *Sārārtha-varṣiṇī* commentary, Viśvanātha elaborates on the nature of this effort as follows: "Just as poverty stricken householders go to rich men's doors to obtain money for their families' maintainence, My devotees go to the assembly of surrendered devotees with the sole intention of collecting treasures of devotional service (such as chanting) from them. On acquiring the science of bhakti they begin to repeatedly practice the tenets of Bhakti yoga, just like a student trying to learn by rote. (*yathā kuṭumba-pālanārthaṁ dīnā gṛhasthā dhanika-dvārādau dhanārthaṁ yatante, tathaiva mad-bhaktāḥ kīrtanādi-bhakti-prāpty-arthaṁ bhakta-sabhādau yatante. Prāpya ca bhaktim adhīyamānam śāstram paṭhata iva punaḥ punar abhyasyanti ca.*)

Viśvanātha further explains the nature of the devotee's resolution (*dṛḍha-vratāḥ*) to practice devotional service: "I resolve to daily chant a fixed number of rounds of the Holy Name on my beads and to offer a fixed number of prostrated obeisances to the Lord and the Vaishnavas. I resolve to regularly do such and such a service. I will maintain my unfailing determination to keep the Ekādaśī fast and other vows. I will pay special attention to controlling my senses." (*etāvanti nāma-grahaṇāni, etāvatyaḥ praṇatayaḥ, etāvatyaḥ paricaryāś cāvaśya-kartavyā ity evaṁ dṛḍhāni vratāni niyamā yeṣāṁ te. yad vā, dṛḍhāny apatitāny ekādaśy-ādi-vratāni niyamā yeṣāṁ te.*)

Ganesh, remover of obstacles on the path of devotion

The Lord helps those who help themselves. When a devotee makes a vow, the Lord helps him maintain his vow. The *bhakti-yogi* must put aside pride in his own will power and understand all his efforts to be totally dependent on the mercy of the guru, the Vaishnavas, and the Lord. Such a person will soon achieve success.

Rūpa Gosvāmī's Upadeśāmṛta

In his *Upadeśāmṛta* Rūpa Gosvāmī explains that there are six impulses to be controlled by the practitioner. They are the impulses of speech, thought, anger, taste, the belly, and the genitals. When these impulses are strong, the unfortunate *jīva* finds himself flailing in the ocean of material suffering.

In connection with the urges of the belly and the tongue, it is noticeable that the food we eat influences our mental processes. The *Sāṅkhya-kārikā* (3.15) reminds us that "according to the *Śruti*, the mind is affected by the food one consumes" (*tad annamayatvaṁ śruteś ca*), or, as it is popularly said, "you are what you eat." For this reason, yogis and other *sādhakas* who try to control the mind pay special attention to the types of food they consume.

Although a devotee knows himself to be pure spirit, he does not eat everything indiscriminately. Nor do other yoga practitioners eat without discrimination. And why not? Because if they eat everything without discrimination their performance of yoga will be adversely affected by the food they take. Yogis of all types engage in their practices with a transcendental objective and if they eat the food of sensual, materialistic persons, these person's tendencies will encroach upon their minds. For example, if one eats the food offered by a sexually promiscuous person, then that defect will have an effect on his thought processes. To avoid this problem, devotees only take *mahāprasāda*, food first offered to Krishna.

"The Lord helps those who help themselves. When a devotee makes a vow, the Lord helps him maintain his vow"

Rūpa Gosvāmī lists six kinds of activities that adversely affect the mind, robbing it of its peace, and interfere with the achievement of devotional perfection:

atyāhāraḥ prayāsaś ca
prajalpo niyamāgrahaḥ
jana-saṅgaś laulyaṁ ca
ṣaḍbhir bhakir vinaśyati

> "The following activities cause one's devotion to be destroyed: overeating, overexertion, gossip, overenthusiasm for or neglect of regulations, indiscriminate associating, and greed." (*Upadeśāmṛta* 2)

A devotee's downfall is caused by overconsumption, by seeking to enjoy things other than Krishna, by attachment to discussing mundane topics, by either completely rejecting the scriptural injuctions or being overattached to scriptural rules without taking account of their purpose—to remember Krishna. Downfall also comes from making vows which are beyond one's capacity to maintain. When a devotee tries to make a show in this way, he jumps from the frying pan into the fire (*ito nastas tato bhrastah*). Not only does he fail in his attempts at devotional service, but his efforts at material happiness are defeated as well.

"A devotee's downfall is caused by making vows that are beyond his capacity to maintain"

Rūpa Gosvāmī, an ocean of compassion, is distressed by the suffering of others. In his *Upadeśāmṛta*, he mercifully shows how a devotee can increase his devotional wealth.

utsāhān niścayād dhairyāt
tat-tat-karma-pravartanāt
saṅga-tyāgāt sato vṛtteḥ
ṣaḍbhir bhaktiḥ prasidhyati

> "Six attitudes are necessary on the part of the practitioner if bhakti is to reach its perfection. He must have enthusiasm for devotional practice, faith that he will achieve Krishna, patience in the attainment of the goal of *prema*; he must perform devotional activities as they have been given by the previous authorities, avoid bad company, and accept the principles of a saintly life." (*Upadeśāmṛta* 3)

When the *jīva* accepts these positive qualities and rejects the six impulses and six principles unfavorable to bhakti, then he will lead a life of Krishna consciousness.

The mind contaminated by bad association and polluted through constant contact with the sense objects is the source of our troubles. For this reason we must take all care to remain in the association of advanced sadhus, struggling to keep ourselves in the cultivation of

Krishna consciousness. Otherwise, we will be engaged in sinfulness and that is like suicide.

The Higher Taste

According to the *Bhagavad-gītā*, by experiencing the higher taste of spiritual pleasure one naturally discards the temporary and insignificant pleasures of this world. If the mind is engaged in the culture of Krishna consciousness, it automatically becomes indifferent to other engagements. In the *Bhāgavatam* the Lord says to Uddhava:

viṣayān dhyāyataś cittaṁ
viṣayeṣu viṣajjate
mām anusmarataś cittaṁ
mayy eva pravilīyate

> "The mind which meditates on sense objects becomes attached to sense objects. The mind which constantly remembers Me becomes absorbed in Me."
> (*Śrīmad Bhāgavatam* 11.14.27)

"We must take all care to remain in the association of advanced sadhus, struggling to keep ourselves in the cultivation of Krishna consciousness"

Indeed, there is no more powerful an agent for self-purification than devotion to Krishna. By providing a higher taste of spiritual ecstasies, pure devotion eliminates all material desires from the heart. Such is the secret to self-purification and control of the mind.

Madana Mohana Temple

The Lord supplies the conditioned souls with human bodies so they can cross over the ocean of material existence. He then personally comes in the form of the guru to act as the captain of the vessel for crossing over this ocean of material suffering. The winds of Krishna's grace blow abundantly. If, however, the *jīvas* do not make sufficient efforts to traverse the waters of *māyā* despite all the favorable conditions, they should consider themselves to be the most unfortunate and least intelligent persons in the world. Therefore, in *Srimad Bhāgavatam* Śukadeva says to Mahārāja Parīkṣit:

saṁsāra-sindhum atidustaram uttitīrṣor
nānyaḥ plavo bhagavataḥ puruṣottamasya
līlā-kathā-rasa-niṣevanam antareṇa
puṁso bhaved vividha-duḥkha-davārditasya

> "O king! A person who, suffering the various kinds of miseries in this world, desires to cross over the unlimited ocean of material existence, has no alternative but to take a boat in the form of relishing the joys of hearing Krishna's pastimes."
> (*Śrīmad Bhāgavatam* 12.4.40)

Vyāsa begins the *Bhāgavatam* with the following verse:

nigama-kalpa-taror galitaṁ phalaṁ
śuka-mukhād amṛta-drava-saṁyutam
pibata bhāgavataṁ rasam ālayaṁ
muhur aho rasikā bhuvi bhāvukāḥ

> "O devotees! O you who know the transcendental joys of love for the Lord! O

you who have attained the wisdom that comes from meditating on your particular relation with the Lord! Even though you are already fully liberated, drink repeatedly the *Bhāgavata*, the ripened fruit of the desire tree of the Vedas; no part of it is to be rejected like the skin or seed of a mango. Its juice is pure transcendental bliss; it has come down to us from Śukadeva who first spoke it in its present form. It was then repeated by his disciples and grand-disciples in the disciplic succession. The great liberated souls reject the pleasures of heaven but do not reject the pleasures of the fruit of the *Bhāgavata*, constantly relishing its flavor." (*Śrīmad Bhāgavatam* 1.1.3)

Once the demigods came to Dvārakā where they beheld the Lord and offered Him extensive prayers and praise. Those prayers confirm the exceptional power of devotion to purify the heart.

"By providing a higher taste of spiritual ecstasies, pure devotion eliminates all material desires from the heart. Such is the secret to self-purification and control of the mind"

śuddhir nṛṇāṁ na tu tatheḍya durāśayānāṁ
vidyā-śrutādhyayana-dāna-tapaḥ-kriyābhiḥ
sattvātmanām ṛṣabha te yaśasi pravṛddha-
sac-chraddhayā śravaṇa-sambhṛtayā yathā syāt

"O Worshipable One! O Supreme Person! Devotees engaged in hearing Your glories with a pure and mature faith are more quickly purified than those who harbor personal desires even while worshiping, hearing explanations of the Vedic learning, studying the scriptures, giving in charity, performing penances or engaging in other ritual processes of purification."
(*Śrīmad Bhāgavatam* 11.6.9)

With the following words Śrīla Prabhupāda Bhaktisiddhānta Sarasvatī emphasizes the contrast between dry learning and the faithful study of devotional texts: "Hearing the glories of the Lord fills the devotees with ever-increasing faith. It is through such faith that the heart is genuinely purified. Material knowledge and learning simply fill the heart with pride."

However the devotee achieves constant remembrance of Krishna, that remembrance is the true secret of achieving self-purification.

avismṛtiḥ kṛṣṇa-padāravindayoḥ
kṣīṇoty abhadrāṇi ca śaṁ tanoti
sattvasya śuddhiṁ paramātma-bhaktiṁ
jñānaṁ ca vijñāna-virāga-yuktam

"The Supreme Lord's lotus feet are the greatest source of auspiciousness. By never forgetting them, all inauspiciousness is destroyed and peace finally settles on the mind. One's being is genuinely purified, devotion to the Lord is awakened, and one attains knowledge combined with realization and renunciation."
(*Śrīmad Bhāgavatam* 12.12.55)[2]

In the following verses, Krishna explains to His dear devotee Uddhava important aspects of the process of purification:

dharmaḥ satyādayopeto
vidyā vā tapasānvitā

mad-bhaktyāpetam ātmānaṁ
na ca samyak punāti hi

"Religious life ruled by truthfulness and other principles, and learning accompanied by self-discipline cannot completely purify one whose heart is devoid of devotion to Lord Hari." (*Śrīmad Bhāgavatam* 11.14.22)

kathaṁ vinā romaharṣaṁ
dravatā cetasā vinā
vinānandāśru-kalayā
śuddhyed bhaktyā vināśayaḥ

"How can a person's heart be purified without the ecstatic devotion that causes his hair to stand on end, his mind melting with love, and tears flowing from his eyes?" (*Śrīmad Bhāgavatam* 11.14.23)

yathāgninā hema-malaṁ jahāti
smātaṁ punaḥ svaṁ bhajate ca rūpam
ātmā ca karmānuśayaṁ vidhūya
mad-bhakti-yogena bhajaty atho mām

"Just as heated gold is freed of its impurities and retrieves its natural brightness, so does the soul become purified of its accumulated karmic reactions through Bhakti yoga. When one is thus purified and regains his natural identity, he worships Me." (*Śrīmad Bhāgavatam* 11.14.25)

yathā yathātmā parimṛjyate'sau
mat-puṇya-gāthā-śravaṇābhidhānaiḥ
tathā tathā paśyati vastu sūkṣmaṁ
cakṣur yathaivāñjana-samprayuktam

"As the spirit soul is cleansed of all sin by hearing about My holy pastimes, he is able to clearly see the most subtle truths, just as an eye which has been treated with collyrium can see physical objects more clearly." (*Śrīmad Bhāgavatam* 11.14.26)

"Hearing the glories of the Lord fills the devotees with ever-increasing faith. It is through such faith that the heart is genuinely purified"

There are hundreds of such statements in the devotional scriptures showing that the only true process of self-purification takes place through the performance of devotional service.

The mind's presiding and worshipable deity is Lord Vāsudeva. Since the principal function of the mind is to search (*anveṣaṇātmikā*), and since the self is the object of all research (*sa ātmā anveṣṭavyaḥ*), the mind remains pure as long as it searches out the Supreme Self, Vāsudeva. On the other hand, if the mind, led by desire to search for other fruits, fluctuates from Vāsudeva to any other object of attention, it is considered to be contaminated. In other words, the mind cannot be considered pure if it chases after liberation, sense gratification, mystic perfection or material gain.

The mind is quickly purified by the influence of pure bhakti. If one engages in the culture of Krishna consciousness, voiding oneself of all other objectives but devotion itself, not mixing it with other superfluous disciplines like *jñāna* and *karma*, then one experiences such purification.

Out of His mercy for the extremely foolish conditioned souls, the Lord instructed Arjuna and Uddhava in the *Bhāgavata* religion. His words and teachings are to be always remembered by everyone:

"One should recognize the spiritual master as one's only true friend and well- wisher; the most worshipable manifestation of the Lord in one's life"

> *man-manā bhava mad-bhaktaḥ*—"Always think of Me and become My devotee." (*Gītā* 18.65)
> *mām ekaṁ śaraṇaṁ vraja*—"Take shelter of Me alone." (*Gītā* 18.66)
> *mayy eva mana ādhatsva*—"Fix your mind exclusively on Me." (*Gītā* 12.8)
> *mayi buddhiṁ niveśaya*—"Use your intelligence to understand Me." (*Gītā* 12.8)
> *bhaktyā mām abhijānāti*—"One can know Me as I am through devotion." (*Gītā* 18.55)
> *bhaktyāham ekayā grāhyaḥ*—"I can be attained only through devotion." (*Śrīmad Bhāgavatam* 11.14.21)

One should recognize the spiritual master as one's only true friend and well-wisher; the most worshipable manifestation of the Lord in one's life. In order to learn the *Bhāgavata-dharma*, the process by which Lord Hari can be pleased, one should surrender to the spiritual master, asking submissively from him about one's duty, and serve him.

The following are some of the teachings one should hear from the spiritual master: characteristics of devotion (*Śrīmad Bhāgavatam* 11.11.34-41); principal practices of devotion (*Śrīmad Bhāgavatam* 11.19.20-24); and the nature of one who qualifies for the practice of devotion (*Śrīmad Bhāgavatam* 11.20.27-34). All these teachings were delineated by the Lord to Uddhava.

Sri Chaitanya, the worshipable deity of Rupa and Raghunatha dasa Goswami

Narottama dāsa prays for the devotees' mercy to cross over the ocean of the illusory energy.

ki rūpe pāiba sevā mui durācāra
śrī-guru-vaiṣṇave rati nā haila āmāra
aśeṣa māyāte mana magana haila
vaiṣṇavete leśa-mātra rati nā janmila
viṣaye bhuliyā andha hainu divā-niśi
gale phāṅsa dite phire māyā se piśācī
māyāre kariyā jaya chāṛāno nā jāya
sādhu kṛpā vinā āra nāhika upāya
adoṣa-daraśi prabho patita uddhāra
ei bāra narottame karaha nistāra

"How can a wicked soul like myself attain service to the Lord? I have no affection for the service of the spiritual master and the Vaishnavas. My mind remains merged in an unlimited world of illusion and has not developed even a drop of attachment for the association of the Vaishnavas. I have forgotten myself in sense gratification and have become blind; in the meantime, that witch Maya follows me around, looking for a chance to place a noose around my neck. There seems to be no way I can be freed of her. Other than the mercy of the

> saintly, there is nothing to help me conquer maya. O Lord, you see no fault in anyone, you deliver even the most fallen. Please, O Lord, it is now time to save Narottama dāsa."

While living in Purī, Mahāprabhu set an example by going to Gadādhara Pundit to hear the stories of Dhruva and Prahlāda from the *Bhāgavatam*. Following Mahāprabhu's example we must hear the stories of the ideal devotees from the mouths of the saintly and the spiritual masters.

"While living in Puri, Mahaprabhu set an example by going to Gadadhara Pundit to hear the stories of Dhruva and Prahlada from the Bhagavatam"

bhakta-pada-dhuli bhakta-pada-jala
bhakta-bhukta-śeṣa tina sādhanera bala
ei tina sādhana haite kṛṣṇa premā haya
punaḥ punaḥ sarva-śāstre phukāriyā kaya

> "Three things give strength to one's spiritual practices: the dust of the devotees' lotus feet, the water which has washed their feet, and the remnants of their food. All the scriptures loudly proclaim that love for Krishna comes from these three things." (*Chaitanya Charitāmṛta* 3.16.60-61)

If one follows these instructions of the great authorities and engages one's senses in the service of the spiritual master and the Vaishnavas, the external-looking, superficial vision of the world disappears and an inward-looking, introspective vision of things arises.

Śrī Raghunātha dāsa Gosvāmī, Bhaktivinoda Ṭhākura, and other great authorities set the example of writing, "Teachings to the Mind" (*Manaḥ-śikṣā*). These works should be regularly studied and followed. Through them, control of the mind will be possible and one will then make rapid spiritual advancement. Other spiritual practices—*karma, jñāna,* or *yoga*—are dependent on bhakti. Independently they cannot bestow any fruits on the practitioner. Bhakti on the other hand, is fully independent. Through the devotional path, all the partial and inadequate results of *karma, jñāna,* and *yoga* are incidentally achieved. But the devotee treats everything other than pure devotional service of the Lord as worthless. Even if the Lord gives to the devotee sense gratification, liberation, or yogic powers he refuses them, thinking them obstacles to his devotional service. All the goals of human life, whether religiosity, material success or sense enjoyments, and even liberation itself, fold their hands and pray for service to the Lord's devotee.

Mahāprabhu unequivocally states that of all the devotional activities, the chanting of the Holy Names is topmost. In His *Śikṣāṣṭaka*, the Lord describes seven different auspicious results of chanting the Names. One of the secondary consequences of chanting the Holy Names is the cleansing of the mind and of the heart—*ceto-darpaṇa-mārjanam.* The reflected manifestation of the Holy Name's mercy brings about control of the mind. Through hearing and discussing the names, form, qualities, and activities of the Lord with a service attitude to the devotees, the mercy of the Holy Name manifests like a rising sun, destroying the darkness of ignorance. As the mode of ignorance recedes, control of the mind is easily attained. The mind cannot be completely controlled through any path of spiritual advancement other than bhakti.

Chapter XIII

Practice and Preaching

namo mahā-vadānyāya
kṛṣṇa-prema-pradāya te
kṛṣṇāya kṛṣṇa-caitanya-
nāmne gaura-tviṣe namaḥ

"I offer my respectful obeisances unto Lord Śrī Krishna who comes with a golden effulgence and carries the name of Krishna Chaitanya. In this form, He is more magnanimous than any other avatar, even Krishna Himself, because He freely distributes what no one has ever given before—pure love of Krishna."
(*Chaitanya Charitāmṛta* 2.19.53)

With this verse Śrīla Rūpa Gosvāmī summarizes the mood of Chaitanya Mahāprabhu, paying homage to Lord Chaitanya's identity, name, form, qualities, and pastimes. Rupa identifies Mahāprabhu as Krishna Himself in the most perfect form as the lover of the Vraja *gopī*s, and explains that Mahāprabhu is known by the name Krishna Chaitanya. Similarly, Krishnadāsa Kavirāja Gosvāmī wrote:

śeṣa-līlāya dhare nāma śrī-kṛṣṇa-caitanya
śrī-kṛṣṇa jānāye saba viśva kaila dhanya

"In the latter part of His life He was known as Śrī Krishna Chaitanya. The purport of His name is that He blesses the whole world by giving it consciousness (*caitanya*) of Krishna." (*Chaitanya Charitāmṛta* 1.3.34)

Mahāprabhu's form is described by the words *gaura-tviṣe,* "to Him whose body is of a golden hue."

Svarūpa Dāmodara describes the Lord as *rādhā-bhāva-dyuti-suvalita*—possessing the color of molten gold like that of Śrīmatī Rādhārāṇī. Mahāprabhu's principal qualities of compassion and munificence are revealed with the words *mahā-vadanyāya*, and His pastime of distributing love of God, the *prema* which is not possessed even by gods like Brahmā and Shiva, is described by the words *kṛṣṇa-prema-pradāya*.

THE PURPOSE OF MAHĀPRABHU'S INCARNATION

Sri Chaitanya Mahaprabhu

After completing His magnanimous pastimes full of sweetness, the Supreme Person, Vrajendranandana Śrī Krishna, left the earth along with His eternal associates the cows, cowherders, and cowherd girls. On returning to His eternal abode, Goloka, He began to think as follows: "All this time I have not bestowed pure love of Myself on the world. By studiously reading the scriptures, the *jīva* souls may come to understand their true identity and engage in My service by following the *vidhi-mārga*. But by following only this method of devotional service, no one can ever reach the supreme level of devotion as found in the residents of Vraja. On the *vidhi* path, the devotee is constantly aware of My majesty and thus his love does not reach the pinnacles of intensity that are common in Vraja. Devotion diluted by consciousness of My divine majesty is not so pleasing to Me.

sakala jagate more kare vidhi-bhakti
vidhi-bhaktye vraja-bhāva pāite nāhi śakti
aiśvarya-jñānete saba jagat miśrita
aiśvarya-śithila-preme nāhi mora prīta
aiśvarya-jñāne vidhi-bhajana kariyā
vaikuṇṭhake jāya catur-vidha mukti pāñā

"The complete, potent Lord took on the golden color and the spirit of His beloved Radha, His complete potency, and appeared in Nabadwip-Mayapura as the son of Jagannatha Misra and Saci Devi"

"Everyone throughout the world worships Me according to scriptural injunctions; but by this process of *vidhi bhakti* one cannot attain the loving moods of Vraja. The whole world looks upon Me with awe and veneration, but devotion diluted by such consciousness of My majesty is not preferred by Me. One who worships according to the scriptural injunctions in a mood of awe and veneration attains the four kinds of liberation and goes to Vaikuṇṭha.

(*Chaitanya Charitāmṛta* 1.3.15-7)

"A devotee who follows the *vidhi* path will no doubt attain one of the four kinds of liberation in Vaikuṇṭha, *sārṣṭi* (possessing riches identical to Mine), *sāmīpya* (residing close to Me), *sālokya* (residing on the same planet as I) or *sārūpya* (having a form like Mine). But even Vaishnavas on the *vidhi-mārga* have no desire for *sāyujyā mukti,* for it means merging into My impersonal aspect and losing their identity as My servants.

sāyujyā śunite bhaktera hay ghṛṇā lajjā bhaya
naraka vāñchaya tabu sāyujya nā laya

"When a devotee hears of *sāyujyā mukti*, he feels disgust, shame, and fear. He would rather go to hell than merge into the formless Brahman.

(*Chaitanya Charitāmṛta* 2.6.268)

"My exclusive devotees desire nothing but the joy of serving Me and do not think anything else can bring happiness. It is My desire to preach throughout the world a path of pure love which transcends the *vidhi-mārga*. I will preach the fundamental religious activity of the Kali Yuga, the chanting of My Holy Names, and by mixing the Name with the different relational moods of servitorship, friendship, protectiveness, and erotic love, I will make the world dance in ecstasy. I too will take on the mood of a devotee and, by experiencing this loving ecstasy Myself, will teach the path of pure love to the world. One who does not put a particular religious teaching into practice cannot expect to preach it effectively.

yuga-dharma pravartāmu nāma-saṅkīrtana
cāri bhāva-bhakti diyā nācāmu bhuvana
āpani karimu bhakta-bhāva aṅgīkāre
āpani ācari bhakti śikhāimu sabāre
āpane nā kaile dharma śikhāna nā yāya
ei ta siddhānta gītā-bhāgavate gāya

"I shall personally inaugurate the religion of the age, *nāma-saṅkīrtana*, the congregational chanting of the Holy Name. By giving ecstatic love of God to the world, I will make it dance. I shall take the part of a devotee, and I shall teach devotional service to all by practicing it Myself. No one can teach religious activities to others without putting them into practice himself. The *Gītā* and *Bhāgavatam* both confirm this truth. (*Chaitanya Charitāmṛta* 1.3.19-21)

yuga-dharma-pravartana haya aṁśa haite
āmā vinā anye nāre vraja-prema dite

"I establish the religious principles for each age through My plenary portions. I alone, however, can bestow the kind of loving service found in Vraja.
(*Chaitanya Charitāmṛta* 1.3.26)

"The preaching of the religious principles of an age can be propagated by any of My unlimited expansions, partial or plenary portions. However, the supreme gift of *vraja-prema* cannot be given by anyone other than Me, Vrajendranandana. Consequently, I will descend to the surface of the earth with My closest associates and, engaging in various delightful pastimes with them, I will distribute the chanting of the Holy Names and *vraja-prema*." (*Anubhāṣya* 1.3.13-28)

After so deciding, the complete, potent Lord took on the golden color and the spirit of His beloved Radha, His complete potency, and appeared in Nabadwip-Māyāpura as the son of Jagannātha Miśra and Śacī Devī. This event took place at the dawn of Kali Yuga.

The dawn or first part of the age of Kali (*kali-kāle prathama sandhyāya*) is explained by our worshipable Śrīla Prabhupāda in his *Anubhāṣya* as follows: "The word *sandhyā* refers to the sixth part of the age at its beginning and end. The *prathama-sandhyā* is thus the beginning of the age and is one-twelfth of its entire period. The *śeṣa-sandhyā* is the same length of time at the end of the age. Since the Kali Yuga lasts 432,000 solar years, its *prathama-sandhyā* continues for 36,000 years. Lord Chaitanya appeared in Nabadwip Māyāpura after 4,586 solar years of Kali Yuga had passed."

In the first part of His life, Mahāprabhu went by the name Viśvambhara, "He who maintains the world." He lived up to this name by distributing love of God. Similarly, in the latter part of His life He was known as Krishna Chaitanya, "Krishna consciousness." By making the people of the world conscious of Krishna He brought good fortune to all.

"In the first part of His life, Mahaprabhu went by the name Visvambhara, 'He who maintains the world.' He lived up to this name by distributing love of God. Similarly, in the latter part of His life He was known as Krishna Chaitanya"

prathama līlāya tāṅra viśvambhara nāma
bhakti-rase bharila dharila bhūta-grāma
ḍubhṛñ dhātura artha poṣaṇa dhāraṇa
puṣila dharila prema diyā tri-bhuvana
śeṣa-līlāya dhare nāma śrī-kṛṣṇa-caitanya
śrī-kṛṣṇa jānāye saba viśva kaila dhanya

"In His early pastimes, Lord Chaitanya was known by the name Viśvambhara because He inundated (*bhara*) the world (*viśva*) with the nectar of devotion and thus saved all living beings. The verb root *ḍubhṛñ* [which is the root of the word *bhara*] indicates nourishing and maintaining. So this name indicates that Mahāprabhu nourishes and maintains the three worlds by distributing love of God. In His later pastimes, He was known as Śrī Krishna Chaitanya. He blessed the whole world by teaching about Lord Śrī Krishna."

(*Chaitanya Charitāmṛta* 1.3.32-34)

Śrī Chaitanya Mahāprabhu accepted the mood of a devotee in order to preach the great treasure of elevated and effulgent love for Krishna through His own acts of relishing it. This great example is indeed the standard we should follow.

Mahāprabhu, the Gardener in the Orchard of Love

"In this spirit of munificence, the compassionate Lord Gauranga played the role of a gardener who planted an orchard of love-fruit trees in Nabadwip"

Krishna's Vraja pastime is one of munificence (*audārya*) in which sweetness (*mādhurya*) predominates, while His Nabadwip pastime as Gaura is one of sweetness in which munificence predominates. In this spirit of munificence, the compassionate Lord Gaurāṅga played the role of a gardener who planted an orchard of love-fruit trees in Nabadwip. Mahāprabhu is sometimes said to be the tree of ecstatic love for Krishna, but by a divine twist, He is also the one who enjoys the fruits of this tree and distributes them. While the Lord relished the taste of these fruits, He also gave them away with such enthusiasm that He used both hands. As He did so, He said,

ekalā mālākāra āmi kāhāṅ kāhāṅ jāba
ekalā vā kata phala pāṛiyā bilāba
ekalā uṭhāñā dite haya pariśrama
keha pāya keha nā pāya rahe mane bhrama
ataeva āmi ājñā diluṅ sabākāre
jāhāṅ tāhāṅ prema-phala deha jāre tāre

"As I am the only gardener, to how many different places can I go? And since I am all alone, how many fruits can I pick and give away? It is extremely tiring to gather up the fruits and distribute them alone; it disturbs Me to know that some people will receive My fruit and others will not. Therefore I order everyone to distribute these fruits of love to everyone they see, wherever they go."

(*Chaitanya Charitāmṛta* 1.9.34-6)

In this way, Mahāprabhu asked those who received His mercy to help Him. In this way they can render service to Him.

ātma-icchāmṛte vṛkṣa siñci nirantara
tāhāte asaṅkhya phala vṛkṣera upara

ataeva saba phala deha jāre tāre
khāiyā hauk loka ajara amare

"I constantly water the tree with the nectar of My personal desire. As a result, there are countless fruits of love upon it. Therefore, I ask all of you to distribute these fruits to everyone everywhere so that by eating them, all can become free from old age and death."
(*Chaitanya Charitāmṛta* 1.9.38-9)

Deity of Kurma Avatar, Kurmakshetra

Mahāprabhu further specifies that it is the special duty of those who are born in India to take up this service:

bhārata-bhūmite haila manuṣya janma jāra
janma sārthaka kari kara para-upakāra

"Whoever has taken a human birth in the land of Bhārata should make his life successful and engage in welfare work for others."
(*Chaitanya Charitāmṛta* 1.9.41)

Lord Chaitanya Mahāprabhu thus so compassionately distributed the fruits of love of God in this effort to make the world fortunate. But we are so wretched that we are indifferent to this matchless gift and refuse to accept it—what to speak of participating in the service of preaching.

Mahāprabhu's Instructions to Kūrma and Vāsudeva

When Lord Śrī Chaitanya Mahāprabhu went on pilgrimage to southern India, He distributed Krishna's name and Krishna *prema* to the inhabitants, making them into Vaishnavas. One of the first holy places He visited in South India was the abode of Kūrma, a deity form of the Lord's turtle incarnation.

In that town lived a Vedic brahmin named Kūrma Vipra. When Kūrma saw Mahāprabhu, he was very impressed by His spiritual effulgence and invited Him to his house for meals. He and his entire family served Mahāprabhu devotedly, charming the Lord with their humility and faith. Kūrma became so enchanted with the Lord that when it was time for Him to leave, he felt unable to bear His separation. He fell down at the Lord's feet and begged to be allowed to accompany Him wherever He went. The Lord was extremely pleased with Kūrma's attitude, but nevertheless answered him with the following words:

prabhu kahe aiche bāta kabhu nā kahibā
gṛhe rahi kṛṣṇa-nāma nirantara laibā
jāre dekha tāre kaha kṛṣṇa upadeśa
āmāra ājñāya guru hañā tāra ei deśa
kabhu nā bādhibe tomāya viṣaya taraṅga
punar api ei ṭhāi pābe mora saṅga

"Never make such a suggestion again. You should rather remain at home and constantly chant the holy name of Krishna. Instruct whomever you see in the religion of Krishna. Become a spiritual master on My order and deliver every-

> one in this land. Do this and you will never again be entangled in the waves of materialistic life. Indeed, one day you will have My company again, here in this very place." (*Chaitanya Charitāmṛta*, 2.7.127-9)

This was the way that the Lord spread Krishna consciousness on His travels from Puri to Setubandha at the southern tip of the subcontinent, purifying the way with the touch of His lotus feet. He would mercifully stop at the houses of brahmins like Kūrma and shower them with grace by instructing them to chant the Holy Names and to instruct others in the chanting.

On that night, the Lord stayed in Kūrma's home and the next morning, after bathing, prepared to continue on His way. Kūrma Vipra followed Him part of the way until the Lord told him to go back home. In the meantime, a leper named Vāsudeva was also on his way to Kūrma's house. He had heard that Mahāprabhu was there and was hoping to get a glance of the Lord. When Vāsudeva learned from Kūrma that the Lord had already departed, he was so disappointed that he fell down on the ground and fainted, lamenting his misfortune.

The Lord, as the omniscient indweller of all beings, was fully aware of Vāsudeva's distress. Even though He had already walked a great distance from Kūrma's house, He returned to grant the leper the opportunity to see him. Not only did He allow Vāsudeva to see Him, but even embraced him affectionately. Mahāprabhu is the friend of the distressed and His miraculous touch immediately cured Vāsudeva of his leprosy and turned him into a healthy and handsome young man.

Vāsudeva Vipra was amazed to see the limitless mercy of the Supreme Lord and with tears in his eyes he glorified the Lord with a verse spoken by Sudāmā Vipra from the *Bhāgavatam*:

kvāhaṁ daridraḥ pāpīyān
kva kṛṣṇaḥ śrī-niketanaḥ
brahma-bandhur iti smāhaṁ
bāhubhyāṁ parirambhitaḥ

> "Just see the difference between a miserable sinner like myself and the abode of the Goddess of Fortune, Śrī Krishna! Although I am a most unqualified brahmin, He has mercifully embraced me in His arms."
> (*Śrīmad Bhāgavatam* 10.89.16)

When Vāsudeva had become a beautiful young man as a result of Mahāprabhu's miraculous touch, he realized that Śrī Chaitanya was none other than the ocean of all virtue and master of the most fallen, the Supreme Person Hari Himself. He said, "Even the lowest classes of society were disgusted at seeing the open sores of my leprous body. They would run away whenever they saw me coming. The only person who could possibly be so merciful as to touch me is the supremely independent Lord, whose only distress is to see the distress of others. O most merciful Lord! I think, however, that I was better off as an untouchable leper. Now that you have made me handsome, I will no doubt become intoxicated with vanity and unable to remember your lotus feet."

Mahāprabhu considered Vāsudeva Vipra to be most qualified due to his humility, and with a choking voice, ecstatically instructed him to act as an *ācārya*, just as He had ordered Kūrma:

prabhu kahe kabhu tomāya nā habe abhimāna
nirantara kaha tumi kṛṣṇa kṛṣṇa nāma
kṛṣṇa upadeśi kara jīvera nistāra
acirāte kṛṣṇa tomā karibena pāra

"You will never become vain if you constantly chant Krishna's name. Deliver the fallen souls by instructing them about Krishna, and Krishna will very quickly deliver you from the material world." (*Chaitanya Charitāmṛta* 2.7.147-8)

After giving these assurances to Vāsudeva, the supremely merciful Mahāprabhu left the pilgrimage town of Kūrmakṣetra. Kūrma Vipra and Vāsudeva embraced each other and sang Mahāprabhu's glories, their eyes filled with tears of sadness at His departure. Krishnadāsa Kavirāja Gosvāmī has described this story as "the deliverance of Vāsudeva," and named Mahāprabhu, *Vāsudevāmṛtaprada*, "the giver of ambrosia to Vāsudeva."

Preaching Does Not Require Renouncing Home

Śrīla Prabhupāda Bhaktisiddhānta Sarasvatī Ṭhākura has commented on Mahāprabhu's instructions to Kūrma Vipra with the following words: "For those who are determined to abandon everything to take shelter of Him and serve Him exclusively, the Supreme Lord Śrī Chaitanya Mahāprabhu here gives the instruction to remain in the home, i.e., to give up the pride of being a heroic performer of *bhajana* and to adopt a regular practice of chanting the holy name of Krishna and, with the humility characteristic of those who remain in the householder station, instruct others in chanting the Holy Names. If one takes up the duties of a spiritual master in this way, he will never become entangled in the 'waves of materialistic life' in the form of the desire for self-aggrandizement.

"Many foolish people think that preaching through the writing of books as done by Rūpa Gosvāmī, Sanātana Gosvāmī, Jīva Gosvāmī or Raghunātha dāsa Gosvāmī, or taking on large numbers of disciples like Madhvācārya, Rāmānujācārya or Narottama dāsa Ṭhākura, is an impediment to spiritual practice. Indeed, these less intelligent persons even claim that such activities are materially entangling. By adhering to such erroneous ideas, they become offenders to the many unalloyed devotees who have nothing to do with the material world and yet preach. This teaching of the Lord to Kūrma and Vāsudeva is intended for such people. If they analyze these teachings carefully, they will give up their pride in a false show of humility and advance the cause of genuine *bhajana* by instructing rather than showing disdain for those who are without devotion to the Lord."
(*Anubhāṣya* 2.7.130)

Śrīla Prabhupāda continues: "Śrī Krishna Chaitanya bestowed consciousness on the unconscious living beings. After He had done so, He instructed those who had been brought to consciousness and attracted to the service of the Lord to take on the role of teachers or *ācāryas* and do for others what He had done for them. Through this pastime of preaching the scriptural path and bringing more souls into the fold of the Lord's infallible family, Gaurasundara fully revealed the glories of His incarnation." (*Anubhāṣya* 2.7.152)

"Sri Krishna Chaitanya bestowed consciousness on the unconscious living beings. After He had done so, He instructed those who had been brought to consciousness and attracted to the service of the Lord to take on the role of teachers or acaryas and do for others what He had done for them"

Some people have difficulty understanding the meaning of the instruction of the Lord to take up the practice of chanting the Holy Names and to simultaneously preach it. If such persons go on to dress up as gurus, they take on demoniac qualities like pride, egotism, and arrogance, and walk through the gates of hell. For this reason, a devotee should take the vow of engaging in personal devotional practice headed by chanting and preaching activities in the spirit of humble service to the servants of the Lord. By so doing, one will be free from any worries about the influence of demoniac qualities. Mahāprabhu Himself taught that the real identity of the individual is not related to the bodily concept of life; "I am the servant of the servant of the servant of the Lord of the *gopīs*." One who keeps this consciousness alive while seeking his own welfare and that of others is free from any fear of falldown. Otherwise, one may well succumb to the temptation of pride.

Bhaktivinoda Ṭhākura has sung about the danger of pride for someone who is otherwise engaged in preaching activity:

āmi ta vaiṣṇava ei buddhi haile
amānī nā haba āmi
pratiṣṭhāśā āsi hṛdaya duṣibe
haibo niraya-gāmī

nije śreṣtha māni ucchiṣṭādi-dāne
abhimāna habe bhāra
tāi śiṣya tava thākiba sarvadā
nā laiba pūjā kāra

> "If I think that I have become a Vaishnava then I will never be prideless. The desire for prestige will descend on my heart and contaminate it and I will go to hell. Thinking myself to be superior to others, I will leave them the remnants of my food and this will fill me with arrogance. Therefore, O Vaishnava Ṭhākura, I promise to always remain your disciple and to never accept worship from anyone." (*Kalyāṇa-kalpa-taru*)

If we disregards this instruction of the great authority Bhaktivinoda Ṭhākura, then we will be affected by our offensive behavior. One may easily deceive innocent people by mouthing the teachings of devotional service while internally thinking "I am a spiritual master" or "I am a Vaishnava," but no one can fool the Lord who dwells within the heart and knows every thought. How can we expect to deceive Him? By ignoring Him, we commits offenses that will result in our degradation to lower species of life and hellish suffering.

Sanātana's Praise of Haridāsa Ṭhākura

Mahāprabhu's most beloved associate Sanātana Gosvāmī praised Haridāsa Ṭhākura, the great teacher of the Holy Name, as the ideal example of the ability to harmonize the practices of chanting the Holy Name and educating people about chanting.

sanātana kahe tomā-sama kebā āche āna
mahāprabhura gaṇe tumi mahā-bhāgyavān
avatāra-kārya prabhura nāma-pracāre
sei nija-kārya prabhu karena tomāra dvāre
pratyaha kara tina-lakṣa nāma-saṅkīrtana
sabāra āge kara nāmera mahimā kathana
āpane ācare keha nā kare pracāra
pracāra karena keha, nā karena ācāra
ācāra pracāra nāmera karaha dui kārya
tumi sarva-guru tumi jagatera ārya

Sanātana Gosvāmī asked, "Haridāsa Ṭhākura, is anyone your equal? You are the most blessed of the associates of Śrī Chaitanya Mahāprabhu. The purpose of the Lord's incarnation is to spread the chanting of His holy names, but He is doing this work through you. You daily chant 300,000 Holy Names and you tell everyone of the glories of chanting. Some carry out the injunctions of spiritual life but do nothing to spread these teachings, whereas others preach but do not follow the principles themselves. You, however, do both things and therefore you are the spiritual master of all, a truly religious person in this world."

(*Chaitanya Charitāmṛta* 3.4.99-103)

In his *Anubhāṣya,* our most worshipable Śrīla Prabhupāda, made the following comments on these verses: "Haridāsa Ṭhākura is the spiritual master of the entire universe and the object of veneration for everyone. As a brahmin through the process of initiation, he chanted the pure Name and is thus qualified to be an *ācārya*, or one who presents the ideal standard of practice. Furthermore, through loudly chanting these names and their glories, he initiated all the living beings in the world in the sacrifice of the Holy Name. By so doing, he qualified as a *pracāraka* or preacher. In this way Haridāsa engaged in the practice and in the dissemination of the teaching." (*Anubhāṣya* 3.4.103)

ACQUIRING THE AUTHORITY TO PREACH

We have seen that Mahāprabhu Himself gave notice that Haridāsa kept to this standard in preaching the Holy Names. The importance of authority in teaching is further explained by Krishna in His instructions to Arjuna in the *Bhagavad-gītā*:

yad yad ācarati śreṣṭhas
tat tad evetaro janaḥ
sa yat pramāṇaṁ kurute
lokas tad anuvartate

"The behavior of superior people is imitated by the ordinary; that which they accept as authoritative is followed by the rest of society." (*Gītā* 3.21)

The words "superior people" (*śreṣṭha*) mean those who are genuine authorities, or *mahājanas* maintaining the highest standards of morality. Their path is the one we must follow, as was stated by Yudhiṣṭhira in answer to the questions of Yamarāja: *mahājano yena gataḥ sa panthā*—"The path of the *mahājanas* is the one everyone should follow."

Mahājanas, or great authorities, are free from the four defects: (1) *bhrama* (error), or the tendency to take the real for the unreal or the unreal for the real, such as a rope for a snake, etc.; (2) *pramāda*, mistakes arising from carelessness or inattention; (3) *karaṇā-paṭava*, limitations on the senses which result in erroneous perceptions; and (4) *vipralipsā*, the desire to deceive. When one has the desire to deceive, then even though he knows his knowledge is inadequate he makes a pretense of knowing, or even though in the possession of the truth, he hides it from others. Anyone free from these defects should be considered authoritative. One should learn from a person who is learned in the scriptures and who is disciplined by saintly behavioral standards; who is experienced in the practices of devotional service and is free from anger, enviousness, and hatred. One may be capable of citing hundreds of verses from scripture and make glorious and eloquent speeches, but if he has not adopted the standards of behavior set by Śrī Chaitanya Mahāprabhu, his rhetoric alone will have no effect. Preaching without practice is futile.

The *Bhāgavatam* tells the story of how Mahārāja Parīkṣit[2] came upon the personified form of Kali Yuga, who at the beginning of the age of Kali, was wreaking havoc on earth. Parīkṣit wished to banish Kali completely from the earth, but Kali prayed to be given a place of his own. Parīkṣit then gave him five places where he could live, and these are known as the abodes of irreligion. They are: (1) the gambling den, or anywhere betting takes place; (2) the places of intoxication—taverns, opium dens, or any place where drugs (including tobacco) are consumed; (3) anywhere illicit sex is practiced, i.e., wherever there are sexual relations outside of marriage or even excessive attachment to one's lawful wedded partner; (4) wherever violence to animals is practiced, i.e., slaughterhouses and all places where meat is consumed by humans as food; and (5) wherever large amounts of gold are accumulated. Any place where money is spent for purposes other than the service of the Lord, it is being misused and results in undesirable entanglement. Prabhupāda Bhaktisiddhānta Sarasvatī states that gambling destroys truthfulness; intoxication results in the destruction of austerity; illicit sex destroys inner and outer purity; and meat-eating destroys mercy. Avoidance of these sinful activities is the pillar of religiosity, and tolerance of them means the establishment of irreligion. The possession of great wealth lays the way to a sinful life. Therefore, wherever there is a large accumulation of riches, untruth, arrogance, lust, and violence are found.

"One may be capable of citing hundreds of verses from scripture and make glorious and eloquent speeches, but if he has not adopted the standards of behavior set by Sri Chaitanya Mahaprabhu, his rhetoric alone will have no effect. Preaching without practice is futile"

athaitāni na seveta
bubhūṣuḥ puruṣaḥ kvacit
viśeṣato dharma-śīlo
rājā loka-patir guruḥ

> "Thus, one who desires his own well-being should refrain from engaging in the above-mentioned sinful activities. The pious, kings, leaders, and teachers should especially be careful to avoid them." (*Śrīmad Bhāgavatam* 1.17.41)

One who dwells in any of the five abodes of Kali will not be able to maintain the appropriate standards of conduct, or ever expect to see his preaching fructify. For this reason Mahāprabhu repeatedly warned devotees against the association of non-devotees and sensualists. The conclusion is that a non-Vaishnava, despite his learning, his intelligence, or his eloquence as a speaker, can never expect to be an effective preacher if he is a debauchee, even if he makes claims of loyalty to Mahāprabhu. Mahāprabhu's associate Jagadānanda Pundit said,

gorāra āmi gorāra āmi mukhe balile nā cale
gorāra ācāra gorāra pracāra laile phala phale

"It is not enough to simply advertise repeatedly that one is a devotee of Mahāprabhu, saying, 'I am Gaura's, I am Gaura's.' Those who take up the practices taught by Mahāprabhu as well as His preaching mission get the results of being the Lord's follower." (*Prema-vivarta*)

Srila Narottama dasa Thakura

Narottama dāsa Ṭhākura, in his *Prema-bhakti-candrikā,* also criticizes the association of non-devotees. Narottama dāsa's prayers and hymns are collected in *Prārthanā* and *Prema-bhakti-candrikā,* while those of Bhaktivinoda Ṭhākura's are found in *Śaraṇāgati, Kalyāṇa-kalpa-taru, Gītāvalī* and *Gīta-mālā.* The songs of these *ācāryas* contain the essence of all the devotional scriptures. One should study these books after taking shelter of a genuine spiritual master and accepting the principles of Vaishnava behavior from him. As one goes on to become a genuine, pure devotee, he may greatly benefit the conditioned souls by preaching the message extracted from these texts.

TAKING SHELTER OF THE LORD: THE LIFE OF THE DEVOTEE

The first song in Bhaktivinoda Ṭhākura's *Śaraṇāgati* is as follows:

śrī kṛṣṇa caitanya prabhu jīve dayā kari
sva-parṣada svīya dhāma saha avatari
atyanta durlabha prema karibāre dāna
śikhāya śaraṇāgati bhakatera prāṇa
dainya, ātma-nivedana, goptṛtve varaṇa
avaśya rakṣibe kṛṣṇa viśvāsa pālana
bhakti-anukūla mātra kāryera svīkāra
bhakti-pratikūla-bhāva varjanāṅgīkāra
ṣaḍ-aṅga śaraṇāgati haibe jāṅhāra
tāṅhāra prārthanā śune śrī-nanda-kumāra
rūpa sanātana pade dante tṛṇa kari
bhakativinoda paṛe dui pada dhari
kāṅdiyā kāṅdiyā bale āmi ta adhama
śikhāye śaraṇāgati karahe uttama

"Out of compassion for the fallen *jīvas,* Śrī Krishna Chaitanya appeared in this world with all of His eternal associates and His eternal abode. Wishing to bestow on them the most rare love for Himself, He taught the process of taking shelter of the Lord which is so important for the devotees. Humility, self-surrender, accepting Krishna as your protector, belief that Krishna will save you in all circumstances, undertaking only activities conducive to development of love for Krishna, and rejecting everything that is detrimental to it; these are the six elements of taking shelter. The son of Nanda, Krishna, listens to the prayers of anyone who takes shelter of Him in this way. I fall down and take hold of the feet of Rūpa and Sanātana in all humility. Crying, 'I am most fallen.' I beg, 'Please teach me how to take shelter of Krishna so that I can perfect my human life.' "

Without taking shelter in this way, one cannot perfect his human life and become free of the darkness of material conditioning. But if doing so, we will be able to properly preach about Krishna's name, form, qualities, and pastimes.

As Śrīla Prabhupāda wrote, *prāṇa āche tāṅra se-hetu pracāra*—"One who has life, preaches." (*Vaiṣṇava ke?*) Therefore, even before preaching, the devotee's first duty is to take up this process of surrender, which is the life of the devotee. Only then will he receive Krishna's blessings and be worthy of preaching the message which was given by Mahāprabhu Himself. Otherwise, he will be nothing more than a cadaver, and his preaching will benefit neither oneself nor others. We may be able to profit and gain fame from mundane people in this world, but that will hold no value on the transcendental platform. Śrīla Prabhupāda further wrote in his poem *Vaiṣṇava ke?*

Srila Prabhupada Bhaktisiddhanta Saraswati Thakura

śrī dayita-dāsa kīrtanete āśa
kara uccaiḥsvare hari-nāma-rava

"Your only hope is in the performance of *harināma-saṅkīrtana*, so chant the Holy Names as loudly as you can."

It is clear that Śrīla Prabhupāda, with these words, is asking us to chant the Holy Names loudly. If we chant without life, would that not be a source of disappointment to him?

Many offenses may be committed by aspirants to spiritual perfection. Thinking of the guru as an ordinary mortal is the gravest offense. One who thinks this way can never successfully preach the Lord's message. Can anyone who makes a pretense of preaching without putting the message into practice be truly pleasing to Mahāprabhu, who Himself stated, "I Myself put the religious principles into practice and then preach them"?

"Even before preaching, the devotee's first duty is to take up this process of surrender, which is the life of the devotee"

We pray to the spiritual master that he give us the strength and intelligence to become truly fixed in the practice of devotional service and then distribute Mahāprabhu's message everywhere. May He give us the nectar of *prema* to drink. Once intoxicated with this *prema*, we will be truly able to sing His glories.

As far as devotees on the *rāgānugā* path are concerned, they may aspire to serve Krishna in a relationship of servitude, friendship, protectiveness or conjugal love, but their aspiration must not be counterfeit. It must follow the directions of the spiritual master and only then will it result in the great fortune of service to the Lord. Rather than simply making a pretense of possessing transcendental greed, an initiated devotee should consider chanting without offenses as the principal internal, or confidential devotional practice. Then, by the grace of his guru, this transcendental greed awakens. This is the principal activity of the devout *bhakta* and this is the teaching that one should try to spread. From such practice and such preaching, one's own ultimate good will be achieved as well as the ultimate good of everyone in the world. This is absolutely certain.

The Lord's affection for His devotees is boundless

CHAPTER XIV

THE PATH OF PASSIONATE LOVE

It is clear from the previous chapter that the purpose of Mahāprabhu's appearance on this Earth was to distribute the love of the residents of Vrindavan, especially the mood of the *gopīs*, to the entire world. And He preached this love through close associates such as Rāmānanda Rāya.

gaurāṅgera madhura-līlā jāṅra karṇe praveśilā
hṛdaya nirmala bhela tāra

"Purified is the heart of one who has heard the delightful pastimes of Lord Gaurāṅga."

Lord Gaurāṅga's name, form, qualities, and activities are all delightful and sweet.

madhuraṁ madhuraṁ vapur asya vibhor
madhuraṁ madhuraṁ vadanaṁ madhuram
madhu-gandhi mṛdu-smitam etad aho
madhuraṁ madhuraṁ madhuraṁ madhuram

"What a delight is this transcendental body of the majestic Lord, what a delight!
What a delight is His beautiful face! What a delight! What a delight!
His gentle smile is as sweet as honey, how sweet, how sweet, how sweet!"
(*Chaitanya Charitāmṛta* 2.21.136)

All of Mahāprabhu's pastimes are transcendentally delightful. His pastime of meeting the world's foremost scholar and logician, Sārvabhauma Bhaṭṭācārya, is an example of such transcendental delight. For an entire week the Lord heard in silence the explanations of Vedanta given by Sārvabhauma Bhaṭṭācārya, and in the end enlightened Sārvabhauma by giving the correct interpretation of the Vedanta as well as 18 different explanations of the *ātmārāma* verse of the *Bhāgavata*. At first Sārvabhauma was deflated and disappointed in himself after witnessing the Lord's unparalleled scholarship, but taking shelter of the Lord's lotus feet, he glorified the Lord, who compassionately granted him a vision of His six-armed form.

Conversation between Sri Chaitanya Mahaprabhu and Ramananda Raya

Delightful, too, was Mahāprabhu's reciprocation with King Pratāparudra, culminating in His hearing the *Gopī-gīta* verses from from the King, embracing him and glorifying him as *bhūrida*—"most charitable"—and then granting him too a vision of His six-armed form.

tava kathāmṛtaṁ tapta-jīvanaṁ
kavibhir īḍitaṁ kalmaṣāpaham
śravaṇa-maṅgalaṁ śrīmad-ātataṁ
bhuvi gṛṇanti ye bhūridā janāḥ

"My Lord, the nectar of Your words and the descriptions of Your activities are like nectar for those who are parched in this dry material world. Transmitted by exalted personalities, these narrations eradicate all sinful reactions. Whoever hears them attains all good fortune. Those in this world who broadcast these delightful topics are certainly the most munificent altruists."
(*Śrīmad Bhāgavatam* 10.31.9, *Chaitanya Charitāmṛta* 2.14.14)

Mahāprabhu's pastime of teaching the theology of *sambandha, abhidheya,* and *prayojana* to Rūpa Gosvāmī at Prayāga and to Sanātana Gosvāmī at the Daśāśvamedha Ghāṭ in Benares is another source of nectar. But perhaps the most delightful of all His pastimes is that of His hearing from Rāmānanda Rāya about the ultimate goal of spiritual life and the process for attaining it.

MAHĀPRABHU'S CONVERSATION WITH RĀMĀNANDA

In His first meeting with Rāmānanda Rāya, Mahāprabhu feigned ignorance and asked Rāmānanda about various spiritual practices and their goals. In answer, Rāmānanda Rāya gradually explained the different levels of philosophical understanding until he finally came to the highest understanding of spiritual life, the ecstatic loving interchanges between Radha and Krishna.

The spiritual methods Mahāprabhu progressively heard from Rāmānanda Rāya were: (1) practice of one's prescribed duty according to the *varṇāśrama-dharma*; (2) giving up the results of one's activities by offering them to the Lord, or devotional service mixed with other disinterested activity; (3) renunciation of one's *varṇāśrama* duties, or *karma-sannyāsa*; and (4) devotional service mixed with the search for knowledge (*jñāna-miśrā bhakti*). As Rāmānanda proposed each of these practices and their results, Mahāprabhu rejected them, saying, "This is superficial. Go more deeply and reveal something more substantial." Rāmānanda proceeded to describe *jñāna-śūnyā bhakti*, i.e., devotional service with no desire for liberation. At this Mahāprabhu expressed approval but asked Rāmānanda to go still deeper.

As Mahāprabhu played the role of a curious seeker, Rāmānanda, out of a desire to serve and answer the Lord, played the role of a teacher. He then described devotional service in the mood of passiveness as the goal of spiritual life. Mahāprabhu approved, but nonetheless, he again asked Ramananda to go deeper. Rāmānanda then described devotion in the spirit of service, then in the moods of friendship and protectiveness, whereupon Mahāprabhu grew more and more enthusiastic saying, "This is excellent, but please go deeper." Finally, Rāmānanda spoke of the love of Krishna's mistresses as the supreme goal of spiritual life, at which the Lord approved ecstatically. He said, "Yes! This is the limit of spiritual achievement, there can be no doubt. But, if there is anything more than this, please tell Me."

Rāmānanda Rāya then began to describe the love of Radha for Krishna as the crowning experience of divine love. The Lord's joy then increased beyond bounds and He kept asking Rāmānanda to go on speaking. Rāmānanda now began to describe the modalities of Radha and Krishna's loving exchanges, quoting verses from the *Gītā-govinda* and other texts which describe the unequalled character of Radha's most competent love for the Lord. At this, Mahāprabhu said to Rāmānanda in great satisfaction:

ebe se jāniluṅ sādhya-sādhana-nirṇaya
āge āra āche kichu śunite mana haya

> "Now I have what I came to learn from you; the goal of life and the process of achieving it. Nevertheless, I think that there is still something more and I desire greatly to hear it." (*Chaitanya Charitāmṛta* 2.8.118)

PREMA-VILĀSA-VIVARTA

As Mahāprabhu specifically asked to hear more about Radha and Krishna, and Their relations and pastimes, Rāmānanda continued to recount all he knew on the subject. Still Mahāprabhu continued to plead with him to go on, further and further. Finally, Rāmānanda gave a description of a most delightful state of ecstatic love called *prema-vilāsa-vivarta.* In this particular transformation of the loving mood, he explained, Radha is overcome by her most elevated ecstatic feelings and, even though separated from Krishna, thinks He is in fact present.

Radha and Krishna's divine love affairs are conducted in two modes: that of separation and that of union. Separation, or *vipralambha,* is a particular transformation of Radha and Krishna's pastimes which serves to increase the pleasure of union. In the *prema-vilāsa-vivarta,* however, due to the intensity of Her *adhirūḍha-mahā-bhāva,* Radha experiences hallucinations of union even in the state of separation. The ecstatic beauty of Radha in this condition is indescribable.

For Mahāprabhu's pleasure, Rāmānanda Rāya sang a song of his own composition describing this situation. Mahāprabhu was so overcome by emotion on hearing Ramananda's song that He covered Rāmānanda's mouth with His hand. The song portrayed Rādhārāṇī's words when in this exalted mood of love:

pahilehi rāga nayana-bhaṅge bhela
anudina bāḍhala, avadhi nā gela
nā so ramaṇa, nā hāma ramaṇī
duṅhu-mana manobhava peṣala jāni'

e sakhī, se-saba prema-kāhinī
kānu-ṭhāme kahabi vichurala jāni'
nā khoṅjaluṅ dūtī, nā khoṅjaluṅ ān
duṅhukeri milane madhya ta pāṅca-bāṇa
ab sohi virāga, tuṅhu bheli dūtī
su-purukha-premaki aichana rīti

"O *sakhī*! In the very beginning, Our eyes met and Our love took birth. Day by day it grew, never finding a limit. He is not My husband and I am not His wife; it is as though Cupid himself ground our minds into powder and mixed them together. O *sakhī*, now that We are separated, if Krishna has forgotten all these things, then remind Him of this: When We first met, We didn't have to seek out a go-between or anyone else. The only one who brought Us together was Cupid with his five arrows, no one else. Now that We are apart, that love has gone and He has had to engage you as a messenger. That is the way of love with good-looking men like Krishna."
(*Chaitanya Charitāmṛta* 2.8.194, See also *Chaitanya Charitāmṛta* 2 13.46)

Our most worshipable predecessor *ācārya* Śrīla Ṭhākura Bhaktivinoda paraphrases this song as follows: "Prior to our first meeting, during the period known as *pūrva-rāga* or incipient affection, through the mutual exchange of glances, something called *rāga* or love suddenly came into existence. This *rāga* was born of both our natures and it kept on growing and growing without reaching any limit. Krishna is the lover or *ramaṇa,* but in this case He was not the cause of the *rāga*; neither was I, the beloved or *ramaṇī*, its cause. The love that arose when We first looked at each other was created by Cupid, who is known as Manobhava, or 'mind-born.' He appeared and ground our minds into a powder. If you think, O *sakhī*, that Krishna has forgotten all this love now that We are separated from each other, then tell Him the following: Previously, We sought out no messenger at the time of union—We asked no one to intercede. The only mediator We had was Cupid himself with his five arrows. Now that We are separated, the *rāga* has become *virāga. Virāga* means *viśiṣṭa-rāga*, or 'a special kind of love,' or *viccheda-gata raga*, 'love in separation.' In this case it has become *adhirūḍha mahā-bhāva,* or the most elevated stage of divine love. Now you are acting as the *dūtī*, or messenger. You will see that handsome men always behave in this way."

Śrīla Ṭhākura Bhaktivinoda continues: "The purport of this song is as follows: during the time of union, love (*rāga*) takes the form of desire and itself takes the role as the messenger. At the time of separation, love becomes a *dūtī* in the form of *adhirūḍha-mahā-bhāva*. This highest platform of divine love is the messenger of *prema-vilāsa-vivarta*, in which there is an experience of union even during separation. Thus Rādhārāṇī addresses this love as a messenger. This indicates that loving affairs are as relishable during separation as they are during enjoyment. *Prema-vilāsa-vivarta* is like a hallucination, similar to one's taking a piece of rope to be a snake, such as when Radha takes a tamāla tree to be Krishna. In this state of confusion born of the *adhirūḍha mahā-bhāva,* She experiences a type of union." (*Amṛta-pravāha-bhāṣya* to *Chaitanya Charitāmṛta* 2.8.193)

In his *Anubhāṣya*, our most worshipable Gurudeva, Prabhupāda Bhaktisiddhānta Sarasvatī Ṭhākura, gives further comments about Rāmānanda's song: "With the words *na so ramaṇa nā ham ramaṇī* ('He is not My lover and I am not His beloved.') Mahāprabhu has revealed the *acintya-bhedābheda-tattva*. It is on this basis that Jīva Gosvāmī gave this name to his philosophical doctrine in the *Sarva-saṁvādinī*. In this song, there is subjective confusion between the identities of the lovers. Ordinary conditioned souls should be warned not to adopt the process of worship known as *ahaṁgrahopāsanā*, identifying themselves with one of the eternal associates of the Lord or the Lord Himself. The philosophy of *ahaṁgrahopāsanā* is a product of the foolishness of those who believe that all is only one spiritual energy. It is the inverse of the spiritual pastimes of the Divine Couple. Mahāprabhu descended from that part of Goloka where His eternal pastimes are going on in order to demonstrate the error of those who think that nondual supreme truth does not experience the subjective (*āśraya*) aspect of divine love."

(*Anubhāṣya* to *Chaitanya Charitāmṛta* 2.8.19)

"Mahaprabhu descended
from that part
of Goloka where
His eternal pastimes
are going on in order
to demonstrate
the error of those
who think that
nondual supreme truth
does not experience
the subjective (ashraya)
aspect of divine love"

The Sadhana for Achieving the Highest Goal

Mahāprabhu accepted that there was no higher achievement than *prema-vilasa-vivarta* in spiritual life, and He then asked Rāmānanda what was the sadhana, or process for achieving it. Rāmānanda began his answer by first denying he was the true speaker.

mora mukhe vaktā tumi tumi hao śrotā
atyanta rahasya śuna sādhanera kathā

> "You are speaking through me and at the same time You are listening. Now hear the extremely confidential explanation of how this goal can be attained."
>
> (*Chaitanya Charitāmṛta* 2.8.200)

Rāmānanda then explained how Radha and Krishna's transcendental pastimes are dependent on Radha's girlfriends for their development. Only these *sakhīs* have the right of entry into Radha-Krishna's confidential pastimes, and they are the ones who expand these *līlās*. Without them, the *līlās* would be limited. The *sakhīs* not only participate in these pastimes, but they also are the first to relish them. Without their leadership, no one can enter these confidential pastimes. Thus they must be accepted before the acceptance of Radha and Krishna.

sakhī vinā ei līlāya anyera nāhi gati
sakhī-bhāve je tāṅre kare anugati
rādhā-kṛṣṇa-kuñja-sevā sādhya sei pāya
sei sādhya pāite āra nāhika upāya

> "Indeed, other than the *gopīs* no one can enter Radha and Krishna's confidential pastimes. Only those who follow in the *gopīs*' footsteps, worshiping the Lord in their mood, can realize the ultimate goal of service to Śrī Śrī Radha-Krishna in the forest bowers of Vrindavan. There is no other procedure for achieving this goal."
>
> (*Chaitanya Charitāmṛta* 2.8.204-5)

A notable feature of Rādhārāṇī's girlfriends is that they have no personal desire to enjoy intimately with Krishna. Their pleasure is derived entirely from seeing the Divine Couple united, and helping Them to experience the joy of union.

sahaja gopīra prema nahe prākṛta kāma
kāma-krīḍā-sāmye tāra kahi kāma-nāma

"The natural love of the *gopīs* for Krishna is not mundane sensuality. Nonetheless, because their transcendental love for Krishna resembles the attraction between men and women in this world, it is sometimes given the name *kāma*, or lust." (*Chaitanya Charitāmṛta* 2.8.214)

"The sakhis not only participate in these pastimes, but they also are the first to relish them. Without their leadership, no one can enter these confidential pastimes. Thus they must be accepted before the acceptance of Radha and Krishna"

The *Tantra* and Rūpa Gosvāmī in his *Bhakti-rasāmṛta-sindhu* similarly state:

premaiva gopa-rāmāṇāṁ
kāma ity agamat prathām
ity uddhavādayo 'py etaṁ
vāñchanti bhagavat-priyāḥ

"The divine love of the cowherd women came to be known as lust. Even so, Uddhava and other great beloved devotees of the Lord desire to attain it."
(*Chaitanya Charitāmṛta* 1.4.163; *Bhakti-rasāmṛta-sindhu* 1.2.285-6)

The following two *Bhāgavatam* verses exemplify Uddhava's appreciation for the *gopīs*' love for Krishna.

vande nanda-vraja-strīṇāṁ
pāda-reṇum abhīkṣṇaśaḥ
yāsāṁ hari-kathodgīrṇaṁ
punāti bhuvana-trayam

"I constantly glorify the dust of the feet of the women of Nanda's cowherd pastures. Their chanting of the activities of Lord Krishna purify the entire universe."
(*Śrīmad Bhāgavatam* 10.47.63)

āsām aho caraṇa-reṇu-juṣām ahaṁ syām
vṛndāvane kim api gulma-latauṣadhīnām
yā dustyajaṁ sva-janam ārya-pathaṁ ca hitvā
bhejur mukunda-padavīṁ śrutibhir vimṛgyām

"Ah! Let me become one of Vrindavan's herbs and plants and be regularly sprinkled with the dust of the *gopīs*' feet, for the *gopīs* abandoned their families and their religious principles, both extremely difficult to give up, in order to worship Mukunda, the ultimate objective of all the Vedic literatures."
(*Śrīmad Bhāgavatam* 10.47.61)

Kubjā and other devotees who did not have the same degree of intense desire for Krishna's pleasure as the *gopīs* but similarly manifested erotic feelings for Him, are said to possess *kāma-prāyā rati*—a love that only resembles that of the *gopīs*. This conclusion is due to Kubjā's (and other devotees in similar mood) high degree of desire for her own pleasure. The presence of such desire for personal enjoyment when near Krishna indicates that the love is less pure. For this reason it has been qualified as *kāma-prāyā* (See also *Bhakti-rasāmṛta-sindhu* 1.2.287). Elsewhere, Kubjā's love for Krishna is said to be mundane (*sādhāraṇī rati*), a far cry from the selfless love demonstrated by Radha and the *gopīs*.

Radha is metaphorically spoken of as the creeper of divine love for Krishna; the *sakhīs* are her twigs, branches, leaves, and fruits. Just as the flower blossoms by receiving water through the roots of the bush, similarly, the *sakhīs* and *mañjarīs* feel joy through the pleasure of Śrīmatī Rādhāraṇī and not independently from Her. There is a Bengali aphorism that says, *mūlete siñcile jala, śākhā pallavera bala, śire vāri nāhi kāryakārī*—"If one sprinkles water on the root, the branches and leaves gain strength. Pouring water on the top of the plant is ineffective." The *sakhīs* thus gain greater pleasure from Radha and Krishna's meeting than they would from personally enjoying a tryst with Krishna. Radha, on the other hand, though knowing this indifference of her girlfriends, still sends them to Krishna so that they can experience the bliss of union with Him. This gives Her millions of times more pleasure than Her own personal happiness. Such is the nature of the divine pastimes of the *gopīs* and Krishna and the reason it is said that their love cannot be viewed as material lust.

Sakhis

nijendriya-sukha-hetu kāmera tātparya
kṛṣṇa-sukha-tātparya gopī-bhāva-varya
nijendriya-sukha-vāñchā nāhi gopīkāra
kṛṣṇe sukha dite kare saṅgama-vihāra

"Lust is to be understood as a desire for one's own sensual pleasure. In contrast, the superior mood of the *gopīs* is a desire to satisfy Krishna's senses. The *gopīs* have not a pinch of desire for their own sensual pleasure and only engage in intimate relations with Krishna to give Him happiness."

(*Chaitanya Charitāmṛta* 2.8.216-7)

Following in the Gopīs' Footsteps

Having established the supreme purity of the *gopīs*' love, Rāmānanda proceeds to stress the necessity of following in their footsteps:

sei gopī-bhāvāmṛte jāṅra lobha haya
veda-dharma-loka tyaji se kṛṣṇe bhajaya
rāgānuga-mārge tāṅre bhaje jei jana
sei-jana pāya vraje vrajendra-nandana
vraja-lokera kona bhāva lañā yei bhaje
bhāva-yogya deha pāñā kṛṣṇa pāya vraje
tāhāte dṛṣṭānta upaniṣad śruti-gaṇa
rāga-mārge bhaji pāila vrajendra-nandana

"One who has a strong desire to taste the nectar of the *gopīs*' loving mood abandons all consideration of adhering exclusively to the religious principles of the Vedas, caring not for public opinion, but simply worshiping Krishna. Whoever worships the Lord on the *rāgānuga* path soon attains the son of Nanda Mahārāja in the land of Vraja. Whoever worships Krishna in any of the moods of the residents of Vraja attains a suitable spiritual body to serve Him there. The exam-

"I constantly glorify the dust of the feet of the women of Nanda's cowherd pastures. Their chanting of the activities of Lord Krishna purify the entire universe"

ples of this are the personifications of the holy *Upanishads*; by worshiping the Lord on the path of spontaneous love, they attained the lotus feet of Vrajendranandana." (*Chaitanya Charitāmṛta* 2.8.219-22)

vidhi-mārge nā pāile vraje kṛṣṇacandra
ataeva gopī-bhāva kari aṅgīkāra
rātri-dina cinte rādhā-kṛṣṇera vihāra
siddha-dehe cinti kare tāhāṅñi sevana
sakhī-bhāve pāya rādhā-kṛṣṇera caraṇa

"One cannot obtain Krishna in Goloka Vrindavan simply by serving Him according to regulative principles. Therefore one should accept the mood of the gopīs and meditate night and day on the pastimes of Śrī Radha and Krishna. One should meditate on one's eternal spiritual body and use it to serve Radha and Krishna; by so doing one attains the direct association of Their lotus feet." (*Chaitanya Charitāmṛta* 2.8.227-8)

There is no hope of attaining *prema* without accepting the leadership of the *gopīs*, for it is inaccessible to one who looks upon Krishna as an object of awe and veneration. Lakṣmī is an example of such a person; She worships the Lord but cannot attain Him in Vraja due to Her perception of Him as being the Lord of Vaikuṇṭha.

gopī-ānugatya vinā aiśvarya-jñāne
bhajileha nāhi pāya vrajendra-nandane
tāhāte dṛṣṭānta lakṣmī karila bhajana
tathāpi nā pāila vraje vrajendra-nandana

"If one does not follow in the footsteps of the *gopīs* and remains absorbed in the consciousness of the Lord's majesty, one cannot attain the service of the lotus feet of the son of Nanda Mahārāja, even though one may be engaged in devotional service. An example of this is the goddess of fortune who worshipped Lord Krishna in order to attain His pastimes in Vrindavan, but failed." (*Chaitanya Charitāmṛta* 2.8.229-30)

In confirmation, the *Bhāgavatam* states:

nāyaṁ śriyo'ṅga u nitānta-rateḥ prasādaḥ
svar-yoṣitāṁ nalina-gandha-rucāṁ kuto 'nyāḥ
rāsotsave 'sya bhuja-daṇḍa-gṛhīta-kaṇṭha-
labdhāśiṣāṁ ya udagād vraja-sundarīṇām

"In the *rāsa* dance, the Lord showed His favor to the beauties of Vraja by placing His powerful arms on their shoulders and dancing with each of them individually. This benediction of extreme love was never experienced by even Lakṣmīdevī, what to speak of the goddesses in the heavenly planets—though the delightful fragrance of lotus flowers emanates from their bodies." (*Śrīmad Bhāgavatam* 10.47.60)

Rāgānugā bhakti

Devotion that follows in the footsteps of the residents of Vraja is called *rāgānugā bhakti*. This kind of devotion alone is truly pleasing to Krishna, whereas *vaidhī bhakti* leads not to Vraja but to Vaikuṇṭha. What then is the means for attaining *rāga-bhakti*? One who has experienced the awakening of unblemished faith is eligible to take up the 64 different practices of the *vidhi-mārga*. However, greed is the only currency that can purchase consciousness drenched in the various flavors of Krishna bhakti. By continuously hearing about the natural, impetuous affection of the residents of Vraja for the Lord, one who develops such a desire, free from trickery, becomes eligible to attain the nectarean mood of the *gopīs*. Such a person is qualified to worship on the *rāgānuga* path.

In Vrindavan, Krishna has countless servants like Raktaka, Patraka, Citraka, Bakula, Bhṛṅgāra, Bhaṅgura, Jambula, Rasāla. His friends include Śrīdāma, Sudāmā, Vasudāma, Stokakṛṣṇa, and Subala. His parents are Nanda and Yaśodā assisted by other elderly gopas and *gopīs*. Each of these persons worships Krishna according to his or her particular desire. The devotional mood fully demonstrated by these residents of Vraja is called *rāgātmikā bhakti*. The devotion which follows in this mood is called *rāgānugā*.

Devotees on the *rāgānugā* path engage in unalloyed devotion to Krishna in the moods of servitorship, friendship, parenthood, or conjugal love. Rūpa Gosvāmī quotes the following verse from the *Nārāyaṇa-vyūha-stava*:

pati-putra-suhṛd-bhrātṛ-
pitṛv an mitravad dharim
ye dhyāyanti sadodyuktās
tebhyo'pīha namo namaḥ

> "I pay my repeated obeisances to all those devotees who meditate with great eagerness on the Lord as their husband, son, companion, brother, father, or friend." (*Bhakti-rasāmṛta-sindhu* 1.2.308, *Chaitanya Charitāmṛta* 2.2.163)

In the course of worshiping Krishna in Vraja, the *rāgānuga-bhakta* intensely desires to attain the mood of one of these devotees. In consequence he attains a spiritual body appropriate to his selected service and finally, upon attaining perfection, gains the personal association of Krishna. The example is given of the *Śrutis* who accepted the *gopīs* as their guides and thus attained Krishna by following the *rāga-mārga*.

iṣṭe svārasikī rāgaḥ
paramāviṣṭatā bhavet
tanmayī yā bhaved bhaktiḥ
sātra rāgātmikoditā

> "The intense and spontaneous absorption in the object of one's adoration (*iṣṭa*) is called *rāga*. Devotion characterized by such *rāga* is called *rāgātmikā bhakti*." (*Bhakti-rasāmṛta-sindhu* 1.2.272)

In his *Durgama-saṅgaminī* commentary Jīva Gosvāmī explains that the cause of intense and spontaneous absorption is *prema-mayī tṛṣṇā*, or divine loving desire. When one's devotion is dominated by such strong desire, it is called *rāgātmikā bhakti*. This *rāgātmikā bhakti* is further subdivided into two categories, *kāma-rupā* ("erotic") and *sambandha-rūpā* ("relational"). When the *rāga*, or intense and spontaneous absorption, is given shape by erotic desire, it is called *kāma-rūpā*; when it is the result of another type of relation, it is called *sambandha-rūpā*.

Sri Sri Radha and Krishna

Although *kāma-rūpā bhakti* implies a relation, it is the only relation dominated by erotic desire—an exclusive desire to please all the Lord's senses. For this reason, although it has the external appearance of ordinary lust, it is completely pure, otherwise, why would great devotees like Uddhava pray to experience it, as shown in the verses quoted above?

Relational love (*sambandha-rūpā*) is that which is experienced by those who pride themselves in being Krishna's parents or having other relationships with Him, such as a friend or servant. All these eternal associates are indicated by the *Bhāgavata* verse (*Śrīmad Bhāgavatam* 7.1.30) where it is said that the Vṛṣṇis attained perfection simply through being related to Krishna. Because of their lack of awareness of Krishna's divine power, the love of the cowherders of Vraja is even greater than that of the Vṛṣṇis or Krishna's other relations in Mathurā and Dvārakā; they are thus even more exalted.

LOBHA, OR INTENSE DESIRE, MAKES ONE ELIGIBLE FOR RĀGĀNUGĀ BHAKTI

Like *rāgātmikā bhakti, rāgānugā bhakti* has two subdivisions. Those who intensely desire (*lobha*) to achieve the *gopīs*' love for Krishna are qualified to practice *rāgānugā bhakti*.

kṛṣṇa-bhakti-rasa-bhāvitā matiḥ
krīyatāṁ yadi kuto'pi labhyate
tatra laulyam api mūlyam ekalaṁ
janma-koṭi-sukṛtair na labhyate

"Since Krishna consciousness soaked with devotion cannot be achieved even after the practice of hundreds of thousands of pious acts, one must pay the only price by which it can be bought: intense greed to have it. Should one come across this greed, one should grab it eagerly."

(*Padyāvalī* 14, *Chaitanya Charitāmṛta* 2.8.70)

The word *laulya* (greed), mentioned in the verse above, is a synonym for *lobha*, a word used by Rūpa Gosvāmī to explain the required qualification for entrance into the path of *rāgānugā-bhakti*. Another synonym for *laulya* is *lālasā*, also used to express this qualification. We must try to understand the meaning of this term. When one's faith is firmly based on a submissive attitude toward scriptural injunctions, one takes up the various activities of devotional service on the *vidhi-mārga*. Gradually then one progresses through the stages described by Rūpa Gosvāmī namely, faith, association with devotees, devotional activities, freedom from deficiencies of character, strong determination, taste, attachment, and finally, ecstatic symptoms and love. The beginning of the ecstatic state comes after one attains the stage of attachment (*āsakti*). This is then followed by the attainment of pure love or *prema*.

Devotional service on the path of *rāgānugā bhakti* is based on faith that has intense desire (*lobha*). Such greed or intense desire is extremely rare; Rūpa Gosvāmī explains that when a devotee hears the divinely inspired scriptures like *Śrīmad Bhāgavatam* and *Padma Purana* from the lips of a realized guru, or other descriptions of the sweet pastimes of the Lord with His Vrindavan devotees in the five relations, he becomes affected by the delightful moods expressed by these eternally perfected associates of the Lord. Not only that, he is also delighted by the beauty of the Lord's form and His attributes; when he sees the Lord's deity form, he is enchanted by His beauty as well. Even the slightest amount of such experience causes him to become more and more indifferent to the scriptural injunctions and other theological arguments that encourage service to God. His desire to continue experiencing the sweetness of the Lord and His devotees becomes spontaneous and natural. These are said to be the symptoms of what Rūpa terms "the outbreak of greed" (*lobhotpatti*).

Rūpa says that those who are on the path of regulative principles continue to depend on scriptural injunctions and logical arguments up to the point of establishing a solid sense of relationship, i.e, *rati*. From this stage, which is equivalent to the dawning of ecstasies called *bhāva*, they no longer require any external impetus. The practice of the *rāgānugā* devotee, however, is based on an internal motivation, called intense desire or greed, from its very inception. He has no need of arguments and ordinances to feel motivated. Nevertheless, it should be pointed out that precisely because he feels such an intense desire, he continues to seek out information from various sources in order to facilitate his attaining the object of his desire. Indeed, he will consider this a duty.

Krishnadāsa Kavirāja Gosvāmī summarizes this as follows:

iṣṭe gāḍha-tṛṣṇā rāgera svarūpa-lakṣaṇa
iṣṭe āviṣṭatā ei taṭastha-lakṣaṇa
rāgamayī-bhaktira haya rāgātmikā nāma
tāhā śuni lubdha haya kona bhāgyavān
lobhe vraja-vāsīra bhāve kare anugati
śāstra-yukti nāhi māne rāgānugāra prakṛti

> "The essential characteristic of *rāga*, or deep attachment, is a strong thirst for the Supreme Lord. Complete absorption in Him is its marginal characteristic. Devotional service pervaded by such *rāga* is called *rāgātmikā bhakti*, spontaneous loving service. One is most fortunate if, after hearing about it, one covets such aspiration. If, out of such transcendental desire, one follows in the footsteps of the inhabitants of Vrindavan, one does not care for the injunctions or reasonings of *śāstra*. Such is the nature of the path which seeks spontaneous love."
> (*Chaitanya Charitāmṛta* 2.22.151-3)

"Following in the footsteps" should not be taken for imitation. The following verses from Rūpa Gosvāmī's *Bhakti-rasāmṛta-sindhu* defining *rāgānugā bhakti* clearly endorse this notion:

virājantīm abhivyaktāṁ
vraja-vāsi-janādiṣu
rāgātmikām anusṛtā
yā sā rāgānugocyate

"*Rāgātmikā bhakti,* or devotional service in spontaneous love, is vividly expressed and manifested by the inhabitants of Vrindavan. Devotional practices that follow in the wake of this spontaneous loving attitude are called *rāgānugā bhakti.*"
(*Bhakti-rasāmṛta-sindhu* 1.2.270; *Chaitanya Charitāmṛta* 2.22.154)

tat-tad-bhāvādi-mādhurye
śrute dhīr yad apekṣate
nātra śāstraṁ na yuktiṁ ca
tal lobhotpatti-lakṣaṇam

"The sadhaka-rupa is the body of the practitioner, or the body one occupies while externally practicing devotional service. The siddha-rupa is the spiritual body; the desired form suitable for executing the service to Krishna which is dear to one's heart"

"On hearing about the sweet moods and activities of Krishna and His devotees in Vraja, one whose mind becomes attracted in such a way that he no longer depends on the instruction of revealed scripture, logic or argument, possesses the symptom indicative of the outbreak of greed."
(*Bhakti-rasāmṛta-sindhu* 1.2.292, *Chaitanya Charitāmṛta* 2.22.155)

sevā sādhaka-rūpeṇa
siddha-rūpeṇa cātra hi
tad-bhāva-lipsunā kāryā
vraja-lokānusārataḥ

"The devotee who intensely desires to attain the *rāgātmikā* mood of the Vrajavāsī associates of Krishna, should engage in the practices of devotional service in his external body as a practitioner, and internally in his spiritual body, always following in the footsteps of the residents of Vraja."
(*Bhakti-rasāmṛta-sindhu* 1.2.295; *Chaitanya Charitāmṛta* 2.22.158)

kṛṣṇaṁ smaran janaṁ cāsya
preṣṭhaṁ nija-samīhitam
tat-tat-kathā-rataś cāsau
kuryād vāsaṁ vraje sadā

"Remembering Krishna and one of His dearest and closest devotees, one should constantly remain absorbed in hearing about their loving relations. In this way, one should make one's permanent residence in Vraja."
(*Bhakti-rasāmṛta-sindhu* 1.2.294, *Chaitanya Charitāmṛta* 2.22.160)

Krishnadāsa Kavirāja Gosvāmī's rendition of these verses is as follows:

bāhya antara ihāra dui ta sādhana
bāhye sādhaka-dehe kare śravaṇa-kīrtana
mane nija-siddha-deha kariyā bhāvana
rātri-dine kare vraje kṛṣṇera sevana
nijābhīṣṭa kṛṣṇa-preṣṭha pācheta lāgiyā
nirantara sevā kare antarmanā hañā

"*Rāgānugā bhakti* is practiced both externally and internally. In the external body, the practitioner engages in hearing and chanting; in his mind, however, he meditates on his spiritual body and serves Krishna in Vrindavan, day and night. In his mind, he constantly serves Krishna following closely in the mood of his favorite devotee in Vraja, one who is most dear to the Lord."

(*Chaitanya Charitāmṛta* 2.22.156-7, 159)

The *sādhaka-rūpa* is the body of the practitioner, or the body one occupies while externally practicing devotional service. The *siddha-rūpa* is the spiritual body; the desired form suitable for executing the service to Krishna which is dear to one's heart. In both of these bodies one must follow the particular devotee beloved of the Lord whose mood one has great eagerness to achieve, such as Śrīmatī Rādhārāṇī, Lalitā, Viśākhā or Śrī Rūpa Mañjarī on one level, and on another, Śrī Rūpa and Sanātana Gosvāmīs and their entourage. One should follow these personalities, and serve the Lord on both those levels. In the external body one should engage in the types of service executed by Rūpa and Sanātana. In the meditation body, or *siddha-deha*, one should serve in the way shown by Radha, Lalitā, Viśākhā, and Rūpa Mañjarī. Never is a practitioner to imitate these devotees, on either level.

The daughter of Śrīnivāsa Ācārya, Śrīmatī Hemalatā Ṭhākurāṇī, had a disciple whom she later excommunicated for his unorthodox views—which he taught in Assam's Surma Valley area. This deviant disciple, Rūpa Kavirāja, taught that since the *gopīs* did not take shelter of a guru, observe the Ekādaśī fast, or worship the Śālagrāma and Tulasī Devī, it wasn't necessary for their followers to do so either. Viśvanātha Cakravartī strongly refuted this doctrine (which he named the *Sauramya-mata*, after the region where it was popular). This doctrine interprets the words *vraja-loka* in Rūpa Gosvāmī's verse to mean Krishna's mistresses in Vraja like Rādha and Candrāvalī. This school of though still has its representatives in Vrindavan today at Ghoṅtār Kuñj. Like the Atibāṛī school, its adepts wear only one strand of *tulasī* neck beads and are also known as Vāmākaupinīs. Because they are mere imitators of the eternal associates of Krishna, they are excluded from pure Vaishnava society.[1]

Genuine *rāgānuga-bhaktas* remain devotedly engaged in the type of service they desire according to the direction of the guru. Thus, their love for Krishna quickly develops and they attain the stage of ecstasies and pure love. The first stage of love's manifestation is called *bhāva-bhakti*; later intensified, it becomes the full manifestation of love called *prema-bhakti*.

ei mata kare jebā rāgānugā-bhakti
kṛṣṇera caraṇe tāṅra upajaya prīti

"One who engages in *rāgānugā bhakti* in this way develops love for the lotus feet of Krishna."

(*Chaitanya Charitāmṛta* 2.22.164)

Srila Prabhupāda Bhaktisiddhānta Sarasvatī Ṭhākura, my most revered spiritual master, wrote in his *Anubhāṣya* commentary to these verses, "One must serve in one's devotee form by repeating the *hari-kathā* heard from his spiritual masters, and mentally serve Radha and Krishna directly in Vraja in a spiritual body appropriate to that service and one's own mood. One who serves in this way is no longer on the *vaidhī bhakti* path, and is no longer motivated exclusively by the words of the guru and the scripture. Rather, on the strength of his naturally awakened taste (*ruci*) for devotional service, he is travelling on the path of *rāgānugā bhakti* and soon reaches the destination of intense love for

Krishna. When one comes to the level of ecstatic moods (*bhāva*) on the *rāgānugā* path, one quickly brings Krishna under his influence and at this point attains Krishna's loving service."

HARINĀMA: THE MEANS TO AWAKENING LOBHA

It is generally believed that *rāga-mārga* condones licentiousness, that it is antinomian. Naturally, such belief is incorrect. One cannot follow the *rāgānugā* path without first attaining the required qualification of intense eagerness. When such intense eagerness arises, then love alone gives the practitioner direction. At this point, the underlying purpose of all activities of the *vidhi-mārga* becomes clear to the practitioner, so even if he becomes less consistent in some of his practices, his heart and soul are constantly, indefatigably engaged in the culture of Krishna consciousness. Although he may become somewhat lak in other areas of devotional life, he never diminishes his interest in hearing and chanting the Holy Names.

The awakening of the *lobha* which qualifies one for *rāgānugā bhakti* is not to be taken cheaply, as if easy to attain. Does this mean the *jīva* has no chance of experiencing it? In answer, Bhaktivinoda Ṭhākura wrote as follows:

> *vidhi-mārga-rata jane svādhīnatā ratna dāne*
> *rāga-mārge karān praveśa*
> *rāga-vaśa-vartī haye pārakīya rasāśraye*
> *labhe jīva kṛṣṇa premāveśa*

"To the person fixed in the regulative principles, the Holy Name gives the jewel of independence and places him on the path of spontaneous devotion. That person, overcome by spontaneous attachment to the Lord, takes shelter of the *parakīyā* mood and thus attains absorption in love for Krishna."

Mahāprabhu invested all His energies into His holy name. The five *rasas*—neutrality, servitude, friendship, parenthood, and consorthood, are present in full splendor in the Name of Him who embodies all the unlimited moods of loving exchange. Thus Bhaktivinoda also sings, *akhila-rasera khani kṛṣṇa nāma cintāmaṇi*—"Krishna's name is a philosopher's stone. It is a gold mine filled with the unlimited moods of loving exchange."

If one wishes to win the treasure of love of God, one must accept the leadership of Chaitanya Mahāprabhu in every way. One must take initiation and inspiration in His line of teachings, chiefly taking to the chanting of the Holy Names—the 16 names and 32 syllables of the Hare Krishna *Mahā-mantra*.

In the *Bhāgavatam*, the ninth Yogīndra, Karabhājana, states that Mahāprabhu is the full incarnation of the Lord.

> *kṛṣṇa-varṇaṁ tviṣākṛṣṇaṁ*
> *sāṅgopāṅgāstra-pārṣadam*
> *yajñaiḥ saṅkīrtana-prāyair*
> *yajanti hi su-medhasaḥ*

"Mahaprabhu invested all His energies into His holy name. The five rasas—neutrality, servitude, friendship, parenthood, and consorthood, are present in full splendor in the Name of Him who embodies all the unlimited moods of loving exchange"

"In the Age of Kali, the golden Lord, upon whose lips the name of Krishna always remains, appears in the company of His expansions, portions, weapons and associates. Those who are very intelligent will worship Him through the sacrifice of congregational glorification (*saṅkīrtana-yajña*)." (11.5.32)

This prediction contains much information about Mahāprabhu's avatar: the words *kṛṣṇa-varṇaṁ* indicate that the two syllables (*varṇa*), *kṛ-ṣṇa*, are constantly being glorified by the Lord. That is, through *kīrtana*, He is always instructing the world in Krishna consciousness. It also means that in His devotional mood, He is constantly seeking Krishna by calling His Name. The words *sāṅgopāṅgāstra-pārṣadam* refer to the Lord's associates. His *aṅgas,* or "bodies," are Nityānanda Prabhu and Advaita Prabhu, who are different forms of the Lord. His *upāṅgas,* or minor limbs, are the Lord's devotees like Śrīvāsa Pundit who have taken shelter of Him. His *astra,* or "weapon," is the Holy Name; and His *pārṣadas*, "associates," are His energies such as Gadādhara, Svarūpa Dāmodara, Rāmānanda, Sanātana, and Rūpa. The Lord's bodily color is *akṛṣṇa,* or "not black," which in combination with other statements in the *Bhāgavatam* indicates that He is golden in hue. Thus, although internally black (Krishna), externally He is golden (Gaura). The meaning of gold in this verse is that Lord Gaurāṅga has taken the color of Śrīmatī Rādhārāṇī as well as Her internal mood. In the Age of Kali, the most intelligent people will worship Lord Krishna in this form through the chanting of the Holy Names.

Deity of Chaitanya Mahaprabhu, Imli Tala Temple, Vrindavan

When Mahāprabhu wrapped His arms around His intimate associates Rāmānanda and Svarūpa Dāmodara and ecstatically told them that the Holy Names are the only means for entering into an understanding of *bhakti-rasa,* He most clearly indicated that His teaching is centered on the chanting of the Holy Names. He said: "My dear Svarūpa Dāmodara and Rāmānanda Rāya, know from Me that chanting of the Holy Names is the most feasible means of salvation in this age of Kali. In this age, the process of worshiping Krishna is to perform sacrifice by chanting the Holy Name. One who does so is certainly very intelligent, and attains shelter at the lotus feet of Krishna. Simply by chanting the holy name of Lord Krishna, one is freed from all undesirable habits. This is the means of awakening all good fortune and bringing about the flow of waves of love for Krishna."
(*Chaitanya Charitāmṛta* 3.20.8-9,11)

Mahāprabhu explained to Svarupa Damodara and Ramananda Raya the attitude one should have while chanting:

tṛṇād api sunīcena
taror iva sahiṣṇunā
amāninā mānadena
kīrtanīyaḥ sadā hariḥ

"One should chant the holy name of the Lord while thinking oneself to be lower than straw in the street. He should be more tolerant than the tree, expect no respect for oneself and give all respect to others."
(*Chaitanya Charitāmṛta* 3.20.21)

If one can chant the Holy Name in this spirit, the auspicious awakening of intense desire for love of Krishna in the mood of the Vrajavāsīs will soon develop in one's heart. A person who is deprived of this wealth is truly poor and wretched. The devotee therefore prays:

prema-dhana vinā vyartha daridra jīvana
dāsa kari betana more deha prema-dhana

"Without love for Krishna, my life is poverty-stricken and meaningless. Therefore I pray that You make me your servant and for my salary pay me with ecstatic love of God." (*Chaitanya Charitāmṛta* 3.20.37)

The chanting of the Holy Names is the best and most powerful of all spiritual practices. Alone, it not only destroys all the contaminations that sully the consciousness of the practitioner, but can bestow upon him the most valuable possession, love for God. One who possesses this love for the Divine Couple, Radha and Krishna, is the wealthiest. If one's ambition is to achieve these riches, then he should wholeheartedly glorify the chanting of the Holy Name as above everything. All of Mahāprabhu's associates set this example by their own behavior.

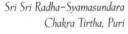

Sri Sri Radha-Syamasundara
Chakra Tirtha, Puri

Our most worshipable spiritual master Śrīla Prabhupāda often quoted Jīva Gosvāmī from the *Bhakti-sandarbha*: "First it is expected that one should hear the Lord's names in order to purify the inner self" (*prathamaṁ nāmnaḥ śravaṇam antaḥkaraṇa-śuddhy-artham apekṣyam*).

Prabhupāda explains that only after one's mind and intelligence are purified by the chanting of the Holy Names can one hear about Krishna's form, qualities, associates, and finally, pastimes. One who has not yet reached the stage of *ruci*, or taste for devotional service, may prematurely go to a pretender guru to take initiation and instruction in *rāgānugā bhakti* without first making an effort to chant the Holy Name without committing offenses. Such a person may then make a pretense of relishing Krishna's *līlā* while still affected by materialistic contamination, but such an attempt will not succeed in bringing him love for the Divine Couple and service for Them in the spiritual abode."

The *sādhya-sādhana-tattva* is fully explained in the teachings of Rāmānanda Rāya, but it is clear from the words of Śrīla Prabhupāda mentioned above that the practices that lead to the supreme goal of service to the Divine Couple, are only possible through the purificatory process of chanting the Holy Name. The Lord Himself confirmed this statement when He said *ihā haite sarva-siddhi haibe sabāra*: "From the chanting of the Holy Name, all perfections will come to everyone." "All perfections" refers to the perfections of spiritual life. Even though the love of the inhabitants of Vraja described by Rāmānanda Rāya is the most secret treasure of the Vedic storehouse of knowledge, the impossible feat of winning this great prize can be accomplished by the mercy of the Holy Name; it can achieve miracles. Mahāprabhu stated to Tapana Miśra, Raghunātha Bhaṭṭa Gosvāmī's grandfather: "The object of life and the means to attain it are found through the chanting of the Holy Names," and "As you repeatedly practice the chanting of the Holy Name, the seedling of love will sprout and you will then know both the goal of life and the means to attain it." [2]

To Sanātana Gosvāmī, Mahāprabhu said that although the nine processes of devotional service are capable of bestowing Krishna *prema*, the chanting of the Holy Names is still the topmost process (*Chaitanya Charitāmṛta* 3.4.70-1). This statement clearly confirms that the ultimate goal of life and all perfection are attained through the Holy Name. Thus, worshiping the Holy Name should be given priority over all other devotional activities, and should be recognized as the supreme means of attaining perfection.

The Names of the Divine Couple possess unequaled characteristics. Both are the means and the goal of spiritual life. To reveal this truth, the Lord Himself descended onto this earth in the form of the Holy Name, and as Mahāprabhu, showed that the chanting of the Holy Name is the supreme form of worship.

nāma cintāmaṇiḥ kṛṣṇaś
caitanya-rasa-vigrahaḥ
pūrṇaḥ śuddho nitya-mukto
'bhinnatvān nāma-nāminoḥ

> "The Holy Name is a transcendental philosopher's stone, for it is the embodiment of all conscious delight. It is complete, pure, and eternally liberated, being nondifferent from Krishna Himself. It is not a material name therefore there is no difference between the Name and the One who is named."
> (*Padma Purana, Bhakti-rasāmṛta-sindhu* 1.2.233; *Chaitanya Charitāmṛta* 17.133)

The *Brahma-saṁhitā* states, "That which you meditate on in your life of sadhana will be achieved in the perfectional stage" (*yādṛśī bhāvanā yasya siddhir bhavati tādṛśī*). In his *Prema-bhakti-candrikā*, Narottama dāsa says, "*sādhane bhābibe jāhā, siddha dehe pābe tāhā.*" One should, therefore, continuously reveal to the Holy Name one's desire for *vraja-prema* while chanting under the direction of Śrī Guru, Rūpa and Svarūpa Dāmodara, without offenses. As one chants in this way, the Holy Name will be merciful and grant one the perfection of *vraja-prema*, for the Lord Himself has stated that all perfections come to one by the grace of the Holy Name (*ihā haite sarva siddhi haibe sabāra*).

Great authorities teach that one should remember the pastimes of the Lord according to the eight times of day in relation to the eight verses of the *Śikṣāṣṭaka*. In his *Bhakti-sandarbha* Jīva Gosvāmī states that in Kali Yuga any type of devotional service must be done in conjunction with the chanting of the Holy Name (*yadyapi anyā bhaktiḥ kalau kartavyā tadā kīrtanākhya-bhakti-saṁyojanenaiva*). One should not give up *kīrtana* in order to engage in *smaraṇa*. The essence of Mahāprabhu's teachings in relation to *sambandha, abhidheya,* and *prayojana* are all contained within His *Śikṣāṣṭaka,* the essence of all scriptures.

The Necessity of Gaura-Nitāi's Mercy

In his *Nāmāṣṭakam* (verse 7), Rūpa Gosvāmī indicates that the Name is even more merciful than the Named:

vācyo vācakam ity udeti bhavato nāma svarūpa-dvayaṁ
pūrvasmāt param eva hanta karuṇā tatrāpi jānīmahe
yas tasmin vihitāparādha-nivahaḥ prāṇī samantād bhaved
āsyenedam upāsya so'pi hi sadānandāmbudhau majjati

"O Lord! You manifest in two different forms, as He who is Named and as the Name. Of the two, I consider the second to be more merciful than the first. Even if one has committed countless offenses to the Named, one can still be immersed in an ocean of ambrosia by worshiping the Name."

"The worship of Gauranga is not difficult—it is easy to gather all its fruits. Prema comes looking for one who cries while calling out the name of Gauranga."

However, in the *Padma Purana*, clear distinctions are drawn between three categories of chanting: the pure Name (*śuddha-nāma*), the reflection of the Name (*nāmābhāsa*), and offensive chanting (*nāmāparādha*). The following verses spoken by Chaitanya Mahāprabhu clearly indicate that only one who chants without offenses is qualified to receive the riches of love for Krishna.

bhajanera madhye śreṣṭha nava-vidhā bhakti
kṛṣṇa-prema, kṛṣṇa dite dhare mahā-śakti
tāra madhye sarva-śreṣṭha nāma-saṅkīrtana
niraparādhe laile nāma pāya prema-dhana

"Of the many ways of executing devotional service, there are nine varieties which are considered to be the best, for they possess a great capacity to deliver love for Krishna and thus Krishna Himself. Of these nine processes of devotional service, the most important is the chanting of the Lord's holy name, for if one chants without committing offenses one obtains the treasure of love for the Lord." (*Chaitanya Charitāmṛta* 3.4.70-1)

One should exercise all caution not to incur any offense to the Holy Name. In taking shelter of the most merciful and munificent Gaura-Nitāi, within a very short time one will have one's heart purified and will be eligible then to attain Radha-Krishna *prema*.

gaurāṅga-bhajana sahaja ati
sahaja tāra phala vitati
gaurāṅga baliyā krandana kare
suvimala prema anveṣaya tāre

"The worship of Gaurāṅga is not difficult—it is easy to gather all its fruits. *Prema* comes looking for one who cries while calling out the name of Gaurāṅga."

Mahāprabhu and Nitāi Prabhu are the most benevolent. That They saved the brothers Jagāi and Mādhāi is not considered a very great thing—it would only take one of Their merciful glances to save the brothers even though they were offenders. The most merciful Gaurahari, through various tricks, delivered even Devānanda Pundit, who committed a serious offense to the Vaishnava Śrīvāsa Pundit.

Remembering Their mercy, one who wishes to advance in the path of *rāgānugā bhakti* should constantly pray humbly to Lord Chaitanya and Lord Nityānanda as Narottama dāsa Ṭhākura prays in his *Prārthanā*:

āra kabe nitāi cāṅdera karuṇā haibe
saṁsāra-vāsanā mora kabe tuccha habe
viṣaya chāṛiyā kabe śuddha habe mana
kabe hāma heraba se śrī-vṛndāvana

rūpa-raghunātha pade haibe ākuti
kabe hāma bujhaba se yugala pīriti

"When will Nitāi Cāṅda be merciful to me? When will my desires for material enjoyments and family life become insignificant? When will I give up the sense objects and have a pure mind? When will I see the land of Vrindavan? When will I have eagerness to beg the mercy of Rūpa and Raghunātha? And when will I be able to understand the love of the Divine Couple?"

Distressed at how, despite the Lord's mercy, we still deceive ourselves and remain bereft of the great gifts He came to give, Narottama prays to Gaurāṅga as follows:

gorā pahuṅ nā bhajiyā mainu
prema-ratana-dhana helāya hārāinu
adhane jatana kari dhana teyāginu
āpana karama doṣe āpani ḍubinu
sat-saṅga chāṛi kainu asate vilāsa
te kāraṇe lāgala karma-bandha phāṅsa
viṣama viṣaya biṣa satata khāinu
gaurāṅga kīrtana rasa magana nā hainu
kena vā āchaye prāṇa ki sukha lāgiyā
narottama dāsa kena nā gela mariyā

Sri Nrsimhadeva

"I did not worship Lord Gaurāṅga and so I succumbed. I have carelessly cast away the treasure of love for Krishna. Thus I have lost the most valuable treasure and only made efforts to gain what is valueless. Due to this fault of mine, I have sunk to the lowest level. Disregarding the association of the holy, I have amused myself in the company of the wicked. Is it any wonder that the noose of karmic reaction is dangling around my neck? I have eaten the horrible poison of material sense gratification and have not become absorbed in the taste of *saṅkīrtana* taught by Gaurāṅga Mahāprabhu. What pleasure still keeps me alive today? Narottama dāsa wonders, 'Why have I not died from this misery?'"

Bhaktivinoda's Prayer to Nṛsiṁhadeva

One who becomes greedy for the mood experienced by the residents of Vraja spontaneously takes to the practice of *rāgānugā bhakti*. A very rare phenomenon, it only comes about through the mercy of an advanced devotee. Such good fortune is achieved only when one takes shelter of a devotee who is exclusively committed to chanting the Lord's holy names. One who makes a pretense of qualification is a self-deceiver, forever deprived of the mercy of Nityānanda-Balarāma, and loses the valuable opportunity of ever attaining the jewel of love for Radha and Krishna.

nitāiera karuṇā habe vraje rādhā-kṛṣṇa pābe
dhara nitāira caraṇa du'khāni

"When Nitāi shows one His mercy, then one attains Radha and Krishna in Vraja. So hold on tightly to Nitāi's lotus feet." (*Prārthanā*)

If desirous of entering the path of advanced worship, a devotee must first strive to eliminate his flaws in the form of lust, anger, and greed. Narottama dāsa Ṭhākura instructs us that if we have the association of advanced devotees we will be protected from the influence of lust, anger, and greed. But association of devotees who are expert in the process of devotional service, knowledgeable in the art of sacred rapture, attached to Krishna, and free from material contamination, is rare. Therefore, the most merciful spiritual authority, Śrīla Bhaktivinoda Ṭhākura, in the *Navadvīpa-bhāva-taraṅga,* prays to Nṛsiṁhadeva—who puts an end to all obstacles on the spiritual path. Prayers such as this are the only hope for fallen, conditioned souls like us. The prayer is part of a description of the Nṛsiṁha temple situated in Devapallī, a village on the island of Godruma, in Nabadwip *dhāma*.

Mahaprabhu's sankirtana in Jarikhanda forest

"When will I see the beauty of the village known as Devapallī and roll in the dust of the temple of Nṛsiṁhadeva in ecstatic love? I will sincerely beg Nṛsiṁha to give me love for Krishna and pray to Him to clean my heart of the six enemies, starting with lust, dishonesty, hope for prestige, and corruption. I will fall at Nṛsiṁha's feet crying and praying for desire to serve Krishna. I will ask to engage in the worship of Nabadwip's Divine Couple without any obstacle. Fear itself is afraid of Lord Nṛsiṁha. When will He be pleased and merciful to me? Even though Nṛsiṁha's form is fearsome to the wicked, He is extremely gentle to Prahlāda and other devotees of Krishna.

"When will He be kind to me and speak compassionately, promising to protect me from all dangers even though I am a fool and without any worth? He will say to me, 'Go and freely reside in the land of Śrī Gaurāṅga. You shall have affection for the Holy Name and you shall engage in *yugala-bhajana*, the service of the Divine Couple. By the grace of My devotees, all obstacles shall be removed. Now go and experience the ecstasy of worshiping Radha and Krishna with a pure mind.'

"Gaurahari is the deity of love. One who attains the good fortune of discussing His pastimes of distributing the fruits of love of Godhead attains the goal of life"

"When will Lord Nṛsiṁha, having said words such as these, place His lotus feet upon my head? There, at the gates of Nṛsiṁha's temple, I will roll in the dust in the ecstasy of love for the Divine Couple which will suddenly descend upon me by His mercy."

When, out of His kindness, Nṛsiṁhadeva mercifully eliminates the obstacles of devotional life, one advances fearlessly and unobstructed on the spiritual path designated by the guru. When the spiritual master is merciful, one obtains the fortune of attaining love for Radha and Krishna.

The Supreme Lord Krishna felt so intensely indebted to Radha's love that He took on Her mood and bodily hue and descended to Jagannātha Purī where He called out:

kāhāṅ kṛṣṇa prāṇanātha muralīvadana
kāhāṅ jāṅ kāhāṅ pāṅ vrajendranandana

> "Where is my beloved Krishna? Where is the flute-player? Where can I find the son of Nanda?" (*Chaitanya Charitāmṛta* 2.12.5)

Calling out for Krishna in this way, and crying so intensely that His tears washed over His chest, Mahāprabhu embraced His close associates, Rāmānanda Rāya and Svarūpa Dāmodara, and revealed to them the most intimate aspects of Rādhārāṇī's mood in separation from Her Lord. Such is the secret essence of *bhajana*. If the Lord Himself had not taken on the mood of His personal potency, Śrīmatī Rādhārāṇī, and demonstrated to the people of the world how She worships Him, such truth wouldn't be known. Therefore, no other gift can compare with the gift from Śrī Chaitanya Mahāprabhu. Even by a brief glimpse into the nature of His gift, the greatest benefit to the conditioned living entities of this world is brought about.

Gaurahari is the deity of love. One who has the good fortune of discussing His pastimes of distributing the fruits of love of Godhead attains the goal of life. Historians will look in time and see that even during the periods when Hindus and Muslims were engaged in conflict, the preaching of Mahāprabhu's teachings of love of God went on with great force. Nothing stopped it or even slowed it down. The entire land of Bharatavarṣa was inundated with the flood of *prema*; the sounds of the Holy Name were everywhere and even many non-Hindus like the Muslims were initiated into His religion of love. Thus it is proved that, to the extent that people engage in discussing Mahāprabhu's munificent pastimes of distributing love to even the lowest members of human society, things like hatred, jealousy and violence will be driven away. People will become more generous, and develop a sense of universal fraternity, embracing everyone in the understanding that the entire world is a single family—*vasudhaiva kuṭumbakam*. Thus, the understanding of the conditioned souls' eternal identity will be awakened and everyone will then engage in the worship of the Supreme Lord Śrī Krishna. In a world formed by this consciousness, the true ideal of communism will be easily achieved and supreme peace will reign.

If wealthy with the love of the Divine Couple, one is eternally freed from the distress of any kind of poverty.

Chapter XV

The Disciple's Mentality

The word *dīkṣā* refers to the process of surrendering to a spiritual master. The genuine spiritual master is one who is most dear to the Supreme Lord, one who is His intimate associate. A person who takes shelter of such a spiritual master is recognized by Krishna as one of His own. The Lord immediately bestows a transcendental body on such a surrendered soul and, in this body, the disciple has the good fortune to serve the divine form of the Lord.

The primary characteristic of a disciple who has received initiation and direction in the practice of worship from his spiritual master is *viśrambha*, an honest desire for faithful and loving service to the spiritual master, the Vaishnavas and the Supreme Lord. The secondary characteristic is that he seeks to destroy all his sinful activities.

The *divya-jñāna,* the transcendental knowledge of *sambandha, abhidheya,* and *prayojana,* is received by the disciple as part of initiation. The self-revealed scriptures, the Vedas, are the supreme authority (*pramāṇa*) on spiritual subject matters. The scripture and the nine *prameya* (teachings) based on scripture are collectively called *daśa-mūla*, the ten basic elements of spiritual knowledge. The nine *prameya* consist of the seven aspects of relationships (*sambandha*)—Krishna Himself, Krishna's energies, Krishna's divine mood (*rasa*), the soul, its bondage and its liberation, and the inconceivable oneness and difference of the Lord and the individual soul. To these seven are added *abhidheya,* bhakti, and *prayojana,* love of God.

Along with all of this knowledge comes an important side effect: the destruction of one's sinful reactions. Thus the direct result of initiation is love for Krishna. Mahāprabhu confirms this in the following statement to to His own spiritual master:

kibā mantra dile gosāñi kibā tāra bala
japite japite mantra karila pāgala

"What mantra have you given me, O Gurudeva! What powers does it possess? As I chant this mantra, I feel that it is turning me into a madman."
(*Chaitanya Charitāmṛta* 1.7.81)

"A lack of interest in the Supreme Lord Sri Krishna is the conditioned soul's chief defect"

If one does not develop love for Krishna nor feels any attachment to the chanting of the Holy Names after being initiated, but remains inclined to sinful activities, falling down from time to time, it is then clear that either knowingly or unknowingly, that person has committed terrible offenses to the Lord, the guru or the Vaishnavas. One should then think: "I have only made a pretense of surrendering myself. I have used my initiation simply as an excuse to engage in sense gratificatory activities."

IGNORANCE MEANS REJECTING THE LORD

A lack of interest in the Supreme Lord Śrī Krishna is the conditioned soul's chief defect. The basis of all sin is ignorance, whose symptom is the rejection of Krishna. The seed of all sin, i.e., the tendency to sin, is present in the flaw of ignorance. From there, sinful activity is inevitable.

Krishnadāsa Kavirāja Gosvāmī compares this deficiency in the conditioned *jīvas* to coming under the influence of a witch's spell.

sei doṣe māyā piśācī daṇḍa kare tāre
ādhyātmikādi tāpa-traya tāre jāri māre
kāma krodhera dāsa hañā tāra lāthi khāya
bhramite bhramite jadi sādhu-vaidya pāya
tāṅra upadeśa-mantre piśācī palāya
kṛṣṇa-bhakti pāya tabe kṛṣṇa nikaṭe jāya

Sri Chaitanya Mahaprabhu

"For rejecting Krishna, the witch of illusion punishes the *jīva*, causing him to suffer the three kinds of misery—*ādhyātmika*, *ādhibhautika*, and *adhidaivika*. The unfortunate conditioned soul then becomes the slave of his desires and his frustrations, suffering their kicks and abuse. After wandering through the universe in this condition, if he somehow finds a saintly person to act as an exorcist, then through his powerful instructions, the witch's mastery is overcome and she runs for her life. The fortunate individual then finds pure devotion to Krishna and goes to Him."
(*Chaitanya Charitāmṛta* 2.22.13-15)

The devotee then turns to Krishna and prays as follows:

kāmādīnāṁ kati na katidhā pālitā durnideśās
teṣāṁ jātā mayi na karuṇā na trapā nopaśāntiḥ
utsṛjyaitān atha yadupate sāmpratam labdha-buddhis
tvām āyātaḥ śaraṇam abhayaṁ māṁ niyuṅkṣyātma-dāsye

"I carried out so many evil orders of my wicked masters—lust, anger, greed, bewilderment, intoxication, and envy—that I have lost count. Yet, despite my faithful service, these masters have never taken pity on me. I am so shameless that the faintest desire for devotional service has never once manifested in my heart. O Lord of the Yadus, today I have finally come to my senses and I throw off my shackles to take shelter of Your fearless lotus feet; please engage me in Your personal service."

(*Bhakti-rasāmṛta-sindhu* 3.2.25, *Chaitanya Charitāmṛta* 2.22.16)

Characteristics OF Purity

Parīkṣit Mahārāja made the following significant statement about how one can recognize purity in a devotee's character: "The person whose self has been washed clean never abandons Krishna's lotus feet (*dhautātmā puruṣaḥ kṛṣṇa-pāda-mūlaṁ na muñcati—Śrīmad Bhāgavatam* 2.8.6)."

"The sign of a pure heart is the inability to abandon the service to Krishna's lotus feet"

Viśvanātha further clarifies: "The sign of a pure heart is the inability to abandon the service to Krishna's lotus feet" (*mat-pāda-sevā-tyāgāsamārthyam eva śuddha-cittatva-cihnam*). If somehow or other one sees that such a devotee is affected by lust or anger, such incidental characteristics should be considered like the bite of a snake with broken teeth; an insignificant setback which does not have long-term effects on the devotee's devotional life (*ataḥ kvacit kāma-krodhādi-sattve'pi utkhāta-daṁṣṭroraga-daṁśanavat tasyākiṁcitkāratvaṁ jñeyam*). There is no poison in a snake's broken fangs, so its bite is not considered a significant problem, even though it appears very dangerous to the uninformed observer. Similarly, lust, anger and greed may cause some disturbance in a devotee's mind, but do not result in his mind being permanently contaminated."

The Lord accepts the offerings of those devotees of purified mind. Other than the association of such pure devotees, the *jīva* has no other hope of attaining any value of significance in life.

One should not think, however, that all one has to do is to sit and listen to the spiritual master's instructions. One has to act according to those instructions. If a disciple does not take up the devotional practices or sadhana recommended by the guru then how can he expect to achieve spiritual perfection?

In the *Chaitanya Charitāmṛta* (2.22.25), the Lord says that, on receiving initiation from the spiritual master, one should worship Krishna and serve the guru. Then one becomes free from the control of maya and attains Krishna's lotus feet.

tāte kṛṣṇa bhaje kare gurura sevana
māyā-jāla chuṭe pāya kṛṣṇera carana

In his commentary to the above-mentioned verse, Śrīla Prabhupāda Bhaktisiddhānta Sarasvatī Ṭhākura writes: "It is through a combination of *bhajana* and service to the spiritual master that one becomes free of maya's net and attains Krishna's lotus feet."

Śrīla Prabhupāda also says, "Our eternal spiritual identity is to be the dust of the lotus feet of Rūpa and Raghunātha." Therefore, we have no other duty in life than to follow their example. He has further affirmed, "Without the performance of *harināma-saṅkīrtana*, no other practices of Bhakti yoga such as residence in Mathurā or association with devotees are complete. However, even if I only engage in *harināma-saṅkīrtana*, I will win all the fruits of residence in Mathurā, associating with devotees, serving the deity in loving faith, and listening to the *Bhāgavatam*. Simply through *harināma-saṅkīrtana*, all perfections come to the *jīva*."

The orders of our gurus are never to be debated

Our spiritual master instructed us to chant 100,000 Names daily without offense, keeping our objectives clear. If we cannot follow this instruction, how can we expect to become free of all the contamination in our hearts? As stated by Śrī Chaitanya Mahāprabhu, the performance of *harināma-saṅkīrtana* is glorious in seven ways. It cleans the mirror of the heart (*ceto-darpaṇa-marjanaṁ*); it extinguishes the conflagration of material life (*bhava-mahā-davāgni-nirvāpaṇam*); it distributes the cooling moon rays of auspiciousness (*śreyaḥ-kairava-candrikā-vitaraṇam*); it is the life of transcendental knowledge, which is like its consort (*vidyā-vadhū-jīvanam*), it increases the ocean of divine bliss (*ānandāmbudhi-vardhanam*); at every step, it gives a taste of the full ambrosia for which we have always been anxious (*pratipadaṁ pūrṇāmṛtāsvādanam*); and it bathes the entire self in divine ecstasy (*sarvātma-snapanam*). Mahāprabhu Himself repeatedly stated that there was no worship superior to the worship of the Holy Names. "All will attain perfection through the chanting of the Holy Names. Chant these Names constantly; I give you no other rules." (*Chaitanya Bhāgavata* 2.23.78)

Do we have any hope of attaining the supreme good if we ignore these instructions of the Lord and the spiritual master?

THE SERVANT'S VOW OF SERVICE

The devotee who desires to reach the level of *niṣṭhā* should make the following vow:

"According to the instruction of my spiritual master, I must absolutely complete chanting a fixed number of Names on my japa beads daily, as well as daily offer a fixed number of obeisances to the devotees and to the deity form of the Lord. I absolutely must perform my prescribed service at certain fixed times of the day. I must observe the fortnightly Ekādaśī fast. Upon rising in the *brahma-muhūrta* period, before dawn, I shall remember Krishna and His devotees' lotus feet in a particular way, then bathe. After this, I will sit down and meditate on the mantra into which my guru has initiated me. Then I will perform puja to the deity, study the devotional scriptures, and sing the hymns written by the great authorities. All these things I shall do every day without fail.

"I shall never entertain thoughts of anything other than Krishna. I shall absolutely give up all useless controversy and gossip. Every day, I shall unfailingly hear the spiritual instructions of my guru and advanced devotees and then discuss those topics with my godbrothers, rather than wasting time in fruitless conversations. I will not allow any of the valuable time given to me in this human form of life to be wasted by giving way to sloth and laziness. I will therefore not lose a moment to sleep that is not absolutely necessary for maintaining my body, but will employ every moment in a way that is spiritually profitable.

"I will be very careful to avoid the association of anyone who is overly attached to material enjoyments, or of the wives of other men, or of womanizing men. Indeed, I shall avoid the company of anyone who is not a devotee of Krishna, for it is said:

asat-saṅga tyāga ei vaiṣṇava ācāra
strī saṅgī eka asādhu kṛṣṇābhakta āra

"'The essence of Vaishnava behavior is to give up the association of the unsaintly. By unsaintly it is meant those who are attached to the opposite sex and those who are non-devotees.' (*Chaitanya Charitāmṛta* 2.12.195)

"Every day without fail I will complete chanting the *Mahā-mantra* consisting of 16 names and 32 syllables a fixed number of times. Even when not chanting on my beads, I will constantly repeat these names without counting. Without completing my japa and chanting my *iṣṭa-mantra*, I will not even touch water, what to speak of taking food. My spiritual master who has initiated me with the *iṣṭa-mantra* is my only true friend in both this world and the next. If I cannot win his pleasure, then all my spiritual practices are for nought. Through his mercy I can win the mercy of the Supreme Lord. If I displease him I have no other recourse. If Krishna is displeased with me, my spiritual master can intervene on my behalf, but if the spiritual master is angry or dissatisfied with my actions, then all my spiritual practices are as worthless as oblations of clarified butter poured on the remains of a fire sacrifice. The service of my spiritual master's lotus feet is the real treasure of my spiritual life. Any spiritual practice performed independently of him is without value. Whatever hearing or chanting I engage in should be done for the pleasure of my spiritual master alone. I should always meditate on these words sung by Narottama dāsa:

sei vrata, sei tapa sei mora mantra japa
sei mora dharama karama

"'The feet of Śrī Rūpa Mañjarī are my real wealth. They are the object of my vows. They are the goal of my austerities and penances, they are the goal of my mantra and my japa. They are the purpose of my religious observances, my every activity.' (*Prārthanā* 8)

"If my guru rebukes or criticizes me, I should take it as a great fortune. I should remember that whatever spiritual practice I engage in, all is being done for his pleasure. I should give this consideration pride of place in my consciousness, remembering Sārvabhauma's words to Mahāprabhu: *ājñā gurūṇāṁ hy avicāraṇīyā*: 'The orders of our gurus are never to be debated.' (*Chaitanya Charitāmṛta* 2.10.145)

"Our eternal spiritual identity is to be the dust of the lotus feet of Rupa and Raghunatha"

"I pray that my intelligence never becomes so contaminated that I criticize the words of my spiritual master. May such a wicked mentality never manifest in my heart, not even in my dreams. Any arrangement he makes for me is for my ultimate good. I pray that I never consider him to be an ordinary mortal by entertaining negative judgements of his words or actions. I will always remain on my guard against such a disaster.

"Because the guru is affectionate towards his disciples, if I approach him with my doubts, he will lay those doubts to rest with his answers. May I never forget for even a moment that my spiritual master is the source of all auspiciousness. The Supreme Lord has taken the form of my guru in order to give me the mercy of initiation and spiritual teaching. May I never forget at any time this manifestation of compassion of the Lord's revealed form as the guru. The duty of the disciple is to always seek the pleasure of his spiritual master, whose only purpose is to carry out the orders of the Supreme Lord Śrī Chaitanya Mahāprabhu on this earth. I should always consider the servants of my guru to be worthy of my respect. Whoever is dear to my guru is dear to me.

"If I can keep on doing my devotional service with this attitude of unswerving, constant

"I should always consider the servants of my guru to be worthy of my respect. Whoever is dear to my guru is dear to me"

faith in my spiritual master, then through his satisfaction I will quickly become qualified for all perfections. My spiritual master has assured me that through the Holy Name I can attain all perfection, therefore, I will faithfully chant the Holy Names without committing offenses, while always making a determined effort to strictly follow his orders. On the strength of the Holy Names in which my guru has instructed me, I will become eligible for the treasure of *rāgānugā bhakti* and for the great fortune to taste the sweet flavors of the most elevated spiritual relations, never given prior to the appearance of Śrī Chaitanya Mahāprabhu."

THE DEVOTEE'S PRAYER

Śrī Guru's mercy is everything—*guru-kṛpā hi kevalam.* Therefore one should pray as follows:

"I am most fallen and useless, O Lord. May my spiritual master be pleased with me. May he give me the spiritual strength to follow his directions. May all the obstacles in my worship of the Lord be removed so that at the end of my sojourn in this world, I may sit alone far from the hustle and bustle of the material world, and with a steady mind, chant the Holy Names with feeling. May the Lord be merciful and allow me to give up my last breath in this way. Knowingly or unknowingly I have committed so many offenses to His lotus feet, and even now I continue to commit such offenses. O Lord, please forgive all such offenses and give me a place at Your lotus feet. Make my life complete by allowing me to associate with those who are dear to You.

"For so long I have simply made a pretense of being initiated. In fact, I have not done that which a surrendered soul should do; I have not strictly followed my spiritual master's instructions, thus I have not made even a little advancement in spiritual life. All the contaminations in my heart prior to initiation are still there today, so how is there any hope of my attaining the divine realization which is said to be the real sign of initiation? Like a lump of iron my heart is without feelings. Even though I chant the Holy Names, it does not melt. Thus I am thinking,

Hanuman

aparādha phale mama citta bhela vajra-sama
tuwā nāme nā labhe vikāra

"Due to offenses, my heart has become as hard as a thunderbolt. Therefore no ecstatic transformations take place when I chant your name."
(Bhaktivinoda Ṭhākura)

tabe jāni tāhe aparādha āchaye pracura
kṛṣṇa-nāma bīja tāhe nā haya aṅkura

"Thus I know I have committed so many offenses to the Holy Name; for though I have planted the seed of the Name, no creeper of love has sprouted."
(*Chaitanya Charitāmṛta* 1.8.29)

"O Gurudeva! Now in the evening of my life, I have become so forlorn and hopeless. O Lord! O You who see no fault in anyone! Be generous to me and give me your mercy. Help me to be free of all offenses so I develop a taste for the Holy Names which you have instructed me to chant. Allow me to earn the right to be called the genuine servant of your servants. With your divine vision, you see me perfectly, externally and internally. You know everything I do; therefore I pray that everything I do—my behavior, my devotional service—be a source of pleasure to you.

"O Lord, forgive all my offenses, whether I have committed them willingly or unwillingly. Forever give me a place among all your servants, at your lotus feet, where there is no more lamentation, no more fear, no more death. Your feet are the only shelter for one like me who has found no refuge anywhere in this world. Your feet are the source of ultimate good for one like me who has found no value anywhere else in this world."

bhūmau skhalita-pādānāṁ
bhūmir evāvalambanam
tvayi jātāparādhānāṁ
tvam eva śaraṇaṁ prabho

> "Those who trip and fall have only the ground as an aid to again get up. O Lord, those who commit offenses to You, have no one but You as a recourse."

So, my dear devotees, tread carefully the path of devotion. Always pray for the mercy of Krishna, the guru, and the Vaishnavas. Remember that progress in devotion depends on progress in humility—that is the art of sadhana.

Epilogue

saiveyaṁ bhuvi dhanya-gauḍa-nagarī velāpi saivāmbudheḥ
so 'yaṁ śrī-puruṣottamo madhu-pates tāny eva nāmāni ca
no kutrāpi nirīkṣyate hari hari premotsavas tādṛśo
hā caitanya kṛpā-nidhāna tava kiṁ vīkṣye punar vaibhavam

"This is the same city of Gauḍa, blessed on earth,
this too the very same ocean beach,
this, the town of Puruṣottama (Purī)
and these, the very same Holy Names, Hare Krishna;
but, alas! Nowhere can I see the same festival of love.
Oh, Chaitanya, source of all compassion,
will I ever again see Your glories?"
(Prabodhānanda Sarasvatī's *Chaitanya-candrāmṛta*, 140)

gorāra āmi mukhe balile nā cale
gorāra ācāra gorāra pracāra laile phala phale

"It is not enough to simply advertise repeatedly that one is a devotee of Mahāprabhu saying, 'I am Gaurā's, I am Gaurā's.' The results of being the Lord's follower come to one who takes up Mahāprabhu's preaching mission as well as the practices taught by Him." *(Prema-vivarta)*

Some of us affirm, with conviction, that we follow Śrī Chaitanya Mahāprabhu, have faith in Him, and are devoted to Him. When we interact with Vaishnavas from other traditions that do not have the same regard for Mahāprabhu that we do, we strongly rebuke them; and criticize them in articles and speeches.

There is indeed a general notion among ordinary people today that Mahāprabhu is accepted throughout the world and that no one truly rejects Him. However, if we look deeply we find that very few of us truly follow Mahāprabhu. In fact, fearing to be called atheists for not offering respect to the Vedic scriptures and the Supreme Lord or of being vilified by the public in general, we claim to honor Mahāprabhu, but all we are really interested in is our own prestige...

There is, these days, a class of people who, leading a reckless private life and following the partial discipline of the *smārtas*, act permissively and whimsically and still dare to publicly criticize the true followers of Mahāprabhu. Dismissing Mahāprabhu's teachings as sectarian, they neglect the standards of Vaishnava conduct and yet profess to know the Lord better than His devotees do. Thus they criticize in their publications the great personalities who have dedicated their lives to Mahāprabhu's service, making Him the ultimate goal of their lives.

"The results of being the Lord's follower come to one who takes up Mahaprabhu's preaching mission as well as the practices taught by Him"

However, the honest inquirer finds that these people are affected by the disease of self-deception, of weakness of character, of dishonesty. The arrogance of these people has nothing to do with true acceptance of Mahāprabhu and His message, but is only proof of sickening attachment to personal prestige and sense gratification.

If we ask ourselves, "Are we truly following Mahāprabhu?" and then honestly seek the answer, we must first examine not only Mahāprabhu's own teachings and conduct, but those of His personal associates, through whom the Lord spread His message. We must then ask ourselves how closely we follow those teachings, especially in times of personal difficulty or social disapproval.

Sadly, some people accept as Mahāprabhu's teachings only those portions that are convenient to their life styles or frame of mind. Such people believe that Śrī Rūpa, Śrī Sanātana, Śrī Jīva, Krishnadāsa Kavirāja Gosvāmī, Vrindavan dāsa Ṭhākura and other intimate associates of the Lord profess doctrines that in reality are different from Mahāprabhu's. They even go so far as to claim that Mahāprabhu's followers are narrow-minded sectarians who have made many exaggerated claims about the Lord's person and teachings. Thus they refuse to accept the statements of Mahāprabhu's associates as authoritative. But when genuine teachers of the doctrines of Vaishnavism expose these people's mock following of Mahāprabhu, showing that, for all intents and purposes, it is actually opposition to the Lord, they become angry and verbally attack the devotees.

The foolish attitude of these people is comparable to the logic of half a hen—Mahāprabhu cannot be separated from His entourage. One cannot cut off the Lord's hands and feet and then pay respects to His head. When devotees quote the voices of authority from the disciplic succession, these self-styled followers of Mahāprabhu call it the Vaishnava sect's fanaticism and narrow-mindedness. As an example they quote the *Chaitanya Bhāgavata* verse in which Vrindavan dāsa Ṭhākura condemns Nityānanda Prabhu's critics:

eta parihāreo je pāpī nindā kare
tabe lāthi māroṅ tāra śirera upare

"I will take a stick and beat on the head those sinners who, ignoring everything I have said, continue to blaspheme Nityānanda Prabhu."
(*Chaitanya Bhāgavata* 1.9.225; 17.158; 2.11.63; 2.18.223; 2.23.522)

The self-styled followers of Mahāprabhu call these utterances of Vrindavan Dāsa Ṭhākura violent and intemperate, and proof of the fanaticism of Vaishnavas in general. Their imaginary approval of Mahāprabhu is based on a rejection of the Lord's associates which is deep rooted in malice and malevolence. They, convinced that devotion is nothing but sentimentalism and unfounded enthusiasm, consider Mahāprabhu's devotees incapable of understanding the Lord's true nature. But they believe themselves, as independent third parties, capable of such understanding. The extent of the arrogance manifest in such a claim is completely beyond even their own comprehension. Such is the type of person that prominently propagates its ideas today on the editorial pages of newspapers and from the podiums of various public assemblies.

Other illegitimate modern-day followers of Mahāprabhu also are those who make a show of accepting Mahāprabhu and His associates, but actually profess all manners of heterodox views. Like wolves in sheep's clothing, these pseudo-Vaishnavas pose as orthodox thinkers, making a hypocritical display of devotion while actually being infected by caste consciousness, monism, or the so-called philosophy of synthesis (*samanvaya-vāda*). These characters make a show of accepting Mahāprabhu and His close associates, but protest either openly or anonymously when Mahāprabhu's surrendered devotees fearlessly preach the Lord's message as it is.

Srila Raghunatha dasa Goswami

These duplicitous frauds tolerate the brow-beating of the impersonalists or the caste brahmins, but when a bonafide *ācārya* speaks out they are unable to tolerate it. Due to excessive sentimentalism and lust, these *sahajiyās* have become so inflated in their egotism that when told that Mahāprabhu's teaching and example direct one to give up bad association, they object, unwilling to give up their sensuous ways.

In the *Chaitanya Charitāmṛta,* the story of Choṭa Haridāsa is told as a lesson for potentially deviant followers. Certain aspects of Choṭa Haridāsa's conduct were displeasing to Mahāprabhu and are to be avoided.

"We must first examine not only Mahaprabhu's own teachings and conduct, but those of His personal associates, through whom the Lord spread His message"

When Krishnadāsa Vipra was tempted away from Mahāprabhu's association by the Bhaṭṭathāri women, he was not acting as a branch of the Chaitanya desire tree of divine love. Giving up the direct service of the Lord to consort with these women, he was not keeping with what is expected of an eternal associate of the Lord.

When in Vraja, the Lord's companion, Balabhadra Bhaṭṭācārya, wanted to leave the service of Mahāprabhu—Krishna Himself—to see the supposed reincarnation of Krishna in Kālīya lake, his behavior was not in accordance with the true standard of an eternal companion of the Lord.

Sārvabhauma Bhaṭṭācārya supported the *smārta* and Māyāvāda philosophies and even refused to accept Mahāprabhu as an incarnation of Lord Krishna. His is another example of conduct uncharacteristic of the branches of the Chaitanya tree of divine love. Many such examples are found throughout the accounts of Lord Chaitanya's *līlā*. There is the instance of Jagāi and Mādhāi's sinful existence and their violent behavior towards Nityānanda Prabhu and Haridāsa Ṭhākura, and their opposition to the chanting of the Holy Name. There is Gopīnātha Paṭṭanāyaka, who stole from the royal treasury. Kamalākānta Viśvāsa, Advaita Prabhu's disciple, perceived Advaita to be in debt. Brahmānanda Bhāratī, one of the roots of the desire tree of divine love, wore a deerskin, the dress of a Māyāvādī sannyasī; and Mahāprabhu did not approve of this and corrected him. Vallabhācārya, who is identified in the *Gaura-gaṇoddeśa-dīpikā* as an incarnation of Śukadeva, proclaimed his own commentary on the *Bhāgavatam* to be superior to that of Śrīdhara Svāmī—this kind of arrogance is not characteristic of a Śukadeva.

Devānanda Pundit, also counted among the branches of the Chaitanya tree, tolerated offenses to Mahāprabhu's dear associate, Srīvāsa Pundit, he contemplated liberation; and interpreted the *Śrīmad Bhāgavatam* in ways that opposed its true purport of devotion to Krishna. This is certainly not befitting an eternal companion of the Lord.

Sentimentalist *prākṛta-sahajiyās* find it painful to hear such criticism of conduct that was disapproved by Mahāprabhu Himself. But just as a good doctor does not hide his diagnosis in order to please the patient, the devotees of the Lord do not hide the fact that progress in spiritual life is dependent on giving up attachment to bad company, sense gratification, and immediate pleasures. The devotee does not withhold good advice out of a desire to deceive and flatter. If the straightforward, direct and honest devotee says that engaging in illicit sexual activity is detrimental to spiritual life and advises one to give it up; or if he tells someone overly attached to wife and children to give up that attachment, these are beneficial instructions. When spoken, the truth may cause pain, but the devotee would rather speak the truth out of kindness than add more fuel on the fire of people's material attachments.

We may be very vocal about following Mahāprabhu, but when He declares that the essence of Vaishnava conduct is to give up bad association such as the company of womanizers and non-devotees, shall we call Him cruel and unkind? Mahāprabhu called Choṭa Haridāsa a "monkey renunciate," one who has given up the appearance of interest in sensual life but goes on to flirt with women and do other things contrary to the Vaishnava rules of conduct. Mahāprabhu said about Choṭa Haridāsa that the only atonement for this grievous deviation was to drown himself. Shall we then call Mahāprabhu cruel and unkind? Shall we deny that He ever said such a thing? Shall we rather try to establish that Mahāprabhu approves of our own loose standards of worldly behavior? If we go about giving speeches in public assemblies to this end, is it not simply proof of our own dishonesty?

We may say, "I accept and follow Mahāprabhu," but despite point-by-point evidence in Mahāprabhu's teachings, we do not accept that the only way of attaining God is devotion characterized by chanting the Holy Names. Nor do we accept that *karma*, *jñāna* and *yoga* are indirect and troublesome paths full of hornets, ghosts, and poisonous snakes. Mahāprabhu and His followers sometimes called other spiritual paths "poison chalices," or "worse than hell," but we insist that these statements are not to be taken literally and that Mahāprabhu was making exaggerated claims in order to promote His doctrine. Is this accepting Mahāprabhu as He is? We want to fit Mahāprabhu's doctrines into the mold of our own subjectivity. Are we then not giving more weight to our own fancies or to current public opinion than to Mahāprabhu? When we put bhakti on the same platform with *jñāna* or *karma*, are we not in effect rejecting bhakti?

Mahāprabhu used the word *satītva*, or wifely chastity, to describe the attitude of a devotee who does not mix his devotional service with *jñāna* or *karma*, or obscure his devotion with desires for sense enjoyment or gratification, all of which He compares to marital infidelity. When we say that bhakti is just one of many different ways of attaining the Supreme, we are saying, in effect, that a wife who cheats on her husband and one who is chaste and faithful are equal. No doubt those sects that promote illicit sexual activities will be glad to hear such tidings, for this liberal attitude gives their transgressions legitimacy. But normally, a respectable person objects to the idea that his chaste mother is on the same level as a prostitute. Of course, a wicked individual or a prostitute has no problem with a righteous man or a chaste woman being derided in this manner! They simply think, "Welcome to the club!"

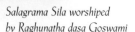

Salagrama Sila worshiped by Raghunatha dasa Goswami

Privately and publicly, the world has introduced infidelity as part of Chaitanya Mahāprabhu's pure doctrines. Thus, quite naturally, many misled persons try to put their infidelity on the same level as the behavior of the chaste pure devotees of the Lord. This they call "the doctrine of synthesis." Like an infectious disease, this philosophy has spread from a few individuals to the society at large. Is it any surprise that Māyāvāda is rapidly proliferating in the world?

So this is how we "honor" Mahāprabhu. We call our opposition to Mahāprabhu's doctrines "honoring" Him in order to keep up our public image.

Some of us actually believe that by making a public show of accepting Mahāprabhu we are doing *Him* a service rather than ourselves one: "I am a brahmin and I honor Mahāprabhu. I have studied so much and I accept Mahāprabhu. I have a big, important job and I follow Mahāprabhu. I am a rich man and I accept Mahāprabhu. So Mahāprabhu is beholden to me."

Others say that they will boycott Mahāprabhu if He opposes their imaginary concept of what is true religion, truth, service, or welfare work, even if His devotees can show from scripture that Mahāprabhu's position is orthodox. How can anyone claim this so-called acceptance of Mahāprabhu as authentic? Aren't we rather accepting our own whims and preferences as our authority? The teachings of Mahāprabhu cannot be changed to suit our own whimsical ideas.

In the *Chaitanya Charitāmṛta* Mahāprabhu says:

harer nāma harer nāma
harer nāmaiva kevalam
kalau nāsty eva nāsty eva
nāsty eva gatir anyathā

"In this age of quarrel and hypocrisy the only means of deliverance is the chanting of the holy names of the Lord. There is no other way; there is no other way; there is no other way." (*Bṛhan-nāradīya Purana, Chaitanya Charitāmṛta* 1.7.76)

SMĀRTAS AND PAÑCOPĀSAKAS

In another verse of *Chaitanya Charitāmṛta* Mahāprabhu says:

ekale īśvara kṛṣṇa āra saba bhṛtya
jāre jaiche nācāya se taiche kare nṛtya

"Lord Krishna alone is the supreme controller, all others are His servants. As He makes people dance, so do they dance." (*Chaitanya Charitāmṛta* 1.5.142)

And Mahāprabhu adds: "The goddesses Gaṅgā and Durgā are My servants. Shiva is My servant." This is stated in the most authoritative text, the *Brahma-saṁhitā*:

sṛṣṭi-sthiti-pralaya-sādhana-śaktir ekā
chāyeva yasya bhuvanāni bibharti durgā
icchānurūpam api yasya ca ceṣṭate sā
govindam ādi-puruṣaṁ tam ahaṁ bhajāmi

Sri Chaitanya Mahaprabhu

"The external potency Maya, who is of the nature of the shadow of the *cit* potency, is worshiped by all people as Durgā, the creating, preserving and destroying agency of this mundane world. I adore the primeval Lord Govinda in accordance with whose will Durgā conducts herself."

(*Brahma-saṁhitā* 5.44)

kṣīraṁ yathā dadhi vikāra-viśeṣa-yogāt
sañjāyate na hi tataḥ pṛthag asti hetoḥ
yaḥ śambhutām api tathā samupaiti kāryād
govindam ādi-puruṣaṁ tam ahaṁ bhajāmi

"Just as, by the action of acids, milk is transformed into curd but yet the effect curd is neither the same as, nor different from its cause, viz., milk, so I adore the primeval Lord Govinda of whom the state of Śambhu (Shiva) is a transformation for the performance of the work of destruction."

(*Brahma-saṁhitā* 5.45)

yat-pāda-pallava-yugaṁ vinidhāya kumbha-
dvandve praṇāma-samaye sa gaṇādhirājaḥ
vighnān vihantum alam asya jagat-trayasya
govindam ādi-puruṣaṁ tam ahaṁ bhajāmi

"I adore the primeval Lord Govinda, whose lotus feet are always held by Ganesh upon the tusks of his elephant head in order to obtain power for his function—destroying obstacles on the path of progress of the three worlds."

(*Brahma-saṁhitā* 5.50)

yac-cakṣur eṣa savitā sakala-grahāṇāṁ
rājā samasta-sura-mūrtir aśeṣa-tejāḥ
yasyājñayā bhramati sambhṛta-kāla-cakro
govindam ādi-puruṣaṁ tam ahaṁ bhajāmi

"The sun, king of all the planets, full of infinite effulgence, the image of the good soul, is as the eye of this world. I adore the primeval Lord Govinda in pursuance of whose order the sun performs his journey mounting the wheel of time."

(*Brahma-saṁhitā* 5.52)

In all these verses we find endorsement of Mahāprabhu's rejection of the *smārta* doctrine of Pañcopāsakas, or worship of the five deities—Shiva, Durgā, Ganesh, Surya, and Vishnu. But despite the clear evidence from *Brahma-saṁhitā* quoted in Mahāprabhu's teachings, Pañcopāsakas cling to their doctrine, arguing that the Vedas themselves authorize this process of polytheistic worship. They affirm that Mahāprabhu Himself visited the temples and holy places connected to these deities, prayed to them, and danced before them. They further argue that if Mahāprabhu did not accept a type of worship that is authorized in the Vedas, then the Vaishnava religion must be considered out of line with the Vedic literature. Indeed, some foolish deviants declare that Mahāprabhu's religion is not Vedic.

Influenced by public opinion, we toss all these heterodox ideas about in our heads. There are indeed many names of gods in the Vedic literature, but only Vishnu is referred to as the supreme deity above all others, and independent of them. The most ancient of the Vedas, the *Ṛgveda-saṁhitā*, clearly states that Vishnu is superior to all gods.

agnir vai devānām adhamaḥ
viṣṇuḥ paramaḥ
tad-antarā hy anya-devatāḥ

> "Agni is the least of the gods; Vishnu is supreme. All other gods are somewhere in between these two."

The *Bhagavad-gītā* and other Vedic scriptures clearly state that the worship of any god other than the Supreme Lord is incorrect and goes against the Vedic principles. Gaurasundara may have visited numerous temples dedicated to gods and goddesses, and shown them respect, but He never considered them to be independent or supreme. Rather, He considered all the gods and goddesses to be servants of Vishnu, and therefore devotees, or Vaishnavas. In this sense only He considered them worshipable. Otherwise, according to the *Pañcopāsanā* understanding, the five gods are worshiped purely functionally and within the temporal world. The goal of the *Pañcopāsanā* is to go beyond these deities' various forms and merge into the impersonal Brahman. At the end of the puja, the five deity forms are ultimately abandoned in the *visarjana* ceremony.

Mahāprabhu accepted that Vishnu and the Vaishnavas have transcendental forms of eternity, bliss, and knowledge. Shiva, Durgā, Ganesh, and Sūrya worshipped by Mahāprabhu are the order-carriers of the Supreme Lord Vishnu in His abode of Goloka-Vaikuṇṭha. There these deities are His eternal associates, and thus never purely functional and to ever be discarded. Who then are the true followers of the Veda, the Vaishnavas or the Māyāvādīs and Pañcopāsakas? And who truly shows greater respect to the gods, the Vaishnavas or the Māyāvādīs and Pañcopāsakas who simply consider these forms imaginary and as convenient objects of worship to ultimately be discarded? Who showed greater respect to Shiva, Rāvaṇa or the Pracetas? Therefore the question: Are we truly following Mahāprabhu? Or are we following Him according to our own convenience, our own tastes and imagination?

Notes

Introduction

[1] Īśodyāna is an area in the holy land of Navadvīpa *dhāma* near the birthplace of Chaitanya Mahāprabhu, Śrī Māyāpura. The maṭha and temple founded by Śrī Bhakti Promode Puri Maharaj, Śrī Gopinath Gaudiya *Math*, is situated there.

Chapter I: Perfection in Worship

[1] *apir atra garhāyāṁ | garhito'tra pūrva-pakṣaḥ | saṁrādhane samyag-bhaktau satyāṁ cakṣuṣādinā pratyakṣeṇa grāhyo'sau bhavati | kutaḥ | pratakṣeti śruti-smṛtibhyām ity arthaḥ* | Baladeva's *Govinda-bhāṣya.*

[2] *Tasmāt samyag-bhaktyā grāhyaḥ śrī-harir iti siddham | cakṣur-ādīni tu tayā bhāvitāni | atas taiḥ sa vedyaḥ |*

[3] *tapasvibhyo 'dhiko yogī*
jñānibhyo 'pi mato 'dhikaḥ
karmibhyaś cādhiko yogī
tasmād yogī bhavārjuna

yoginām api sarveṣāṁ
mad-gatenāntar-ātmanā
śraddhāvān bhajate yo māṁ
sa me yuktatamo mataḥ

The yogi is considered by Me to be greater than the ascetics, greater than the man of knowledge and greater than the ritualist. Therefore, O Arjuna, become a yogi. And of all yogis, the faithful person who worships Me with all his soul, surrendering to Me, is most closely united with Me. (*Gītā 6.46-7*)

[4] The *Pañcarātra* refers to the Vaishnava texts which describe the various ritualistic performances such as initiation, deity worship, etc. The *Pañcarātra* is also sometimes called the Vaishnava tantra. The *Bhāgavatam* is more concerned with theology and descriptions

of the eternal nature of the Supreme Lord.

5 Such repetition is typical of many *upanishads* and is found in most of them to signal the end of a section or a book. A case in point is the text quoted above from the *Chāndogya Upanishad*, 8.15.1.

6 The words used here by Srila Purī Mahārāja are *pravartaka*, *sādhaka* and *siddha*. This is an allusion to the *sahajīyā* doctrine which lays particular stress on these terms. A *pravartaka* is someone who engages in the external practices of devotional service, while a *sādhaka* is one who engages in the esoteric sexo-yogic practices of the *sahaja-tantra*. (Translator)

CHAPTER II: THE PURIFYING POWER OF SERVICE

1 See Chapter 6.

CHAPTER III: THE BEGINNINGS OF SERVICE

1 The seven upper planets are Bhūḥ, Bhuvaḥ, Svaḥ, Mahaḥ, Jana, Tapaḥ, and Satya; the seven lower planets are Tala, Atala, Vitala, Nitala, Talātala, Mahātala, and Sutala.

CHAPTER VII: THE GURU AND INITIATION

1 *śiva-saṁstutaṁ dīkṣitam ity arthaḥ | pradhānatvena śrī-viṣṇu-dīkṣā-grahaṇāt śrī-śivasyāpi samyak-stuti-viṣayam iti bhāvaḥ | evaṁ ca dīkṣāṁ vinā pūjāyām anadhikārāt tathā*
śālagrāma-śilā-pūjāṁ vinā yo'śnāti kiñcana
sa cāṇḍālādi-viṣṭhāyām ākalpaṁ jāyate kṛmiḥ
ity ādi vacanair pūjāyāś cāvaśyakatvād dīkṣāyā nityatvaṁ sidhyati | śrī-śālagrām-śilād-hiṣṭhānaṁ vargeṣu mukhyatvāt sarvāṇy eva bhagavad-adhiṣṭhānāny upalakṣayati | nityatvam eva brahma-vacanena ca sādhayati te narā iti | janārdano yair nārcita iti dīkṣāṁ vinār

CHAPTER VIII: DUTIES OF AN INITIATED DISCIPLE

1 Śrīla Sanātana Gosvāmī explains the words *viśuddhāhata-yug-vastra-dhāraṇaṁ* as follows: *viśuddhaṁ pavitram āhataṁ ca nūtanaṁ. Pāṭhāntare viśuddhena janena āhṛtam ānītaṁ yad yugaṁ vastraṁ vastra-yugmaṁ tasya dhāraṇam.* "The cloth should be pure and new. There is, however the following alternative reading: one should wear a pair of garments which have been brought by someone who is pure."

2 A *nyāsa* is a process of assigning various parts of the body to their titulary deities through touch and special mantras. This is a part of the process of self-purification which is part of the devotee's preparation for worship.

3 Some commentators take 32 and 33 to be one single *samaya*, and later divide number 45 in two.

4 Sanātana's commentary reads: *daśamy-ādi-dina-trayeṣu daśamy-ekādaśī-dvādaśīṣu yad vrataṁ ca bhakṣaṇādi-niyamas tasmin niyamena svāsthyaṁ śraddhayā sthairyam ity arthaḥ.*

5 Sanātana's commentary quotes the following verse: *prauḍha-pāda-lakṣaṇam uktam | āsanārūḍha-pādas tu jānunor vātha jaṅghayoḥ | kṛtāvasakthiko yas tu prauḍha-pādas tathocyate ||* The word *prauḍha-pāda* refers to someone who places his feet on his seat and then either kneels or sits on his hams.

6 Another meaning of *kalañja* is tobacco. This is more likely to be the meaning here as meat has already been prohibited earlier.

7 These red and white flowers are commonly seen in India, poisonous—they are unsuitable to be offered.

CHAPTER IX: DIKSA MANTRA AND THE HOLY NAME

[1] These *saṁskāras* are explained at further length in *Hari-bhakti-vilāsa 1.228ff*. *Janana* refers to the inscription of the formula in the yantra such as the one described in *Nārada-pañcarātra 3.15.26-44*. *Jīvana* refers to chanting the mantra with the *praṇava oṁkāra*. *Tāḍana* means to sprinkle each letter of the mantra with a mixture of water and sandalwood while uttering the *vāyu-bīja-mantra*, "*iṁ*". Offering the same number of Oleander (*karavīra*) flowers as there are syllables in the mantra is called *rodhana*. *Abhiṣeka* refers to sprinkling water with *aśvattha* leaves for the same number of times as there are syllables in the mantra. *Vimalīkaraṇa* means mentally purifying the three roots of the mantra by burning it with the *jyoti-mantra* (*oṁ haṁ raṁ oṁ*). *Āpyāyana* refers to the sprinkling of water with *kuśa* grass onto every syllable of the mantra. *Tarpaṇa*, *dīpana*, and *gopana*. *Tarpaṇa* is sprinkling water on the yantra while chanting the mantra; *dīpana* means chanting the mantra with the addition of the seed syllables, *oṁ*, *hrīṁ* and *śrīṁ*; and *gopana* means keeping the mantra secret.

[2] The words *amuka-dravyaka* ("this certain item") is to be replaced by the items which one is going to offer in the fire sacrifice. Similarly, the word *iyat* is to be replaced by the exact number of mantras one intends to chant each day.

[3] *premāñjana-cchurita-bhakti-vilocanena*
santaḥ sadaiva hṛdayeṣu vilokayanti
yaṁ śyāmasundaram acintya-guṇa-svarūpaṁ
govindam ādi-puruṣaṁ tam ahaṁ bhajāmi

[4] *nanu bhagavan-nāmātmakā eva mantrāḥ | tatra viśeṣeṇa namaḥ-śabdādy-alaṁkṛtāḥ śrī-bhagavatā śrīmad-ṛṣibhiś cāhita-śakti-viśeṣāḥ śrī-bhagavatā samam ātma-sambandha-viśeṣa-pratipādakāś ca | tatra kevalāni śrībhagavan-nāmāny api nirapekṣāṇy eva parama-puruṣārtha-phala-paryanta-dāna-samarthāni | tato mantreṣu nāmato 'py adhika-sāmarthye labdhe kathaṁ dīkṣādy-apekṣā | ucyate | yadyapi svarūpato nāsti tathāpi prāyaḥ svabhāvato dehādisambandhena kadartha-śīlānāṁ vikṣipta-cittānāṁ janānāṁ tat-tat-saṁkocīkaraṇāya śrīmad-ṛṣi-prabhṛtibhir atrārcana-mārge kvacit kvacit kācit kācin maryādā sthāpitāsti |*

[5] Prabhupāda Bhaktisiddhānta Sarasvatī Ṭhākura's language in this section is based on the *Bhakti-rasāmṛta-sindhu 2.1.7-10*. These verses trace the development of the devotee's capacity to relish transcendental mellows.

CHAPTER X: EXPERTISE IN BHAJAN

[1] See also *Śrīmad Bhāgavatam 1.12.14, 2.1.5* and *2.2.36*. See also *Caitanya Caritāmṛta 3.4.70-1*.

[2] This is a reference to the Muslims who were vehemently opposed to so-called "idol" worship, which in Persian and Urdu is called *but-parastī*.

[3] *nanv atra śāstre bhaktir abhidheyety avagamyata eva | tatrāpi bhakty-aṅgeṣu madhye mahārāja-cakravartivat kim ekaṁ mukhyatvena nirṇīyate | tatrāha nāmānukīrtanam iti | sarveṣu bhakty-aṅgeṣu madhye śravaṇa-kīrtana-smaraṇāni trīṇi mukhyāni tasmād bhārateti ślokenoktāni | teṣu triṣv api madhye kīrtanam | kīrtane'pi nāma-līlā-guṇādi-sambandhini tasmin nāma-kīrtanam | tatrāpy anukīrtanaṁ sva-bhakty-anurūpa-nāma-kīrtanaṁ nirantara-kīrtanaṁ vā | nirṇītaṁ pūrvācāryair api | na kevalaṁ mayaivādhunā nirṇīyata iti | tenātra pramāṇaṁ na praṣṭavyam iti bhāvaḥ | kīdṛśam | akutobhayam iti | kāla-deśa-pātropakaraṇāviśuddhy-aśuddhi-gata-bhayābhāvasya kā vārtā | bhagavat-sevādikam asahamānā mlecchā api yatra naiva vipvenerationpadyanta iti bhāvaḥ | kiṁ ca sādhakānāṁ siddhānāṁ ca nātaḥ param adhikaṁ śreya ity āha nirvidyamānānām arthān mokṣa-paryanta-sarva-kāmebhya iti | icchatām iti | arthāt tān eva kāmān iti praviśa piṇḍīn itival labhyate |*

tataś ca nirvidyamānānām ekānta-bhaktānām icchatāṁ svarga-mokṣādi-kāminām yoginām ātmārāmāṇāṁ ca etad eva nirṇītam | yathāyogyaṁ sādhanatvena phalatvena ceti bhāvaḥ.

4 A book recounting the life of Srīla Prabhupāda Bhaktisiddhanta Sarasvatī Ṭhākura with articles by many of his disciples which first appeared in 1940. The above section is found on page 177.

Chapter XII: Controlling the Mind

1 The *Vedanta-sāra* ("Essentials of Vedanta") is a book by Sadānanda Yogīndra of the Śaṅkara *sampradāya*. The book summarizes all of the principal doctrines of the Vedanta school of thought.

2 *bhakta-niṣṭhā bhajanotthā śrāntis tad-darśanotthā sva-niṣṭhā kṛpā ceti dvābhyām eva bhagavān baddhaḥ.*

3 *yathā kuṭumba-pālanārthaṁ dīnā gṛhasthā dhanika-dvārādau dhanārthaṁ yatante, tathaiva mad-bhaktāḥ kīrtanādi-bhakti-prāpty-arthaṁ bhakta-sabhādau yatante. Prāpya ca bhaktim adhīyamānam śāstram paṭhata iva punaḥ punar abhyasyanti ca.*

4 *etāvanti nāma-grahaṇāni, etāvatyaḥ praṇatayaḥ, etāvatyaḥ paricaryāś cāvaśya-kartavyā ity evaṁ dṛḍhāni vratāni niyamā yeṣāṁ te. yad vā, dṛḍhāny apatitāny ekādaśy-ādi-vratāni niyamā yeṣāṁ te.*

5 In its second line this verse has an alternative reading. Instead of *ca śaṁ*, its reading has *śamaṁ*. The word *śamaḥ* ("tranquility") has been defined elsewhere (*Śrīmad Bhāgavatam* 11.19.36; See also *Chaitanya Charitāmṛta* 2.19.210-212) *man-niṣṭhatā buddheḥ*, by the Lord Himself as "attachment of the intelligence to Me." In this case, rather than "brings peace of mind" we should understand it as "brings attachment of the intelligence to Me."

Chapter XIII: Practice and Preaching

1 Ganjam is a district of Orissa. Today, the Chikakola Road station is found in the state of Andhra Pradesh and has been renamed as Śrī Kākulam Road. The BNR railway line is now India's South Eastern Railway. For more information on this pastime of Śrī Rāmānuja, one can turn to the thirty-sixth chapter of *Prapannāmṛtam*, the biography of the founder of the Śrī *sampradāya*.

2 Our worshipable spiritual master Śrīla Bhaktisiddānta Sarasvatī Ṭhākura gave the following information about this place, known as Kūrma-sthāna, in his *Anubhāṣya* commentary on the *Chaitanya Charitāmṛta*: "On the BNR railroad line there is a station named Chikakola Road in the district of Ganjam. Eight miles east of this station is a place known as Kūrmācala (Kūrma's mountain), or Śrī Kūrmam. This is the most popular pilgrimage site for those who speak the Telugu language. When Rāmānuja was flung there by Lord Jagannātha in the 11th century of the Śaka era, he thought that the Kūrma deity was a Shiva-liṅga and so started a fast. Later, when he learned that it was in fact an image of the tortoise avatar of Vishnu, he arranged for it to be worshiped.

Chapter XIV: Path of Passionate Love

1 See Viśvanātha's Bhaktisāradarśinī commentary to *Bhakti-rasāmṛta-sindhu 1.2.295.*

2 This passage is found in *Caitanya Caritāmṛta 1.6.10-17* and *Caitanya Bhāgavata 1.2.128-47*: Verse 140: *sādhya sādhana tattva je kichu sakala | harināma saṅkīrtane milibe sakala ||* "The object of life and the means to attain it are found through the chanting of the Holy Names." Verse 147: *sādhite sādhite nāma premāṅkura habe | sādhya sādhana tattva jānibā se tabe ||* "As you repeatedly practice the chanting of the Holy Name, the seedling of love will sprout and then you will know both the goal of life and the means to attain it."

About the Author

Vaishnava Sarvabhauma Sri Srila Bhakti Promode Puri Goswami Maharaja

Om Visnupada Srila Bhakti Promode Puri Founder President & Acharya
Sri Gopinath Gaudiya Math

Tridaṇḍī Swami Śrīmad Bhakti Promode Puri Goswami Maharaja appeared in the village of Ganganandapur, District Jessore (now in Bangladesh), as the son of Śrī Tarini Charan Chakravarty and Śrīmatī Ram Rangini Devi. Born on October 8, 1898 during the auspicious *brahma-muhūrta* hour, he was given the name Śrī Promode Bhushan Chakravarty.

Promode Bhushan's reverent service mood was evident even as a young man. Along with the study of Sanskrit, he worshiped the family deities of Śrī Śrī Radha Gopīnātha. Once, during the winter, he forgot to cover the Lord with a blanket. That night he himself began to shiver uncontrollably with fever and chills. The Lord appeared to him in a dream and showed him that He had been left without a blanket. The young Promode Bhushan woke up and immediately covered the Lord, after which his fever subsided.

Promode Bhushan completed his high school education in Baruipur near Diamond Harbour and then went on to study chemistry at Bangabasi College, Calcutta. In 1917, he met his Guru, Prabhupada Śrīla Bhaktisiddānta Sarasvatī Goswami Ṭhākura. From the first meeting Śrī Promode Bhusan accepted Prabhupada in his heart as his eternal master. His strong attachment to spiritual life brought him regularly to his Guru's lectures at the Calcutta ashram of the Gaudiya Math. In 1923, on the holy occasion of Śrī Krishna Janmāṣṭamī, he surrendered at his Guru's lotus feet and received *harināma* and *mantra-dīkṣā*. He was thenceforth known as Śrī Praṇavānanda Brahmacārī.

Śrī Praṇavānanda's service attitude was so exemplary that soon Prabhupada Śrīla Sarasvatī Ṭhākura engaged him as the editor of Gaudiya Math publications. Praṇavānanda Brahmacārī would summarize Śrīla Sarasvatī Ṭhākura's lectures, elaborate on them, and with Prabhupada's approval, publish them in various periodicals including *Dainika Nadiyā Prakāśa*, the world's only daily spiritual newspaper. In recognition of his scholarship and historical researches, Sarasvatī Ṭhākura honored him with the title, *Mahopadeśaka Pratna-vidyālaṅkara*. He served in close association with his Guru for thirteen years.

At the time of Prabhupāda's *aprakaṭa-līlā*, Śrī Praṇavānanda Brahmacārī held his guru's lotus feet to his chest so that they might remain forever enthroned in his heart. After Śrīla Prabhupāda's disappearance, he began extensive traveling and preaching.

In 1942, Śrīla Prabhupāda Sarasvatī Ṭhākura appeared to him in a dream and gave the divine order to accept Tridaṇḍī-sannyāsa. Śrīla Prabhupāda had requested him to accept Tridaṇḍī-sannyāsa earlier in1933, yet considering himself unfit he humbly declined. At this time he accepted sannyāsa initiation and its symbol, the *daṇḍa* (staff) from his godbrother Śrīla Bhakti Gourava Vaikhanasa Maharaja at the Śrī Śrī Gaura-Gadādhara temple in Champahati. He was given the name Tridaṇḍī Swami Bhakti Promode Puri.

For more than seven years, Tridaṇḍī Swami Bhakti Promode Puri Goswami Maharaja served as the head pujari and temple president of Śrī Yogapīṭha, the birthplace of Śrī Chaitanya Mahaprabhu discovered by Śrīla Bhaktivinoda Ṭhākura. During that time, the deities were internally urging him to take up a more intense study of the scriptures and a life of solitary worship or bhajana.

He moved to a humble cottage on the banks of the Ganges at Kalna in the district of Burdwan, where he lived with his beloved deities Śrī Śrī Radha Gopīnātha. The King of Burdwan was extremely impressed with the saintly character of this ascetic. On the appearance day of Śrīmatī Radharani in 1958 he presented Śrīla Puri Maharaja the large and ancient Ananta Vāsudeva temple of Kalna. He accepted this offering and engaged in service at the temple for several years.

Later, Śrīla Puri Maharaja's godbrother, His Holiness Om Viṣṇupāda Tridaṇḍī Swami Śrīla Bhakti Dayita Madhava Goswami Maharaja requested him to come to his *maṭha* and assist him as the editor of spiritual publications. Puri Maharaja then entrusted the Kalna temple to his younger brother and went to Calcutta to take up his new service. Madhava Maharaja particularly requested that he take full charge of the monthly magazine, *Śrī Chaitanya Vāṇī*. He also became editor-in-chief of *Śrī Gauḍīya* published monthly from Śrī Chaitanya Math, Mayapur. Śrīla Puri Maharaja continued to fulfill this role with great care and devotion until the advanced age of 97.

Presently, Śrīla Puri Maharaja is the seniormost living disciple of Śrīla Bhaktisiddhanta Saraswati Ṭhākura. In addition, he was the lifelong intimate associate of His Divine Grace Śrīla Bhakti Rakshaka Śrīdhar Deva Goswami Maharaja, whom he considered to be the benign guardian of the celestial wealth of Śrīla Rūpa Goswami.

Śrīla Puri Maharaja was well known as the best *kīrtana* leader in the early days of Śrī Gaudiya Math and often sang on radio programs. He also gained a wide reputation for extensive knowledge and meticulous practice of deity worship and the rituals for deity installation and temple consecration. His service to Śrīla Sarasvatī Ṭhākura in these areas resulted in his being widely know as *Pūjāpāda*.

Over and above his senior position and high qualifications, many are attracted to Tridaṇḍī Swami B. P. Puri Goswami by his divine personality. He emanates sweetness and love. He is seen by them as a well-wishing guide to the spiritual domain. The opening of the Śrī Gopīnātha Gaudiya Math in Ishodyan during the 1989 Gaura Pūrṇimā provided a doorway to that spiritual domain.

Our humble prayer is that we may always be situated at the holy lotus feet of Śrīla Bhakti Promode Puri Goswami Maharaja, which are our only access to the predecessor acharyas and their divine teachings. We pray that we may be engaged in the eternal service of Śrī Guru and Gauranga and Śrī Śrī Radha-Gopinath under his divine direction.